African Americans and Post-Industrial Labor Markets

African Americans and Post-Industrial Labor Markets

Edited by
James B. Stewart

Transaction Publishers
New Brunswick (U.S.A.) and London (U.K.)

331.6396073
A2582

This book is printed on acid-free paper that meets the American National Standard for Permanence of Paper for Printed Library Materials.

Library of Congress Catalog Number: 96-26899
ISBN: 1-56000-920-9
Printed in the United States of America

Library of Congress Cataloging-in-Publication Data
African Americans and post-industrial labor markets / edited by James B. Stewart.
      p.   cm.
    Includes bibliographical references and index.
    ISBN 1-56000-920-9 (pbk. : alk. paper)
    1. Afro-Americans—Employment. 2. Labor market—United States. 3. Unemployment—United States. I. Stewart, James B. (James Benjamin), 1947– .
HD8081.A65A673   1996   96-26899
331.6'396073—dc20   CIP

This book is dedicated to the members of the National Economic Association, whose research, teaching, and professional activities continue to provide the data and analyses necessary to develop efficient and humane policies to improve the economic status of African Americans. It is also dedicated to the past editors of *The Review of Black Political Economy* who have provided the most useful medium in existence for the dissemination of high quality scholarship examining the economic circumstances of peoples of African descent—Robert Browne, Lloyd Hogan and Margaret Simms. Special thanks is due to Eileen Williams for her help in assembling this volume and for her dedicated work as editorial assistant during my tenure as editor of *The Review of Black Political Economy.*

CONTENTS

PART III: OCCUPATIONAL CROWDING

PART IV: BLACK WOMEN IN THE LABOR MARKET

PART V: STRUCTURAL UNEMPLOYMENT
AND JOB DISPLACEMENT

PART VI: SECTORAL ANALYSES

PART VII: STRATEGIES TO INCREASE EMPLOYMENT

The chapters in this book originally appeared in various issues of *The Review of Black Political Economy:*

Chapter	Issue
1, 12	Winter 1995
2, 14, 16	Spring 1995
3, 7, 9	Spring 1993
4, 22	Summer 1994
5	Fall 1992
6	Summer 1993
8, 11, 13	Summer 1992
10	Summer 1991
15, 17, 18, 20	Winter 1994
19, 21	Fall 1994

INTRODUCTION

James B. Stewart

The collection of analyses presented in this volume documents the disproportionate vulnerability of African Americans to the dislocations associated with the ongoing transformation of the U.S. economy as the dawn of the twenty-first century approaches. All of the chapters have been published previously in *The Review of Black Political Economy* between 1991 and 1996. The collection thus represents one of the best sources of up-to-date perspectives on the circumstances facing African Americans in post-industrial labor markets.

The volume is organized into seven sections: "The Intersection of Race, Power, Culture, and Economic Discrimination," "Black-White Wage Differentials," "Occupational Crowding," "Black Women in the Labor Market," "Structural Unemployment and Job Displacement," "Sectoral Analyses," and "Strategies to Increase Employment." A brief description of the analyses presented in each section is provided below.

THE INTERSECTION OF RACE, POWER, CULTURE, AND ECONOMIC DISCRIMINATION

This section lays the groundwork for the remainder of the volume, focusing attention on the fact that the contemporary circumstances facing African Americans in labor markets are conditioned by the general status of race relations and, in particular, by fallout from the ongoing debate in various popular and professional media about the causes of persisting racial inequities and how such inequities should be addressed in public policy. This debate is catalyzing dramatic changes in policies that have had a significant impact on the status of African American workers, including affirmative action and job training. Opponents of these and other policies are claiming not only that the policy outcomes have been suboptimal, but also that notions of race and culture reflected in policy designs are outmoded. Economists have tended to avoid discussions about the nature of race and culture and how these affect individual and collective behavior in economic arenas. Such avoidance is sanctioned by the assumption that these matters are issues of tastes and preferences and, consequently, belong to the province of other disciplines. The introductory essay offers a framework designed to prod economists into reassessing the value of the standard approaches used by economists to discuss race and culture with the hope that economists' perspectives can provide some additional clarity to the ongoing dialogue.

One of the concepts that has emerged in the "new" dialogues about race and culture is "cultural capital." This concept is used to expound the thesis that many of the social ills affecting African American communities derive from the deterioration in individual and family values, an erosion presumably associated with social welfare programs that originated during the 1960s. The analysis by James Johnson, Elisa Bienenstock, and Jennifer Stoloff finds that although such factors do affect employment, this effect is not statistically significant when controls are introduced for human capital. This leads to their recommendation of additional investments in public education and expanded efforts to reduce racial discrimination in labor markets, as opposed to a focus on some type of "values re-education."

The analysis by Jeremiah Cotton also provides useful insights regarding the utility of a shift in emphasis away from economic discrimination toward cultural characteristics as barriers to economic advancement. He examines factors affecting wage differences among Hispanic black, Hispanic white, and non-Hispanic black males. This tripartite comparison scheme allows a determination of the relative degree to which race and culture contribute to the observed pattern of variation. Cotton finds significant differences between the earnings of white and black Hispanics that, in his words, "do not bode well for the culture-over-color argument."

Public policy debates about issues of racial disparities are often handicapped by the absence of solid evidence to inform discussion. Empirical studies of discrimination related to labor markets still rely heavily on indirect measurement, treating discrimination as a residual after controlling for other factors expected to influence outcomes. In contrast, in studies of housing discrimination one of the more effective techniques involves controlled experiments in fair housing audits in which carefully matched testers of different races enter into randomly selected housing transactions and record all treatment. The overall level of discrimination encountered by the testers provides a measure of the extent of racial segregation in that particular housing market. The analysis by Marc Bendick, Charles Jackson, and Victor Reinoso uses a similar technique to examine employment discrimination. They find that in over 20 percent of the cases, African American applicants were treated less favorably than equally qualified nonminorities.

If changes in public policies that have the potential to alter the relative well-being of different groups are on the horizon, then there is a need to consider more directly how employers are likely to adapt to changes in regulations, such as affirmative action, that affect employment decisions. The analysis by Thomas Hyclak, Larry Taylor, and James Stewart offers a useful historical perspective on this issue. The authors examine the impact of affirmative action policies on application and hiring patterns in Detroit firms using data for 1972. They find that firms subject to affirmative action reporting requirements were more likely to hire black male managers than other firms, but that such requirements, at least during this time period, had less effect on the hiring of female managers.

Together, the chapters in this section present a picture of complex but persistent patterns of discrimination in labor markets that can be altered, to some extent, through well-designed public policies. The design of such policies, however, requires refinement of the tools used by economists to allow examination of the intersection of race, power, culture, and economic discrimination.

BLACK-WHITE WAGE DIFFERENTIALS

The most prevalent type of exploration of differential circumstances facing black and white workers is the analysis of factors contributing to observed differentials in earnings. In 1994 the median weekly earnings of year-round full-time wage and salary workers was $467 for all workers, $371 for African Americans, and $354 for Hispanics. The two chapters in this section address issues about both the appropriate design of wage differential studies and the public policy implications that can be derived from these investigations. Jeremiah Cotton's analysis focuses on differences in wages between black and white males across geographic regions. Most wage differential studies use national samples and attempt to control for regional differences solely by including dummy variables in the estimating equation. Cotton uses a more sophisticated technique and finds that both the relative labor market outcomes and relative labor market treatment of black male workers differed significantly across regions during the period 1976-1984. He suggests that to the extent that such regional variation continues "policies designed to improve racial equity in labor markets (and thereby labor efficiency) will need different emphases in different regions."

Kwabena Gyimah-Brempong and Rudy Fichtenbaum focus on the relative extent to which wage differentials result from differences in human capital and labor market structure. Labor market structure is defined as labor market conditions that affect the wage structure but "are neither the traditional productivity characteristics nor personal characteristics of the worker." They find that discrimination against black males and females accounted for substantially more of the difference in wages than human capital differences. The principal public policy implication emerging from their analysis is that while narrowing human capital gaps is necessary, it is more important to enforce policies designed to increase the accessibility of African Americans to higher-wage industries.

The combined findings suggest that there is a need for flexible approaches to reducing wage disparities that take into account differences across regions in economic conditions and labor market structure. Such policies should focus particular attention on increasing access to higher-paying occupations.

OCCUPATIONAL CROWDING

The findings reported above reflect, in part, continuing patterns of occupational crowding, that is, the overrepresentation of some groups of workers into easily identifiable groups of low-wage occupations. The concept of occupational crowding has been employed most typically in studies of labor market experience of women, but as the chapters in this section demonstrate, it can also be used to gain useful insights about the labor market status of males.

Susanne Schmitz and Paul Gabriel examine the relationship between occupational segregation and local labor market dynamics. They find evidence that the relative occupational distributions of white women and black males are systematically related to changes in specific local labor market conditions. Two very interesting conclusions are: (a) that the unemployment rate of white males "is directly related to differences between the occupational distributions of white males" and other population groups, and (b) that "increases in the relative supply of black males and white females are associated with greater differences in their occupational distributions compared to white males."

Augustin Fosu explores whether black and white women working in the clerical and service sectors hold different jobs. This study considers what might be described as "second-tier" occupational segregation, since the overrepresentation of women in these occupations is itself a manifestation of a broader pattern of occupational segregation. Fosu finds that in 1961 there was strong evidence that black women were overrepresented in the lowest-paying lowest-status jobs. By 1981, however, there was little evidence that this pattern continued to persist.

Andrés Torres compares the determinants of wage differences among both men and women between African Americans and Puerto Ricans in New York City over the period 1960 to 1980. Torres identifies divergent paths of economic mobility for the two groups. Changes in labor market segmentation combined with the use of political power contributed significantly to wage gains for African Americans. In contrast, changes in human capital accounted for most of the wage gains for Puerto Ricans and changes in labor market segmentation had a negative effect on wage changes.

In general, then, occupational segregation remains a problem that increases the vulnerability of black workers to major shifts in sectoral growth within the economy. There is an interactive effect among groups not captured by focusing on individual workers alone. The optimal means to combat group vulnerability to existing patterns of occupational segregation may differ across different subpopulations.

BLACK WOMEN IN THE LABOR MARKET

The status of black women in labor markets was first addressed systematically by *The Review of Black Political Economy* through co-sponsorship of the symposium that provided the content for the 1986 monograph entitled, *Slipping Through the Cracks, the Status of Black Women.* Since that time there have been many additional studies that have examined the labor market circumstances facing African American women, including many of the investigations in other sections of this volume. Prior to the mid 1970s the labor market participation of married black women significantly exceeded that of white women. The phenomenon of stagflation in the mid-1970s induced a significant increase in the labor force participation of married white women. The study in this section by

David Macpherson and James Stewart uses 1980 data to broach the subject of whether labor force participation of women differ in interracial marriages involving blacks and whites compared to women in homogeneous black and white marriages. Two of the major conclusions are that labor force participation rates were higher for women in interracial than in endogamous marriages and that after adjusting for differences in personal and family characteristics, the labor force participation of women in interracial marriages was approximately halfway between that of women in white and black homogeneous marriages.

The chapter by Emily Hoffnar and Michael Greene examines the relative earnings of black women compared to white women and black and white men, controlling for residential location. They find that black women in suburbs and central cities have lower earnings than the relevant comparison groups. Interestingly, living in the central cities was not associated with an earnings penalty for either black or white women compared to suburban residence, while inner city black and white male residents did earn less than their suburban counterparts.

These analyses underscore the need for gender specific studies that control carefully for familial composition and variation in gender role configurations across households in efforts to understand how ongoing changes in the labor markets will affect African American women. Without such detailed analyses, expectations regarding the labor market participation effects of policy changes such as welfare reform may not match popular expectations. The number of interracial marriages has expanded substantially, complicating our understanding of the labor force participation decisions of women. Moreover, the development of targeted public policy efforts could be adversely affected by proposals to include a multiracial category in the next population census. The pattern of responses to such a question could complicate substantially efforts to explore trends in economic adjustment across groups as traditionally defined.

STRUCTURAL UNEMPLOYMENT AND JOB DISPLACEMENT

Between March 1991 and April 1994 fourteen major corporations alone announced planned reductions of 370,000 jobs. Between 1991 and 1993 4.5 million workers were displaced who had previously been employed three or more years. Among these displaced workers 19 percent were unemployed at the time of the survey, 13 percent were out of the labor force, 23 percent were working full-time but earning less than before displacement, and 5 percent were self-employed. Only 26 percent were working full-time for equal or higher pay. Various studies have found that blacks are overrepresented among displaced workers.

Since 1979 total job losses in the U.S. economy have numbered 43 million. These losses have been offset by a robust record of job creation. The total number of jobs has increased from 90 million in 1979 to 117 million in 1995. Since 1991 annual job loss has been no less than 3.25 million annually. In contrast, prior to 1991 there was only one year where job loss exceeded 3 million (1983). During the period 1981-83 blacks accounted for 12 percent of layoffs, while whites and Hispanics accounted for 79 percent and 6 percent respectively. Comparable percentages for the period 1991-93 were blacks 10 percent, whites 75 percent, and Hispanics 11 percent.

The analysis by Don Mar examines the effects of changes in the vacancy-to-unemployment ratio on black and white earnings over the period 1956-1983. He finds that black women's wage earnings are less sensitive to changes in national vacancy-to-unemployment ratios than white earnings, which means that black women are less likely to experience wage gains when new jobs are created. The results were inconclusive for black males.

Thomas Hyclak and James Stewart explore the unemployment rate responses of black, white, and Hispanic workers to shifts in labor demand across industries during the period 1980-1984. They find that black unemployment rates are much more sensitive to changes in aggregate demand and wage flexibility than is the case for whites and Hispanics. They also report that the unemployment rate of blacks is more severely affected by structural changes in labor demand than is the case for white and Hispanic workers.

M. V. Lee Badgett investigates the effects of changes in flows into and out of unemployment on the growing gap between black and white unemployment rates in the 1970s and 1980s. He finds that job instability increased for blacks at the same time that employment opportunities declined, while the reverse occurred among white women. One of the interesting policy assessments in Badgett's analysis is that equal employment opportunity enforcement and affirmative action "had little discernible impact on racial differences in macro-level unemployment components, either when policy enforcement was at its peak or when it dropped off dramatically during the Reagan administration."

The collective message emerging from these studies is that black employment is highly sensitive to changes in both aggregate and local economic conditions. As a consequence, policy changes designed to promote macro-level economic stabilization could well have the unintended effect of further increasing job instability among blacks.

SECTORAL ANALYSES

The phenomenon of growing job instability described previously is obviously exacerbated by large-scale sectoral shifts in economic activity and associated employment dislocation. The most massive shift, of course, has involved erosion in manufacturing employment coupled with rapid employment expansion in service industries. Total employment in U.S. manufacturing declined from 21 million in 1979 to 18.4 million in 1991. During the same period total nonfarm employment grew by 26.7 million jobs, mostly in the service sector.

A significant proportion of the employment shifts are related directly to patterns of international trade. International trade affects various sectors but its influence has been most pronounced in the manufacturing sector. In the early 1980s the United States enjoyed a trade surplus in manufactured goods. However, between 1980 and 1994 this pattern shifted to the point that there was a deficit of $156 billion and manufacturing imports increased from 54 percent to 84 percent of all imports.

There are, however, other sectors that have experienced and are experiencing long-term employment declines that require scrutiny, including the armed forces and the federal government. Other sectors, such as so-called "high tech" industries have experienced cycles of employment growth and decline. The decline in manufacturing employment and the associated growth in service sector jobs can be distinguished from the other sectoral shifts by the degree of market influence. Employment shifts in high tech industries, particularly those that are defense related, the armed forces, and federal government are caused directly by public policy decisions. Both the armed forces and the federal government have been downsizing for several years and these reductions are of concern because of the disproportionate representation of blacks in these sectors. In general, blacks tend to be concentrated into relatively low-paying agencies and occupations in the federal government.

Bartholomew Armah examines the demographic characteristics of manufacturing and service workers affected by changes in the configuration of international trade over the period 1987-1990. In manufacturing

industries the workers most positively affected by trade shifts were unionized white males in technical occupations with high levels of educational
attainment. In service industries young, non-unionized workers with less
education experienced the most positive outcomes.

Roger Williams examines the effect of the reduction in defense expenditures on black employment across states. He finds that, with the exception of New York, black job losses are particularly acute in a few specific
Southern states. In discussing the impacts of planned reductions in the
size of the military forces, Williams predicts that if the overall entry rate
into the military decreases by 20 percent, the percentage representation
of blacks could decline by 36 percent. He suggests that without military
training and experience, many young blacks will have difficulty obtaining civilian jobs.

Don Mar and Paul Ong analyze industrial employment losses in Silicon Valley, California, one of the "meccas" for high-tech firms. They
examine the probabilities of permanent layoffs across racial groups following the 1985 recession in the Silicon Valley semiconductor industry.
Black workers were less likely to be rehired than other workers, particularly in white-collar occupations.

Michael Greene and Emily Hoffnar compare the earnings of black and
white males in public sector employment. They find that African American males are no better off in the private than in the public sector. In
contrast, white male public sector workers earn significantly less than their
private sector counterparts. Greene and Hoffnar suggest that this difference in experiences may be the result of the fact that earnings declines
experienced by African American workers in the private sector during the
1980s may have eliminated any pre-existing private sector earnings premium.

The chapters in this section indicate that black workers are particularly
at risk in those industries where significant job losses have occurred.
This suggests the need for the development of mechanisms to track the
effects of federal government downsizing and anticipated increased hiring at the state and local levels due to "new Federalism" policies to
determine whether black and other minority group workers are being
treated equitably. The results also raise the question of whether planned
changes in programs providing assistance to workers dislocated as a
result of international trade patterns will have a disproportionate impact
on black workers.

STRATEGIES TO INCREASE EMPLOYMENT

The various studies discussed in the preceding sections paint an ominous picture and invite the question of what types of programs are available to reduce the problems experienced by black workers. The need for targeted programs is evidenced, for example, by the fact that in April 1995 the unemployment rate for black teenagers was 35.6 percent compared to 17.5 percent for all teens. Another indication of the desirability of focused initiatives is that in 1993 the poverty rate for blacks in the labor force most of the year was 13.9 percent versus 6.7 percent for all workers. These data are a particular cause for concern in the context of current efforts to reduce funding for many vocational training programs, including vocational and adult education, and extended unemployment benefits. Some analysts note that the type of dislocations discussed in the previous sections are being offset to a significant degree by new sources of job creation, in particular small enterprises. In fact, over 50 percent of jobs created in the 1980s occurred in enterprises employing less than 100 workers. This phenomenon has led to suggestions that job creation strategies should revolve around efforts to reduce barriers to small business formation and operation.

The analysis by Maurice Mongkuo and William Pammer examines the employment impacts of a specific public program. They explore the outcomes relative to minority employment associated with the Urban Development Action Grants targeted partnership development initiative in Pittsburgh, Pennsylvania, between 1978 and 1988. Mongkuo and Pammer find no significant increase in employment resulting from this initiative and suggest that the program benefits were captured by other groups.

In a similar vein, Joan Fitzgerald and Wendy Patton scrutinize the outcomes of the "High Unemployment Program," a job training program implemented in Ohio in 1987 that targeted young African American males for focused on-the-job training. They find that the potential impact of the High Unemployment Program was blunted by weak staff commitment to the program objectives. One of the telling conclusions drawn by the authors is that "in the currently racially charged environment [weak staff commitment] is likely to affect many new government programs throughout the 1990s."

Timothy Bates analyzes the employment of minority workers in black- and nonminority-owned small urban enterprises. He finds that black-owned businesses rely heavily on minority workers in contrast to their minority counterparts. Bates argues that the findings point to the possible existence of "a small business world of network hiring in which job accessibility is a function of the small business owner."

One of the messages emerging from these studies is that the potential benefits of many employment enhancing programs have been unrealized due to flaws in program design and poor management due, in part, to lukewarm commitment to program goals. Given the current racial schisms and the expectations that governmental equal employment enforcement mechanisms will be further weakened, it is unlikely that small nonminority-owned business enterprises will constitute a major source of new employment opportunities for blacks. Although significant increases in the number of black-owned businesses has occurred in the last decade, it is critical to keep in mind that the characteristics of black businesses limit the extent to which they constitute vehicles for upward mobility of large numbers of people. To illustrate, approximately 94 percent of black-owned firms are sole proprietorships and two-thirds operate in the service or retail trade areas. Only 10 percent have paid employees and only about 340 have 100 or more employees.

The limitations associated with existing programs, the questionable viability of some proposed alternative policy directions, along with the current political mind-set suggest the need for developing a new approach to policy design with a long-term rather than a short-term focus. Here the work of various futurists can provide useful insights. For example, it is projected that 35 percent of the work force will be comprised of contingent workers by the year 2000. Aside from the fact that contingent workers do not receive benefits, these predictions are troubling because part-time workers earn 20-40 percent less than full-time workers. This raises the question of whether blacks will be disproportionately relegated to the status of contingent workers and whether, even in this tenuous status, they will be compensated differentially.

Some futurists suggest that as the global economic transformation proceeds, fewer and fewer workers will be needed to produce the goods and services for the global population and that it will be necessary for society to reorganize some activities such that they are compensated via wage payments. The Tofflers argue in *The Politics of the Third Wave*, for example, that "As . . . new jobs are not likely to be found in what we still think of as manufacture, we will need to prepare people through schooling apprenticeships and on-the-job learning for work in such fields as the human services."[1] They maintain further that "if . . . wages are low in the service sector, then the solution is to increase service productivity and to invent new forms of work-force organization and collective bargaining."[2] In a similar vein, Aronowitz and DiFazio claim there is a need for society to provide subsidies in the form of tax deductions for shadow wages for voluntary community service work.[3]

This latter suggestion underscores the fact that employment policy and community development policy must be developed in parallel. To pursue any other approach will ensure that the labor market problems facing African Americans examined in this volume will only worsen as the transformation of the post-industrial economy proceeds.

NOTES

1. A. Toffler and H. Toffler, *Creating a New Civilization, the Politics of the Third Wave* (Atlanta: Turner Publishing Co., 1995) p. 53.
2. Ibid.
3. S. Aronowitz and W. DiFazio, *The Jobless Future, Sci-Tech and the Dogma of Work* (Minneapolis: University of Minnesota Press, 1994), pp. 256-58.

I

THE INTERSECTION OF RACE, POWER, CULTURE, AND ECONOMIC DISCRIMINATION

1

NEA PRESIDENTIAL ADDRESS, 1994

TOWARD BROADER INVOLVEMENT OF BLACK ECONOMISTS IN DISCUSSIONS OF RACE AND PUBLIC POLICY: A PLEA FOR A RECONCEPTUALIZATION OF RACE AND POWER IN ECONOMIC THEORY

James B. Stewart

INTRODUCTION

Recently I was contacted by the *Wall Street Journal* to discuss what could be described as the "value added by black economists to public policy discussions related to race." I was queried as to why most black economists, other than selected neoconservatives like Thomas Sowell and Walter Williams, seem to be invisible in contemporary visible public discussions about race and American society that are occurring in the popular media.

As outgoing editor of *The Review of Black Political Economy*, I find such an assessment particularly galling; nonetheless it is in fact accurate. With the possible exception of the writings of Julianne Malveaux, there is little continuing public exposure of the perspectives that black economists have advanced on issues of race and economics in venues like *The Review,* the publications of the Joint Center for Political and Economic Studies, *Black Enterprise,* and the Urban League's annual *State of Black America.*[1]

This situation can be explained partially, of course, by the presence of imperfections in the policy discussion market. There clearly are barriers to entry that limit the access of "progressive" black economists. One set of these imperfections is demand driven. The existing demand outside the black community for inputs from black economists is limited largely to conservative, pro-market, anti-government intervention policy recommendations.

Another set of imperfections is largely associated with the supply side.

The current production of what might be described as alternative progressive policy perspectives is dominated by liberal think tanks where the role of black economists and other black social scientists is often marginal or largely symbolic. As an example, consider the production of *A Common Destiny,* presumably the publication of the update of the classic Gunnar Myrdal study, *An American Dilemma.*[2] The marginalization of black researchers from this project led to the formation of a counter study group by Charles Willie and Wornie Reed of the Monroe Trotter Institute at the University of Massachusetts-Boston. This collective produced four volumes—again receiving little public attention.[3]

The situation I am describing would be less problematic if these externally imposed imperfections were the sole explanation for the invisibility of black economists. Unfortunately this is not the case. When the African American Summit was held in Baltimore earlier this year, I wrote now former NAACP Executive Director Benjamin Chavis and offered the expertise of the National Economic Association to help in formulating strategies to pursue economic empowerment of black communities. I received no answer. Now while this may have been simply an artifact of Chavis's internal problems, it is not the sole reason because the experience was largely replicated when the same offer was made to Hugh Price, the new head of the Urban League. And recently another leadership summit was held and again black economists, as a collective, were not invited to participate.

These experiences are problematic principally because the primary theme of the leadership summits has been "economic empowerment," an area where black economists presumably have some expertise. This leads me to ask the question, are there other factors that contribute to black economists' marginalization from the race and public policy arena that are related directly to the analytical tools that we employ, creating the perception of irrelevance to outsiders?

The position I want to argue briefly is that our analytical tools do not speak effectively to some of the important economic issues of the day that concern peoples of African descent. Specifically, I will claim that the models currently employed do not address adequately issues of group identification and its effects on economic behavior. Yet these issues are clearly salient to the black community at large as evidenced, for example, by the renewed popularity of black nationalist ideologies and the tensions surrounding what I would describe as the re-Africanization and ethnicification of the black population of the United States through immigration from Africa and the Caribbean. These issues are also being played out on a global scale as demonstrated by so-called "ethnic conflicts" in the former Yugoslavia, the former Soviet Union, the British Isles, Somalia, etc.

There are at least two problems with the existing frameworks typically used to examine racial issues from an economic perspective. First, the models focus principally on the concept of discrimination. Admittedly, discrimination is one of the most critical issues facing people of African descent. But, unless the framework of analysis coherently specifies a model of group identification, then predictions about the outcomes of reducing discrimination will be flawed.

The need for such a model is underappreciated, in part, because of the standard assumption that individual economic interests will dominate interpersonal attachments if the market mechanism is allowed to condition social relationships. The key issue, however, is the extent to which the market in fact shapes social relations and whether its influence is unidirectional.

A second problem with the standard treatment is that even when an attempt is made to model collective behavior, it is usually informed by a simplistic metaphor that is implicitly based on an analogy to paid membership in voluntary organizations, ignoring the myriad of insights that have been generated by other social and behavioral sciences. Again, this shortcoming is rarely appreciated by economists.[4]

To understand how issues of collective identity have been submerged in standard economic models consider the following statement by Kenneth Arrow in a 1974 publication:

The black steel worker may be thought of as producing blackness as well as steel, both evaluated in the market. We are singling out the former as a special subject for analysis because somehow we think it is appropriate for the steel industry to produce steel and not for it to produce a black or white work force.[5]

The devaluing of group identification in economic affairs is pervasive in the writings of conservative black economists. To the extent that the impression has been created that this is the modal position of black economists, then a serious barrier to dialogue with the black community exists. The work of Thomas Sowell is notorious for its simplistic comparisons across racial and ethnic groups. In his writings race and ethnicity are confusingly conflated and reduced to issues of differences in income and age distributions and differences in occupational specialties and political strategies used to establish entrées to the market. Once entrance and mobility are achieved, presumably these distributional differences erode among members of sophisticated groups.[6]

The models developed by Sowell and other black economists have interesting precedents. In *A Theory of Racial Harmony,* Alvin Rabushka argues that

> under conditions of voluntary exchange in free markets, racial tensions and conflict are kept to a minimum. Individuals, as members of specific racial groups, stand to gain or lose on the basis of their marginal value of productivity (which may be conditioned by genetic, historical, political or cultural reasons). Groups of individuals with low marginal values of productivity attempt to compensate by gaining public control over resources, thereby using political power and the decision making authority of government to re–allocate wealth to their own advantage.[7]

He also writes:

> The public activities of government in the multiracial environment thus convert private economic competition among individuals in markets into social and political conflict between races. . . . Efforts by governments to do away with racial conflict tend to intensify it further. Moreover, the blame for existing racial problems can be attributed to prior government activity, such as licensing slavery, establishing apartheid, imperialism or enforcing segregation. Hence, governments should be seen as a chief cause of racial conflict, rather than as a promoter of racial harmony.[8]

The devaluation of group identification in Rabushka's analysis is obvious. In addition, however, he conveniently overlooks the fact that government action is the collective expression of the individual tastes and preferences of those in power, not the oppressed.

Suppose, however, that we take Rabushka's argument at face value. The critical question is what options are available for oppressed groups. The conservatives' preferred option is that everyone take their lumps in the marketplace and accept the outcomes as somehow reflecting a just distribution. A second option would be to secede from the system and attempt to establish an independent regime.

Unfortunately, Gary Becker informs us in *The Economics of Discrimination* that the second option provides no relief. Becker purports to demonstrate that "retaliation" by minority groups is counterproductive "since effective discrimination occurs against them, not because of the distribution of tastes, but because of the distribution of resources," i.e., majorities have a more balanced distribution of labor and capital than minorities.[9] In sum, he maintains that "complete segregation reduces the absolute and relative income of the minority and therefore increases, rather than decreases, the market discrimination against it."[10] In Becker's view, "effective discrimination occurs against a minority because it gains so much by 'trading' with the majority; accordingly, complete segregation does not avoid the bad economic effects of discrimination but only multiplies them."[11]

If these assertions are accurate, then how does one explain the large number of contemporary international efforts focused on carving up larger, heterogeneous jurisdictions into smaller, presumably less efficient jurisdictions that are either religiously, ethnically or racially homogeneous? Are the actors pursuing such aims irrational in economic terms? Or does group identity have some value that is being overlooked by the standard model?

It could certainly be the case that agents are incorrect in their valuations as a result of incomplete or inaccurate information. But such widespread misinformation seems unlikely. Trends in other disciplines suggest that it is the economists' devaluation of race that is problematic. As an example, even William Julius Wilson, the prominent sociologist who wrote *The Declining Significance of Race,* later modified his position in the face of widespread counterfactual evidence.[12]

The model of group identity employed by economists undervalues group identity, in part, because it reflects attempts to adapt an analogy from the study of collective bargaining dynamics. Prior to the formation of a local union there is a group of workers united by a common experience of oppression. Through collective action they produce countervailing power and this bargaining relationship becomes sanctioned by an external authority (the NLRB). Over time unions face the problem of free riders, i.e., those who benefit from the contracts negotiated by the union but choose to have no other association. Given this weak demand for membership, it is possible for employers to offer incentives that make workers as well off without the union. The "official" status of the union, ascribed by external forces then becomes a barrier to economic efficiency.

The adaptation of this scenario by conservatives to model racial group identification typically proceeds along the following lines. The historical exploitation of blacks produced collective efforts to overcome oppression but there was no more natural solidarity underlying this collective action than was the case for workers. The civil rights movement successfully produced countervailing power that generated various civil rights legislation and enforcement mechanisms and, most important, the enshrinement of race as a social category. Now that discrimination has been eliminated, most blacks no longer desire to be ascribed an official racial status, but government policies, e.g., "affirmative action," keep the ascribed status in the public conscience, thereby creating institutional barriers to harmonious race relations, i.e., social inefficiency.

The critical question is whether such a model accurately captures the dynamic nature of group composition, the historical reality of the experiences of peoples of African descent, the current pattern of intensified group identification manifested in the conflicts mentioned previously, or the general status of race relations. Contrast the "weak" model of identification described above with one suggested by anthropologist John Szwed, who argues: "What we may have thought of as behavior caused by physical form is, rather, learned behavior organized at many communicative levels, each cross-referencing each other. It is possible to see from this way of looking at the world that we have been confusing cultural styles with race."[13] One implication of such a perspective is that the simplistic assumption advanced by Sowell et al. that diminished racial identification can occur akin to the declining ethnic identification that characterized the historical experience of European immigrants in the United States is precluded if racial identity differs in important respects from ethnic identity within a given "racial" group. A more important implication, however, is that a model of group identification generated from concepts and analytical tools associated with economic science should focus on how the traditional concerns with efforts to maximize satisfaction in the context of the allocation of resources are related to patterns of interaction among individuals who are part of a group. In addition, a useful model should be able to specify the differences between within-group and intergroup interactions. The standard models of discrimination employed by economists focus almost solely on the impacts of a static configuration of inter-group conflict on the inter-group income distribution, assuming a given mix of factor endowments. Group identity is assumed to be given and immutable and the intensity of conflict is treated as constant over time.

With these weaknesses in mind, suppose we suspend Arrow's value judgment and ask what are the implications of assuming that the production of collective identity has value to members of a group and is a normal activity undertaken jointly by individuals and groups? Assume also that this collective identity is a joint product of other productive activities and has the potential to generate negative externalities for other groups. Elsewhere, I have presented the basic hypotheses underlying a formal specification of such a model using, ironically, the theory of social interactions based on a household production function framework developed by Gary Becker.[14] For present purposes, however, a summary discussion will suffice.

The magnitude of externalities produced by the production of collective identity could be expected to depend on a variety of factors including the degree of overlap in the composite racial, sexual, religious and class profiles of groups, the relative weights assigned to various commodities in individuals' utility functions, the degree of physical proximity of groups with different cultural production functions, and most important, differences in the relative political and economic resource bases that determine production possibilities.

A similar approach has been suggested by Okonkwo in a 1973 article that appeared in *The Review*, in which the presence of whites in a particular area who discriminate against blacks was assumed to inflict an external diseconomy on a community of "aware" blacks.[15] The term "aware" can be interpreted to mean those for whom the production of cultural identity has explicit value. From this vantage point, discriminatory behavior by groups in conflict becomes one manifestation of efforts to adjust the social environment to reduce the impact of perceived externalities associated with cultural production by other groups. Okonkwo, in fact, suggests such an interpretation: "The assumption that discrimination is an externality will in general cut both ways, so that blacks will appear as a public bad. . . . "[16]

One of the implications of this model is that individuals with similar cultural production functions have an incentive to engage in collective behavior to reduce the negative externalities associated with others' cultural production. Such inter-group competition can lead to tensions even

in the absence of competition for, or maldistribution of, economic resources, but persisting resource maldistributions will inevitably exacer-
bate inter-group tensions, as demonstrated by Hirschman.[17] Using the
framework developed by Breton, the decision to devote resources to the
use of political instruments such as voting and lobbying can be modeled
using standard economic theory.[18]

One of the most important implications of Breton's model is that differences in resource endowments will generate differences in the types of
political instruments that are used. This model can be used to demonstrate, for example, why African Americans have shown a preference for
political instruments such as demonstrations over other instruments such
as voting.[19] If the pattern of inequality in relative income and wealth
distributions exhibits some variation as opposed to increasing monotoni-
cally as assumed by Hirschman, then the pattern of usage of particular
political instruments over time will also exhibit variation.[20] The upshot
of the preceding discussion is that within this alternative framework, the
critiques advanced by Rabushka and Sowell of political strategies employed by African Americans are invalid.

Competition for economic resources will typically be layered onto
competition for social space. Thus when so-called "middle class" blacks
seek to escape the cultural production environment in central cities they
often wind up residing in racially segregated suburban enclaves. Although income and socialization differences alter aspects of the technology of cultural production, negative externalities are still perceived by
whites that increase with the size of the local black population.

This framework also suggests why school desegregation efforts typically entail relocation of black students in relatively small numbers to
predominantly white districts. This pattern minimizes the negative externalities on white students associated with the activities of the relocated
students while allowing the existing cultural production process to proceed with minimal disruptions. Of course it totally disrupts the cultural
production processes of the relocated black students, but that is often an
unspoken objective.

In general, concentrations of individuals with similar cultural production functions allow economies of scale to be exploited. As an example,
if there are enough residents in a given area then a black church can be
established, or an independent black school. Thus the size of the local
black population and its characteristics become important parameters for
highly mobile black professionals. And black middle class parents are

increasingly selecting historically black institutions of higher education for their offspring although their class status would presumably allow so-called "integrated" options. This behavior can be easily explained using the framework I am outlining. The goal seems to be to ensure that some minimal level of group identity is produced concurrent with the acquisition of general human capital. Further, parents seek to avoid their children's exposure to the negative externalities and derivative intergroup conflicts associated with cultural production processes operative in traditionally white institutions.

Treating the production of racial identity and culture as a process that generates negative externalities is consistent with other specifications of externalities. As an example, Wheaton suggests that "we might view an externality–laden good as being composed of two goods; one's own consumption (a regular good) and the benefit or harm to others of that consumption—a public good."[21]

As the foregoing suggests, this model forces a reconceptualization of the relative economic welfare associated with heterogeneous and homogeneous jurisdictions. Using analyses presented by Mishan and McGuire it can be shown that homogeneous jurisdictions can, under certain conditions, in fact maximize rather than reduce collective welfare.[22] To illustrate, Mishan argues that " . . . an optimal solution emerging from conflicts of interests is optimal only with respect to an implicit constraint requiring the area in question to be used in common by groups or persons having conflicting interests. Once separate areas, or separate facilities are introduced, solutions appear that are Pareto superior to the familiar constrained outcomes."[23] McGuire's analysis suggests that if efficient delivery of public goods can be accomplished in smaller jurisdictions, and there are distinct groups with different demand functions for the public good, then it is Pareto optimal to allow homogeneous groups to organize separate jurisdictions.[24] This conclusion is relevant, of course, for the contemporary debates about electoral districts deliberately drawn to maximize the probability that people of color are elected. The logic of such jurisdictions is that, in the words of Breton, "voluntary or coercion free organization to supply public policies is basically impossible for the large group, though in smaller groups, cooperation between individuals may lead to a coercion free situation."[25]

There are obviously numerous ancillary conditions that must exist to make a separate jurisdictions regime viable where units are given greater autonomy to exercise political and economic self-determination. These include a reasonably balanced resource base, and equitable terms of trade, à la Becker. The continuing interest in exploring the feasibility of homogeneous jurisdictions stems, in part, from the fact that in heterogeneous jurisdictions the likely result is the manipulation of policy instruments. This manipulation often entails creation of institutional arrangements that restrict the availability of high-value public goods to smaller numbers than would be technologically possible. As an example, within some large urban school districts, it is not unusual to find well-endowed public schools populated principally by nonminority students while the majority of schools are resource poor.

This is not to say that separate jurisdictions are always the optimal solution. In some cases reductions in intergroup differences in the technology of cultural production can be achieved. As an example, one of the most popular forms of music for some young whites is hip-hop. To the extent that technologies of cultural production and the produced identity structures are similar there will be less conflict in heterogeneous jurisdictions. It is also important to recognize that the type of externalities I am discussing are more important in some arenas than others. These externalities are particularly important in the marriage market, in competition for positions with high levels of prestige and power and in the case of religious differences. They are less important, as already indicated, in the workplace and also in athletics. In McGuire's framework, if distinct representative demand functions for different groups cannot be constructed, then homogeneous jurisdictions are not Pareto optimal. Thus greater intragroup variation in characteristics that affect the degree of attachment to an original reference group are likely to be associated with greater overlap in the commodity production functions of different groups, reducing welfare gains that can emerge with homogeneous jurisdictions.

The model I am outlining is consistent with the thrust of the Community Economic Development literature that appeared frequently in the pages of *The Review* during the 1970s.[27] It formalizes ideas that undergirded the types of community-based self-help intervention efforts that were proposed, but were not often stated explicitly. But the model also allows us to understand why the legal system plays such a crucial role in the area of race relations. As Mishan has observed, "in cases of conflicting interests, according as the law, deliberately or by default, places the burden of reaching optimal arrangements on one party or group rather than the other, both the characteristics of the optimal outcome and the costs of its attainment are altered. And the more important, as a component of welfare, are the external effects in question the greater in these respects, is the impact of the law."[28] Thus, the present perspective reverses the conclusion advanced by Rabushka et al. regarding the appropriate role of government in addressing racial conflicts.

What does this model have to say about traditional concerns, for example discrimination and conflict in the workplace? In general, employers attempt to create a quasi-artificial enterprise identity that serves as an alternative or complement to the core identification of workers with other collectives. This process is most obvious in Japanese enterprises but it proceeds as well in most large U.S. corporations. Similar to the process described previously for individuals, this identity is a joint product, an externality generated concurrent with the production of the firm's output. Individuals are expected to structure their cultural production functions so that negative externalities that adversely affect productivity and worker solidarity are minimized. Alternatively the work environment is structured so that conflicts do not impact the production process. Various techniques are used to accomplish this end. Historically, racial segregation and occupational crowding were popular instruments. More recently, diversity training has become the principal technique for avoiding intergroup conflicts. Individuals who are unable to modify cultural production functions run the risk of termination. The military is the best example of the process I have described. For the military, the mission is paramount and when racial conflicts intensified in the late 1960s and early 1970s, a race relations institute was created to provide human relations training for all of the services.

There are several conclusions that emerge from this discussion. First, in a world characterized by cultural differences and inequitable distribution of economic resources, intergroup conflict in both economic and noneconomic settings is an endogenous characteristic of the social space rather than a nefarious exogenous contamination of market allocation processes and individual decisionmaking. Second, collective identity has value and groups are often willing to forego income and wealth increments to ensure that a desirable level of solidarity and autonomy exist. Third, reductions in intergroup income and wealth differentials will not automatically lead to the erosion of traditional patterns of collective identification.

None of these conclusions is of earth-shattering significance. However, the framework I have outlined does allow black economists to participate in contemporary dialogues about race and culture in ways precluded by the standard framework and on terms compatible with the interests of our constituency. Kenneth Arrow and his colleagues can afford to restrict the range of their investigation of race and economics to the status of blacks as de–cultured workers, but black economists can afford no such luxury. Borrowing a line from an E.F. Hutton commercial, who knows, perhaps, if we can formulate a viable alternative to the standard discourse in the spirit of the preceding discussion, when black economists talk about issues of race and culture maybe more people will listen.

NOTES

1. On an annual basis *Black Enterprise* features perspectives from members of its Board of Black Economists. The National Urban League's annual publication, *The State of Black America,* typically features one or more analyses prepared by black economists.

2. Gerald Jaynes and Robin Williams, eds., *A Common Destiny: Blacks and American Society* (Washington, D.C.: National Academy Press, 1989); Gunnar Myrdal, *An American Dilemma, The Negro Problem and Modern Democracy,* Twentieth Anniversary Edition (New York: Harper and Row, 1962). Originally published in 1944 by Harper and Row. See also the critique of *A Common Destiny* presented in James B. Stewart, "Did They Come to Bury Gunnar Myrdal—Or to Praise Him?" *Forum For Social Economics,* Vol. 20, No. 1 (Fall 1990), 16–32.

3. Charles V. Willie, Antoine M. Garibaldi and Wornie L. Reed, eds., *The Education of African–Americans* (Westport, CT: Auburn House, 1991); Wornie L. Reed, ed., *African–Americans, Essential Perspectives* (Westport, CT: Auburn House, 1993); Wornie L. Reed with William Darity, Sr. and Noma L. Roberson, *Health and Medical Care of African–Americans* (Westport, CT: Auburn House, 1993); and Robert Hill, with Andrew Billingsley, Eleanor Engram, Michilene F. Malson, Roger H. Rubin, Carol B. Stack, James B. Stewart, and James E. Teele, *Research on the African American Family, A Holistic Perspective* (Westport, CT: Auburn House, 1993).

4. The timeliness of the current inquiry is suggested by the recent publication of a special issue of the *Personality and Social Psychology Bulletin* focusing on the self and the collective (October 1994). The introduction by Dale Miller and Deborah Prentice discusses the evolution of psychologists' interests from the issue of how individuals behave in small groups to the issue of how "groups behave within individuals" (p. 451). They correlate this shift in emphasis with a similar thrust in anthropology, asserting that anthropologists are increasingly treating culture in cognitive terms, as a "conceptual structure." Miller and Prentice suggest that with this shift "the boundary between the self and culture for anthropologists, like the boundary between the self and the group for social psychologists, has become blurred. It is no longer possible to assert confidently where one ends and the other begins" (p. 451). Turner et al. argue in one article that the emergent properties of group processes entail a shift in self–perception from personal to social identity (John Turner, Penelope Oakes, S. Alexander Haslam, and Craig McGarty, "Self and Collective: Cognition and Social Context," *Personality and Social Psychology Bulletin,* special issue, The Self and the Collective, 20 (5) (October 1994), 454–463. These authors

maintain that this self–categorizing "is inherently variable, fluid, and context dependent, as self–categories are social, comparative and are always relative to a frame of reference" (p. 454). This general perspective is consistent with specific work on the formation of racial identity among blacks by William Cross, who originally posited that individuals with an initial limited attachment to collective racial identity are moved as a result of negative racially based encounters to develop a strong racial group orientation (see William Cross, "The Negro–to–Black Conversion Experience," *Black World* (July 1971), 13–27. Similar to the pieces cited earlier, Cross's update of his work places greater emphasis on the ambiguity between individual identity and group identity (see William Cross, *Shades of Black, Diversity in African-American Identity* (Philadelphia: Temple University Press, 1991). This update also explores the implications of individual deviations from modal indicators of group identity. See also Janet Helms, ed., *Black and White Racial Identity, Theory, Research and Practice* (Westport, CT: Greenwood Press, 1990).

5. Kenneth Arrow, "The Theory of Discrimination," in O. Ashenfelter and A. Rees, eds., *Discrimination in Labor Markets* (Princeton, NJ: Princeton University Press, 1974), 4.

6. See for example Thomas Sowell, *Race and Economics* (New York: David McKay Company, 1975); Thomas Sowell, *Markets and Minorities* (New York: Basic Books, 1981); and Thomas Sowell, *Ethnic America: A History* (New York: Basic Books, 1982).

7. Alvin Rabushka, *A Theory of Racial Harmony* (Columbia, SC: University of South Carolina Press, 1974), 4–5.

8. Rabushka, 6.

9. Gary S. Becker, *The Economics of Discrimination* (Chicago: University of Chicago Press, 1957).

10. Becker, 16.

11. Becker, 16.

12. William Julius Wilson, *The Declining Significance of Race* (Chicago: University of Chicago Press, 1980).

13. John F. Szwed, "Race and the Embodiment of Culture," *Ethnicity 2* (1975), 25. Szwed's perspective is an example of anthropologists' treatment of culture as a cognitive construct referenced in note 4.

14. Gary S. Becker, "A Theory of Social Interactions," *Journal of Political Economy* 82 (1974), 1063–1093. The foundations of the present discussion can be found in James B. Stewart, "The Political Economy of Race Relations: Toward an Explanatory and Predictive Theory of Black/White Conflict," unpublished (1984).

15. Ubadigbo Okonkwo, "The Economics of Ethnic Discrimination," *The Review of Black Political Economy* 3, No. 2 (1973), 1–18.

16. Okonkwo, 15.

17. Albert O. Hirschman, "The Changing Tolerance for Income Inequality in the Course of Economic Development," *Quarterly Journal of Economics* 87 (1973), 544–566.

18. Albert Breton, *The Economic Theory of Representative Government* (Chicago: Aldine Publishing Company, 1974). See Appendix for an explanation of the Breton framework.

19. See Appendix.

20. See Appendix.

21. William C. Wheaton, "On the Possibility of a Market for Externalities," *Journal of Political Economy* 80 (1972), 1039–1044.

22. E. J. Mishan, *Welfare Economics: Ten Introductory Essays* (New York: Ran-

dom House, 1969); Martin McGuire, "Group Segregation and Optimal Jurisdictions," *Journal of Political Economy* 82 (1974), 112–132.

    23. Mishan, 227.

    24. McGuire, "Group Segregation."

    25. Breton, "Economic Theory," 57.

    26. McGuire.

    27. See for example, *The Review of Black Political Economy*, Special Issue, "Black Community Revitalization: Implementation," 10, No. 1 (Fall 1979).

    28. Mishan, 226.

APPENDIX

The more formal specification that follows of some of the concepts discussed in the preceding presentation is based on a synthesis of constructs adapted from Becker (see note 14), Hirschman (see note 17) and Breton (see note 18). Becker's standard household production framework is modified to allow examination of the implications of the production of individual and collective identity on the well being of agents. The concepts of "the tunnel effect," "the reverse tunnel effect," and "institutionalized envy" and associated analyses used by Hirschman are used to examine changes in intra- and inter-group conflict and association over time related to temporal trends in income distribution. Finally, Breton's framework is used to discuss how conflicts engender particular forms of political responses.

The basic household production function takes the general form:

(1) $U_i = U_i(Z_1, \ldots, Z_m)$

In this formulation U_i is the utility function of the ith individual and the Zs are defined by Becker as basic wants or commodities such as distinction, a good name, etc. For the moment the major implication of the approach is that the concerns of this analysis, i.e., individuals' sense of who they are and how they are related to a group are analogous to the types of commodities that Becker's analysis was designed to examine. This treatment is also consistent with the emerging approaches to the study of group identity as a cognitive phenomenon discussed in note 4.

The production of a given commodity, Z_j, is assumed to involve some combination of an individual's time, t_j, and goods and services obtained through markets, x_j. Each individual, i, is assumed to use an individual–specific technology of production, E^i in the production of commodities that is identical for each commodity produced by i. Becker defines this technology as a combination of the agent's personal attributes, e.g., age and experience, and what are described as "environmental" variables. This yields the general specification:

(2) $Z_j = f_j(x_j, t_j; E)$

Becker then incorporates interactions with others into the model by assuming that the monetary value of others' relevant characteristics affect the production of commodities. Formally,

(3) $Z_j = f_j(x_j, t_j, R^1, \ldots, R^m; E)$

In (3) the R's denote the inputs of others to the production of commodity j by individual i. Becker then goes on to analyze the simple case of a single commodity produced by a single input, ignoring time inputs. In this case maximizing utility is equivalent to maximizing the production of the commodity, or:

(4) $U_i = Z(x, R)$

These simplifications enable Becker to generate first-order equilibrium conditions associated with interperson transfers and other interesting mathematical results.

The approach adopted here is less mechanical. We seek to modify the apparatus to allow examination of the relationship between identity construction and economic forces and determine if and how this relationship changes.

As a starting point, consider the following scenario:

Individual i was reared in a predominantly black inner city environment and developed a particular affinity for barbecued spare ribs and music videos on BET. Upon high school graduation s(he) enrolled in an HBCU. After taking a black studies course s(he) decided to become active in community-based economic development efforts. Local community members lauded this participation and s(he) received a special award at the time of graduation. S(he) pursued graduate study at a traditionally white institution located in a small town. There were no soul food restaurants and all the radio stations played country and western music. For a while s(he) called relatives weekly to get soul food recipes. After some time country and western music didn't seem to sound so bad and the telephone calls home became too expensive. S(he) moved to a large city after graduation and rented a suburban apartment. S(he) adorned the living room with an impressive collection of African artifacts. One day s(he) found out by accident that a colleague with comparable human capital had a salary advantage of $10,000. That evening s(he) came home to find a cross burning in front of the apartment. After some soul searching s(he) moved to the inner city and joined an organization fighting neighborhood gentrification. S(he) doesn't have the time or interest to go out with colleagues from work anymore. They wonder what is wrong and have started making disparaging comments in private. The local black residents were suspicious at first but have warmed up somewhat since the demonstration last week that focused on the efforts of the new residents to have the City Council change the neighborhood zoning regulations.

To guide the modifications to the basic model to allow discussion of the above scenario, the following assumptions are introduced:

(a) An individual's racial/cultural identity can be modeled as a commodity produced through the use of market goods and services and own time;

(b) Racial/cultural identity is interrelated with other dimensions of an individual's core identity, e.g., gender, religion, class, and individuals prioritize identity dimensions and choose technologies of commodity production to maximize well-being;

(c) Individuals produce racial/cultural identity using a technology of production consisting of customary processes identified from a public stock of preexisting cultural knowledge and modifications to those processes introduced as a result of current efforts to enhance identity;

(d) Individuals' private production of racial/cultural identity concurrently produces an externality with public good characteristics that augments the stock of collective racial/cultural identity for group members; and

(e) Both the private production of racial identity by members of one group and the negative externalities associated with that private production (collective identity) can diminish the production of identity by other groups.

Most of these assumptions can be incorporated into a modified model as follows:

(5) $RCI_i^A = RCI_i^A \{x_i, t_i, EDUC_i, AGE_i, GEOG_i; h_i(RCI^{A*}),$
      $k_i(RCI^B, RCI^{B*})\}$

In this formulation RCI_i^A denotes racial/cultural identity of individual i belonging to group A. For the purpose of simplifying the exposition the simultaneity among identity dimensions are ignored, although as suggested in note (4), there appears to be substantial fluidity in self-categorization. The formulation incorporates selected demographic variables, i.e., education (EDUC), age (AGE) and geographical location (GEOG) in a manner that assumes that any influence on racial/cultural identity is unidirectional. The argument $h_i(RCI^{A*})$ is i's technology for producing racial/cultural identity based on i's understanding of historical approaches and i's own interpretation of contemporary alternatives. This is the contemporary impact of group A's history on the current identity construction by individual i. It is a public good and each individual's production function and desired level of identity construction determines the amount of the public good that is used in commodity production. This logic of this treatment is based on the analysis by Wheaton referenced in note 21 and the bi-directional synergy between individual and group identity discussed in note 4.

The function $k_i(.)$ can be thought of as a cultural filter that mediates the direct historical (RCI^{B*}) and contemporary (RCI^B) effects of the production of racial/cultural identity by members of group B on individual i. This is the negative externality of differing other's racial/cultural identity production suggested by Okonkwo, referenced in note 15.

Using the notational convention employed above, the contribution of i's production to collective identity that becomes part of the usable collective cultural repertoire available during the next period is RCI_i^{A*}. The aggregate net augmentation of cultural repertoire available to members of group A in period t+1 can be defined as follows:

(6) $\Delta RCI^{A*,\,t+1} = v\,(RCI_i^{A,t}, \ldots RCI_n^{A,t}, RCI_i^{A*,t}, \ldots$
     $RCI_n^{A*,\,t}) - \gamma(RCI^{A*,\,t-1})$

In (6) v is a technology that assimilates the functional racial/cultural identity construction of individuals, i = 1, ..., n, into the corpus of group A's aggregate cultural repertoire or storehouse of hermeneutic knowledge. We assume the existence of a mechanism to filter out dysfunctional adaptations from becoming important features of group identity. Such a mechanism might accomplish this, for example, by varying the degree of information disseminated among adaptations. γ is a technology for filtering out obsolete practices from the pre–existing cultural repertoire.

The preceding discussion provides sufficient tools to discuss some of the basic features of the scenario. The first implication of the specification that should be emphasized is that there is no a priori predicted direction of the effect of characteristics such as educational attainment, geographical location, or age on the production of racial/group identity. In technical terms, the signs of $\partial RCI_i/\partial EDUC_i$, $\partial RCI_i/\partial AGE_i$, and $\partial RCI_i/\partial GEOG_i$ are indeterminate. In the scenario the agent's pre–college human capital accumulation had little impact on racial/cultural identity development, the Black Studies course taken in college had a significant effect and post-graduate studies had limited effects. In a similar vein, the identity response to aging and geographical location had cyclical characteristics. This pattern reflects the fact that the effects of these characteristics depends on (a) the technology of commodity production, (b) the resources available for identity production, (c) the effectiveness of cultural filters, and (d) the relative priority of racial/cultural identity in the individual's identity matrix. For the sake of brevity only one example of each effect will be cited.

The agent in the scenario modified the technology of commodity production after leaving graduate school using symbolic representations in the form of artifacts to substitute for direct interactions with other group members. Clearly the market restrictions affected the agent's identity production by inducing an involuntary substitution of own prepared foods for soul restaurant fare. Over time the effectiveness of the agent's cultural filters eroded and the cultural production of others, in specifically country and western music, began to create noise in the production of the agent's core racial/cultural identity. This was facilitated by the agent's diminished access to the cultural repertoire of African Americans, resulting, in part, from reduced contact with family members. The agent began to reduce the weight assigned to core racial/cultural identity and to develop an enlarged identity. This implies a change in the sign of the impact of the racial/cultural production of members of other groups on the agent's racial/cultural identity production.

A second implication flowing from the basic specification and the scenario is that traditional forms of economic discrimination affect identity production in several ways. In the scenario there are examples of discrimination in the provision of public goods (elementary and secondary education), human capital discrimination (lower valuation placed on human capital acquired through an HBCU), and wage/income discrimination.

In the scenario, the agent was unaware while enrolled in public school that a differential level of provision of public education was occurring. However, subsequent information obtained about such discrimination can affect identity production at a later point in time. In addition, absence of opportunities to interact with individual members of other groups can adversely affect the development of effective cultural filters.

Assuming that the agent's salary decrement is due in part to a lower valuation on human capital obtained from an HBCU, this is the cost associated with avoiding the negative externalities generated by others' cultural production and the lesser positive contribution to core identity production associated with attending a predominantly white institution.

The income discrimination experienced by the agent reduces the mix of market goods and services available for identity production and the production of other commodities. However, prior to the agent experiencing an overt racial act and acquiring information about the salary differential, it may well have been the case that the substitution effect would have overwhelmed the income effect relative to core identity production. The relative magnitudes of the income and substitution effects on the production of core identity are determined primarily by the parameters of h_i and k_i. Finally, it is important to note that the agent's subsequent involvement in collective efforts to strengthen group identity and pursue economic empowerment might not have occurred without the experience of overt discrimination and a "shock" to the system that the cultural filters could not absorb.

Next we wish to examine the intra- and inter-group interactions reflected in the scenario. To facilitate this discussion consider the racial/cultural identity production functions of three individuals indicated below:

(7a) $RCI_1^A = RCI_1^A \{x_1, t_1, EDUC_1, AGE_1, GEOG_1; h_1(RCI^{A*})$
$k_1 (RCI^B, RCI^{B*})\}$

(7b) $RCI_2^A = RCI_2^A \{x_2, t_2, EDUC_2, AGE_2, GEOG_2; h_2(RCI^{A*}),$
$k_2(RCI^B, RCI^{B*})\}$

(7c) $RCI_3^B = RCI_3^B \{x_3, t_3, EDUC_3, AGE_3, GEOG_3; h_3(RCI^{B*}),$
$k_3(RCI^A, RCI^{A*})\}$

Individuals 1 and 2 belong to group A and individual 3 belongs to group B. In this example group A is meant to represent African Americans and group B, white Americans. For the purposes of simplicity, the superscripts A and B will be dropped.

Let X_1, X_2, and X_3 represent the total incomes of 1, 2 and 3 respectively. Assume that the following initial conditions exist: $X_3 > X_2 > X_1$; $EDUC_3 > EDUC_2 > EDUC_1$; $AGE_3 = AGE_2 = AGE_1$; and $GEOG_3 = GEOG_2 = GEOG_1$.

The issue of concern is how these relationships influence the functions h (.) and k (.) of each individual, but it is first important to understand the direct effects of income inequality on patterns of racial/cultural identity production. Useful hypotheses regarding the relevant relationships can be generated by adapting the analysis of Hirschman (cited in note 17).

(i) $\partial RCI_1/\partial X_2 > 0$; $\partial RCI_2/\partial H_1 > 0$;

This prediction is based on Hirschman's "tunnel effect," which entails a high degree of tolerance for income inequality initially, in part because "advances of others supply information about a more benign external environment; receipt of this information produces gratification; and this gratification overcomes, or at least suspends, *envy*." It is assumed here, then, that individual 3 views individual 2's higher income as an indicator of future increases in own income.

(ii) $\partial RCI_1/\partial X_3 = 0; \partial RCI_2/\partial X_3 > 0.$

The first condition assumes that individual 3 perceives that economic advance is associated only with group B. In such cases Hirschman argues that "those who are left out and behind are unlikely to experience the tunnel effect." However, individual 2 assumes initially that economic advance is possible and views individual 3's higher income as a signal that advancement is possible. The second condition is based on Hirschman's view that "the most effective homogenizing agent is perhaps an intensive historical experience that has been shared by all members of a group." Thus even though $X_1 > X_2$ and $EDUC_1 > EDUC_2$, these class differences are assumed not to erode 2's racial/cultural solidarity with 1 or vice versa.

Also assume that initially:

(iii) $\partial RCI_3/\partial X_2 = 0; \partial RCI_3/\partial X_1 = 0$

These conditions simply indicate that individual 3's racial/cultural identity production is unaffected by individuals 1 and 3's income generating activities. This is a reasonable assumption given the initial conditions set on $GEOG_1$, $GEOG_2$ and $GEOG_3$.

Now assume that at time t_1 the following conditions exist relative to the initial period t_0: $(X_2^{t_1} / X_2^{t_0}) > (X_3^{t_1} / X_3^{t_0}) > 1; (X_1^{t_1} / X_1^{t_0}) = 1;$ and that $GEOG_3 = GEOG_2 = GEOG_1$.

It is reasonable to make the following predictions regarding the implications for the agents' racial/cultural identity production:

(iv) $\partial RCI_2/\partial X_1 > 0; \partial RCI_1/\partial X_2 > 0.$

The first prediction is based on Hirschman's "reverse tunnel effect" whereby an agent observes nonimprovement in the status of a member of his/her reference group and takes this as a signal of likely trends in one's own status. The second prediction assumes that the tunnel effect is still in operation relative to individual 1's view of individual 2's progress.

It is also likely that:

(v) $0 < \partial RCI_2/\partial X_2 < \partial\ RCI_2/\partial\ X_3$;

This condition implies that although the intra-group income trends are important to individual 2's racial/cultural identity production, the characteristics of the produced identity are altered as a result of 1's identification with individual 3. It is important to note that this phenomenon is not the negative externality effect on racial/cultural identity production described earlier, as individual 2's identity production is enhanced rather than retarded through the identification with individual 3.

(vi) $\partial RCI_3/\partial X_2 < 0$; $\partial RC_1\ 1\ \partial/\ X_3 < 0$.

These predictions are based on Hirschman's argument that the tolerance for income equality erodes over time possibly leading the nonmobile group to expect that "as a result of another group's advance, it will expect to be *worse* off." Thus, it is assumed that individual 3 perceives that individual 2's more rapid income growth has occurred at 3's expense. In a similar vein, individual 1 makes the same evaluation about individual 3's income growth. In addition, however, it is reasonable to expect that negative externalities from 2's racial/cultural identity production are now affecting 3's racial/cultural identity production. This occurs through the change in $GEOG_2$ as follows:

(vii) $\partial RCI_3/\ \partial k_3(\ .\ ) < 0$ (initially $= 0$ at t_o when $GEOG_3$
      $= GEOG_2$)

From the vantage point of individual 3:

(viii) $\partial RCI^A/\partial\ GEOG_2 > 0$

However, it may well be the case that from the vantage point of individual 1, the following expectation may exist:

(ix) $\partial RCI^A\ /\ \partial GEOG_2 < 0$

Hirschman argues that in situations where the upwardly mobile become integrated into a higher class structure "the immobile may lose hope of eventual advance." He argues that this produces a shift in allegiance "from supporter to enemy" that comes about purely as a result of the passage of time. This would imply that in addition to the relationship implied in (ix), the following conditions now exist from the vantage point of individual 1:

(x) $\partial RCI_1/\partial X_2 < 0; \partial RCI_3/\partial X_2 > 0$

There are two critical implications of the situation reflected in (ix) and (x). First, there is now additional "noise" in the production of racial/ cultural identity of group A that affects not only its own racial/cultural identity production but also that of group B. This noise directly affects the functions h_1, and h_2 as well as the efficiency of the cultural filters k_1, k_2 and k_3. The upshot of this situation is that all agents are motivated to expend time and resources to produce a commodity that can be described as "political comfort."

Hirschman suggests that situations of the type described above have the potential to foment revolution in developing countries. Here we wish to consider conflicts of lesser magnitude of the type examined by Breton (see note 18). Breton's concern is the difference between the amount of a public policy supplied and that desired by a citizen, which is defined as the degree of coercion. This concept of coercion can be treated as a correlate of the political comfort commodity introduced above.

Breton assumes that if the level of coercion exceeds a certain threshold then an individual will attempt to reduce that coercion through the use of political instruments. Individuals are assumed to select among alternative political instruments with differing time/resource input mix requirements subject to cost constraints. The cost of using a given political instrument is the sum of money and time required to achieve a unit reduction in coercion.

One implication of Breton's analysis is that higher income individuals will choose less time-intensive political instruments, such as voting or regulating own economic behavior, while lower income individuals are more likely to use time-intensive instruments such as joining social movements or pressure groups. Moreover, individuals who are members of a group that is a numerical minority have an incentive to use instruments requiring collaboration with other agents to exploit economies of scale. The immediate implication of Breton's analysis is that the critiques of the political strategies used by blacks that have been advanced, for example by Rabushka and Sowell (see notes 6, 7 and 8) are misguided because the observed patterns reflect differences in inter–group resource endowments.

To apply Breton's analysis to the case at hand, it is only necessary to recognize that there is a subset of public policies that simultaneously impact racial/cultural group identity production and the income and/or wealth and/or human capital distributions. These policies include affirmative action, public school desegregation and minority business set-asides. It is reasonable to expect that individuals will respond to coercion perceived to be associated with such policies in a manner roughly analogous to that described by Breton. The credibility of this hypothesis is strengthened since many of the adverse affects of racial/cultural identity production are hypothesized to be manifested as negative externalities with public goods characteristics. Breton's analysis is designed to examine the factors affecting the provision of public goods.

In the scenario used to motivate discussion of the formal model, the situation is further complicated by the fact that a group of whites have relocated into a neighborhood previously populated overwhelmingly by blacks ($GEOG_1 = GEOG_3$). Both groups experience coercion and use different political instruments in attempting to reduce that coercion. This introduces the issue of the welfare implications of homogeneous versus heterogeneous jurisdictions discussed in note 22.

The particular conclusions derived from the preceding exploration are, of course, driven by the specific assumptions that were introduced. What is more important than the specific conclusions, however, are (a) the extent to which the general framework is useful for motivating collaborative exploration of critical policy issues with specialists in other fields, and (b) the general foci that emerge that can guide further exploration.

Assuming that the framework has some heuristic value, some of the topics that emerge as worthy of additional scrutiny include: (1) human capital accumulation optimization strategies that reflect both direct income-generating and identity-related characteristics; (2) the impacts of the manner in which income is generated, e.g., transfers, employment, illicit activities on collective identity production; (3) identification of social mechanisms that reinforce those dimensions of the aggregate cultural repertoire that jointly maximize economic well-being and collective identity; and (4) development of mechanisms to foster efforts to enhance economic–well being and identity development as income stratification and residential heterogeneity increase.

2

AN EMPIRICAL TEST OF THE CULTURAL CAPITAL HYPOTHESIS

James H. Johnson, Jr., Elisa Jayne Bienenstock, and Jennifer A. Stoloff

Using data from the Multi-City Survey of Urban Inequality, an exploratory, empirical analysis of the cultural capital hypothesis was conducted. The analyses indicate that, while the types of cultural influences cited by proponents of this thesis clearly have negative effects on employment when viewed in isolation from other factors, they are not significant when statistical controls for human capital variables are incorporated into the model. Our findings suggest the need to invest more resources in the public education system and in efforts to combat racial discrimination in the labor market.

INTRODUCTION AND CRITICAL BACKGROUND

A wide range of theories have been advanced to explain the steadily deteriorating quality of life in U.S. inner-city communities. Yet one perspective—the so-called cultural capital hypothesis—has held sway in recent public policy debates. It holds "that a deterioration in individual responsibility and family morals and values, rooted primarily in liberal social welfare policies and programs of the 1960s, is principally responsible for rising rates of concentrated and persistent poverty, joblessness, family disruption, out-of-wedlock births, and gang- and drug-related lethal violence in urban America over the last two decades."[1]

Based on this view, policymakers, with widespread public support, have instituted a set of, arguably, paternalistic and punitive public policies to "change welfare as we know it" and to foster normative behavior among the inner-city poor. In response to the high rates of lethal violence, for example, policymakers have instituted a series of "get tough, lock them up and throw away the key" crime policies. To reduce welfare dependency and to foster responsibility and strengthen family values and morals, policies designed to teach the inner-city disadvantaged the importance of staying in school (Learnfare), of not having children until marriage (Wedfare and Bridefare), and of getting and maintaining a job (Workfare) have been implemented in many states and are currently being contemplated at the federal level.[2]

Some researchers and social policy analysts have argued that the foregoing assessment of the underlying causes of contemporary poverty is a misspecification of the problem and that the aforementioned policy prescriptions are aimed not at *reducing poverty* per se, but, rather, at *reducing dependency* on the government dole.[3] This argument seems highly plausible and may indeed be valid. But its proponents have failed to provide ample empirical evidence to support this view and thus have contributed to the political ideological quagmire in which the contemporary poverty debate is mired.

That the concept of "cultural capital" is difficult to operationalize and measure—in a statistical sense—is largely responsible for this state of affairs. It is clear from the recent writings of its proponents that cultural capital is a multi-dimensional concept not easily captured in a single variable or indicator. The issues of measurement and operationalization, therefore, must be resolved before the hypothesis can be subjected to rigorous empirical testing—both independent of and relative to alternative explanations of the contemporary poverty problem in urban America.[4]

RESEARCH OBJECTIVES AND DATA

In this article, we conduct an exploratory empirical analysis of the cultural capital hypothesis. We attempt first to operationalize this theoretical construct, and second to assess the statistical effects of a set of empirically derived dimensions of cultural capital on the labor market experiences of a sample of able-bodied, working-age men.

To address these issues, we utilize data from a new interdisciplinary research initiative, the Multi-City Study of Urban Inequality (MCSUI). The theoretical underpinnings and research design of the MCSUI have been described in detail elsewhere.[5] Suffice it to note that the major goal was to gather primary data from a large sample of households and employers in four cities (Atlanta, Boston, Detroit, and Los Angeles) that would enable researchers to determine the extent to which three sets of forces—changing labor market dynamics, racial attitudes and polarization, and racial residential segregation—contributed, singularly and in concert, to the growing schisms between the "haves" and the "have-nots" in urban America over the last two decades.

For the purpose of this study, we limit these exploratory analyses to data from the Los Angeles component of the MCSUI for two reasons. The first pertains to the demand-side and the supply-side features of the Los Angeles labor market.[6] On the one hand, the Los Angeles labor pool is large and extremely diverse—nearly 60 percent of the population is non-white (black, Asian, or Hispanic); on the other, while there was substantial job growth during the 1980s—732,000 jobs were added to the Los Angeles economy—labor demand was insufficient to accommodate the burgeoning supply of labor. Moreover, the demand that did exist during the 1980s was highly concentrated in two economic sectors—producer services (high-wage jobs) and personal services (mainly low-wage jobs) (Table 1), which contributed to the growing gap between the haves and the have-nots in Los Angeles.[7]

Further, since 1990, the demand for labor in all sectors of the Los Angeles economy has been on a downward trajectory. This is due, in part, to major federal cuts in defense spending and partly to a more general trend in corporate America toward downsizing, re-engineering, and capital flight, especially from the state of California, in an effort to facilitate efficiency and competitiveness in the global marketplace. Mainly as a consequence of these forces, it has been estimated that the state of California lost 700,000 jobs at the outset of this decade.[8] Business failures and capital flight from the Los Angeles metropolitan area accounts for much of this job loss. Unfortunately, on the supply side, the number of job seekers arriving in Los Angeles, primarily from abroad, has not declined accordingly.[9]

When the foregoing demand-side and supply-side realities are juxtaposed, Los Angeles emerges as a labor surplus environment, a community in which there are far more job seekers than there are available jobs. In contrast to their counterparts in tight labor markets, where the number of job applicants roughly approximates job vacancies, employers in labor surplus environments can be far more selective in recruitment and hiring; that is, they can screen out job seekers whom they deem—rightly or wrongly—to possess inappropriate cultural capital attributes.[10] Thus, the Los Angeles labor market context, where there is enormous competition for available positions,[11] is ideal for an empirical test of the cultural capital hypothesis.

The second reason relates to the unique features of the Los Angeles component of the MCSUI dataset.[12] It is a large sample that is highly representative not only of the dominant ethnic groups—Asians, blacks,

TABLE 1
Comparison of LASUI Data with 1990 Census
of Population and Housing Data

Race and Ethnicity

Group	LASUI RAW	LASUI Weighted	LA County Eligibles*	LA County
White	21.4	43.2	49.4	47.0
Black	27.8	11.0	10.9	10.3
Asian	26.2	7.7	6.5	6.2
Latino	24.5	38.1	33.2	31.5
Other	-	-	-	5.0
TOTAL	4,025	3,133	5,787,991	6,090,712

Neighborhood Poverty Status

Neighborhood Poverty Level	LASUI RAW Sample	LASUI Weighted Sample	LA County Eligibles*
<20%	52.7	75.2	72.6
20-40%	31.5	22.2	24.7
40+	15.8	2.6	2.6
TOTAL	4,025	3,133	6,108,478

Source: U.S. Bureau of the Census,
1990 Census of Population and Housing, STF3A
 * Population 21 years of age or older

Hispanics, non-Hispanic whites—in the local labor market, but also of the population residing in both poor and nonpoor neighborhoods in Los Angeles (Table 2).[13]

Our decision to focus on males in the Los Angeles sample reflects our research interest in the steadily declining economic status of young black males nationally, and in urban America in particular. It has been argued elsewhere that the black male jobless problem must be critically evaluated within the context of the broader changes occurring on both the demand side and the supply side of the labor market.[14] The MCSUI data are ideal for such analyses.[15]

ANALYSES AND FINDINGS

Unpacking the Cultural Capital Box

Cultural capital theorists have specific explanations for the relative success or failure of the various ethnic minorities—Chinese Americans, Koreans, Japanese Americans, Hispanics and blacks—who are represented in the MCSUI data from Los Angeles. It is useful to briefly review these explanations.

Proponents argue that the poor performance of blacks in the labor market is due in large measure to the debilitating effects of slavery and, subsequently, of the southern sharecropper system. Writing about the effects of slavery, Sowell states, for example, that "As workers, blacks had little sense of personal responsibility under slavery. Lack of initiative, evasion of work, half done work, unpredictable absenteeism, and abuse of tools and equipment were pervasive under slavery, and these patterns did not suddenly disappear with emancipation."[16] The slavery experience, according to cultural capital theorists, inculcated in blacks, "values that are impediments to work, savings, education, and upward mobility, impediments that operated with stultifying effects. . . . "[17] Further, Harrison contends that these values and behaviors persisted under Jim Crowism in the South,[18] and Lemann argues that blacks who migrated from the South brought these behavioral traits with them to the urban North, where they were once again reinforced by the liberal social-welfare policies of the 1960s.[19]

In a similar vein, Harrison argues that immigrants from Latin America lag behind in economic performance due to their traditional Iberian culture and values, which he characterizes as the direct opposite of the cultural values that European immigrants brought to this country. He

TABLE 2
Employment Change by Industry 1980–1990

	Total Employment	Transformative Activities	INDUSTRY Distributive Services	Producer Services	Personal Services	Social Services
Los Angeles County						
1980	3,471,764	1,038,751	948,524	492,278	254,320	694,150
1990	4,203,792	1,107,917	1,150,053	709,066	365,534	810,096
Change '80-'90	732,028	69,166	201,529	216,788	111,214	115,946
%	21.0%	16.6%	21.0%	44.0%	44.0%	16.7%
Los Angeles City						
1980	1,394,855	376,656	365,858	229,350	129,901	275,733
1990	1,670,488	405,447	437,548	315,409	184,850	302,367
Change '80-'90	275,633	28,791	71,690	86,059	59,949	26,634
%	19.7%	7.6%	19.6%	37.5%	42.3%	9.7%
Balance of County						
1980	2,076,909	662,095	582,666	262,928	124,419	408,417
1990	2,533,304	702,470	712,505	393,657	180,684	507,729
Change '80-'90	456,395	40,375	129,839	130,729	56,265	89,312

Source: Census of Population, 1980 and 1990. Note: Transformative activities include manufacturing and construction; distributive services include transportation, communication, wholesale and retail trade; producer services include finance, insurance, real estate, and business services; personal services include entertainment, repairs, eating and drinking; and social services include medical, education, and government.

states further that the "Mexicans who migrate to the United States bring with them a repressive culture that is disconcertingly persistent."[20] Sowell contends that the goals and values of Mexican-Americans have never been centered on education,[21] and Mead argues that they have less industrious work attitudes.[22]

Unlike blacks and Hispanics, who are perceived to possess the wrong set of cultural capital attributes, Harrison argues that "the Chinese, Japanese, and the Koreans who have migrated to the United States have injected a dose of the work ethic, excellence, and merit at a time when those values appear particularly beleaguered in the broader society."[23]

The success of these three groups, he contends, is rooted in a set of "culturally derived" characteristics flowing from their Confucian value system, which emphasizes education, hard work, excellence, risk taking, and frugality. Further, in contrast to blacks and Hispanics, these groups are perceived as having a strong future orientation and a sense of self as part of a collectivity that extends the radius of trust outside the family to the community.[24]

Specifically with respect to work or employment outcomes, then, cultural capital theorists argue that the high rate of joblessness in urban America is due neither to structural constraints in the labor market, as posited by Wilson,[25] nor to employer discrimination, as postulated by Kirschenman and Neckerman.[26] Rather, they contend that the joblessness problem reflects character deficiencies and deviant values of inner-city residents, especially males. They argue that inner-city residents actually choose not to work regularly and that this unwillingness to work is embedded in the nature and culture of the inner city. Negative attitudes toward work, cultural capital theorists assert, are rooted in:

> *ghetto life* (the breakdown of authority and lack of disapproval of antisocial behavior); *ethnicity* (the lack of value placed on getting ahead by some ethnic groups); *culture* (a history of slavery and dependence on Whites created a world view among Blacks that makes them uniquely prone to anti-hero attitudes); and the *Third World origins of immigrants* (less industrious work attitudes shaped by African and Latin rather than the European origins of today's poor).[27]

The foregoing descriptions of "culturally derived" characteristics purportedly explain who prospers and who does not in American society. Based on this, we selected fifteen questions from the MCSUI, which were designed to capture the forces that shape an individual's morals, values, and work orientation. These questions are grouped into five categories in Table 3, which also indicates how the responses to each question are coded.

The categories are: *geographical influences,* including the respondent's place of birth and place of residence most of the time, up to age sixteen; *family background influences,* whether the respondent lived with both parents most of the time until age sixteen, the employment status of the respondent's father and mother during his formative years (i.e., until age

TABLE 3
Cultural Capital Indicators

Concept	Variables	Specific Measures
Geographic Influences	Where was your mother living when you were born?	Recoded: (1) Third World Country, (2) Other foreign country, (3) Southern U.S., (4) Elsewhere
	In what city and state did you live most of the time before you were age 16?	Recoded: (1) Third World Country, (2) Other foreign country, (3) Southern U.S., (4) Elsewhere
Family Background Influences	Did you live with both of your parents most of the time until you were 16 years old?	Coded: (1) yes (2) no
	What is the highest grade of school or year of schooling your father completed?	Coded: absolute years
	Did he usually work during the year when you were age 16?	Coded: (1) yes (0) no (B) DK
	What is the highest grade of school or year of schooling your mother completed?	Coded: absolute years
	Did she usually work during the year when you were age 16?	Coded: (1) yes (0) no (B) DK
	Most of the time when you were 16 years old did you and (SELECTED SIB) grow up in the same household?	Coded: (1) yes (0) no
	Does (SELECTED SIB) WORK?	Recoded: (1) yes (0) no
	Was there ever a time up to when you were 16 years of age when your family received AFDC, public assistance, or welfare?	Coded: (1)
Religious Influences	Are you:	Coded: (1) Protestant, (2) Catholic, (3) Jewish, (4) Other, (5) No preference
	What category best describes how often you attend religious services?	Coded: (1) If attends church at least once a month or more, (0) else
Political Influences	Generally speaking, do you think of yourself as:	Coded: (1) Republican, (2) Democrat, (3) Independent, (4) Some other, (5) No preference, (6) No preference for religious reasons
	We hear a lot of talk about liberals and conservatives. Where would you place yourself on this scale?	Recoded: (1) Liberal, (2) Moderate, (3) Conservative, (4) Haven't thought about it
	Are you a U.S. citizen?	Recoded: (1) yes (0) no
	Are you registered to vote?	Coded: (1) yes (0) no
Race/Ethnic Identity	Please choose from this page the number that best describes your race:	(1) White, (2) Black/African American, (3) Asian American (4) American Indian, (5) Other
	Are you of Spanish or Hispanic origin?	(1) yes (0) no
	Please look at the card and tell me which group you belong to:	(1) Mexican, (2) Mexican American, (3) Puerto Rican, (4) Cuban, (5) Salvadorian, (6) Dominican, (7) Guatemalan, (8) Nicaraguan, (9) Other
Language Skills	How would you rate the respondent's ability to understand English?	Coded: (1) Excellent, (2) Very Good, (3) Good, (4) Fair, (5) Poor
	How would you rate the respondent's ability to speak clearly in English?	Coded: (1) Excellent, (2) Very Good, (3) Good, (4) Fair, (5) Poor

sixteen), and whether the respondent's family ever received welfare or lived in public housing during his formative years; *educational influences,* years of school completed by the respondent's father and mother, and years of school completed by the respondent prior to coming to the United States; *religious influences,* church affiliation and frequency of church attendance; *political influences,* party affiliation, political leaning, citizenship status, whether the respondent was a green card holder, and whether the respondent was registered to vote. Table 3 also includes indicators of *ethnic identity* and *language skills.*

To identify the underlying structure in these data, we first transformed the responses to each of the items/questions in Table 3 to dummy variables. This re-coded dataset was then subjected to a principal component analysis that reduced the individual variables to a smaller, more manageable number of "principal components" representing the underlying structure of the original responses. Those principal components with eigenvalues greater than one—a total of fifteen—were considered to be significant and thus were rotated using the varimax solution to identify more clearly the cluster of variables loading on each component. Together these fifteen components accounted for 69 percent of the total variance in the original set of cultural capital indicators.

We shall describe only seven of the principal components here—those which proved to be highly correlated with the employment status of males in the Los Angeles labor market. They are reproduced in Table 4.

The first component, accounting for 16.1 percent of the variance, distinguishes U.S. citizens (−.869) who vote (−.769) and speak standard English (−.765) from individuals who were born in a Third World country (.861), who lived in a Third World country most of the time before they were sixteen years old (.852), and who have a green card (.753). Individuals with positive scores on this component are documented aliens from the Third World, while those with negative scores are U.S. citizens. Given this pattern of loadings, we labeled this component *Citizenship.*

The next two components tap into other dimensions of immigrant cultural influences in Los Angeles. One (Component 2) captures Mexicans (.864) whose primary language is Spanish (.801), and the other (Component 3) captures individuals who were born in a foreign country outside the Third World (.857) and who lived primarily in that region prior to age sixteen (.885). Component 2, labeled *Mexican Immigrants,* accounts for 6.4 percent of the total variance, and Component 3, labeled *Non-Third World Immigrants,* accounts for 5.8 percent of the total variance.

TABLE 4
Principle Components

Variable	Loading	Communality
Component 1: Citizenship		
(16.1% of total variance)		
Born in Third World	0.861	0.899
Lived in Third World	0.852	0.855
Educated Outside of U.S.	0.867	0.857
Green Card	0.753	0.637
U.S. Citizen	-0.869	0.829
Voter	-0.769	0.679
Speak Standard English	-0.765	0.789
Component 2: Mexican Immigrants		
(6.4% of Total Variance)		
Mexican	0.525	0.864
Spanish Speaking	0.559	0.801
Component 3: Non-Third World Immigrants		
(5.8% of Total Variance)		
Born in Foreign Country	0.915	0.857
Lived in Foreign Country	0.920	0.885
Component 4: Southern Roots		
(4.8% of Total Variance)		
Born in South	0.905	0.862
Lived in South	0.905	0.847
Component 5: English Proficiency		
(3.4% of Total Variance)		
Understands English Well	0.898	0.906
Speaks English Well	0.883	0.888
Component 6: Parental Education Influences		
(3.1% of Total Variance)		
Mother's Education	0.792	0.705
Father's Education	0.772	0.650
Component 7: Family Dependency		
(3.0% of Total Variance)		
Lived in Public Housing as a child	0.563	0.931
Family Received AFDC when respondent was a child	0.619	0.505

Component 4, labeled *Southern Roots,* captures individuals who were born in the southern United States (.857) and who lived primarily in that region prior to age sixteen (.885). This factor taps those individuals who, according to cultural capital theorists, have poor attitudes toward work, especially if they are black.[28]

Whereas Components 1 through 4 reflect geographic influences, Component 5 is a measure of *English Proficiency.* Accounting for 3.4 percent of the total variance, this component identifies individuals who, according to ratings by the interviewer, understand English well (.898) and are able to speak English clearly (.883).

Components 6 and 7 capture household and family influences. Years of school completed by the survey respondent's mother (.792) and years of school completed by the respondent's father (.772) loaded on Component 6. Two indicators of growing up in a household that received government assistance loaded on Component 7: whether the survey respondent lived in public housing as a child (.431) and whether the family received AFDC when the respondent was a child (.505). Component 6, labeled *Parental Educational Influences,* accounted for 3.1 percent of the variance in the original set of variables, and Component 7, labeled *Family Dependency,* accounted for 3.0 percent.

Together this subset of principal components capture several specific types of influences—including geographic, historical, and family background effects—that cultural capital theorists contend shape one's morals, values, and attitudes toward family, community, and work. The crucial empirical question here is: to what degree do these factors statistically influence an individual's employment status—that is, whether able-bodied men work or not?

Cultural Capital and Employment: Is There a Link?

To answer this question, we recoded the male responses to a question in the MCSUI regarding present work status as a dichotomous variable, after excluding individuals who were in school, disabled, or retired. Those who were employed part time or full time, or who were temporarily laid off, were classified as *working,* and those who were unemployed or not attached to the labor market were classified as *not working.* Using logistic regression analysis, we then tested the statistical effects of four sets of independent variables.

In addition to the empirically derived principal components of cultural capital, we also included several human capital, contextual, and social status variables, which are defined in Table 5. The goal here is to determine the effects of cultural capital independent of, and controlling for, other factors that have been posited as determinants of employment status in urban labor markets.[29]

We entered the variables into the logit model in blocks beginning with the empirically derived cultural capital indicators, followed by the human capital variables, the contextual variables, and the social status variables. Within each block, we used the backward stepwise selection procedure to identify the statistically significant predictor variables. The results of the logistic regression analyses are summarized in Table 6.

As block one in Table 6 shows, three of the seven empirically derived components of cultural capital—Mexican immigrants, southern roots, and family dependency—emerged as statistically significant predictors of the employment status of our sample of Los Angeles men. Moreover, the signs of the corresponding beta values on each of these variables are consistent with the cultural capital hypothesis. Being a Spanish-speaking Mexican immigrant (b = −.147), born in the South, and spending most of your formative years in this region (b = −.211), and having lived either in publicly subsidized housing and/or in a family that received welfare as a child (b = −.175) all have negative effects on the likelihood of working. Translating the exponentiated betas in Table 6 into odds or probabilities, the findings indicate that, in comparison to their male counterparts who do not share these traits, Mexican immigrants are 14 percent less likely to be working, males with southern roots are 19 percent less likely to be working, and those in the Los Angeles sample who grew up in publicly subsidized family situations are 17 percent less likely to be working.

Do these findings hold up when statistical controls for individual human capital attributes such as age, marital status, years of school completed, and job training are introduced into the model? Block two in Table 6 provides an answer to this question.

Two of the human capital variables, marital status (b = .672) and years of school completed (b = .138), emerged as statistically significant predictors of the employment status of men in our sample. Every additional year of school completed increased the odds or likelihood of working by 14 percent, and married men in our sample were 95 percent more likely to be working than were unmarried men.

What impact did these two variables have on the cultural capital components of the model? When these two human capital variables were introduced, two of the cultural capital variables, Mexican immigrants and family dependency, were rendered statistically insignificant. Only one of

TABLE 5
Variables Used in Analysis

Type of Variable	Attributes	Variables	N	Working (%)	Not Working (%)
Independent	Cultural Capital	Mexican Immigrants	218	89.0	11.0
		Southern Roots	87	73.6	26.4
		English Proficiency (low)	457	88.2	11.8
		Parental Educational (father or mother 13+ yrs.)	685	85.1	14.9
		Family Dependency	152	76.3	23.7
		Citizenship (non-U.S. citizen)	564	88.1	11.9
		Third World Immigrants	690	89.0	11.0
		Non-Third World Immigrants	58	94.8	5.2
Control	Human Capital	Age (Mean)	1363	37.0	37.0
		Marital Status (married)	1364	91.7	8.3
		Job Training (yes)	365	85.8	14.2
		Years of School Completed	1184	14.0	12.0
	Contextual	Neighborhood Poverty Rate			
		High (>40%)	223	88.3	11.7
		Medium (20-39%)	457	86.4	13.6
	Social Status	Criminal Record (yes)	168	66.0	33.0
		Black (yes)	255	76.9	23.1
		Non-Hispanic White	306	88.6	11.4
		Asian-American	365	93.4	6.6
		Latino/Hispanic	438	85.8	14.2
		Skin Tone (dark)	233	79.0	21.0
		Skin Tone (med.-light)	1135	87.4	12.6
Dependent	Employment Status	Working	1369	86.0	14.0

the empirically derived cultural capital attributes, southern roots (b = −.158, p = .07), maintained its statistical significance; however, its effect declined (see Table 6, block two).

The next set of variables that we entered into the model consisted of one social status variable (i.e., whether the respondent had a criminal record) and two contextual variables (i.e., neighborhood poverty status). As block three in Table 6 shows, neither of the poverty indices was significant, but the crime variable was highly significant (b = −1.24). In fact, the effects of this variable were so strong that it rendered the influence of southern roots statistically insignificant. The results indicate that having a criminal record reduces the likelihood, or odds, of an individual's working by 72 percent, as compared to someone without a criminal record.

TABLE 6
Logistic Regression Results

Variables	Block 1			Block 2			Block 3			Block 4		
	B	Sig	Exp(B)	B	Sig	Exp(B)	B	Sig	Exp(B)	B	Sig	Exp(B)
Constant	2.0338			-0.1165			0.2528			0.4598		
Mexican Immigrants	-0.1471 (0.0861)	0.0876	0.8632	0.1190 (0.1127)	0.2907	1.1264	0.0579 (0.1146)	0.6133	1.0596	0.0320 (0.1154)	0.7814	1.0325
Southern Roots	-0.2106 (0.0849)	0.0131	0.8101	-0.1579 (0.0866)	0.0684	0.8539	-0.0880 (0.0902)	0.3293	0.9158	-0.0360 (0.0951)	0.705	0.9646
Family Dependency	-0.1749 (0.0846)	0.0386	0.8396	-0.1110 (0.0869)	0.2014	0.8949	-0.0650 (0.0893)	0.4668	0.9371	-0.0182 (0.0943)	0.8473	0.982
Marital Status				0.6720 (0.2066)	0.0011	1.9581	0.5462 (0.2120)	0.0100	1.7267	0.5294 (0.2121)	0.0126	1.6979
Years of School Completed				0.1384 (0.0322)	0.0000	1.1485	0.1316 (0.0330)	0.0001	1.1407	0.1228 (0.0264)	0.0000	1.1307
Criminal Record							-1.2398 (0.2498)	0.0000	0.2894	-1.2304 (0.2458)	0.0000	0.2922
Black & Dark Skinned										-0.7307 (0.2963)	0.0136	0.4816

Standard errors appear in parentheses below each coefficient.

Given the enormous racial disparity in joblessness in our urban centers, we entered into the model, as the final set of independent variables (block 4 in Table 6), a measure of race (black) and skin tone (dark), both of which might be viewed as indicators of social status. Neither variable was statistically significant independent of the other, but the interaction effect between these two variables was statistically significant. Being dark in skin tone *and* black (b = −.731) has a negative impact on the likelihood, or odds, of working.

Table 7 summarizes the findings of the logistic regression analyses. None of the empirically derived principal components of cultural capital, in the final analysis, were statistically significant predictor variables. The most influential variables in distinguishing who was working or not working in our Los Angeles sample included whether or not the individual had a criminal record, the years of school the individual completed, and his marital status. However, it is noteworthy that, after controlling for these and other cultural capital and contextual variables, being a dark skinned black male, rather than a light skinned non-black, reduced an individual's odds of working by 52 percent.

DISCUSSION AND CONCLUSIONS

There are multiple and competing explanations, with varying degrees of plausibility, for the growing schism between the haves and the have-nots in urban America.[30] What we have characterized in this paper as the cultural capital hypothesis appears to be the most popular explanation among both the public and political and civic leaders: *the trend toward continued inequality in American society is due not to structural changes in the economy, employer discrimination, or increasing social isolation and economic marginalization of the most disadvantaged elements from the mainstream of the society, but, rather, to a deterioration in values, morals, and personal responsibility.*

It is this view that undergirds the sweeping changes in the U.S. Congress in the recent mid-term elections. These elections have enabled the new Republican majority to forge its "Contract With America."[31] And it was this view that served, throughout the 1980s, as the basis for the enactment, at both the federal and state levels, of a wide range of arguably paternalistic and punitive public policies as a means to deal with the seemingly intractable problems of drugs, crime, and long-term welfare dependency in our cities.[32]

Yet our exploratory analyses of the MCSUI data, based on the ethni-

TABLE 7
Summary Results of Logistic Regression Analysis

		Working		Not Working		
		B	Exp(B)		B	Exp (B)
Statistically Significant	Marital Status	1	(70%)	Criminal Record	(1)	(71%)
	Years of School Completed	.123	(13%)	Black & Dark Skinned	-.731	(52%)
		B	Exp(B)		B	Exp (B)
Not Statistically Significant	Non Third World Immigrant	.152	(16%)	Parental Educational Influence	-.01	(1%)
	English Proficiency	.146	(15%)	Age	-.01	(2%)
	Citizenship	.146	(20%)	High Poverty Tract	-.02	(3%)
	Medium Poverty	.182	(20%)	Skin Tone	-.114	(11%)
	Black	.063	(6%)	Southern Roots	-.037	(4%)
	Mexican Immigrant	.034	(3%)	Family Dependency	-.018	(2%)

cally diverse Los Angeles sample, do not support the cultural capital hypothesis, and they question the attention that this school of thought has been receiving in the public policy arena. The types of cultural influences—geographical (e.g., being born in the South or in the Third World), historical (e.g., slavery and sharecropper system), and familial (e.g., growing up in a household dependent on government assistance)—cited by proponents of this thesis clearly have negative effects on employment *when viewed in isolation from other factors.* But the negative effects of the cultural capital variables disappeared once statistical controls for a range of human capital (education and marital status) and social status (race, skin tone, and criminal record) variables are incorporated into the model.

That the likelihood of working is positively influenced by years of school completed and marital status is not surprising. The crucial question is: what are the policy implications of these findings?

If, as Wilson and others suggest,[33] the key to marriage is having a good job which, in turn, enables one to form and maintain a stable family; and if the odds of securing employment increase with years of school completed, then the policy implications are fairly straightforward: we need to invest far more resources in improving the public education system, especially school-to-work transition programs, for non-college-bound youth.

On the other hand, it is clear from our preliminary explorations of the MCSUI data that a criminal record is a major impediment to employment. And it is also clear from this research that a criminal record is not necessarily a function of one's package of cultural capital attributes, as some conservative policy analysts would lead us to believe.[34]

Rather, it reflects, we believe, this nation's obsession with punishment, as opposed to prevention and rehabilitation, not just for major crimes but for most minor offenses as well, especially if the offenses occur in economically distressed inner-city communities.[35] We believe the crime epidemic is related, in part, to the fact that the kinds of personal resources and so-called mediating institutions that once encouraged young men to pursue mainstream avenues of economic and social mobility, and that discouraged them from engaging in dysfunctional behavior, are no longer effective or available in inner-city communities.[36] Previous research indicates that such community-based institutions as the Boy's and Girl's Club and the YMCA and YWCA lost much of their financial support during the 1980s, and thus became less effective precisely at the time that the problems confronting disadvantaged youth were worsening.[37]

In addition, emerging evidence suggests that programs designed to mend the social fabric of economically distressed communities will go a long way toward resolving the urban crime problem. For example, a recent evaluation of a Midnight Basketball League in Milwaukee, Wisconsin, revealed that the program (1) created a safe haven in which the participants and the fans could engage in positive social activities, (2) channeled the energy of gang members in a positive direction, and (3) significantly improved the educational and career aspirations of program participants. In addition, according to Milwaukee Police Department statistics, crime rates in the target area decreased by 30 percent during the program's first year of operation.[38]

Moreover, the program achieved these highly desirable outcomes with a modest investment of $70,000—roughly the same amount required to maintain two inner-city males in prison for one year. One does not have to be an investment banker to realize that programs like Midnight Basketball will contribute far more to the revival of economically distressed inner-city communities than will any or all of the enormously popular punitive and/or paternalistic policies currently advocated at all levels of government.[39]

Finally, the preliminary results of this study suggest that discrimination is still alive and well in the Los Angeles labor market. Even after controlling for a range of cultural capital attributes, human capital attributes, and contextual variables, the results indicate that a dark-skinned black is 52 percent less likely to be employed.

This finding is consistent with the results of a recent study by Bluestone, Stevenson, and Tilly, which documents the disparity in employment for black and white males, controlling for age and education.[40] During the mid-1980s, according to their study, the jobless rate for twenty-year-old black men (21.6 percent) was almost five times higher than was the rate for their white counterparts (4.8 percent). And for twenty-year-old men with less than a high school education, the racial disparity in the jobless rate was even greater: 10.3 percent for white men and 36.1 percent for black men.[41]

Moreover, the findings of this study suggest that, over the last twenty years, race-based discrimination has been increasing rather than decreasing in the U.S. labor market. Their data indicate that the disparity in the jobless rates of young black and white men, with and without a high school diploma, was not nearly as stark during the 1960s as it was in the 1980s.

Our findings with respect to the effect of race (black) and skin-tone (dark) on the odds of working in Los Angeles are also consistent with the results of recent public opinion surveys, face-to-face interviews with employers, and focus group discussions held with black, white, Latino, Korean, and Chinese residents of Los Angeles County.[42] These studies indicate that black males, in particular, are viewed negatively not only by whites but also by other non-white minority groups (especially Asians); they are perceived as being less intelligent, more prone to violence, and more likely to rely on the government dole than to prefer to work. The evidence indicates that black men are substantially disadvantaged in the labor market because these negative stereotypes are often applied categorically.[43]

These findings should give pause to those who, in the current debate about affirmative action, advocate class-based[44] as opposed to race-based[45] remedies for past discrimination, especially in the labor market. The Los Angeles data suggest that even if one has played by the rules—gone to school, avoided trouble with the law, and gotten married, etc.—race still matters,[46] and it matters a great deal if one is a dark-skinned black male.

NOTES

This research was supported by grants from the Ford, Russell Sage, and Haynes foundations. The authors are solely responsible for all findings and conclusions.

1. See Michael Darby (ed.), *Reducing Poverty in America* (Thousand Oaks, CA: Sage Publications, 1996).

2. See ibid. Also see Walter C. Farrell, Jr., and James H. Johnson, Jr., "Access to Local Resources is Key to Problems in the Inner City," *Wisconsin Review* 2 (1994): 23; Joan Petersilia, "Crime and Punishment in California: Full Cells, Empty Pockets, and Questionable Benefits," in J.B. Steinberg, D.W. Lyon, and M.E. Vaiana (eds.), *Urban America: Policy Choices for Los Angeles and the Nation* (Santa Monica: Rand Corporation, 1992).

3. See James H. Johnson, Jr., "The Real Issue for Reducing Poverty," in M. Darby (ed.), *Reducing Poverty in America* (Thousand Oaks, CA: Sage Publications, 1996), pp. 374–96.

4. Bordieu, P. "Les Trois Etats du Capital Culture," *Actes de la Rechereche en Sciences Sociales* 30(19793-5); M.P. Fernandez-Kelley, "Towandas Triumph: Social and Cultural Capital in the Urban Ghetto," in A. Portes (ed.), *Economic Sociology of Immigration* (New York: Russell Sage Foundation, 1995). Also see, Thomas Sowell, *Race and Culture: A World View* (New York: Basic Books, 1994); and Lawrence E. Harrison, *Who Prospers? How Cultural Values Shape Economic and Political Success* (New York: Basic Books, 1992).

5. See James H. Johnson, Jr., Melvin L. Oliver, and Lawrence D. Bobo, "Unraveling the Paradox of Deepening Urban Inequality: Theoretical Underpinnings and Research Design of a Multi-City Study," *Urban Geography* 15 (1994): 77–89.

6. James H. Johnson, Jr., and Melvin L. Oliver, "Structural Changes in the U.S. Economy and Black Male Joblessness: A Reassessment," in G.E. Peterson and W. Vroman (eds.), *Urban Labor Markets and Job Opportunity* (Washington, D.C.: The Urban Institute Press, 1992).

7. James H. Johnson, Jr., and Walter C. Farrell, Jr., "The Fire This Time: The Genesis of the Los Angeles Rebellion of 1992," *North Carolina Law Review* 71(1993): 1403–20.

8. Mark Shields, "Pete Wilson's Ungolden State," *Liberal Opinion* 6 (March 27, 1995): 7.

9. William H. Frey, "Immigration and Internal Migration Flight: A California Case Study," *Population and Environment* 16 (1995): 351–75.

10. For a complete discussion of issues surrounding "tight" versus "slack" labor markets, see Richard B. Freeman, "Employment and Earnings of Disadvantaged Young Men in a Labor Shortage Economy," in C. Jencks and P. Peterson (eds.), *The Urban Underclass* (Washington, D.C.: The Brookings Institution, 1991).

11. Melvin L. Oliver and James H. Johnson, Jr., "Interethnic Minority Conflict in an Urban Ghetto: The Case of Blacks and Latinos in Los Angeles," *Research in Social Movements, Conflict, and Change* 6(1984): 57–64; James H. Johnson, Jr., and Melvin L. Oliver, "Interethnic Minority Conflict in Urban America: The Effects of Economic and Social Dislocations," *Urban Geography* 10 (1989): 449–63; and James H. Johnson, Jr., Cloyzelle K. Jones, Walter C. Farrell, Jr., and Melvin L. Oliver, "The Los Angeles Rebellion: A Retrospective View," *Economic Development Quarterly* 6(1992): 356–72.

12. See Johnson, Oliver, and Bobo, "Unraveling the Paradox of Deepening Urban Inequality."

13. For a detailed discussion of the survey and sample procedures employed in

the LASUI, see James H. Johnson, Jr., Melvin L. Oliver, and Lawrence D. Bobo, *The Los Angeles Study of Urban Inequality: Theoretical Underpinnings, Research Design, and Preliminary Findings* (Los Angeles: UCLA Center for the Study of Urban Poverty, 1995), Appendix A.

14. See Harry J. Holzer, "Black Employment Problems: New Evidence, Old Questions," *Journal of Policy Analysis and Management* 13 (1994): 699–722.

15. Johnson, Oliver, and Bobo, "Unraveling the Paradox of Deepening Urban Inequality."

16. Thomas Sowell, *Ethnic America* (New York: Basic Books, 1981), p. 200.

17. Harrison, *Who Prospers*, p. 194.

18. Ibid.

19. Nicholas Lemann, *The Promised Land* (New York: Alfred Knopf, 1991).

20. Harrison, *Who Prospers*, p. 223.

21. Sowell, *Ethnic America*; and Sowell, Race and Culture.

22. Lawrence Mead, *The New Politics of Poverty* (New York: Basic Books, 1992).

23. Harrison, *Who Prospers*, p. 223.

24. Harrison, ibid.

25. William Julius Wilson, *The Truly Disadvantaged* (Chicago: University of Chicago Press, 1987).

26. Joleen Kirschenman and Kathryn Neckerman, "We'd Love to Hire Them . . . But: The Meaning of Race for Employers," in C. Jencks and P. Peterson (eds.), *The Urban Underclass* (Washington, D.C.: The Brookings Institution, 1991).

27. Mimi Abramovitz, "The New Paternalism," *The Nation* 225 (1992): 368–71 (emphasis added).

28. Lemann, *The Promised Land*; Mead, *The New Politics of Poverty.*

29. Holzer, "Black Employment Problems."

30. Johnson, Oliver, and Bobo, "Unraveling the Paradox of Deepening Urban Inequality."

31. Ed Gillespie and Bob Schellhaus (eds.), *Contract With America: The Bold Plan by Rep. Newt Gingrich, Rep. Dick Armey, and the House Republicans to Change the Nation* (New York: Random House, 1994).

32. Farrell and Johnson, "Access to Local Resources."

33. Wilson, *The Truly Disadvantaged*; and Mark Testa, Nan Marie Stone, Marilyn Krough, and Kathryn M. Neckerman, "Employment and Marriage Among Inner City Fathers," *Annals of the American Academy of Political and Social Sciences,* 501 (1989): 79–91.

34. James Q. Wilson, "How to Teach Better Values in the Inner Cities," *Wall Street Journal* (June 1, 1992): A12; and Robert Woodson, "Transform Inner Cities from the Grassroots Up." *Wall Street Journal* (June 1, 1992): A12.

35. Petersilia, "Crime and Punishment in California."

36. See Fernandez-Kelly, "Towandas Triumph;" and James H. Johnson, Jr., and Melvin L. Oliver, "Modeling Urban Underclass Behaviors: Theoretical Considerations," *CSUP Occasional Paper Series* 1 (1989): 1–25.

37. See David Grant and James H. Johnson, Jr., "Conservative Policymaking and Growing Urban Inequality in the 1980s," in R. Ratcliff, M. L. Oliver, and T. Shapiro (eds.), *Research in Politics and Society* (Greenwich, CT: JAI Press, 1995).

38. Walter C. Farrell, Jr., James H. Johnson, Jr., Marty Sapp, Roger M. Pumphrey, and Shirley Freeman, "Redirecting the Lives of Inner City Black Males: An Assess-

ment of Milwaukee's Midnight Basketball League," *Journal of Community Practice* (1995: forthcoming).

39. For a detailed discussion of the ineffectiveness of "get tough" on crime policies, see Petersilia, "Crime and Punishment in California." For discussions of the value of community-based institutions and other social resources in mending the social fabric of inner-city communities, see Farrell and Johnson, "Access to Local Resources;" and Robert Putnam, "The Prosperous Community: Social Capital and Public Life," *American Prospect* 13 (1993): 37.

40. Barry Bluestone, Mary Huff Stevenson, and Chris Tilly, *An Assessment of the Impact of "Deindustrialization" and Spatial Mismatch in the Labor Market Outcomes of Young White, Black, and Latino Men and Women Who Have Limited Schooling* (Boston, MA: John McCormick Institute of Public Affairs, 1992).

41. Bluestone, Stevenson, and Tilly, ibid.

42. See Lawrence D. Bobo, Camille L. Zubrinsky, James H. Johnson, Jr., and Melvin L. Oliver, "Public Opinion Before and After the Spring of Discontent," in M. Baldassare (ed.), *The Los Angeles Riots: Lessons for the Urban Future* (Boulder, CO: Westview Press, 1995), pp. 103–133; Kirschenman and Neckerman, "We'd Love to Hire Them . . . But;" and Lawrence D. Bobo, Camille L. Zubrinsky, James H. Johnson, Jr., and Melvin L. Oliver, "Work Orientation, Job Discrimination, and Ethnicity: A Focus Group Perspective," in R.L. Simpson and I.H. Simpson (eds.), *Research in the Sociology of Work* (Greenwich, CT: JAI Press, 1995), pp. 45–85.

43. See Kirschenman and Neckerman, "We'd Love to Hire Them . . . But;" Margery A. Turner, Michael Fix, and Raymond Struyk, *Opportunities Denied, Opportunities Diminished: Racial Discrimination in Hiring,* Urban Institute Report 91–9 (Washington, D.C.: The Urban Institute Press, 1991); and Phillip Moss and Chris Tilly, *Why Black Men Are Doing Worse in the Labor Market* (New York: Social Science Research Council, 1991).

44. Mickey Kaus, "Class Is In," *The New Republic* 184 (March 27, 1995): 6.

45. Richard Cohen, "The Right Pick in Piscataway," *Washington Post National Weekly* (March 13–19, 1995): 29.

46. Ellis Cose, *The Rage of a Privileged Class* (New York: Harper Collins Publishers, 1993).

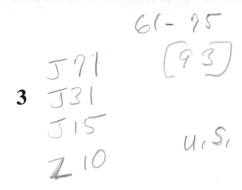

61 - 75

[9 3]

J 71
J 31
J 15
Z 10

U.S.

3

COLOR OR CULTURE? WAGE DIFFERENCES AMONG NON-HISPANIC BLACK MALES, HISPANIC BLACK MALES, AND HISPANIC WHITE MALES

Jeremiah Cotton

The analysis of the determinants of wage differences between Hispanic black, Hispanic white and non-Hispanic black males undertaken
in this research does not support the contention that cultural differences are more significant than color differences in the generation of
racial wage gaps.

Although the human capital investment model is widely accepted as
the major explanation for racial differences in economic outcomes, its
empirical performance has been rather poor. There have been many studies of income, earnings, and wage differences between blacks and whites
in which such theoretically important human capital variables as education and work experience have been controlled for and yet in the over-
whelming majority of these studies a significant portion of the income,
earnings or wage differentials remained unexplained.[1] Most researchers
have attributed much of this unexplained residual to labor market discrimination in one form or another.

This reading of the residual, however, has been met with a good deal
of skepticism by some analysts. Given their belief in the prevalence and
potency of the competitive forces operating in neoclassical labor markets
these analysts contend that labor market discrimination cannot endure for
long under such a regime and therefore rather than discrimination the
residuals are actually the reflections of some heretofore overlooked influence. One of the most popular candidates is unmeasured cultural differences between the races. As William Darity, Jr. noted in a penetrating
critique of their position:

These economists doubt that it is legitimate to interpret the residuals in racial earnings regressions as capturing the effects of discrimination. Instead they argue that the residual is capturing cultural differences that generate the remaining differences in earnings between members of various groups who might otherwise appear to possess the same human capital endowments. If culture is viewed as a component of human capital . . . then previous regression equations have been misspecified and the residuals are picking up the specification error. Cultural differences, it is now alleged, lead to systematic differences in labor market achievement. The "unexplained" residual in the human capital regression equation now finds an origin in ethnic/racial gaps.[2]

Two of the most outspoken proponents of this view are economists Thomas Sowell and Barry Chiswick. Both have compared native born blacks with other minority groups—notably, Jews, West Indians, Irish, Japanese and Chinese—who immigrated to this country poor, were confronted with ethnic and racial discrimination, and were forced into low-paying, menial occupations.[3] But unlike native born blacks they managed to overcome these obstacles and achieve a considerable amount of economic success. According to Sowell and Chiswick, they did this by dint of hard work, self-discipline and sacrifice, and a future orientation manifested in the willingness to forego current income, consumption and leisure in order to invest in the acquisition of labor market skills. In the Sowell-Chiswick lexicon these attitudes and behaviors are culturally determined and predispose the individuals who have them both to accumulate more human capital than those whose cultures fail to transmit similar values and to utilize that capital more efficiently and effectively.

Thus, the cultural advantages whites enjoy not only guarantee they will have on average more human capital than blacks, but even when blacks and whites with the same nominal amount of human capital are compared whites will tend to be more productive. It is this that explains the residual.

Critics counter that Sowell and Chiswick are themselves guilty of a misspecification, having omitted social class from their cultural equations. The Jews who immigrated to the United States at the turn of the century brought with them the wide assortment of productive skills that they had developed and deployed in their countries of origin. Rather than moving up the class ladder, Jews merely reclaimed the middle class status they had enjoyed prior to immigration. Stephen Steinberg observed that

> Despite their poverty . . . Jewish immigrants were concentrated in economically advanced sectors of their countries of origin, and therefore had industrial experience and concrete occupational skills that would serve them well in America's expanding industrial economy.[4]

West Indians in the United States are perhaps the prime exhibits in the culture-not-color argument. Sowell has made much of the fact that though black themselves, West Indians have generally performed better economically than native born blacks. This is ascribed to cultural traits, largely missing among American blacks, that put a high premium on economic achievement.

William Darity, Jr. and Rhonda Williams, however, have cited research that shows West Indians who immigrated to the United States also did better economically than those who immigrated to London or who stayed at home in the Caribbean. It turns out that the former came from a generally higher socioeconomic class than did the latter two.

> How, then, do we explain the less than sterling achievement of this same culture when functioning elsewhere—say at home in the (poverty stricken) West Indies or in Britain? Sowell acknowledges that this same culture has proven less remunerative in the West Indies, but is silent as to the reason.
> Cultural explanations fail in a historical context because they consistently exclude considerations of social class.[5]

These conflicting interpretations of the residuals have profound implications for human capital theory and the bedrock marginal productivity theory of income distribution that underlies it. The latter theory has been identified by E. K. Hunt as one of the three principal tenets that constitute the neoclassical ideological defense of competitive capitalism.[6] If capitalism is to be successfully defended as a system in which individual rewards are distributed equitably commensurate with individual contributions to the production process, then racial differences in economic outcomes must be shown to be due to racial differences in characteristics that directly determine the quantity and quality of those contributions.

If the residuals are the result of omitted cultural traits that differ by race and if these differences are highly positively correlated with productivity differences, then capitalism's essential claims of efficiency and equity cannot thereby be rejected. If, on the other hand, the residuals are largely the result of labor market discrimination then the defense of capitalism on these grounds collapses.

The research embodied in this article seeks to shed further light on the relevance of these two positions, culture and color, by undertaking a cross comparison of wage differences between Hispanic black males and Hispanic white males in an attempt to control for culture, and between Hispanic black males and non-Hispanic black males in an attempt to control for color.[7] Non-Hispanic white males will serve as the benchmark group in the formation of the wage differentials. Moreover, given the socioeconomic diversity among the Hispanic subgroups, the use of all Hispanics for comparisons moots the social class selectivity issue. Finally, by using males alone, the complications arising from inter- and intra-cultural gender differences are set aside.

It may be tentatively concluded that culture has a relatively greater influence on economic outcomes than color if there turns out to be a relatively greater difference in the situation of Hispanic black males and non-Hispanic black males than between Hispanic black and Hispanic white males since the latter two generally experience the same culture through language, art, music, religion and other culture-transmitting mores and forms. This, however, is not to overlook the fact that there is some cultural variation among the Hispanic subgroups themselves. Aside from being racially diverse, they have also been shaped by somewhat differing geographic, historical and sociopolitical forces. Still, it seems reasonable to expect more cultural similarities among Hispanics taken together than with a non-Hispanic group with whom they happen to share some particular demographic characteristic.

On the other hand, if color has a greater impact on the determination of wages than culture then we may expect there to be a greater difference between the fortunes of Hispanic black and white males than between Hispanic and non-Hispanic black males.

DATA AND EMPIRICAL MODEL

The data used to estimate the wage equations on which the comparisons are based were culled from a series of nine Current Population Survey tapes spanning the years 1976 to 1984. The four samples drawn consisted of 463 Hispanic black males, 5,476 Hispanic white males,

TABLE 1
Percent Distribution of Hispanic Populations and Samples by Subgroups

	Total Civilian Population*	Total Male Population*	White Sample	Black Sample
All Hispanics	100.0%	100.0%	100.0%	100.0%
Mexican Americans	60.1	63.7	62.8	1.8
Puerto Ricans	10.8	8.4	9.2	36.3
Cubans	5.8	5.7	6.8	31.4
Central & South Americans	9.4	9.3	7.2	21.9
Other Spanish	14.9	12.9	14.0	8.6
*Civilian and Male Populations are as of 1991–II				

Source: U.S. Bureau of Labor Statistics, *Employment and Earnings,* Vol. 38, No. 7, July 1991 and *Current Population Survey* Computer Tapes for 1976 through 1984.

2,847 non-Hispanic black males, and 17,568 non-Hispanic white males. Table 1 shows the percentage distributions of the Hispanic black and white samples by subgroup with the distributions of the total Hispanic civilian and total Hispanic male populations by subgroup as a reference.

Note that the distribution of the white sample follows the general contours of the civilian and male distributions while that of the black sample is quite different. The black sample is made up of about two-thirds Puerto Ricans and Cubans and the white sample is almost two-thirds Mexican American. Thus, to the extent that the Mexican American "brand" of Hispanic culture differs from that of Cubans and Puerto Ricans the intracultural comparisons will be somewhat skewed.

All persons in the sample were sixteen years and older and worked full-time, year-round. The samples were restricted to full-time workers in order to maximize the human capital effects inasmuch as it is sometimes complained that blacks and Hispanics tend to spend less time in the labor market than whites and consequently invest less in the accumulation and development of their human capital.

Because it is assumed that the wage determination process differs markedly for the four demographic groups, separate wage equations were estimated for each group. Chow tests were performed to substantiate this hypothesis and all were significant at the 0.01 level or less.[8] The wage equations themselves take the semilogarithmic form in order to depict the presumed nonlinearity of the wage-human capital relationship.

The two principal human capital variables are education, and work experience or on-the-job training. Neither of the constructs used here to represent these variables are altogether satisfactory. Education is measured solely by years of school completed and therefore does not take into account differences in the quality of the relative amounts of schooling acquired. This means that the estimated education coefficients may well be upwardly biased. The work experience construct is even less appealing. It is defined as the difference between an individual's age and the number of years of school attended plus 6, the latter being the age at which most schooling begins: WX = Age - (Schooling + 6). This implies that all post-school activity is devoted to the acquisition of on-the-job training, ignoring the periods of voluntary or involuntary withdrawals from the labor market during which time no training occurs. It therefore overstates the amount invested in this important form of human capital. This is a more significant problem for blacks and Hispanics than for whites. The former two tend to have more labor force dropouts as well as more frequent and longer-lasting spells of involuntary unemployment than whites. Of course the use of only full-time workers helps repair this deficiency since they more nearly fit the definition of work experience used here.

RESULTS OF ESTIMATED EMPIRICAL MODEL

Table 2 gives the mean values and regression coefficients of the wage equations and it can be seen that Hispanic blacks had over one-half year more schooling than Hispanic whites and just under one-half a year less schooling than non-Hispanic blacks. However, the payoff to schooling at the margin for Hispanic whites was quite a bit greater than for Hispanic blacks and even slightly greater than that for non-Hispanic blacks. An additional year of schooling increased the Hispanic white average wage by 5.67 percent; the Hispanic black wage by 4.77 percent; and the non-Hispanic black wage by 5.61 percent. As might be expected, both the level of schooling and the rate of return to an additional year were greater for non-Hispanic whites than for all of the other groups.

Wage-experience profiles derived from the work experience quadratics in Table 2 are depicted in Figure 1. The equations on which these profiles are based are generated by subtracting the sum of the mean values of the other independent variables multiplied by their respective regression coefficients from the value of the log wage. This constrains the profiles to pass through the origin and highlights the differences in their respective slopes.

TABLE 2
Mean Values and Regression Coefficients of Model Variables
(Estimated Standard Errors in Parentheses)

Variables	Black Hispanics Mean Values	Black Hispanics Regression Coefficients	White Hispanics Mean Values	White Hispanics Regression Coefficients	Non-Hispanic Blacks Mean Values	Non-Hispanic Blacks Regression Coefficients	Non-Hispanic Whites Mean Values	Non-Hispanic Whites Regression Coefficients
Education	12.21	.0477* (.0094)	11.61	.0567* (.0021)	12.66	.0561* (.0035)	13.40	.0683* (.0014)
Work Experience	19.65	.0203* (.0087)	19.14	.0249* (.0019)	20.40	.0211* (.0025)	19.11	.0294* (.0011)
(Work Experience)^2	533.137	−.00028* (.00002)	528.77	−.00035* (.00004)	599.73	−.00029* (.00005)	532.13	−.00044* (.00002)
Central City	.734	.3711* (.1353)	.451	−.0108 (.0176)	.537	.1566* (.0223)	.267	.0538* (.0102)
In SMSA	.213	.6045* (.1441)	.303	.0261 (.0186)	.204	.2059* (.027)	.354	.1293* (.0094)
Married With Spouse	.738	.1653** (.0992)	.773	.1500* (.0208)	.662	.143* (.0266)	.782	.2081* (.0126)
Once Married	.148	.0926 (.1207)	.079	.0926* (.0304)	.157	.0750** (.033)	.074	.1020* (.0186)
Private Sector Employment	.817	−.1413 (.1052)	.843	.0248 (.0266)	.736	−.0078 (.0299)	.818	.0489* (.0152)
Industry Construction	.030	.3881 (.4894)	.070	.2515* (.0372)	.046	.2262* (.0709)	.070	.2348* (.0239)
Manufacturing Durables	.141	.1935 (.4698)	.199	.1616* (.0316)	.187	.2589* (.0611)	.202	.1835* (.0207)
Manufacturing Nondurables	.122	.1725 (.4689)	.111	.1737* (.0341)	.122	.2401* (.0629)	.110	.1554* (.0221)
Transport. Pub. Util.	.061	.2835 (.4751)	.096	.2639* (.0355)	.119	.2772* (.0642)	.098	.2548* (.0226)
Wholesale-Retail Trade	.190	.0864 (.4665)	.176	.0059 (.0319)	.123	.0318 (.0634)	.168	.0117 (.0210)
Finance, Insurance, Real Estate	.068	−.0459 (.469)	.042	.0496 (.0435)	.046	.0821 (.0723)	.046	.1155* (.0266)

TABLE 2 (continued)

Variables	Black Hispanics Mean Values	Black Hispanics Regression Coefficients	White Hispanics Mean Values	White Hispanics Regression Coefficients	Non-Hispanic Blacks Mean Values	Non-Hispanic Blacks Regression Coefficients	Non-Hispanic Whites Mean Values	Non-Hispanic Whites Regression Coefficients
Public Administration	.046	−.0238 (.4873)	.065	.2324* (.0468)	.111	.2464* (.0706)	.078	.2062* (.0276)
Business & Repair Services	.080	.2554 (.4711)	.041	.0403 (.0430)	.039	.0539 (.0742)	.037	.0287 (.0279)
Personal Services	.038	.2145 (.4818)	.025	−.1457* (.05)	.022	−.0696 (.0836)	.016	−.1514* (.0365)
Entertainment Recreation Services	.019	−.4278 (.5143)	.007	.0175 (.0811)	.015	−.0388 (.0935)	.007	.0099 (.052)
Professional & Related Services	.202	.0002 (.4672)	.104	.0111 (.0375)	.148	.0247 (.0655)	.122	−.0209 (.0237)
Trend								
1977	.086	−.2577 (.1829)	.065	.0298 (.0333)	.109	.0174 (.0401)	.087	.0424** (.0185)
1978	.113	−.0855 (.1537)	.072	.064** (.0323)	.118	.0687** (.0392)	.091	.1194* (.0183)
1979	.106	.1366 (.1499)	.082	.2194* (.0311)	.111	.1447* (.04)	.100	.1919* (.0226)
1980	.160	.0340 (.1416)	.138	.2961* (.0275)	.134	.2066* (.0385)	.137	.3081* (.0210)
1981	.128	.0618 (.1454)	.131	.3856* (.0278)	.131	.3372* (.0387)	.132	.3955* (.0168)
1982	.111	.3794* (.1446)	.154	.4650* (.0269)	.123	.4060* (.0393)	.139	.4615* (.0166)
1983	.10	.4068* (.1998)	.146	.5055* (.0272)	.102	.4783* (.0410)	.124	.5031* (.0170)
1984	.109	.5866* (.1475)	.112	.5394* (.0288)	.081	.5830* (.0434)	.093	.535* (.0182)
Constant	1.000	.2036 (.5497)	1.000	.291* (.0527)	1.000	.1667** (.0862)	1.000	.0316 (.0337)
R^2		.415		.305		.308		.302
Standard Error		.448		.487		.474		.521
Ln Hourly Wage		1.71189		1.8221		1.76513		1.96378
Mean Hourly Wage		$6.407		$7.316		$6.913		$8.567
N		463		5,476		2,847		17,568

*Significant at .01 level or less
**Significant at .10 level or less

FIGURE 1
Wage-Experience Profiles

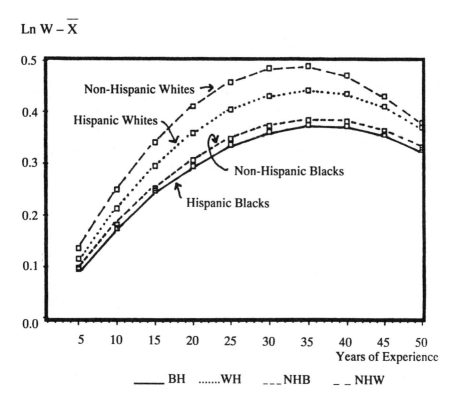

The two white profiles lay everywhere considerably above the black profiles and rose at faster rates up to about thirty-five years of work experience. Thus the gap between the two pairs steadily increased over that period. Somewhat surprisingly, however, both white profiles peaked slightly earlier than the black profiles and appeared to decline more rapidly on the other side of the peaks.

Thus, it would appear that in general the payoffs here for the two major human capital constructs, education and work experience, were greater for the two white groups than for the two blacks groups, with Hispanic black males receiving the lowest returns.

Other variables included in the equations controlled for urban-nonurban residence, marital status, private or public employment, industry, and the year in which the wage was earned. The latter is expected to help dampen some of the cyclical effects that might be assumed to have differential impact on the economic fortunes of the various groups. All of the controls behaved pretty much as expected. Both black groups were more concentrated in central cities than whites, with Hispanic blacks even more urbanized than non-Hispanic blacks. Moreover, living in the urban center or urban ring had a significant and positive effect on the wages of all groups except Hispanic whites.

Marital status was entered in the models as "married, with spouse" and "once married" (i.e., divorced, widowed, or separated), with "single" as the reference group. And with the exception of once married Hispanic blacks, marriage contributed materially to the wages of all groups.

Although the effects were not significant for the three minority groups, the signs on the private sector coefficients suggest that black males benefited most from public sector employment while the very reverse was the case for white males. This is consistent with the notion that non-whites face less obstacles in the public than in the private sector.

Aside from the fact that none of the industry variables and only a few of the later trends were significant for Hispanic blacks, both industry and the trends performed reasonably well. Agriculture, Forestry-Fisheries and Mining was the industry reference group and 1976 was the reference year.

The greater white than black payoffs adumbrated in the performance of the education and work experience variables is confirmed by the fact that the mean hourly wages for Hispanic and non-Hispanic black males, at $6.41 and $6.91, respectively, were lower than those for Hispanic and non-Hispanic whites, at $7.32 and $8.57, respectively.

DECOMPOSITION OF THE WAGE DIFFERENTIALS

A deeper probe into this matter entails the decomposition of the wage differences between non-Hispanic whites and each of the other three minority groups. This decomposition separates the wage differentials into components that are variously called the "explained," "endowment" or "skill" differences and those called "unexplained" or "treatment" differences, the usual proxies for labor market discrimination.

Among the several forms that such a decomposition can take, the most logically and theoretically appropriate one is given by:

$$\ln \overline{W} - \ln \overline{W} = \Sigma B * (\overline{X}^W - \overline{X}^B) + \Sigma \overline{X}^W (B^W - B*) + \Sigma \overline{X}^B (B * - B^B)$$

where the first term on the right-hand side of the equation is the difference between white and minority endowments that would obtain in the absence of discrimination, and the second and third terms are the differences between white and minority endowments as currently valued and how they would be valued in the absence of discrimination. The first term is considered to be the true value of the endowment differences; the second term is the pure treatment advantage, or "benefit," discrimination confers on whites; and the third term is the pure treatment disadvantage, or "cost," incurred by minorities.[9] Table 3 displays the results of these decompositions and indicates that while the gap between the wages of non-Hispanic white males and Hispanic black males was considerably larger than that between non-Hispanic whites and non-Hispanic blacks, approximately the same percentages of the two gaps were attributable to differences in productivity endowments. Similarly, about the same percentages of the two wage gaps represented costs imposed by discrimination on the two black groups. By contrast the non-Hispanic white/Hispanic white wage gap was smaller, the percentage due to endowment differences larger, and the discriminatory disadvantage smaller than those of both black groups.

Translated into the dollars and cents terms of the mean hourly wage gaps, 85¢ of the $2.16 gap between non-Hispanic white and Hispanic black wages, 67¢ of the $1.66 non-Hispanic white/non-Hispanic black wage gap, and 82¢ of the $1.25 non-Hispanic white/Hispanic white gap were due to endowment differences. Discrimination resulted in non-Hispanic white males being overpaid by 13¢, Hispanic black males being underpaid by $1.18, non-Hispanic black males underpaid by 86¢, and Hispanic white males underpaid by 30¢.

In Table 4 the wage differentials are further decomposed to account for the proportional contributions of each of the independent variables. As can be seen, in all of the decompositions educational differences play a major role in all three components of the wage differentials. For example, *ceteris paribus,* educational differences between Hispanic blacks and non-Hispanic whites result in a $2.86 difference in their respective mean hourly wages. However, if there had been no discrimination only 68¢ of that difference would have remained, and therefore $2.18 of the education-determined gap is due to discrimination—with white educational attainment being overvalued by 17¢ and Hispanic black education undervalued by $2.01.

In the cases of work experience, urban residence and the undifferentiated factors contained in the constant term, the wage advantage is in

TABLE 3
Decomposition of Wage Differentials
(Percentage of wage differentials in parentheses, followed by the dollar
value of the mean hourly wage differentials)

	Total Differential	Endowment Differential	White Advantage	Minority Disadvantage
Non-Hispanic White-Hispanic Black	.25189	.09934	.01528	.13727
	(100%)	(39.4%)	(6.1%)	(54.5%)
	$2.16	$.85	$.13	$1.18
Non-Hispanic White-Non-Hispanic Black	.19865	.08044	.01528	.10293
	(100%)	(40.5%)	(7.7%)	(51.8%)
	$1.66	$.67	$.13	$.86
Non-Hispanic White-Hispanic White	.14168	.09258	.01528	.03382
	(100%)	(65.4%)	(10.8%)	(23.8%)
	$1.25	$.82	$.13	$.30

favor of Hispanic black males. Once again all things being equal, being more urbanized than whites causes the Hispanic black wage to be $2.92 larger than the white wage, with $2.83 due to the market's overvaluation of Hispanic black urbanization and 2¢ due to the undervaluation of urban whites.

CONCLUSION

These differential outcomes, particularly among members of the same cultural group—Hispanic black and Hispanic white males—do not bode well for the culture-over-color argument. Hispanic whites with less average schooling and work experience earned higher average wages and suffered less adverse treatment in the labor market than their black counterparts. On the other hand, non-Hispanic black males had slightly higher average educational attainment and work experience than Hispanic black males, and earned a somewhat higher average wage. Both faced nearly similar levels of labor market treatment (or ill-treatment). Thus, culture did not seem to have any active part in distinguishing their comparative wages.

Those who wish to defend and maintain the cultural explanation for

TABLE 4
Portions of Wage Differentials Attributable to Individual Independent Variables by Dollar Value

Non-Hispanic White-Black Hispanic Differential

Variables	Total Differential	Endowment Differential	White Advantage	Minority Disadvantage
Education	$2.86	$.68	$.17	$2.01
Work Experience	−.06	−.15	.07	.02
Urban-Rural Residence	−2.92	−.07	−.02	−2.83
Marital Status	.30	.02	.05	.23
Sector of Employment	1.33	.00	.04	1.29
Industry	.04	.29	−.03	−.22
Trend	1.39	.08	.03	1.28
Constant	−.78	—	−.18	−.60
Total	$2.16	$.85	$.13	$1.18

Non-Hispanic White-White Hispanic Differential

Variables	Total Differential	Endowment Differential	White Advantage	Minority Disadvantage
Education	$2.28	$1.05	$.19	$1.04
Work Experience	.31	−.02	.07	.26
Urban-Rural Residence	.51	−.03	−.03	.57
Marital Status	.42	.01	.06	.35
Sector of Employment	.18	−.01	.05	.14
Industry	.03	.05	−.04	.02
Trend	−.16	−.23	.03	.04
Constant	−2.32	—	−.20	−2.12
Total	$1.25	$.82	$.13	$.30

Non-Hispanic White-Non-Hispanic Black Differential

Variables	Total Differential	Endowment Differential	White Advantage	Minority Disadvantage
Education	$1.72	$.41	$.17	$1.14
Work Experience	.57	−.07	.07	.57
Urban-Rural Residence	−.55	.03	−.02	−.56
Marital Status	.53	.13	.05	.35
Sector of Employment	.38	.03	.04	.31
Industry	−.37	−.03	−.03	−.31
Trend	.51	.17	.03	.31
Constant	−1.31	—	−.18	−.95
Total	$1.66	$.67	$.13	$.86

residual differences in black and white outcomes (and the capitalist labor markets in which they are generated) will need to reconcile the results of this research with their thesis.

NOTES

1. See, e.g., Walter Fogel, "The Effects of Low Educational Attainment on Incomes: A Comparative Study of Selected Ethnic Groups," *Journal of Human Resources* 3 (Fall 1966): 22–40; Alan S. Blinder, "Wage Discrimination: Reduced Form and Structural Estimates," *Journal of Human Resources* 8 (Fall 1973): 436–55; Stanley H. Masters, "The Effect of Educational Differences and Labor Market Discrimination on the Relative Earnings of Black Males," *Journal of Human Resources* 9 (Summer 1974): 342–60; Farrell Bloch and Sharon P. Smith, "Human Capital and Labor Market Employment," *Journal of Human Resources* 12 (Fall 1977): 550–59; James Gwartney and James Long, "The Relative Earnings of Blacks and Other Minorities," *Industrial and Labor Relations Review* 31 (April 1978): 336–46; Mary Corcoran and Greg J. Duncan, "Work History, Labor Force Attachment, and Earnings Differences Between the Races and Sexes," *Journal of Human Resources* 14 (Winter 1979): 3–20; Cordelia Reimers, "Labor Market Discrimination Against Hispanic and Black Males," *The Review of Economics and Statistics* 65 (November 1983): 570–79; Naomi T. Verdugo and Richard R. Verdugo, "Earnings Differentials Among Mexican American, Black and White Male Workers," *Social Science Quarterly* 65 (June 1984): 417–25; Jeremiah Cotton, "The Gap at the Top: Relative Occupational Earnings Disadvantages of the Black Middle Class, *The Review of Black Political Economy* 18 (Winter 1990): 21–38.

2. William Darity, Jr., "What's Left of the Economic Theory of Discrimination," in Steven Shulman and William Darity, Jr., eds. *The Question of Discrimination: Racial Inequality in the U.S. Labor Market* (Middletown, Conn.: Wesleyan University Press, 1989), p. 337.

3. Thomas Sowell, *Race and Economics* (New York: McKay, 1975); *Idem, American Ethnic Groups* (Washington, D.C.: The Urban Institute, 1978); *Idem, Ethnic America* (New York: Basic Books, 1981); *Idem, Knowledge and Decisions* (New York: Basic Books, 1981): *Idem, The Economics and Politics of Race: An International Perspective* (New York: William Murrow and Co., 1983): *Idem, Civil Rights: Rhetoric or Reality?* (New York: William Murrow and Co., 1984); Barry Chiswick, "An Analysis of Earnings and Employment of Asian-American Men," *Journal of Labor Economics* 2 (April 1983); *Idem*, "The Earnings and Human Capital of American Jews," *Journal of Human Resources* 18 (Summer 1983): 313–34.

4. Stephen Steinberg, *The Ethnic Myth: Race, Ethnicity and Class in America* (New York: Atheneum Press, 1981), p. 97.

5. William Darity, Jr. and Rhonda M. Williams, "Peddlers Forever?: Culture, Competition, and Discrimination," *American Economic Review* 75 (May 1985): 259.

6. E.K. Hunt, in *History of Economic Thought: A Critical Perspective* (Belmont, CA: Wadsworth, 1979) described the three tenets as:

> (1) the marginal productivity theory of distribution, which pictured competitive capitalism as an ideal of distributive justice, (2) the "invisible hand" argument, which pictured capitalism as an ideal of rationality and efficiency, and (3) the faith in the automatic, self-adjusting nature of the market, which demonstrated that the principal functions of government should be to enforce

contracts and to defend the powers and privileges of private property (p. 374). He went on to observe that all three propositions are interrelated, forming a mutually consistent whole in which the adoption (rejection) of any two of the propositions necessarily implied the adoption (rejection) of the third. Each of these tenets has been challenged both from without and from within the neoclassical tradition. Indeed it was John Maynard Keynes himself, a stout believer in marginal productivity theory and the allocative efficiency of the market, who urged the abandonment of the assumption of self-correcting markets in order to rescue capitalism from self-destruction.

7. The Hispanics in this study are composed of those individuals who identify their Spanish origin as Mexican American (or "Chicano," "Mexican," or "Mexicano"), Puerto Rican, Cuban, Central or South American, or Other Spanish, and also identify their race as either "white" or "black."

8. The null hypothesis of this test is that the estimated effects of the explanatory variables on wages are no different for Hispanic blacks (HB), Hispanic whites (HW), non-Hispanic blacks (NHB) and non-Hispanic whites (NHW). These effects are represented by the coefficients on the separate wage equations. Six additional tests were also made in order to determine whether any of the four groups were pair-wise similar. The results are:

Combined Samples	HB/HW Samples	HB/NHB Samples	HB/NHW Samples	HW/NHB Samples	HW/NHW Samples	NHB/NHW Samples
5.77*	3.53*	4.32*	7.55*	5.86*	4.12*	6.33*

*significant at .01 level

9. For a discussion of the assumption underlying the derivation of this expression of the decomposition formula, see Jeremiah Cotton, "On the Decomposition of Wage Differentials," *The Review of Economics and Statistics* 70 (May 1988): 236–43.

4

MEASURING EMPLOYMENT DISCRIMINATION THROUGH CONTROLLED EXPERIMENTS

Marc Bendick, Jr., Charles W. Jackson,
and Victor A. Reinoso

Race/ethnic discrimination in hiring can be measured under controlled conditions using matched pairs of minority and nonminority research assistants posing as applicants for the same job. In 149 in-person job applications in the Washington, D.C., labor market, African American applicants were treated less favorably than equally qualified nonminorities more than one-fifth of the time. Employer behavior during these interactions suggest that, within continued public and private efforts against discrimination, particular attention should be accorded to the cognitive underpinnings of bias.

Three decades after the civil rights revolution of the 1960s, policy consensus remains elusive concerning equal employment opportunities for racial and ethnic minorities. Sharp debate continues on anti-discrimination laws and their enforcement, affirmative action, and immigration control. Underlying this lack of consensus is controversy concerning empirical questions such as: To what extent does discrimination operate in the American labor market today? Has the United States achieved a color-blind society, or do personal characteristics still condition the rewards to personal qualifications?

This paper utilizes a new technique for empirical research on these questions, employment "testing" or "auditing." The paper first outlines gaps in empirical information that testing can address. It then describes the testing approach and illustrates its power with results from initial applications. These results demonstrate that hiring discrimination remains far more prevalent than is commonly assumed. The paper concludes with suggested directions for future public and private efforts against bias.

WHAT IS KNOWN ABOUT EMPLOYMENT DISCRIMINATION

During the past several decades, substantial research has been conducted on employment discrimination, the vast majority of it suggesting that racial and ethnic bias survives to a significant extent.

This conclusion is reinforced by the continued operation of race/ethnic distinctions throughout American society. These patterns include widespread segregation in housing and social life, as well as incidents of discrimination experienced by minorities in daily living. Additionally, public opinion surveys indicate that substantial segments of the American population continue to hold stereotyped beliefs and prejudiced attitudes toward minority groups.[1]

Studies of the labor market also suggest the continued presence of discrimination. While some racial and ethnic gaps have diminished over recent decades, econometric research continues to find that minorities do less well than equally qualified nonminorities on such employment outcomes as representation in higher-level occupations, wages, returns on investment in educational credentials, and rates of job dismissal.[2] Public agencies enforcing antidiscrimination laws continue to receive a large flow of complaints annually. In 1988 (the latest year for which detailed data have been released), 50,477 charges alleging race, ethnic, or national origin discrimination in employment were filed with the federal Equal Employment Opportunity Commission (EEOC) and its state and local counterparts.[3]

This accumulated evidence is limited in two important ways. First, much of the information is indirect; rather than observing discriminatory behavior itself, that behavior is inferred from observing its preconditions or its consequences. Second, the magnitude of discrimination remains controversial. Some studies confirm the presence of discrimination but do not estimate its magnitude; others provide quantitative estimates, but these estimates often are not robust with respect to changing assumptions.

Among all aspects of employment, perhaps the greatest uncertainty surrounds estimates of bias in *hiring*. If a job applicant is told that an advertised position has already been filled or that another applicant has been hired who is more qualified, the disappointed job seeker typically does not have sufficient information to confirm or contradict these assertions. Probably reflecting this difficulty in verification, among all race/ethnicity employment discrimination charges filed with the EEOC in 1988, only 6.4 percent concerned hiring.[4]

THE METHODOLOGY OF EMPLOYMENT TESTING

In this context of information gaps, testing represents a promising new empirical technique. Employment testing may be defined as a social science procedure creating controlled conditions under which to measure employers' candid responses to the personal characteristics of job seekers. Its approach is that of a laboratory experiment in which one condition varies while other factors likely to affect a measured outcome are systematically held constant. Testing achieves this circumstance by sending matched pairs of research assistants to apply simultaneously for the same job vacancy. Economists define employment discrimination as "valuation in the labor market of personal characteristics which are unrelated to productivity."[5] In employment testing, applicant characteristics related to productivity are controlled by selecting, training, and credentialing testers to create pairs of job applicants who appear equally qualified for the job they seek. Simultaneously, the effect of characteristics unrelated to productivity are subjected to experimentation by pairing testers who differ in one personal characteristic (in the present case, minority and nonminority). When the testers in these pairs experience substantially different responses to their applications, few assumptions and little analysis are required to infer that the difference is caused by that personal characteristic.

The Fair Employment Council of Greater Washington, Inc. (FEC) has implemented this concept by conducting race-based tests in the Washington, D.C. metropolitan area since the fall of 1990.[6] At that time, six pairs of testers were recruited from among upper-level university undergraduates or recent graduates. Each pair teamed one African American research assistant with a white research assistant of the same sex, approximate age, personal appearance, articulateness, and manner. Testers received training of approximately one week, including an explanation of testing,[7] information on the job-seeking process, coaching on how to be an effective applicant, and practice interviews.

During training, FEC staff worked with each tester pair to develop fictional biographies specifying personal histories, education, work experience, and job-relevant skills. Reflecting information on typical prerequisites for common entry-level occupations,[8] these biographies were designed to make all testers strong candidates for the positions for which they were to apply. Biographies for each pair of testers were made equivalent, with only slight variations to keep their pairing from being apparent to potential employers. A typical pair of testers consisted of persons who were actually recent graduates from the same Ivy League university.

However, their testing biographies described both as having completed two years of college at different nonprestigious schools and possessing approximately two years' entry level work experience in retail and office positions. For vacancies where skills such as typing were relevant, testers offered similar levels of proficiency.

Once trained, testers were dispatched to apply for jobs picked through random sampling[9] from the region's largest-circulation newspaper, the *Washington Post*; from among employment agencies in the telephone "Yellow Pages"; and from other public lists of firms in an industry, such as a directory of local hotels published by the Washington Conventions and Visitors Bureau. From November 1990 to August 1991, six teams of FEC testers completed a total of 149 audits.

In assessing the results of these tests, the most central measure of discrimination is differences in rates of job-seeking success: Who proceeds furthest in the job application process? Who receives a job offer? The hypothesis of an absence of discrimination would be confirmed if equally qualified minority and nonminority testers met with success at equal rates, and discrimination is measured by the extent to which minorities are treated less favorably than their nonminority partners. Of course, instances also arise in which minority job candidates are selected over nonminority candidates, reflecting either random effects where two equally qualified candidates compete for a single opening or employer preference in favor of minorities. Therefore, in this paper, testing outcomes are analyzed by computing the proportion of job applications in which nonminority applicants are successful, the proportion of applications in which minorities are successful, and subtracting the latter from the former to generate a net rate of discrimination against minority job seekers.

While this net rate is an important summary measure of the magnitude of discrimination, testing generates more empirical information than is captured in any single number. Testing allows the recording of detailed information about employer-applicant interactions—for example, what questions are asked, what information is volunteered, and what degree of encouragement is expressed to job candidates. Thus, testing generates behavioral data on institutional and psychological mechanisms of bias that have previously been examined only in case studies. But because testing is structured to eliminate explanations of differences in treatment other than discrimination, the complexity that leads case studies to be difficult to interpret is sharply reduced. At the same time, by repeating the same procedure in dozens or hundreds of job applications, testing moves beyond isolated case studies to statistically analyzable samples.

The testing approach can be applied to a range of demographic groups and sample of jobs, and that process is well underway. Table 1 profiles six studies completed by three different research organizations—the Fair Employment Council of Greater Washington, the Urban Institute, and the University of Colorado—implementing variations of the same core testing design.[10] The table indicates that 1,532 tests have been accumulated in four metropolitan labor markets: Chicago, Denver, San Diego, and Washington, D.C. The job vacancies tested typically have been for entry-level positions ranging in qualifications from less-than-high-school-graduate to college graduate and drawn from a variety of industries. Discrimination against both African Americans and Hispanics has been explored using both male and female testers and job applications by mail and telephone as well as in-person.

THE OVERALL PREVALENCE OF DISCRIMINATION

Selected results from four of these six studies are presented in Table 2.[11] These results indicate that many firms today do operate as equal opportunity employers. This conclusion is based on instances in which a pair of testers contacted companies, and the equal qualifications of the two testers were reciprocated by equal treatment. In some cases, both were turned away because the job had already been filled. In other cases, both were interviewed and then offered equivalent jobs. In cases where only one position was available, even-handedness was reflected in an equal probability that the minority or the nonminority applicant would be chosen. In the four studies reviewed in Table 2, even-handed treatment was observed between 70 and 80 percent of the time.

In the remaining tests, however, the outcomes were different. The first row of Table 2 reports the proportion of tests in which one or more substantial differences in treatment or outcome were encountered by tester teams. It indicates that African American testers were treated significantly worse than their white partners at a net rate of 24 percent in the FEC study;[12] in tests pairing Anglo and Latino applicants, the corresponding figure for net disadvantage to Latinos ranged from 22 percent in the FEC study to 20 percent in the Urban Institute effort. In other words, discrimination adversely affected minority job seekers in more than one job application in five.

The second section of Table 2 focuses on a particularly important

TABLE 1
Characteristics of Six Testing Studies of Racial/Ethnic Discrimination in Hiring, 1989–1992

Charac- teristic	(a) Af.American-White Pairs FEC	(b) UI	(c) UC	(d) Latino-Anglo Pairs FEC	(e) UI	(f) UC
Method of Application	In person	In person	In person	In person	Telephone/ Mail	In person
Number of tests	149	300	145	498	300	140
Tester gender	Male & Female	Male	Male	Male Female	Male	Male
Labor Market	Washington	Washington Chicago	Denver	Washington	San Diego Chicago	Denver
Source of Job Sample	newspaper industry lists walk-ins	newspaper	newspaper	newspaper industry lists walk-ins	newspaper	newspaper
Location City Suburbs	60% 40	-- --	24% 76	21% 79	-- --	23% 77
Employees < 15 ≥ 15	17% 83	-- --	22% 78	-- --	12% 88	19% 81
Education Claimed in Resume high school graduate 1-2 years college college graduate	 100%	 100%	 100%	 50% 50	 100%	 100%
Employment Cluster Retail Office Service Other	22% 5 63 10	23% 21 37 19	37% 20 32 11	34% 46 4 16	16% 10 56 18	37% 17 35 11

outcome measure—the probability that a person applying for a position eventually is offered that position. The table indicates that the net difference between nonminority and minority applicants—all to the disadvantage of minorities—ranges from 10 percent (in the Urban Institute's African American/white study) to 15 percent (in the Urban Institute Hispanic/Anglo study), with the FEC's figure of 11 percent for its African American/white tests falling in between.

TABLE 2

Selected Outcome Measures in Four Testing Studies, 1989–1992

Outcome Measure	(a) White-Af.Am.Pairs FEC	(b) White-Af.Am.Pairs UI	(c) Anglo-Hispanic Pairs FEC	(d) Anglo-Hispanic Pairs UI
Applicants Experienced a Substantial Difference in Treatment or Outcome				
Non-Minority favored	29%	20%	25%	31%
Minority favored	-_5	-_7	-_3	-11
DIFFERENCE	24%	13%@	22%	20%
Probability an Applicant Received a Job Offer				
Non-Minority	15%	15%	--#	22
Minority	-_4	-_5	==	-_8
DIFFERENCE	11%	10%	--	15%

@ Includes only differences in the stage to which job applicants advanced; does not include any differences in treatment.
# Applications were not pursued to the job offer stage.
Details may not add to totals due to rounding.

The rates displayed in Table 2 incorporate the effects of discrimination operating in several different ways and at several different stages of the job-seeking process. In the FEC's African American/white tests, the following rates of prevalence were observed for five of these mechanisms:

- *Opportunities to Interview.* Although the testers in each pair presented their applications at virtually the same moment, one might be turned away "because the job is filled," while the other was interviewed. Overall, 48.3 percent of white testers received interviews, compared to 39.6 percent of their African American partners, a difference of 8.7 percentage points.
- *Job Offers or Referrals.* Although each pair of testers were selected and trained to be equally poised and articulate and carried resumes describing equivalent education and experience, one tester might be rejected while the other received a job offer. Some 46.9 percent of white testers who were interviewed received job offers, compared to 11.3 percent of their black counterparts, a difference of 35.6 percentage points.

- *Compensation.* In 16.7 percent of the tests in which both the African American tester and her/his white partner were offered the same job, the white was offered a higher starting wage; the reverse never occurred. In cases where both testers were offered the same job, the starting wage offered white applicants averaged $5.45 per hour, compared to $5.30 for their African American partners, a gap of $.15 per hour.
- *Steering.* Both applicants might be offered jobs, but one a well paid, upwardly mobile position and the other a low-pay, dead-end post. A total of 2.0 percent of white applicants were "steered" to an alternative job at a lower level than the position for which they initially applied, compared to 5.4 percent of African American applicants, a difference of 3.4 percentage points.
- *Access to Additional Opportunities.* When applying for one position, a job candidate is sometimes considered for other vacancies, often unadvertised ones, at the same level or higher than the job originally advertised. This situation was experienced by 4.0 percent of white testers but only 2.7 percent of African American testers, a gap of 1.3 percentage points.

Among these five differences, only that for job offers is large enough to be statistically significant (at the .01 level) in a sample of 149 tests. However, all five consistently operated to the disadvantage of minority applicants. Furthermore, when expressed as a proportion of the time nonminorities are favored over minorities when the mechanism potentially operates, the differences are substantial. The figures in the previous paragraphs translate into a rate of whites obtaining job interviews that is *22 percent* higher than that for their equivalently qualified African American counterparts; a rate for whites of receiving job offers at the interview stage that is *415 percent* the rate for African Americans; a *17 percent* probability that a white offered a job will receive a higher wage offer than an African American offered the same position; a likelihood for a white applicant of being steered to a lesser-quality job that is *37 percent* lower than that for an African American; and access to additional job vacancies that is *48 percent* greater for a white than an African American. Together, these effects make the labor market experiences of equally qualified minority and nonminority job applicants substantially different.

The following incidents[13] exemplify the forms of discriminatory treatment whose rates of incidence have just been presented:

- *Opportunities to Interview.* The *Washington Post* carried an advertisement for a restaurant supervisor in the Washington suburbs. An African American tester who went to the restaurant was told that he would be called if the restaurant wished to pursue his application. Minutes later, a white tester with equivalent credentials followed the same procedure. He was called later the same day to schedule an interview, interviewed the day after that, and subsequently offered the position. Meanwhile, the African American tester made four follow-up calls to reiterate his interest in the position, including one after the white tester refused the job offer. No response was received to these calls.
- *Job Offers or Referrals.* An African American female tester sought entry-level employment through a large employment agency in downtown Washington. After completing an application and being interviewed briefly, she was told that she would be called if a suitable vacancy became available. Shortly thereafter, her white testing partner arrived seeking similar opportunities. After she completed an application and was interviewed, she was told about a receptionist/sales position at an upscale health and grooming firm. She was coached on interviewing techniques and scheduled for an interview later that day; in that interview, she was offered the position.
- *Compensation.* A major department store chain advertised in the *Washington Post* for sales assistants in the women's clothing department of a branch in an affluent neighborhood. When a pair of female testers applied for the position, both were interviewed by the store's personnel department, and both were offered permanent, full-time employment. However, the starting salary offered to the African American tester was $6.50 per hour, while her white partner was offered $7.50 per hour.
- *Steering.* A major-brand auto dealer in the Washington suburbs advertised in the *Washington Post* for a car salesperson. An African American tester who applied was told that to enter the business, he should accept a position as a porter/car washer. Arriving shortly thereafter with identical credentials, his white testing partner was immediately interviewed for the sales position that had been advertised.
- *Access to Additional Opportunities.* A dating service in the Washington suburbs advertised in the *Washington Post* for a receptionist/typist. When an African American tester applied for the posi-

tion, she was interviewed but heard nothing further. When her white testing partner applied for the receptionist position and was interviewed, the employer offered to create a new position for her, that of personal assistant to the manager. This new position would pay more than the receptionist job, would lead to rapid raises and promotions, and would provide tuition assistance. Follow-up calls by the African American tester elicited no interest on the part of the firm, either for the receptionist position or the newly created opportunity, even after the white tester refused the offer.

RELATING THESE RATES TO THE OVERALL LABOR MARKET

A rate of discrimination exceeding twenty percent is unfortunate, particularly when that rate reflects behavior as blatant as that just illustrated. However, discrimination is even more insidious than these numbers suggest, for four reasons.

First, a typical job seeker applies for a number of jobs in the course of one search for employment.[14] If one job application in five is infected by discriminatory treatment, then the probability that a minority job seeker experiences discrimination during a multiple-application job search approaches 100 percent. Such findings suggest that virtually every minority participant in the non-professional American labor market is likely to be touched by discrimination at some time in her or his working life.

Second, inequality of opportunities often arise after initial hiring—as signaled, for example, by the 67,192 race/ethnic complaints alleging employment bias filed with the EEOC in 1988 that involved assignments, compensation, promotion, dismissal, or other treatment of persons already employed. Indeed, entry-level recruitment and hiring are believed to be the personnel processes in which minorities have made the most progress in many firms, with "glass ceiling" problems in retention and advancement remaining substantially more intractable.[15] Thus, posthiring practices undoubtedly produce instances of discrimination in addition to those counted through testing studies of hiring alone.

Third, while the effects of discrimination are serious for any worker, they are perhaps most destructive for job seekers just entering the world of work; being denied access to the bottom rung of "career ladders" can trap persons in a lifetime of "dead end," low-paying, unstable employment.[16] Testing results demonstrating that discrimination is common are based on samples of jobs disproportionately composed of such career-entry opportunities. Furthermore, the better the job, the greater the likelihood of discrimination. For example, in FEC African American-white tests where both applicants received a job offer, the average starting wage offered to whites was $5.45 per hour; in jobs where white applicants received an offer but their black partner did not, the starting wage averaged $7.13 per hour.

Finally, testing is most readily applied only to job vacancies that are relatively accessible because they are advertised in newspapers or listed with employment agencies. Such vacancies account for only about one-third of all employment opportunities, with the remaining two-thirds filled through more private means of recruitment such as word-of-mouth and personal referrals.[17] It is reasonable to assume that some employers utilize recruitment techniques in which information about vacancies is not publicized to keep away minority and other "undesirable" applicants. Therefore, the extent of discrimination in the overall labor market is almost certainly higher than the rate among vacancies that have been subject to testing.

IDENTIFYING DISCRIMINATION TROUBLE SPOTS

The studies in Table 1 consistently find that discrimination arises at some rate throughout the labor market. Nevertheless, certain circumstances are commonly hypothesized to be more prone to discrimination than others. For example, theory suggests that problems may concentrate in occupations involving customer contact, in better-paid positions, or in suburbs where minorities are discouraged from residing.[18]

Table 3 presents multiple regression analysis addressing such hypotheses, drawn from the two studies conducted in the Washington, D.C. labor market by the FEC (see Columns (a) and (d) of Table 1). In the regressions equations whose coefficients are presented in Columns (a) and (b) of Table 3, the dependent variable is coded +1 if the minority tester was favored, O if the two testers were treated equally, and -1 if the nonminority was favored. In Columns (c) and (d) of Table 3, these regression results are translated into an average probability of encountering discrimination by multiplying the regression coefficients in Columns (a) or (b) by the value corresponding to the circumstance examined (e.g., 1=tester is male) while holding all other variables at their average values.

The first row of Table 3 repeats the average probability of encountering discrimination in these two studies; consistent with Table 2, this

TABLE 3
The Effect of Selected Factors on the Probability that a Minority Tester will Experience Less Favorable Treatment[&]

	(a)	(b)	(c)	(d)
			Average Probability	
	Regression Coefficients		of Discrimination[#]	
Characteristic of	African-		African-	
Job or Applicant	American	Latino	American	Latino
Average of all tests			24.2	22.4%
Intercept	1.2	.4**	—	—
Applicant is male	−18.0*	.2**	13.6	29.3
Applicant is female	@	@	31.6	12.2
In District of Columbia	−1.7	@	18.9	37.2
In Maryland suburbs	@	{−.2**	20.6	{18.5
In Virginia suburbs	16.6	{	37.2	{
Job advertised in metropolitan newspaper	−19.6	−.1	14.7	19.7
Job advertised in suburban newspaper	—	−.1	—	22.3
Unsolicited application to an employer	@	—	34.3	—
Application to an employment agency	80.4**	@	66.7	33.7
Job typically not filled by a college graduate	—	−.1	—	24.8
Job typically filled by a college graduate	—	@	—	19.6
Sales position	43.8**	{.1	30.0	{25.0
Hotel position	30.4	{	16.6	{
Restaurant position	37.3	{	23.5	{
Office position	@	.1	41.9	21.8
Blue collar position	—	@	—	13.6
> 15 Employees	16.6	—	21.9	—
≤15 Employees	−3.6	—	25.5	—
Ad marked "equal opportunity"	—	.0	—	23.0
Ad not marked "equal opportunity"	—	@	—	22.0
R2	.14	.13		
DF	138	457		
F	2.1	6.8		

& = dependent variable is +1=minority favored, 0=treated equally, −1=non-minority favored.
@ = omitted category.
{ = categories combined.
— = not included in regression.
= Product of regression coefficients in columns (a) or (b) and value corresponding to the circumstance examined (e.g., 1=tester is male), holding all other variables at their average values.
* Statistically significant at the .05 level (2 tailed).
** Statistically significant at the .01 level (2 tailed).

figure is 24.2 percent for African Americans and 22.4 for Latinos. The remaining rows of the table then estimate how this probability varies under different conditions:

- *Gender.* It is often hypothesized that minority males are more subject to discrimination than minority females.[19] In the FEC's Latino-Anglo tests, male job seekers were more likely to encounter discrimination than female ones (29.3 percent versus 12.2 percent). However, the FEC's African American-white tests found the opposite pattern (13.6 percent for males, 31.6 percent for females). Only further studies can determine whether these contradictory results are stable, implying that race and gender interact differently for the two minority groups. At the least, both sets of findings document that race/ethnic discrimination is by no means confined to males.
- *City Versus Suburbs.* It is often hypothesized that suburbs are more hostile to minorities than central cities. Results in the FEC's African American-white tests were consistent with this hypothesis (an 18.9 percent rate of discrimination in the District of Columbia, compared to rates of 20.6 percent and 37.2 percent in its two surrounding suburban areas). However, in the FEC's Latino-Anglo tests, the opposite proved true (37.2 percent in the District of Columbia versus 18.5 percent in the suburbs). The difference between the two studies may reflect the fact that in the Washington area, a majority of the population in the central city is African American. At the same time, the distinction between city and suburb itself may be too broad; in the African American-white study, rates of discrimination were similar for the District of Columbia and its Maryland suburbs (18.9 percent and 20.6 percent) but substantially higher in the Virginia suburbs (37.2 percent).
- *Job Advertising.* Jobs advertised in the major metropolitan newspaper (the *Washington Post*) were associated with rates of discrimination between 14.7 and 19.7 percent, lower than the rate for jobs listed in suburban newspapers (22.3 percent) or "walk-in" applications where there was no newspaper advertising (34.3 percent). These patterns are consistent with the hypothesis, stated earlier, that the more closely information about a vacancy is held, the greater the likelihood of discrimination because restricting information is a means of discrimination.
- *Employment Agencies.* Employment agencies are firms whose business is to place workers in other firms, either temporarily or

permanently. Particularly in office and service employment, these agencies control access to a substantial number of job opportunities. In applying to employment agencies, the FEC's African American testers encountered less favorable treatment than their identically qualified white testing partners 66.7 percent of the time. This outcome is consistent with the hypothesis that screening out "undesirable" applicants is one of the services many employment agencies provide to their client firms.

- *Educational Prerequisites.* In the FEC's tests involving Latino and Anglo applicants, discrimination proved somewhat more prevalent for jobs not typically filled by college graduates (24.8 percent) than those typically filled by college graduates (19.6 percent).

- *Firm Size.* It is sometimes hypothesized that large corporations with professional human resource departments and formal policies of equal employment opportunity are less likely to discriminate than small, owner-managed firms. However, in the FEC's tests involving African Americans and whites, only a slightly lower rate of discrimination was observed in large firms than in small ones (21.9 percent versus 25.5 percent). FEC testers experienced biased treatment from some of the nation's largest, best-known retailers, hotel chains, real estate agencies, and service companies.

- *EEO Labeling.* Firms whose vacancy announcements carried statements such as "an Equal Opportunity Employer" were not substantially less likely to discriminate than firms that did not (22.0 percent versus 23.0 percent).

THE CENTRAL ROLE OF STEREOTYPICAL THINKING

One potential use of testing results such as those in Table 3 is in targeting antidiscrimination enforcement efforts; they identify where in the labor market problems are particularly prevalent. Other data generated by testing can address a related issue of targeting, namely: What are the specific mechanisms by which bias operates in the hiring process?

Table 4 illustrates this role of testing using data from the FEC study in Column (a) of Table 1. The table reports five measures comparing how African American and white testers fared in different aspects of the hiring process. These comparisons not only embody the comparability created by the overall testing process (that is, by fielding pairs of equally qualified job applicants); they create additional comparability by reporting results for sets of testers whom employers allowed to proceed to the same stage of the hiring process (e.g, pairs of testers who were both interviewed but neither received a job offer).

The results reported in Table 4 suggest the often subtle nature of discrimination in the 1990s. In the FEC's tests, racially based remarks, obvious hostility, or similar explicit indications of bias have been encountered only rarely. In nearly all cases, minority and nonminority testers were treated with approximately equal politeness. Illustrating this pattern, the first four groups of results in Table 4 report the experiences of African American and white testers in terms of the highest level of employees who interacted with them, the minutes of contact between the applicant and the employer, the number of topics discussed during the application process (e.g., the requirements of the job, the applicant's qualifications), and the number of comments made to testers (e.g., concerning their qualifications, their chances of obtaining the job, or the quality of the job). These indicators register few consistent differences in the experiences of black and white applicants. For example, comparing interviews that resulted in job offers, there was only a slight difference in the proportion of interviews conducted by a line manager rather than clerical or personnel staff (89.5 percent for whites, 83.3 percent for African Americans), and only a one minute difference in the length of these interviews (23.3 minutes for whites, 22.2 minutes for African Americans). No difference on these four variables is statistically significant, and the direction of differences is almost as likely to favor African Americans as whites (seven in favor of whites, five in favor of African Americans).

In contrast to these apparent similarities in treatment during the hiring process, the *judgments* made during the process showed substantial differences consistently favoring nonminorities.

One indicator of employers' judgments of applicants is comments made to testers by the staff screening or interviewing them. As reported in the fourth section of Table 4, interviewers consistently made more comments to white testers than to their African American partners. In the fifth section of the table, these comments are divided into positive ones (e.g., "You are just what we are looking for.") and negative ones (e.g., "This really is a dead-end job; you wouldn't want it anyway."). During job interviews, the proportion of nonminority applicants receiving one or more *positive* comments was 50 percent, while the comparable figure for minorities was 18 percent; the proportion of nonminority applicants receiving one or more *negative* comments was 10 percent, while the corresponding figure for minorities was 23 percent. The fifth section of Table 4 reports that a white tester who was interviewed but did not receive a

TABLE 4
Comparison of Application Processing for African American and White Testers Applying for 149 Jobs in the Washington, D.C. Labor Market, 1990–1991

Indicator	White Testers	African American Testers	Difference (White– Af. Am.)	Ratio (White/ Af. Am.)
Percent of applicants who met with a line manager at each stage, by furthest stage reached:				
Present credentials	26.3%	24.6%	1.7%	1.07
Interview, no offer	73.3	79.2	-5.9	.93
Interview and offer	89.5	83.3	6.2	1.07
Average minutes of contact at each stage, by furthest stage reached:				
Present credentials	15.7	16.1	-.4	.98
Interview, no offer	17.2	13.3	3.9	1.29
Interview and offer	22.2	23.3	-1.1	.95
Average number of topics discussed throughout the application process, by furthest stage reached:				
Present credentials	.80	.82	-.02	.97
Interview, no offer	2.98	3.02	-.04	.99
Interview and offer	3.33	2.50	.83	1.33
Average number of comments recorded throughout the application process, by furthest stage reached:				
Present credentials	.22	.13	.09	1.69
Interview, no offer	.83	.51	.32	1.62
Interview and offer	1.75	1.50	.25	1.17
Ratio of positive to negative comments received throughout the application process, by furthest stage reached:				
Present credentials	.50	.43	.07	1.16
Interview, no offer	2.90	.53	2.37	5.46
Interview and offer	35.54	--#	--	--
Percent of applicants reaching the prerequisite stage who moved to the further stage of:				
Presenting credentials	94.6%	91.9%	2.7%	1.03
Interview, no offer	71.0%	67.9%	3.1%	1.05
Tests	23.6%	15.3%	8.3%	1.54
Interview and offer	46.9%	11.3%	35.6%**	4.15

** = difference statistically significant at .01 level.
\# = no positive comments were received by African Americans at this stage.

job offer experienced 2.9 positive comments for every negative one, while a counterpart African American tester received only .5 positive comments for every negative one.[20]

A second measure of employers' judgments of minority and nonminority job candidates is the stage of the application process to which minorities advance. The final section of Table 4 reports a modest (5 percent) racial difference in the probability of obtaining an interview, and a larger difference (54 percent) in the probability of being allowed to take skills tests. These differences represent limitations on the extent to which minority job applicants can display their qualifications. Then, differences in minority/nonminority outcomes are sealed in hiring decisions. As reported in Table 2, in the FEC's African American-white tests, nonminorities received job offers 15 percent of the time they entered the application process, while the comparable rate for minorities was 4 percent. This pattern is echoed in the final section of Table 4, where it is reported that 46.9 percent of white applicants who advanced to a job interview obtained a job offer, while 11.3 percent of their African American counterparts did so, a rate for whites *4.2 times* that for African Americans.

The juxtaposition of approximately even-handed treatment of job applicants with hiring judgments that are less even-handed seems paradoxical. In some cases, it may reflect the behavior of employers who, although they do not intend to hire minorities, feel social or legal pressure to interview minority applicants. In other cases, however, the outcome seems to reflect more complex cognitive processes.

In particular, it appears to reflect the effect of traditional stereotyped beliefs held by employment decision makers on the way job applicants are judged. Social psychological research suggests that generalizations about a demographic group strongly influence how an individual from that group is perceived. This effect is particularly strong in situations where exposure to that individual is brief and accompanied by limited prior information. For example, in one psychological experiment, two groups of university students were shown videotapes concerning a fourth-grade girl. In a first tape, half the students observed the girl living in a depressed urban neighborhood, while the other half saw her living in an affluent suburb. Both groups were then shown the same videotape of her performing on an achievement test. Students who had previously been exposed to the girl's "high class" background judged her to be of higher ability *and reported her obtaining a higher numerical test score* than did students who had been exposed to her "low class" background.[21]

This experimental situation is analogous to entry-level hiring. Deci-

sions are often made on limited information—typically, a one-page resume and an interview averaging perhaps twenty minutes. It is therefore
not surprising that interviewers' judgments of individuals are influenced
by generalizations about the applicants' demographic group that the interviewer may have formed over a lifetime.

The process of interpreting new data in light of prior information is, of
course, a common mechanism of human thought. It is well known in
labor economics under the label "statistical discrimination."[22] However,
it creates problems for minority job seekers because of the unfavorable
content of generalizations concerning African Americans and Hispanics
held by many Americans. According to public opinion research, widely
held images of both African Americans and Hispanics portray them,
relative to nonminorities, as less intelligent, more lazy and welfare-de-
pendent, and more prone to violence. Company managers and other personnel decision makers readily generalize about ethnic groups, and the
content of these generalizations is highly adverse to most minorities. In
one study in Chicago, for example, common generalizations by employers concerning African American and Hispanic workers emphasized their
shortcomings in terms of work ethic, honesty, attitudes, communication
skills, intelligence, educational preparation, and stability.[23]

When employers and their staffs bring such attitudes into a job-selec-
tion process, every minority candidate enters the process with a substantial handicap. However well a minority individual may perform in the
interview and however impressive his resume, those qualifications are
likely to be discounted or incorrectly perceived based on the prior generalizations.[24] Indeed, stereotypical thinking can even turn applicants' positive attributes into their opposite. For example, a standard piece of advice
to job seekers is to dress well for employment interviews.[25] But when an
African American male tester wearing a suit and tie was interviewed by a
Washington-area employment agency, he was asked whether his ability
to afford such clothes indicated that he participated in illegal activities.

DIRECTIONS FOR PUBLIC POLICY

The persistence of substantial racial/ethnic bias in hiring, documented
by testing, clearly implies the need for continued efforts toward its eradication. Enforcement of antidiscrimination laws—such as is carried out by
the Equal Employment Opportunity Commission, its state and local counterparts, the Office of Federal Contract Compliance, and by private litigation—needs to be maintained. Indeed, testing enhances opportunities

for such efforts in that testers can participate in litigation either as plaintiffs who are victims of discrimination or as witnesses corroborating allegations of discrimination by actual job seekers.[26]

Support by the American voting public and their elected representatives is prerequisite to such efforts. Accordingly, it is unfortunate that, while racial/ethnic minorities within the American population hold perceptions of the prevalence of discrimination matching the empirical findings in this paper, nonminorities predominantly do not. For example, a 1989 nationwide poll reported that 80 percent of African Americans thought that an African American applicant who is as qualified as a white applicant is less likely to win a job that both want—but only 37 percent of whites agreed; and 62 percent of African Americans felt that the chances of an African American to win a supervisory/managerial position were worse than those for whites—but only 41 percent of whites agreed.[27]

Given these perceptions, perhaps it is not surprising that, since the early 1980s, enforcement activities of the federal Equal Employment Opportunity Commission have stagnated under a combination of inadequate resources and leadership that was ambivalent about the agency's mission. Between fiscal year 1982 and fiscal year 1992, the EEOC's backlog of cases grew from 33,417 to 52,856; and the proportion of complaints dismissed by the EEOC for "no cause" rose from 29 percent in 1981 to 59 percent in 1986.[28] In the same era, considerable policy attention was paid to the contention that litigation in the United States on subjects such as employment discrimination was chronically overused and adversely affected the productivity and competitiveness of the American economy;[29] five Supreme Court rulings substantially reduced the power and scope of federal antidiscrimination laws; and passage of the Civil Rights Act of 1991 to reverse these rulings sparked protracted and bitter debate. Had testing studies indicating the continued prevalence of discrimination challenged public perceptions, this course of events might have been different.

While indicating the continuing need for traditional enforcement of civil rights laws, testing results also suggest the desirability of some refocusing of efforts. In particular, traditional enforcement often focuses on instances of blatant, conscious discriminatory behavior (for example, failure to interview minority job candidates) or the discriminatory impact of "objective" selection procedures (for example, racial/ethnic differences in pass rates on written examinations). While not denying the importance of such mechanisms, testing suggests that they represent only part of current problems. It is equally important to focus on the role of less blatant, often unconscious personal judgments and attitudes in generating differences in employment outcomes—for example, how accurately employers evaluate interviews with minority job candidates. The process of examining and modifying such cognitive processes is complex, involving individual consciousness-raising as well as changes in organizational cultures.[30] However, such difficult undertakings are required to address important forms of employment bias in the 1990s.

NOTES

This research was supported by grants to the Fair Employment Council of Greater Washington, Inc., from the Rockefeller, Ford, MacArthur, Public Welfare, and Norman Foundations. The authors are solely responsible for all findings and conclusions.

1. Gerald Jaynes and Robin M. Williams, eds., *A Common Destiny, Blacks and American Society* (Washington: National Academy of Sciences Press, 1989), chapters 2 and 3; Reynolds Farley, Charles Steeh, Tara Jackson, Maria Krysan, and Keith Reeves, "Continued Racial Segregation in Detroit: 'Chocolate City, Vanilla Suburbs' Revisited," *Journal of Housing Research*, Vol. 4, No. 1 (1993), pp. 1–38.; Joe R. Feagin and Melvin P. Sikes, *Living with Racism, The Black Middle Class Experience* (Boston: Beacon Press, 1994); Louis Harris, *The Unfinished Agenda on Race in America* (New York: NAACP Legal Defense Fund, 1989); Tom Smith, *Ethnic Images* (Chicago: National Opinion Research Center, 1990).

2. Andrew Gill, "The Role of Discrimination in Determining Occupational Structure," *Industrial and Labor Relations Review*, Vol. 42, No. 4 (1989), pp. 610–623; Jaynes and Williams, *Common Destiny*, pp. 146–147; K.I. Wolpin, "The Determinants of Black-White Differences in Early Employment Careers: Search, Layoffs, Quits, and Endogenous Wage Growth," *Journal of Political Economy*, Vol. 100, No. 3 (1992), pp. 535–60; Glen Cain, "The Economic Analysis of Labor Market Discrimination: A Survey," in Orley Aschenfelter and Richard Layard, eds., *Handbook of Labor Economics* (New York: Elsevier, 1986), pp. 694–785; Craig Zwerling and Hilary Silver, "Race and Job Dismissal in a Federal Bureaucracy," *American Sociological Review*, Vol. 57, No. 5 (1992), pp. 651–660.

3. *Combined Annual Report, Fiscal Years 1986, 1987, and 1988* (Washington: U.S. Equal Employment Opportunity Commission, 1988).

4. EEOC, *Annual Report*; see also Jomills Braddock and James M. McPartland, "How Minorities Continue to be Excluded from Equal Employment Opportunities: Research on Labor Market and Institutional Barriers," *Journal of Social Issues*, Vol. 43, No. 1 (1987), pp. 5–39.

5. Kenneth Arrow, "The Theory of Discrimination," in Orley Aschenfelter and Albert Rees, eds., *Discrimination in Labor Markets* (Princeton: Princeton University Press, 1973), p. 3.

6. *Annual Report, 1990–1992* (Washington: Fair Employment Council of Greater Washington, Inc., 1993); *Employment Testing Manual* (Washington: Fair Employment Council of Greater Washington, Inc., 1993). The same techniques are also applicable to demographic characteristics other than race and ethnicity. For example, using pairs of applicants age 32 and 57, testing has been applied to hiring discrimination based on age; see Marc Bendick, Jr., Charles Jackson, and Horacio Romero, *Employment Discrimination Against Older Workers: An Experimental Study of Hir-*

ing Practices (Washington: Fair Employment Council of Greater Washington, 1993).

7. Tests might be conducted in a "double blind" format, that is, with testers not being told that discrimination is the subject of the study in which they are participating. This approach was implemented, for example, in a study of discrimination in auto sales practices; see Ian Ayres, "Fair Driving: Gender and Race Discrimination in Retail Car Negotiations," *Harvard Law Review*, Vol. 104, No. 4 (1991), pp. 817–872. However, it is unrealistic to assume that employment testers would not infer the subject of the study from the procedures they were following and the data they were asked to record. Instead, the FEC seeks to ensure the objectivity of tester-generated data by careful tester selection, extensive training, close supervision, data collection procedures that emphasize facts over judgments, and an organizational culture of social science objectivity.

8. *Dictionary of Occupational Titles* (Washington: U.S. Department of Labor, 1991); *Occupational Outlook Handbook* (Lincolnwood, IL: VGM Career Horizons, 1990).

9. In preparing sampling frames for random sampling, positions were excluded if they were part-time or temporary employment; were in government; or required advanced education, extensive experience, specialized skills, or occupational licenses. While sampling within each sampling frame was random, some sampling frames were selected, in part, because of hypotheses that firms in that frame might be particularly bias-prone (e.g., employment agencies). To the extent that this hypothesis was confirmed, caution should be exercised in applying the precise rate of bias estimated from this sample to the general labor market.

10. The core design is set forth in Marc Bendick, Jr., *Auditing Race Discrimination in Hiring: A Research Design* (Washington: Bendick and Egan Economic Consultants, Inc., 1989). For alternative designs, see Jerome Culp and Bruce Dunson, "Brothers of a Different Color: A Preliminary Look at Employer Treatment of Black and White Youth," in Richard Freeman and Harry Holzer, eds., *The Black Youth Employment Crisis* (Chicago: University of Chicago Press, 1986), pp. 233–259; P.A. Riach and J. Rich, "Measuring Discrimination by Direct Experimental Methods: Seeking Gunsmoke," *Journal of Post-Keynesian Economics*, Vol. 14, No. 2 (1991–92), pp. 143–50.; Frank Bovenkerk, *A Manual for International Comparative Research on Discrimination on the Grounds of "Race" and Ethnic Origin* (Geneva: International Labour Organisation, 1992), and George Galster et al., *Sandwich Hiring Audit Pilot Program* (Washington: The Urban Institute, 1994).

Table 1 is based on the following sources: Column (a): FEC, *Annual Report*, chapter 3; Column (b): Margery Austin Turner, Michael Fix, and Raymond Struyk, *Opportunities Diminished, Opportunities Denied* (Washington: Urban Institute, 1991); Columns (c) and (f): Franklin James and Steve DelCastillo, *We May be Making Progress Toward Equal Access to Jobs: Evidence From Recent Audits* (Denver: University of Colorado, 1992); Column (d): Marc Bendick, Jr., Charles Jackson, Victor Reinoso, and Laura Hodges, "Discrimination Against Latino Job Applicants: A Controlled Experiment," *Human Resource Management*, Vol. 30, No. 4 (1991), pp. 469–484; Column (e): Harry Cross, et al., *Employer Hiring Practices: Differential Treatment of Hispanic and Anglo Job Seekers* (Washington: Urban Institute, 1990).

11. The sources for Table 2 are the same as for Table 1 (see Footnote 10).

James and DelCastillo, *We May be Making Progress*, report a testing study in the Denver labor market that estimated a two percent net rate of discrimination against African Americans compared to whites but a ten percent rate in favor of Hispanics over Anglos. These results are contaminated by methodological flaws, including inappropriate pairing of testers, inadequate supervision of field work, and compensation arrangements giving minority testers greater incentives to pursue job openings than nonminorities. These flaws led to differences in the level of effort expended by paired testers (e.g, different numbers of follow-up calls) and also raised general concerns about data validity and reliability; see Michael Fix and Raymond Struyk, eds., *Clear and Convincing Evidence: Measurement of Discrimination in America* (Washington: Urban Institute Press, 1993), appendix. Accordingly, this study is not included in Table 2.

12. The net rate of 24 percent is obtained by subtracting 5 percent of instances in which minorities were favored from the 29 percent of instances in which the nonminorities were favored. The comparable figure in Table 2 for the Urban Institute study of African Americans and whites—13 percent—refers only differences in the stage of application to which the testers progress, not the full range of possible differences in treatment or outcome.

13. These examples, all involving African Americans, are drawn from FEC, *Annual Report*, pp. 5–6. Comparable incidents involving Latinos are presented in Bendick et al., "Discrimination Against Latinos," p. 475.

14. Marc Bendick, Jr., "Matching Workers and Job Opportunities, " in D. Bawden and F. Skidmore (eds.), *Rethinking Employment Policy* (Washington: Urban Institute Press, 1989), pp. 81–108; Harry Holzer, "Informal Job Search and Black Youth Unemployment," *American Economic Review*, Vol. 77, No. 3 (1987), pp. 446–452; Steven M. Bortnick and Michele Harrison Ports, "Job Search Methods and Results: Tracking the Unemployed, 1991," *Monthly Labor Review*, Vol. 115, No. 12 (1992), pp. 29–35.

15. R. Roosevelt Thomas, *Beyond Race and Gender* (New York: American Management Association, 1991); Susan Jackson and Associates, *Diversity in the Workplace* (New York: Guilford Press, 1992); Mary Lou Egan and Marc Bendick, Jr., *Managing Greater Washington's Changing Workforce* (Washington: Greater Washington Research Center, 1991).

16. Freeman and Holzer, *Black Youth*; Marc Bendick, Jr., and Mary Lou Egan, *Jobs: Employment Opportunities in the Washington Metropolitan Area for Persons with Limited Employment Qualifications* (Washington: Greater Washington Research Center, 1988).

17. See Footnote 14.

18. Gary Becker, *The Economics of Discrimination* (Chicago: University of Chicago Press, 1971); Susan Hanson and Geraldine Pratt, "Dynamic Dependencies: A Geographic Investigation of Local Labor Markets," *Economic Geography*, Vol. 68, No. 4 (1992), pp. 610–623.

19. Joleen Neckerman and Kathryn Kirschenman, "'We'd Love to Hire them, But...': The Meaning of Race for Employers," in Christopher Jencks and Paul E. Peterson, eds., *The Urban Underclass* (Washington: Brookings Institution, 1991), pp. 203–234; Freeman and Holzer, *Black Youth Employment*.

20. Job interviews that do not lead to an offer but nevertheless include positive comments may leave job seekers more optimistic and encouraged to continue their job search than interviews dominated by negative comments. Nationwide, minority males who are not employed become "discouraged workers" (that is, leave the labor force rather than actively seek employment) at a substantially higher rate than counterpart white males. This difference is often attributed to their relative chances of obtaining employment, as reflected, for example, in higher unemployment rates for minorities than nonminorities. Testing findings concerning positive and negative comments received during interviews provides an additional explanation of this pattern.

21. J.M. Darley and P.H. Gross, "A Hypothesis-Conforming Bias in Labelling Effects," *Journal of Personality and Social Psychology*, Vol. 44, No. 1 (1983), pp. 20–33. See also J. Krueger and M. Rothbart, "Use of Categorical and Individuating Information in Making Inferences About Personality," *Journal of Personality and Social Psychology*, Vol. 55, No. 1 (1988), pp. 187–195, and R.D. Arvey and J.E. Campion, "The Employment Interview: Survey and Review of Recent Research," *Personnel Psychology*, Vol. 35, No. 2 (1982), pp. 281–322.

22. Dennis J. Aigner and Glen Cain, "Statistical Theories of Discrimination in Labor Markets," *Industrial and Labor Relations Review*, Vol. 30, No. 2 (1877), pp. 175–87; M.A. Spence, "Job Market Signaling," *Quarterly Journal of Economics,* Vol. 87, No. 3 (1973), pp. 355–74.

23. Smith, *Ethnic Images*; Joseph E. Trimble, "Stereotypical Images, American Indians, and Prejudice," in Phyllis A. Katz and Dalmas A. Taylor (eds.), *Eliminating Racism* (New York: Plenum Press, 1988), pp. 181–201; Neckerman and Kirschenman, "We'd Love to Hire Them."

24. A second mechanism that may operate is that the behavior of interviewers may cause minority applicants to perform badly in interviews. In one social psychology experiment, white university students interviewed African American and white job applicants. When the applicant was African American, the interviewers sat further away, terminated the interview 25 percent sooner, and made 50 percent more speech errors than when the applicant was white. Then, in a second experiment, interviewers deliberately duplicated the behavior typical of interviews with African Americans and whites. Neutral judges rated the interview performance of job applicants of any race subjected to the "African American" treatment as more nervous and less effective than that of persons subjected to the "white" treatment; see C.O. Word, M.P. Zanna, and J. Cooper, "The Nonverbal Mediation of Self-Fulfilling Prophesies in Interracial Interaction," *Journal of Experimental Social Psychology*, Vol. 10, No. 1 (1974), pp. 109–120. See also C. G. Lord and D.S. Saentz, "Memory Deficits and Memory Surfeits: Differential Cognitive Consequences of Tokenism for Tokens and Observers," *Journal of Personality and Social Psychology*, Vol. 49, No. 4 (1985), pp. 918–926.

25. John T. Molloy, *Dress For Success* (New York: Warner Books, 1988).

26. Roderic Boggs, Joseph Sellers, and Marc Bendick, Jr., "Use of Testing in Civil Rights Enforcement," in Michael Fix and Raymond Struyk (eds.), *Clear and Convincing Evidence: Measurement of Discrimination in America* (Washington: Urban Institute Press, 1993), pp. 345–376; FEC, *Annual Report*, pp. 10–13; Michael Yelnosky, "Filling an Enforcement Void: Using Testers to Uncover and Remedy Discrimination in Hiring for Lower-Skilled, Entry-Level Jobs," *University of Michigan Journal of Law Reform*, Vol. 26, No. 2 (1993), pp. 404–459.

27. Harris, *Unfinished Agenda*; see also J.R. Kluegel and E.R. Smith, *Beliefs about Equality: Americans' Views of What Is and What Ought to Be* (Hawthorne, NY: Aldine de Gruyter, 1986).

28. Women Employed, *Compilation of EEOC District Office Reports* (Chicago: Women Employed, 1992); Claudia Withers and Judith A. Winston, "Equal Employment Opportunity," in *One Nation Indivisible: The Civil Rights Challenge for the 1990s* (Washington: The Citizens Commission on Civil Rights, 1989), pp. 190–214.

29. Walter Olson, *The Litigation Explosion* (New York, NY: Truman Talley Books, 1992).

30. Thomas, *Beyond Race and Gender*; Jackson, *Diversity*; Egan and Bendick, *Managing*. Several social psychological studies have found that, in laboratory simulations of employment selections, individuals often discriminated in favor of minori-

ties [Arvey and Campion, "The Employment Interview"; Braddock and McPartland, "How Minorities"]. These results contrast with the findings of testing studies involving actual job selections in firms. To understand this contrast, further research is needed to differentiate between discrimination reflecting the attitudes of individual staff members and that reflecting the policies and organizational culture of the firms that employ them.

SOME NEW HISTORICAL EVIDENCE ON THE
IMPACT OF AFFIRMATIVE ACTION: DETROIT, 1972

Thomas Hyclak, Larry W. Taylor, and James B. Stewart

A sample of Detroit area firms in 1972 is used to determine the effects of affirmative action requirements and other firm characteristics on the recruitment and hiring of women and black men. The results suggest that affirmative action changed firm hiring practices with respect to black males. The unique data set also allows for a test of Becker's well-known hypothesis that customer prejudice may influence the hiring of blacks or females.

Despite the existence of a voluminous literature on affirmative action, there have been surprisingly few econometric examinations of the wage and employment impacts of affirmative action programs on minority and female workers. In fact, a recent review by Gunderson identifies just eight studies devoted to this theme.[1] The results of these studies generally indicate a positive impact of affirmative action on minority and female employment opportunities. This has been confirmed in recent papers by Smith and Welch and Donohue and Heckman, who add the interesting conclusion that most of the positive effects of affirmative action appear to have occurred in the early 1970s, even though it is generally acknowledged that strong enforcement of anti-discrimination policy began only after 1973.[2] Given the continued interest in the impact of antidiscrimination policy and the recent emphasis on the existence of "glass ceilings" that limit the upward mobility of women and minority workers in managerial jobs, this article reexamines the effect of affirmative action on the recruitment and hiring of managerial employees in a sample of Detroit area firms during this critical early 1970s period.[3]

While Freeman and others argue that federal anti-discrimination programs have altered the personnel policies of firms, the existing empirical studies on the effects of affirmative action offer only indirect evidence on this question.[4] There have been two types of studies in this literature. The first, exemplified by Heckman and Payner, examines the time series of employment and/or wage shares of various groups to determine if the timing of shifts in the share of target groups coincides with changes in legislation or policy.[5] The second type of study examines cross-section data on firms or establishments to determine if those subject to affirmative action regulations significantly increased their share of minority workers over some time span. Leonard and Smith and Welch carry out such studies using data extracted from EEO-1 forms filed with the Equal Employment Opportunity Commission.[6] Neither of these two types of studies directly examines the effect of federal anti-discrimination programs on the recruitment and hiring practices of firms. In fact, as is argued by Holzer, empirical studies of the recruitment and hiring procedures of firms have been quite rare in the labor economics literature.[7]

This article utilizes a previously untapped data source to study the effect of affirmative action and other establishment characteristics on the rate at which black male and female workers applied for and were hired for managerial jobs in a sample of firms in the Detroit metropolitan area in 1972. While this data source has some limitations which are discussed below, it does allow us to conduct a rigorous empirical examination of the hypothesis that affirmative action programs changed the personnel practices of affected firms in the recruitment and hiring of women and black men.

THE 1972 DETROIT AREA STUDY

The data set contains information collected from interviews with the senior manager, the chief personnel manager and a front-line supervisor at 131 business establishments in the Detroit metropolitan area. Our study of the determinants of minority and female hiring patterns focuses on the personnel manager portion of the survey. Although there are no detailed data on the personal characteristics of the applicants or hires, the personnel manager did supply the race and sex composition of the last twenty applicants and the last twenty hires in various occupations at the establishment. Of course, the fixed number of applicants and hires (twenty each) thus precludes simply counting the number of applicants and hires to respectively derive the demand and supply of workers for the various positions within the firms. Furthermore, a lack of detailed personal characteristics also precludes a labor-supply model analogous to those popularized by Heckman and others.[8] On the other hand, this weakness is shared with all of the previous establishment level examinations of the effect of affirmative action on minority and female employment.

The fixed numbers of applicants and hires also abstracts from the issue of possible timing differences in the application-hiring process across occupations, and the impact of these timing considerations on the composition of applicant pools. As an example, in job classifications where little turnover occurs, the pool of applicants could have little relationship to the pool of hires in comparison to occupations and firms where turnover rates are high.

It is also important to recognize the limitations of the data base in quantifying the micro-level effects of affirmative action. The results will understate the impacts if the average black applicant is less qualified than the average white applicant. Alternatively, the impact will be overstated if the average black candidate is more qualified than the average white applicant. There are two competing patterns that would influence the relationship between the average qualifications of black and white cohorts. First, the presence of employer and employee discrimination certainly increased the probability that the average black hire was more qualified than white counterparts. To the extent that information about the relative strength of employer and employee tastes for discrimination across employers was known to potential applicants, the applicant pools for specific employers would be conditioned by such information. It is unlikely, however, that such a level of disaggregation and quality of information existed.

Second, one important effect of the public policy mix prior to the implementation of Equal Opportunity legislation was to diminish the rate of human capital accumulation by blacks. The result would be a general reduction in the overall qualifications of black applicants for all positions.

The original sample design, based on 212 establishments drawn from 32 size-by-industry cells, was an explicit compromise between a representative sample of Detroit area firms and one representative of the employment locations of the Detroit area labor force.[9] A response rate of 73% yielded 132 establishments willing to permit interviews, and problems with missing data further reduced the number of firms in our sample to 99. Significantly, all of the major auto firms refused to participate. While these factors limit our article to a rigorous case study of a group of Detroit firms, the unique data in the survey and the verdict that the early

1970s represented a critical period for the affirmative action program has convinced us that our information is useful. The strength of this data base is that it permits a dynamic analysis of the application queue and the hiring process at the level of the firm.

THE MODEL

A multinomial logit model is used to determine the joint impact of affirmative action and direct customer contact on the application and hiring patterns of women and minorities. Conditional upon the character-istics of the firm, we are able to estimate the application and hiring probabilities for black males, white males and females for managerial positions, and to estimate these probabilities for white males and black males for skilled blue-collar positions. The multinomial logit model is used because the closed form of the likelihood function implies that the parameters are relatively easy to estimate.

We specify the first set of equations as a reduced form for the prob-ability of an applicant of a given race/sex category:

$$P \text{ (black-male applicant)} = \exp(\beta_1 X) / D,$$

(1) $$P \text{ (female applicant)} = \exp(\beta_2 X) / D,$$

$$P \text{ (white-male applicant)} = 1 / D,$$

where

$$D = 1 + \exp(\beta_1 X) + \exp(\beta_2 X).$$

The conditioning vector, X, contains (weakly) exogenous variables, and the parameters β_1 and β_2 are to be estimated by maximum likelihood.[10] In addition to an affirmative action dummy variable, the set of condition-ing variables includes measures of the recruiting practices by firms, and minimum educational requirements and starting salaries for managerial and skilled blue collar jobs. A complete description of the conditioning variables is found in Table 1.

In particular we include in X the black male percentage (PCTBM) and the female percentage (PCTFEM) of the existing work force. Holzer presents evidence indicating that firms value referrals from current work-ers to fill job openings.[11] Clearly, then, applications from minority and female workers would seem more likely at firms with relatively larger

TABLE 1
Variable List

Variable	Description
AA	dummy set equal to one if the firm is a federal contractor or subject to other affirmative action reporting requirements.
CITY	dummy set equal to one for firms located in the city of Detroit; a zero signifies a suburban firm in the greater Detroit area.
CONT	percentage of managerial workers that have direct contact with customers.
FORREC	dummy set equal to one if the firm relies on newspapers or agencies for managerial applicants.
INTREC	dummy set equal to one if the firm relies on internal recruiting for managerial applicants.
MINED	the minimum education level required for management jobs.
MININC	the lowest salary level earned by managers.
PCTBM	black-male percentage of existing managerial work force.
PCTFEM	female percentage of existing managerial work force.
REVGRO	dummy set equal to one for firms experiencing a positive trend in revenues over the preceding five years.
SINGLE	dummy set equal to one for firms that were single unit corporations.
SIZE	the logarithm of the number of people currently employed as managers.
UNION	dummy set equal to one if the establishment is unionized.

black and female work forces. In addition, firm reputation effects stemming from past hiring patterns are likely to condition the search activities of blacks and women. The predetermined variables PCTBM and PCTFEM are thus included to capture the dynamic aspects of the application process.

Holzer also suggests that formal search methods through agencies or in response to newspaper ads have a higher payoff to minority job searchers.[12] To capture this aspect of the application process, we include dummy variables indicating whether the firm relies on formal recruiting methods to attract applicants.

The second part of the model considers the selection by employers. We specify P (black-male applicant I hire), P (female applicant I hire) and P (white-male applicant I hire) by the multinomial logit equations at (1), but with β_i replaced by Θ_i and another regressor vector, Z, substituted for X[13,14]. While X and Z may overlap, the hiring equations also include the regressors log (PBMA/PWMA) and log (PFA/PWMA), where PBMA, PWMA and PFA are the respective probabilities of current black-male, white-male and female applicants. These regressors are included for two reasons. First, the decision to hire minorities and women is contingent on the odds that they apply. Second, the inclusion of log (PBMA/PWMA) allows us to test whether black-male applications and hires are statistically independent. If so, then (as a group) black-males are indistinguishable from white-males from the perspective of the employer, and thus there is no basis for discrimination according to race. If statistical independence holds true, then the element in Θ_1 corresponding to log (PBMA/ PWMA) is unity, while all other elements are zero. Similarly, female applications and hires are statistically independent if all of the elements in Θ_2 are null except for the (unit) element corresponding to log (PFA/ PWMA). Moreover, although log (PBMA/PWMA) and log (PFA/PWMA) are unobserved, consistent estimates of them can be generated by using the (estimated) applications model at (1). Correct asymptotic standard errors for the hiring model are then derived by employing results found in Amemiya and Pagan.[15]

Becker's well-known model of employment discrimination includes the possibility that the hiring decisions of an unbiased employer might be affected by the tastes for discrimination of the existing workforce and/or of customers.[16] Our conditioning vector Z contains three variables designed to test for these influences. We expect that employee discrimination will be lower the higher percentage of black males and females among the firm's employees. Also, the more experience employers and white employees have with blacks and women in a particular occupation, the less likely they are to rely on sex or race as productivity screening devices. For both of these reasons, we expect PCTBM and PCTFEM to be positively related to the hiring chances of black and female applicants.

At the same time, it should be recognized that during the period covered by this study the workforces of some firms may have been bifurcated across race and skill classification. This type of labor force structure will, of course, reduce the extent to which experience in any particular skill classification becomes generally available to managers operating other units and/or with responsibilities for other job classifications.

To capture the possible effect of customer prejudice on hiring, we include in Z the personnel manager's estimate of the percentage of workers in a given occupation at each firm who have direct contact with customers (CONT). If the employers in our sample felt that customers preferred to deal with white male representatives of their firm, then CONT should have a negative effect on female and black male hiring probabilities.

EMPIRICAL RESULTS

Table 2 presents the empirical multinomial logit results for our models of the application queue and selection process for managerial jobs. Asymptotic standard errors for the hiring model are derived in Appendix A, while the usual information matrix is used to derive the standard errors for the applications model. For the application queue, we find a statistically significant positive effect of affirmative action (AA) requirements on the likelihood of female applications, whereas, affirmative action seems to have little effect on the application rate of black males for managerial jobs at the firms in our sample. This might reflect the fact that in the early 1970s, action to alleviate sex discrimination was just beginning while racial discrimination had been a matter of public policy since the 1960s. Women in our sample may have been responding to the perception that females were a more important target group for satisfying affirmative action mandates.

In the hiring equation, affirmative action appears to have had a positive effect only for black men. Furthermore, the size of the estimated effect suggests a fairly strong impact of affirmative action on black male hiring. While the coefficient for females is negative, this variable is insignificant at conventional levels of significance.

The results for blacks are consistent with those obtained in studies of the effect of the compliance activities of the Office of Federal Contracts Compliance (OFCCP) for the period 1966–73. Ashenfelter and Heckman, Burman, and Heckman and Wolpin all found positive effects of compliance activities on overall black male employment although there was little impact on relative occupational position.[17] Leonard finds a larger effect on employment and occupational upgrading between 1974 and 1980.[18] In part, Leonard's findings reflect greater effectiveness of OFCCP via promulgation of specific guidelines regarding application of policies to contractor establishments.

While affirmative action appeared to work in favor of minorities and women, customer prejudice seemed to work to their detriment. Of considerable interest is the finding that women and black men were less likely to be hired at firms where managerial jobs involved a high degree

TABLE 2
Determinants of Application and Hiring Probabilities
for Managerial Positions

Variable	Applications		Hires		MEAN	Standard Deviation
	Females	Black Males	Females	Black Males		
Constant	−5.8117	−6.8486	−1.0560	−0.4643		
	(5.72)	(7.57)	(0.47)	(0.11)		
AA	1.8241	−0.3381	−0.7805	2.6856	0.84	0.36
	(3.36)	(0.95)	(1.29)	(2.17)		
CITY	−0.1150	0.0323	0.1979	0.0466	0.43	0.49
	(0.51)	(0.16)	(0.89)	(0.11)		
CONT	−0.0005	0.0000	−0.0188	−0.0255	84.22	26.61
	(0.14)	(0.01)	(5.37)	(3.83)		
FORREC	2.1407	0.2790			0.40	0.49
	(4.16)	(0.64)				
INCOME	−0.0741	−0.0246	−0.0206	−0.1112	13.25	6.16
	(2.44)	(1.14)	(0.65)	(1.83)		
INTREC	1.3063	1.0936			0.43	0.49
	(2.44)	(3.05)				
log (PBMA/PWMA)			−0.3715	1.1404	−3.03	1.36
			(1.38)	(2.34)		
log (PFA/PWMA)			0.3413	−0.9983	−3.59	2.00
			(1.82)	(2.49)		
MINED	−0.1787	0.0966	0.0229	−0.2347	12.67	2.67
	(4.36)	(2.24)	(0.38)	(2.04)		
PCTBM	0.0456	0.0847	0.0071	0.0191	4.27	9.38
	(4.46)	(9.62)	(0.25)	(0.39)		
PCTFM	0.0710	0.0134	0.0386	0.1142	8.34	15.09
	(8.75)	(1.49)	(2.27)	(3.08)		
REVGRO	0.7236	0.2414	−0.0735	1.3091	0.59	0.49
	(2.94)	(1.07)	(0.29)	(2.65)		
SINGLE	−1.2727	−1.0000	−2.3826	−3.9100	0.17	0.38
	(3.48)	(1.97)	(3.81)	(2.57)		
SIZE	0.3908	0.5576	0.0981	−0.3220	3.34	1.27
	(3.32)	(6.21)	(0.47)	(0.85)		
UNION	0.3714	0.3918	0.3080	0.9278	0.72	0.45
	(1.43)	(1.40)	(1.08)	(1.57)		
Likelihood Ratio (slopes = 0)		552.47		486.30		

Absolute value of the asymptotic t-ratio in parentheses.

of direct contact (CONT) with customers. Even though Becker's theory of discrimination allowed for the possibility that employers would discriminate in hiring because they expected their customers to have tastes for discrimination, to date there has been very little empirical testing of this hypothesis.[19] Here we have evidence that the hiring of both minorities and women for managerial positions in the Detroit area in 1972 was inversely related to the degree of customer contact on the job. Although the magnitude of the coefficient of CONT is small, the coefficient is robust and the mean percentage of managerial jobs requiring customer contact is large (56.56). Thus the aversion to hiring blacks and women in high-contact managerial jobs may have contributed to occupational crowding.

As expected, the higher the female and minority proportion of the existing work force (see PCTFEM and PCTBM), the more likely were females and black males to apply for managerial jobs. Clearly the prevalence of informal information channels about job vacancies and firm characteristics can account for this, although it is possible that firm reputation effects in the labor market also acted to channel black and female applicants to firms already employing relatively large proportions of these workers as managers.

The female makeup of the existing managerial work force also had significant effects on hiring, while the black male makeup had no significant effects. It appears that a large percentage of women in existing managerial positions is indicative of assertive affirmative action policies for the firms in our sample. In the case of blacks, however, the results show that firms with relatively large black male labor forces were less likely to hire black males for management jobs. This could indicate the presence of quotas or targets that constrain black male managerial hires. In the case of women, both PCTFEM and PCTBM are positive and statistically significant in the hiring equation. The results obtained for the variables PCTFEM, and PCTBM suggest that the positive effects of affirmative action compliance on hires were highly skewed within the establishments in our sample and are consistent with a general pattern of occupational crowding for women and blacks.

In addition to the composition of the managerial work force, recruiting practices had a significant impact on the probability of black male and female applications. The dummy variables for reliance on internal recruitment (INTREC) and formal recruitment (FORREC) procedures are both positive and, with the exception of FORREC for black males, statistically significant.[20] In comparison with the excluded category—informal recruitment through references from current employees—the use of more formal recruitment practices enhanced the chances of attracting minority applicants. This result is consistent with the findings of Holzer.[21]

Interestingly, the minimum education (MINED) required for a managerial job had a significant negative effect on female applications but a significant positive effect on black male applications. This might suggest that mainly well-educated black males were likely to apply for managerial jobs in this sample of firms. On the other hand, the starting income (INCOME) for management jobs had a negative effect on application probabilities for *both* women and black men, and black men were less likely to be hired at firms where managerial jobs required higher education levels or paid higher starting salaries. MINED had a significantly negative effect on the hiring rate of black men and essentially no effect for women. This may reflect greater uncertainty about the quality of education for blacks than for white women and hence a greater use of education as a screening device against black men.

Among firm characteristics, neither unionized firms (UNION) nor city location (CITY) were significant at conventional levels of significance. However, each of these variables had the expected sign. For example, the coefficient for CITY in the applications queue was negative for females and positive for black males. Moreover, the coefficients on UNION were always positive. Large firms and growing firms were more likely to attract women and black men while single unit firms (SINGLE) were significantly less likely to have black male or female applicants. Leonard also found that single unit firms were less likely to have increased minority employment over his study period.[22] Perhaps these firms were less likely to be targeted for compliance reviews or perhaps larger, multi-unit firms are more likely to have formalized personnel policies that limit the exercise of biased hiring decisions. Since SINGLE also had a significant negative affect on the hiring rates for both women and black men, these results suggest an important role for single unit firms in understanding how minority and female employment opportunities are determined.

The final variables of interest are the predicted log odds ratios of black male and female applications derived from the application queue model. As discussed previously, these variables [log (PBMA/PWMA) and log (PFA/PWMA)] are included in the hiring equation to measure the supply of black males and women relative to white males, and to allow us to test whether applications and hires are statistically independent. The likelihood of a black male (woman) being hired for a managerial job was positively related to the likelihood of a black male (woman) being in the applicant pool. Moreover, the significantly negative coefficient on log (PFA/PWMA) for black males suggests some degree of substitution in hiring between black males and women.

To determine whether applications and hires are statistically independent, we used three Wald statistics normalized by the corrected asymptotic covariance matrix found in Appendix A. The first test ascertains whether black male applications and hires are independent by restricting Θ_1 in the manner already described, but with Θ_2 left unrestricted. Similarly, the second test decides whether female applications and hires are independent by restricting Θ_2 but leaving Θ_1 unrestricted. Finally, the third test jointly restricts Θ_1 and Θ_2. All of these tests are asymptotically chi-square, with the first two statistics having 14 degrees of freedom and the latter having 28 degrees of freedom. As the calculated values of the statistics are respectively 38.74, 213.01 and 275.71, we then easily reject the null hypothesis of independence at conventional levels of significance. These statistical tests then indicate that, in general, employers perceived differences in the black male and female applicants relative to the white male applicants. The findings reported in this section are especially significant in the context of the recent report by the Department of Labor.[23] Based on a detailed examination of nine major firms, the report indicates that both "minorities" and women were excluded from the highest levels of management, with minorities restricted to lower management levels than women. In addition, it was found that firms did not have monitoring mechanisms to guarantee equal access to senior management positions and that hiring for upper levels was facilitated via reliance on word-of-mouth communication and employee referral networking. The report suggested a shift in focus in compliance monitoring from examining the highest levels of the corporate structure to analysis of pipelines to the top because glass ceilings appear to exist at lower levels in the organizational hierarchy than previously recognized.

Our findings suggest that the foundations for the Department of Labor conclusions can be identified in the early history of compliance efforts. The compliance response of firms in our sample suggests a strategy of conjoining existing patterns of occupational segregation with limited hiring into the managerial ranks.

CONCLUSION

This article has exploited a unique data set to model the effect of firm characteristics on the probabilities that an establishment would receive applications from minority and/or female workers, and then would hire such workers for managerial positions. In comparison with other recent studies of changes in the demographic makeup of firm or industry employment, our micro level econometric analysis of the race and sex composition of the managerial applicant and hiring pools in a sample of Detroit area firms in 1972 permits a more direct look at the effect of affirmative action requirements on the recruitment and selection process. There are four main conclusions from our empirical analysis:

1. Firms subject to affirmative action requirements were more likely to hire black males for managerial jobs even though these firms were not more likely to attract black male applicants. Thus it appears that the affirmative action program indeed had the effect of changing employer hiring patterns with respect to black workers in the early 1970s, as the work of Smith and Welch and Donohue and Heckman suggests.[24]

2. With respect to women, affirmative action requirements had a highly significant positive correlation with the female application probability for managerial jobs and an insignificant (negative) effect on hiring chances for those jobs. Our interpretation of this finding is that as women began entering career labor markets in large numbers in the early 1970s they were disproportionately attracted to firms following personnel practices influenced by affirmative action even before sex discrimination became a major policy target of that program.

3. Women and black men were far more likely to apply for jobs at firms already employing relatively large proportions of female and black workers in managerial jobs. Part of this effect can be traced to the importance of informal channels of information regarding job openings and firm characteristics operating through the existing workforce that still seems to be a dominant information source in labor markets. Holzer's finding that minority access to jobs is improved by the use of formal search methods is confirmed by our analysis.[25] Firms relying on newspaper ads or employment agencies or on formal procedures for promotion from within received more female and black male applications for managerial jobs than did firms relying on employee references.

4. Perhaps our most interesting result is that firms where managers were more likely to deal directly with customers were also firms at which women and blacks were less likely to be hired.

This is consistent with Becker's hypothesis that customer tastes for discrimination (or employer perceptions of these tastes) could influence the hiring patterns of an unprejudiced employer.[26] As far as we can discern, this represents the first empirical test of this well-known hypothesis.

One of the implications of this study is the need for additional case studies of the effect of anti-discrimination policy on individual markets and/or industries. In assessing the validity of studies examining the effects of OFCCP enforcement, Heckman has observed that general estimates of gains based on comparisons between federal contractors and noncontractors at a given point in time may be biased because both types of firms hire in the same market and noncontractors may maintain diverse workforces in anticipation of bidding for contracts.[27] Similar methodological problems arise in studies that attempt to gauge the impacts of EEOC compliance activity and the general effects of antidiscrimination legislation. The findings of studies using national data can be cross-checked against market-specific studies with detailed information about individual applications, hires, and promotions. Such information, in combination with firm-specific data detailing workforce composition, market characteristics and other relevant information can yield new insights regarding the response of both potential employees and employers to the incentive structure generated by antidiscrimination instruments. In particular, such studies can shed useful insights regarding the dimensions and permeability of glass ceilings and their relationship to patterns of occupational segregation by race and gender. The present study can serve as a partial foundation for such investigations.

NOTES

The authors thank Hugh Wills, Stan Masters, and participants in seminars at the Australian National University, Melbourne University and the Far East Meetings of the Econometric Society for constructive suggestions, and Quing Hui Zhao and Chia-Ying Ma for excellent research assistance.
    1. Morley Gunderson, "Male-Female Wage Differentials and Policy Responses," *Journal of Economic Literature* 27(1) (March 1989): 46-72.
    2. James P. Smith and Finis Welch, "Black Economic Progress after Myrdal," *Journal of Economic Literature* 27(2) (June 1989): 519–564; John Donohue and James Heckman, "Continuous Versus Episodic Change: The Impact of Affirmative Action and Civil Rights Policy on the Economic Status of Blacks," unpublished manuscript, (November 1989); James P. Smith and Finis Welch, "Affirmative Action and Labor Markets," *Journal of Labor Economics* 2(2) (April 1984): 269–301.
    3. U.S. Department of Labor, *A Report on the Glass Ceiling Initiative* (Washing-

ton: USGPO, 1991).

4. Richard B. Freeman, "Black Economic Progress After 1964: Who Has Gained and Why?" in *Studies in Labor Markets,* edited by Sherwin Rosen (Chicago: University of Chicago Press, 1981), pp. 247–294.

5. James Heckman and Brook Payner, "Determining the Impact of Federal Antidiscrimination Policy on the Economic Status of Blacks: A Study of South Carolina," *American Economic Review* 79(1) (March 1989): 138–177.

6. Jonathan S. Leonard, "The Impact of Affirmative Action on Employment," *Journal of Labor Economics* 2(4) (October 1984): 439–463; Jonathan S. Leonard, "The Effect of Unions on the Employment of Blacks, Hispanics and Women," *Industrial and Labor Relations Review* 39(1) (October 1985): 115–132; Smith and Welch (1984), op. cit.

7. Harry J. Holzer, "Hiring Procedures in the Firm: Their Economic Determinants and Outcomes," in *Human Resources and the Performance of the Firm,* edited by Morris M. Kleiner et al. (Madison, WI: Industrial Relations Research Association Services, 1987), pp. 243–274.

8. James J. Heckman, "Shadow Prices, Market Wages, and Labor Supply," *Econometrica* 42(4) (July 1974): 679–694.

9. Robert M. Groves, *Intra-Employer Status Mobility: The Role of the Firm in Wage and Occupational Achievement* (Ph.D. Diss., University of Michigan, 1975).

10. Since we have multiple observations for each firm, it is also possible to estimate β_1 and β_2 by a linear probability model or by minimum chi-square methods (see G.S. Maddala, *Limited Dependent and Qualitative Variables in Econometrics* (New York: Cambridge University Press, 1983), pp. 28–32. These estimation methods essentially entail using the percent black (or female) as the dependent variable. We prefer the maximum likelihood (ML) estimator, however, since it is asymptotically efficient, and because the performances of the other estimators are calibrated relative to ML estimation. For example, it can be shown that the minimum logit chi-square estimator and the (optimal) ML estimator are symptotically equivalent.

11. Holzer, op. cit.

12. Harry J. Holzer, "Informal Job Search and Black Youth Unemployment," *American Economic Review* 77(3) (June 1987): 446–452.

13. The multinomial logit models for both applications and hires are intended as pure probability models for unordered categories. However, it is also possible to view the hiring decision by the employer as a probabilistic choice. The levels of indirect utility for the employer can be written as follows: $U_{bm} = \Theta_1 Z + e_1$, $U_f = \Theta_2 Z + e_2$, and $U_{wm} = \Theta_3 Z + e_3$, where U_{bm}, U_f, and U_{wm} are the indirect utilities from hiring a black male, female and white male, respectively. Define the random variable Y such that Y=1 if U_{bm} is greater than U_f and U_{wm}, Y=2 if U_f is greater than U_{bm} and U_{wm}, and Y=3 if U_{wm} is the largest. Thus, Y=1 (say) indicates that the employer will hire a black male. If the disturbances e_i are independently and identically distributed with the type I extreme-value distribution, then the multinomial logit model is again applicable; see Madadala, op.cit. Note that the parameter vector Θ_3 is not identified and must be normalized to zero for estimation purposes.

14. From our estimated models, it is also possible to calculate P (Hire / Black Male Applicant) / P (Hire / White Male Applicant) = [P (Black Male Applicant | Hire) / P (White Male Applicant / Hire)] x [P (White Male Applicant) / P (Black Male Applicant)]. For the purpose of predicting hiring patterns for individual firms, the above odds ratio would be of interest. The calculations for females are completely analogous.

15. Takeshi Ameniya, "The Estimation of a Simultaneous Equation Tobit Model," *International Economic Review* 20(1) (February 1979): 169–181 and Adrian R. Pagan, "Two Stage and Related Estimators and Their Applications," *The Review of Economic Studies* 53 (August 1986): 517–538.

16. Gary Becker, *The Economics of Discrimination,* 2nd ed. (Chicago: University of Chicago Press, 1971).

17. Orley Ashenfelter and James J. Heckman, "Measuring the Effect of an Anti-Discrimination Program," in *Evaluating the Labor Market Effects of Social Programs* edited by Orley Ashenfelter and James Blum (Princeton: Industrial Relations Section, 1976), pp. 46–84; George Burman, *The Economics of Discrimination: The Impact of Public Policy* (Ph.D. Thesis, Graduate School of Business, University of Chicago, 1973); and James J. Heckman and Kenneth I. Wolpin, "Does the Contract Compliance Program Work? An Analysis of Chicago Data," *Industrial and Labor Relations Review* 29(4) (July 1976): 544–564.

18. Jonathan S. Leonard, "The Effect of Unions on the Employment of Blacks, Hispanics and Women," *Industrial And Labor Relations Review* 39(1) (October 1985): 115–132.

19. Becker, op. cit.

20. The hiring equation excludes the recruitment variables since it is unlikely that these will directly influence the selection process.

21. Holzer, "Informal Job Search and Black Youth Employment," op. cit. and Holzer, "Hiring Procedures in the Firm: Their Economic Determinants and Outcomes," op. cit.

22. Jonathan S. Leonard, "The Impact of Affirmative Action on Employment," op. cit. and Jonathan S. Leonard, "Employment and Occupational Advance Under Affirmative Action," *Review of Economics and Statistics* 66(3) (August 1984): 377–385.

23. U.S. Department of Labor, op. cit.

24. Smith and Welch, op. cit. and Donohue and Heckman, op. cit.

25. Holzer, "Informal Job Search and Black Youth Unemployment," op. cit.

26. Becker, op. cit.

27. James Heckman, "The Impact of Government on the Economic Status of Black Americans," in *The Question of Discrimination: Racial Inequality in the U.S. Labor Market* edited by Steven Shulman and William Darity (Middletown, CT: Wesleyan University Press, 1989), pp. 50–80.

APPENDIX A

Two-Stage Covariance Matrix for the Hiring Equation

There are two generated regressors in the hiring equation: log (PFA/PWMA) and log (PBMA/PWMA). The presence of these (consistently estimated) stochastic regressors necessitates a modification of the usual maximum-likelihood covariance matrix. To derive the correct variances, let X represent the regressors from the applications model, and let Z represent the variables from the hiring model. Then:

$$\log (\text{PFA/PWMA}) = \log (\exp(\hat{\beta}_1 X)) = \hat{\beta}_1 X, \text{ and}$$

$$(1) \quad \log (\text{PBMA/PWMA}) = \log (\exp(\hat{\beta}_2 X)) = \hat{\beta}_2 X,$$

where $\hat{\beta}_1$ and $\hat{\beta}_2$ are the estimated coefficients for females and black males, respectively, in the applications model. If β_1 and β_2 were known with certainty, then the modification presented below would be unnecessary.

Following Amemiya (1979) and Pagan (1986), it can be shown that:

$$(2) \quad (\hat{\Theta} - \Theta) \underset{=}{A} - \left(E \frac{\partial^2 \log L_H}{\partial \Theta \partial \Theta'} \right)^{-1} \left[\frac{\partial \log L_H}{\partial \Theta} + E \frac{\partial^2 \log L_H}{\partial \Theta \partial \beta'} (\hat{\beta} - \beta) \right]$$

where $\beta \equiv \begin{bmatrix} \beta_1 \\ \beta_2 \end{bmatrix}$, $\Theta \equiv \begin{bmatrix} \Theta_1 \\ \Theta_2 \end{bmatrix}$, $\log L_H$ is the log of the likelihood for the hiring model, and $\hat{\Theta}$ is the maximum likelihood estimator of Θ.

Since $\text{Var}\left(\frac{\partial \log L_H}{\partial \Theta} \right) = -E \frac{\partial^2 \log L_H}{\partial \Theta \partial \beta'}$, then

$$\text{Var}(\hat{\Theta}) \underset{=}{A} \left[E \frac{\partial^2 \log L_H}{\partial \Theta \partial \Theta'} \right]^{-1}$$

$$(3) \quad \cdot \left\{ -E \frac{\partial^2 \log L_H}{\partial \Theta \partial \Theta'} + E \frac{\partial^2 \log L_H}{\partial \Theta \partial \beta'} \left(-E \frac{\partial^2 \log L_A}{\partial \beta \partial \beta'} \right)^{-1} E \frac{\partial^2 \log L_H}{\partial \beta \partial \Theta'} + \begin{matrix} \text{Covariance} \\ \text{Terms} \end{matrix} \right\}$$

$$\cdot \left[E \frac{\partial^2 \log L_H}{\partial \Theta \partial \Theta'} \right]^{-1}$$

where $\log L_A$ is the log-likelihood for the applications model.

The above expression is simplified by noting that the covariance terms are zero. These terms take the form,

$$E\frac{\partial^2 \log L_H}{\partial\Theta\partial\beta'} E\left\{\left(\hat{\beta}-\beta\right)\frac{\partial \log L_H}{\partial\Theta'}\right\}.$$

However, from standard asymptotic theory,

$$\left(\hat{\beta}-\beta\right)\underset{\underline{\underline{A}}}{} - \frac{\partial^2 \log L_A}{\partial\beta\partial\beta'}\frac{\partial \log L_A}{\partial\beta}$$

and thus the covariance terms are asymptotically equivalent to

$$E\frac{\partial^2 \log L_H}{\partial\Theta\partial\beta'}\left(-\frac{\partial^2 \log L_A}{\partial\beta\partial\beta'}\right)E\left[\frac{\partial \log L_A}{\partial\beta}\frac{\partial \log L_H}{\partial\Theta'}\right].$$

[Note that $-E\dfrac{\partial^2 \log L_A}{\partial\beta\partial\beta'} = -\dfrac{\partial^2 \log L_A}{\partial\beta\partial\beta'}$ for the multinomial logit model.]

Furthermore, $E\left[\dfrac{\partial \log L_A}{\partial\beta}\dfrac{\partial \log L_H}{\partial\Theta'}\right] = 0$ since the observations in the applications queue are statistically independent from the hires. For example, the last twenty hires for a given firm do not necessarily overlap with the last twenty applicants.

$V(\hat{\Theta})$ is relatively straightforward to calculate. Define the set of dummy variables:

y_{ij}^A = 1 if the ith applicant falls in the jth category

y_{ij}^A = 0 otherwise.

y_{ij}^H = 1 if the ith hire falls in the jth category

y_{ij}^H = 0 otherwise.

Since there are three categories and n observations, then,

$$\log L_A = \sum_{i=1}^{n}\sum_{j=1}^{3} y_{ij}^A \log P_{ij}^A$$

and $\log L_H = \sum_{i=1}^{n} \sum_{j=1}^{3} y_{ij}^{H} \log P_{ij}^{H}$

where $P_{ij}^{A} = \dfrac{\exp(\beta_j X_i)}{1 + \sum_{k=1}^{2} \exp(\beta_k X_i)}$ $j = 1, 2$

(4)   and $P_{i3}^{A} = \dfrac{1}{1 + \sum_{k=1}^{2} \exp(\beta_k X_i)}$.

P_{ij}^{H} $(j = 1, 2)$ and P_{i3}^{H} are defined similarly.

It immediately follows that:

(5) $-E \dfrac{\partial^2 \log L_A}{\partial \beta_k \partial \beta'_k} = \sum_{i=1}^{n} P_{ik}^{A}(1 - P_{ik}^{A}) X_i X'_i$ and

(6) $-E \dfrac{\partial^2 \log L_A}{\partial \beta_k \partial \beta'_h} = \sum_{i=1}^{n} P_{ik}^{A} P_{ih}^{A} X_i X'_i$

while the formulas for $-E \dfrac{\partial^2 \log L_H}{\partial \Theta \partial \Theta'}$ are analogous. Moreover, since

$\dfrac{\partial \log L_H}{\partial \Theta_k} = \sum_{i=1}^{n} \left(y_{ik}^{H} - P_{ik}^{H} \right) Z_i$, then:

(7) $E \dfrac{\partial^2 \log L_H}{\partial \Theta_k \partial \beta'_j} = \sum_{i=1}^{n} -\left[P_{ik}^{H} \Theta_{kj} - P_{ik}^{H} P_{i3}^{H} \sum_{h=1}^{2} \exp(\Theta_h Z_i) \Theta_{hj} \right] Z_{ij} X'_i$

where $\Theta.j$ is the coefficient for log (PFA/PWMA) when j=1, and is the coefficient for log (PBMA/PWMA) when j=2. Likewise, Z_{i1} = log (PFA/PWMA) and Z_{i2} = log (PBMA/PWMA).

Since the covariance terms (above) are zero, the corrected standard errors are always larger than those based solely on the information matrix.

II

BLACK-WHITE WAGE DIFFERENTIALS

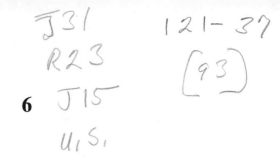

A REGIONAL ANALYSIS OF BLACK MALE-WHITE MALE WAGE DIFFERENCES

Jeremiah Cotton

This research indicates that labor market outcomes for black males in terms of hourly wages differed markedly from region to region over the 1976 to 1984 period. And although black males faced a substantial amount of discriminatory treatment in all regions, the amounts varied significantly by region.

Most empirical studies of differences in black-white labor market performance undertaken in the past have been based on models estimated from national samples. In these studies the effects of the industrially diverse regional and local labor markets on racial earnings and employment differences were accounted for by the use of dummy variables. However, to the degree that the structure of the earnings or employment determination process differs from region to region, such models are misspecified and cloud the issue of racial differences in labor market outcomes and treatment.

A close inspection of Table 1 reveals some of the regional variations in labor market outcomes. The table shows black and white male labor force participation rates, unemployment rates, and employment/population ratios in the recession year of 1982 and the more prosperous 1989.[1] In both years the labor force participation rates and employment/population ratios for black men in the West and South regions were above the national average, while those in the Midwest and Northeast were below the average. The black male unemployment rates in the West, South and Northeast were below the national average and those in the Midwest were above the average.

And while there were also interregional variations in the white male

TABLE 1
Labor Market Outcomes by Region, 1982 and 1989

1982

	LABOR FORCE PARTICIPATION RATES		UNEMPLOYMENT RATES		EMPLOYMENT/ POPULATION RATIOS	
	Black Males	White Males	Black Males	White Males	Black Males	White Males
United States	70.1	77.4	20.1	8.8	56.0	70.6
Northeast	69.0	75.6	19.0	8.5	55.9	69.2
Midwest	69.6	78.5	29.3	10.3	49.3	70.4
South	70.3	76.9	17.6	7.1	57.9	71.4
West	71.8	78.8	17.8	9.6	59.0	71.2

1989

	LABOR FORCE PARTICIPATION RATES		UNEMPLOYMENT RATES		EMPLOYMENT/ POPULATION RATIOS	
	Black Males	White Males	Black Males	White Males	Black Males	White Males
United States	71.0	77.1	11.5	4.5	62.8	73.7
Northeast	70.1	76.1	11.2	4.1	62.3	73.0
Midwest	67.8	78.5	16.4	4.5	56.7	75.0
South	71.8	76.1	10.0	4.4	64.6	72.8
West	74.6	78.0	11.2	4.9	66.2	74.2

Sources: U.S. Dept. of Labor, Bureau of Statistics, *Geographic Profile of Employment and Unemployment,* 1982 and 1989, Bulletins 2170 and 2361.

outcomes, in both years the variation was greater for blacks than for whites. This was mainly due to the disparity in the black and white situations in the Midwest where in 1982 the black unemployment rate was over 9 percentage points higher than the black national average and the employment/population ratio was nearly 7 points lower. By contrast the white Midwest unemployment rate was only 1.5 percentage points greater than the white average and the employment/population ratios were a mere 0.2 points lower. Thus it would appear that the devastating recession that gripped the country in the early 1980s and that was mainly centered in the Midwest had a much more deleterious effect on blacks than it did on whites.[2]

And although things in the Midwest had improved by 1989, blacks still fared worse there than their counterparts in the other regions. Whites in the Midwest in 1989, however, had higher labor force participation rates and employment/population ratios than they did in any of the other regions and unemployment rates that were only slightly higher than those in two of the three regions and lower than those in the third.

Many of the empirical studies on black-white labor market performance found prima facie evidence of labor market discrimination against blacks.[3] In the context of the present argument it is expected that there will be regional variations in such discrimination as well. And indeed, two researchers in the mid-1970s found just that. Nicholas Kiefer and Sharon Smith constructed three "regions" made up of the nine Northeastern states they properly termed the "Northeast" region, five states in the South they called the "Border" region (i.e., Delaware, District of Columbia, Maryland, Virginia and West Virginia), and the other twelve Southern states they labeled the "Deep South" region.[4]

Not surprisingly they reported finding a greater amount of labor market discrimination against blacks in the "Deep South" than in the other two regions, and a greater amount in the "Border" than in the "Northeast" region.

The Kiefer-Smith study, however, was limited in three important respects. First, of course they excluded the important labor markets in the Midwest and West regions from their analysis, almost half the country; second, they investigated labor market conditions in only one year, 1973, and therefore did not attempt to account for any effects the business cycle might have had on racial differences in labor market outcomes by region; and third, they used a version of the method for making quantitative estimates of discrimination, the Oaxaca-Blinder decomposition, that has been shown to be logically flawed.[5] It is to Kiefer and Smith's credit, however, that unlike many who have used the Oaxaca-Blinder method they appear to have recognized the problems inherent in its use.[6]

The trouble arises with the choice of weights in the formulas that are used to decompose racial wage differences into an "explained" component that is assumed to be due to differences in productivity characteristics between the races and an "unexplained" component that is usually taken as an upper bound estimate of wage or labor market discrimination.

Oaxaca in particular suggested two alternative formulas:

(1) $\ln \overline{W}^W - \ln \overline{W}^B = \sum B^W (\overline{X}^W - \overline{X}^B) + \sum \overline{X}^B (B^W - B^B)$

(2) $\ln \overline{W}^W - \ln \overline{W}^B = \sum B^B (\overline{X}^W - \overline{X}^B) + \sum \overline{X}^W (B^W - B^B)$

In both (1) and (2) the first terms on the right-hand sides of the equations are measures of differences in the productivity characteristics, X_i, and the second terms are measures of differences in labor market treatment as represented by differences in the market-derived regression coefficients, B_i.

In (1) the first term is weighted by the white regression coefficients, implying that in the absence of discrimination the market would treat both blacks and whites as whites are currently treated. In (2) the first term is weighted by the black coefficients, implying that if there were no discrimination both whites and blacks would be treated the same as blacks are now treated by the market. The flaws in both readings are readily apparent, for in the absence of discrimination neither whites nor blacks would be treated as they are currently treated in the presence of discrimination. Rather, in the absence of discrimination we would expect whites to receive *less* favorable treatment than they now enjoy and blacks to receive *more* favorable treatment than they now do. Hence, neither of the sets of weights in (1) and (2) are adequate for estimating the true value of productivity differences and discrimination.[7]

The research embodied in this study attempted to repair the deficiencies in previous research by pooling a series of nine Current Population Surveys from 1976 to 1984, a period that spanned the 1981–82 recession and recovery. Separate samples of black and white males, sixteen years and over who were employed full-time, were drawn from each of the four regions identified by the Census (see footnote 3): "Northeast," "Midwest," "South," and "West." The organizing hypothesis that the black and white wage-determining processes differ significantly by region was tested and supported at the 5 percent level of significance by a series of Chow-Fisher F-tests.[8]

Wage equations were then constructed, estimated and decomposed using a decomposition formula that not only permits estimates to be made of the "true" value of black-white productivity differences, but also of the amount of pecuniary benefits discrimination confers on whites and the amount of pecuniary costs blacks incur. This formulation is expressed as:

$$(3) \quad \ln \overline{W}^W - \ln \overline{W}^B = \sum B^*(\overline{X}^W - \overline{X}^B) + \sum \overline{X}^W(B^W - B^*)$$
$$+ \sum \overline{X}^B(B^* - B^B)$$

where the first term on the right-hand side of (3) is the difference between black and white productivity characteristics that would occur in the absence of discrimination, and the second and third terms are the differences in the way the market currently treats whites and blacks, respectively, and the way they would be treated in the absence of discrimination.

The first term of (3) is assumed to be a measure of the true value of racial productivity differences; the second term when positive is a measure of the favored treatment whites receive, or "benefits" conferred on them by discrimination; and the third term when positive is a measure of the unfavorable treatment blacks receive in the labor market, or the "costs" of being black.[9] The second and third components are the "residual" or "unexplained" portion of the wage differential. They are considered by many as constituting an upper bound estimate of wage discrimination since the inclusion in the first component of any relevant, productivity-enhancing characteristic previously omitted from the regression models (e.g., school quality) would necessarily reduce the residual and with it the estimate of discrimination. The residual, however, might also be thought of as a *lower* bound estimate of discrimination since many of the characteristics contained in the first component might very well themselves be the product of discrimination (racial discrimination is widely known to be a major determinant of the different levels of educational quantity and quality obtained by the races).

The principal operational weakness of equation (3) is the fact that the B* vector cannot be observed and must therefore be estimated. The estimator of B* used here is defined as: $B_i^* = f_{bi} B_i^B + f_{wi} B_i^W$, where the f_{bi} and f_{wi} are the average proportions of black and white workers, respectively, in the employed civilian male labor force in the ith region, and B_i^B and B_i^W are the vectors of black and white regression coefficients.[10]

EMPIRICAL RESULTS

The mean values and regression coefficients of the explanatory variables used in the regional wage equations are shown in Tables 2 and 3, respectively. According to the neoclassical theories of human capital investment and marginal productivity, education and on-the-job training, or work experience, are the principal determinants of productivity and hence wages. Because of data limitations they are imperfectly cast here as years of school completed and years of post-school activity.

White males in the Northeast had one full year more schooling than their black counterparts; however, somewhat surprisingly, the situation was reversed in the West where blacks had slightly more than one year more schooling than whites. The smallest white-black schooling gap occurred in the Midwest where whites exceeded blacks by about two-thirds of a year.

TABLE 2
Mean Values of Model Variables

	NORTHEAST		MIDWEST		SOUTH		WEST	
	Black Males	White Males	Black Males	White Males	Black Males	White Males	Black Males	White Males
Education	12.54	13.54	13.10	13.76	12.28	13.17	14.21	13.16
Work Experience	20.83	19.84	20.41	19.32	20.59	19.25	18.44	18.13
Work Experience^2	606.18	563.36	585.72	540.62	625.03	543.40	476.09	484.80
Central City	.77	.34	.68	.22	.41	.28	.46	.23
In SMSA	.18	.39	.22	.38	.19	.32	.31	.32
Married with Spouse	.69	.77	.69	.79	.65	.81	.60	.75
Once Married	.13	.07	.16	.07	.15	.07	.22	.09
Private Sector Employment	.78	.82	.78	.83	.72	.81	.64	.80
INDUSTRY Construction	.03	.05	.01	.06	.07	.10	.04	.07
Mfg. Durables	.15	.22	.35	.28	.16	.15	.12	.17
Mfg. Nondurables	.10	.13	.12	.12	.14	.12	.06	.08
Transportation Public Utilities	.12	.09	.12	.10	.12	.09	.12	.11

TABLE 2 (cont'd)

Wholesale & Retail Trade	.14	.15	.09	.16	.13	.19	.10	.17
F.I.R.E.	.07	.07	.04	₸04	.03	.04	.06	.03
Public Administration	.09	.07	.10	.06	.11	.09	.16	.09
Business & Repair Services	.07	.04	.03	.03	.03	.03	.04	.05
Personal Services	.04	.02	.001	.01	.02	.02	.01	.02
Entertainment & Recreation Service	.01	.01	.001	.001	.01	.01	.10	.01
Professional & Related Services	.18	.14	.13	.12	.14	.11	.16	.12
TRENDS 1977	.09	.11	.11	.11	.13	.13	.01	.01
1978	.12	.11	.15	.11	.12	.13	.07	.02
1979	.11	.11	.13	.11	.13	.15	.01	.03
1980	.13	.13	.13	.13	.13	.10	.17	.20
1981	.13	.12	.12	.13	.12	.09	.18	.19
1982	.12	.11	.08	.12	.14	.15	.12	.17
1983	.08	.10	.07	.09	.11	.14	.16	.16
1984	.12	.10	.11	.11	.03	.01	.20	.15

TABLE 3
Regression Coefficients of Model Variables
(Standard errors in parentheses)

	Northeast		Midwest		South		West	
	Black Males	White Males	Black Males	White Males	Black Males	White Males	Black Males	White Males
Education	.0513*	.0690*	.0438*	.0577*	.0542*	.0740*	.0433*	.0672*
	(.0071)	(.0031)	(.0100)	(.0031)	(.0049)	(.0025)	(.0154)	(.0026)
Work Experience	.0158*	.0248*	.0153**	.03*	.0273*	.0306*	−.0063	.0299*
	(.0058)	(.0025)	(.0068)	(.0022)	(.0033)	(.0020)	(.0090)	(.0024)
Work Experience^2	−.0002**	−.0004*	−.0003**	−.0005*	−.0004*	−.0005*	.0002	−.0004*
	(.0001)	(.0001)	(.0001)	(.0001)	(.0001)	(.0001)	(.0002)	(.0001)
Central City	−.0362	.0259	.0024	.0994*	.1867*	.0729*	−.0061	.0477**
	(.0900)	(.0219)	(.0767)	(.0208)	(.0285)	(.0188)	(.0814)	(.0218)
In SMSA	.0666	.1204*	.098	.1750*	.223*	.1420*	.0241	.0814*
	(.0977)	(.0206)	(.0858)	(.0181)	(.0400)	(.0179)	(.086)	(.0198)
Married with Spouse	.0631	.2161*	.2001**	.2487*	.1302*	.1972*	.3251*	.1843*
	(.0591)	(.0252)	(.0706)	(.0253)	(.0352)	(.0250)	(.0908)	(.0255)
Once Married	.0053	.0824**	.1590*	.0878*	.0553	.1421*	.1980**	.0849*
	(.0749)	(.0391)	(.0867)	(.0376)	(.0445)	(.0366)	(.1005)	(.0359)
Private Sector Employment	−.0068	.0111	−.2585*	.0644**	.0519	.0349	−.0959	.0718*
	(.0623)	(.0307)	(.0869)	(.0310)	(.0414)	(.0289)	(.0888)	(.031)
INDUSTRY Construction	.3978*	.2772*	.0610	.4189*	.1611**	.1852*	.5366**	.2606*
	(.1258)	(.0799)	(.2124)	(.0574)	(.0749)	(.0409)	(.2525)	(.0411)
Mfg. Durables	.0694	.2701*	.00001	.4075*	.2315*	.0785*	.1186	.1409*
	(.0722)	(.0723)	(.0001)	(.0509)	(.0656)	(.0381)	(.223)	(.0348)
Mfg. Nondurables	.0482	.2064*	−.0981	.3778*	.2910*	.1526*	.1496	.1046*
	(.803)	(.0739)	(.0740)	(.0532)	(.0668)	(.0395)	(.236)	(.0406)
Transportation Pub. Util.	.2005*	.3646*	−.0321	.4393*	.2856*	.2055*	.1066	.2143*
	(.0728)	(.0753)	(.0765)	(.0544)	(.0697)	(.0412)	(.2192)	(.0375)
Wholesale & Retail Trade	−.0418	.1252*	−.3385*	.2076*	.031	−.056	.0248	−.0067
	(.0752)	(.0733)	(.0824)	(.0518)	(.0679)	(.0375)	(.2241)	(.0341)
F.I.R.E.	−.0073	.2401*	−.1278	.3725*	.0341	.0076	−.0279	.0673
	(.0858)	(.0770)	(.1183)	(.0623)	(.0888)	(.0497)	(.2399)	(.0536)
Public Administration	.0943	.2853*	−.2868*	.3328*	.31**	.15*	.1451	.2338*
	(.0837)	(.0817)	(.1174)	(.0641)	(.0809)	(.0505)	(.2324)	(.0490)
Business & Repair Service	.0448	.0813	−.054	.2173*	−.0050	−.0536	−.2903	.0593
	(.0918)	(.0825)	(.1351)	(.0665)	(.0932)	(.0526)	(.2499)	(.0469)
Personal Services	−.1611	.0768	−.4281	.0602	−.0828	−.2712*	−.1071	−.2323*
	(.1157)	(.0971)	(.3562)	(.0919)	(.0985)	(.0686)	(.3020)	(.0605)

TABLE 3 (continued)

	Northeast		Midwest		South		West	
	Black Males	White Males	Black Males	White Males	Black Males	White Males	Black Males	White Males
Entertainment & Rec. Service	−.1448	.2659**	−.4675	.1278	−.2149	−.1735**	−.0126	.0067
	(.2033)	(.1252)	(.5073)	(.1197)	(.1575)	(.1001)	(.2254)	(.0903)
Professional & Related Services	.00001	.0862	−.6163*	.1962*	.0651	−.1234*	.0183	−.024
	(.0001)	(.0749)	(.0918)	(.0566)	(.0744)	(.0438)	(.2201)	(.0411)
Trends 1977	−.0112	.0687**	.0201	.0323	.0396	.0814*	.3813	−.1106*
	(.0902)	(.0362)	(.0927)	(.0340)	(.0529)	(.0313)	(.3598)	(.0919)
1978	.0458	.1246*	−.0327	.1386*	.0811	.1302*	.2384	.1435**
	(.0865)	(.036)	(.0882)	(.0339)	(.0536)	(.0311)	(.1580)	(.0700)
1979	.1160	.1998*	.1324	.1938*	.172*	.2192*	.0768	.1725*
	(.0887)	(.0356)	(.0910)	(.0337)	(.0536)	(.0303)	(.2647)	(.0560)
1980	.0855	.3029*	.1398	.3088*	.2608*	.3046*	.3549*	.275*
	(.0851)	(.0348)	(.0912)	(.0330)	(.0532)	(.0336)	(.1294)	(.0333)
1981	.1530**	.3868*	.2924*	.3728*	.4089*	.3979*	.5087*	.3736*
	(.084)	(.0351)	(.0913)	(.0329)	(.0539)	(.0343)	(.1311)	(.0337)
1982	.3640*	.4569*	.4988*	.4402*	.4228*	.4453*	.5130*	.4808*
	(.0858)	(.0358)	(.1027)	(.0336)	(.0530)	(.0302)	(.1366)	(.0341)
1983	.5396*	.5109*	.3494*	.4832*	.4935*	.5059*	.6819*	.4998*
	(.0954)	(.0364)	(.1081)	(.0336)	(.0553)	(.0307)	(.1318)	(.0345)
1984	.5810*	.4742*	.4550*	.5276*	.5733*	.7064*	.6625*	.505
	(.0861)	(.0365)	(.0949)	(.0344)	(.0784)	(.0688)	(.1284)	(.034
Constant	.661*	−.0052	1.1759*	−.0517	.0111	−.0449	.6401**	.117
	(.1728)	(.0949)	(.2098)	(.0754)	(.1049)	(.0613)	(.3171)	(.064
R^2	.29	.272	.265	.313	.356	.355	.274	.276
Standard Error	.47	.528	.489	.499	.458	.497	.461	.548
Ln Hourly Wage	1.77925	1.94734	1.91641	2.02193	1.77401	1.85339	1.97472	2.035
Geometric Mean Hourly Wage	$5.92	$7.01	$6.80	$7.55	$5.89	$6.38	$7.20	$7.66
N	610	4,179	503	4,252	1,472	4,535	370	4,602

*   Significant at .01 level or less
**   Significant at .10 level or less

Not surprising, however, is the fact that whatever the difference in their respective levels of schooling attainment the payoffs to investments in schooling itself were greater for whites than for blacks in all regions. Indeed, the black-white payoff gap was greater in the West, the one region where black educational attainment outstripped that of whites, than in any of the other three regions. And in fact, the rate of return to an additional year of schooling for black males in the West was less than it was for blacks in any other region. Thus it would appear that no matter what their relative levels of educational attainment, the market during this period rewarded white education and productivity better than it did that of blacks.

Wage-experience profiles (not shown) generated from the work experience quadratic tell essentially the same story as did the education construct. White male wage-experience profiles lay everywhere above those of black males in all regions. The West is again particularly notable inasmuch as neither of the black work experience coefficients were significant, implying that work experience yielded relatively little or no returns for blacks there. The results in the South region are also interesting for just as the payoff to an additional year of schooling was greater for blacks in the South than in the other regions, the black wage-experience profile was highest there as well.

With respect to the other variables in the model, as expected, blacks were more concentrated in central cities than whites, with the greatest black concentration occurring in the Northeast and Midwest. However, not only did more whites live outside than inside of central cities, but with the exception of the Northeast a greater proportion lived in essentially rural areas than lived either in the suburbs or the central city.

With the sole exception of the South, the black urban residence coefficients were uniformly insignificant and the signs on the Northeast and West coefficients indicate a negative relationship between wage levels and central city residence. These results are consistent with the increasing outmigration of jobs from urban areas primarily witnessed to by Kasarda.[11]

In all regions a smaller proportion of black than white males were married and living with their spouses, and a larger proportion were in the "divorced, separated, or widowed," category of "once married," with somewhat more married black males in the Northeast and Midwest than in the South and West. The payoff to marital status was significant for blacks in all regions except the Northeast and the "once marrieds" in the South.

Proportionally more whites than blacks were employed in the private sector, with the greatest percentages in the Northeast and Midwest. Only in the latter region did private sector employment have an impact, a negative one, on black wages.

In the Midwest there was a greater concentration of both blacks and whites in the relatively high-paying durable goods manufacturing industries than in the other regions, with blacks more heavily represented than whites (35 percent versus 28 percent). These were the industries in the Midwest that were among the hardest hit by the 1981–82 recession. Average unemployment in such industries in 1982 in the Midwest was 17 percent, the second highest among the broad industry categories shown in the table, and exceeded only by the 24 percent unemployment rate in the Midwest construction industry. There was also substantial employment of blacks in similar industries in the Northeast and South, but not nearly so much as in the Midwest. In the West "public administration" and "professional and related services" were the industries in which the greatest percentage of blacks were employed. Very few of the black industry coefficients were significant, however, and in the Midwest those that were ("wholesale/retail trade," "public administration," and "professional services") had a negative effect on black wages.

Practically all of the white trends were significant and carried the expected, positive signs, while for blacks about half the trends were significant, with most of those occurring in the later years of the period.

The geometric mean hourly wage for black males was highest in the West ($7.20) where black male average educational attainment was also the highest, and lowest in the South ($5.89) where black average educational attainment was lowest. Although this result would seem to support the human capital-productivity-wage argument it has to be tempered by the fact that white male wages were also highest in the West ($7.66), the region where their educational attainment was the lowest.

The widest black-white wage gap occurred in the Northeast where white males earned $1.09 more per hour on average than black males. This was also the region where the difference in black and white schooling was the greatest. The next largest wage gap was in the Midwest, 75 cents, but here the difference between black and white schooling, as noted above, was relatively small. In the South the wage difference was 49 cents, and was lowest in the West at 46 cents.

DECOMPOSITION RESULTS

Within the context of the neoclassical paradigm it is logical to ask how much of these mean hourly wage differences were due to differences in the human capital and associated characteristics represented by the independent variables in the model and how much was due to other, unspecified factors, chief among which perhaps is labor market discrimination.[12] The most frequently employed method for answering these queries is the use of a decomposition formula such as equations (1), (2) or (3). This article employs the latter since it more nearly depicts reality of the wage determination process in an environment in which labor market discrimination is assumed to exist.

The decomposition results are shown in Table 4 and further confirm the somewhat surprising outcome in the West. Pure wage discrimination appears to have been greater by far there than in any other region. The West decomposition in the last row of the table is interpreted as follows: Due to their superior productivity characteristics, black males in the West would have earned 72 cents more per hour than whites *if there had been no discrimination.* Because of discrimination, whites earned 75 cents per hour more than they would have had discrimination not existed, and blacks earned 42 cents less than they would have in the absence of discrimination.

This outcome in the West could be further evidence of the relatively greater discrimination that has been detected against blacks in white collar and other middle-class occupations than against their blue collar and service occupation counterparts.[13] As noted above, blacks in the West were more educated and more concentrated in quasi-white collar industries (public administration, professional services, entertainment and recreational services) than they were in the other regions.[14]

The South is the region where it was expected that the discrimination components would have been the largest. However, 19 cents of the 49-cent wage difference in the South was due to whites' human capital advantages, while 6 cents was the result of the more favorable market treatment accorded whites, and 24 cents was the result of the less favorable treatment blacks received. Thus, about 60 percent of the wage differential was due to discrimination.

In the Midwest nearly two-thirds of the wage differential was due to differential treatment with only about one-third the result of whites' greater human capital endowments. Forty-eight cents of the 75-cent gap can be thought of as "the pure cost of being a black male worker in the Mid-

TABLE 4

Decomposition of Regional Wage Differentials
(Percentage of ln wage differentials in parentheses, followed by dollar
value of mean hourly wage differentials)

	Total Differential	Productivity Characteristic Differential	White Male "Benefit"	Black Male "Cost"
NORTHEAST	.16808	.08633	.00687	.07488
	(100%)	(51.4%)	(4.1%)	(44.5%)
	$1.09	$.56	$.04	$.49
MIDWEST	.10552	.03539	.00287	.06726
	(100%)	(33.5%)	(2.7%)	(63.8%)
	$.75	$.25	$.02	$.48
SOUTH	.1904	.07409	.02258	.09373
	(100%)	(38.9%)	(11.9%)	(49.2%)
	$.49	$.19	$.06	$.24
WEST	.06121	-.09484	.09994	.05611
	(100%)	(-155.0%)	(163.3%)	(91.7%)
	$.46	-$.71	$.75	$.42

west," and the other 2 cents as "the pure benefit of being a white male worker in the Midwest."

Productivity differences between whites and blacks were greatest in the Northeast, accounting for 56 cents of the $1.09 wage gap. Blacks earned 49 cents per hour less than they would have in the absence of discrimination and whites earned 4 cents per hour more.

CONCLUSION

It is evident that both the relative labor market outcomes and relative labor market treatment of black male workers differed markedly by region during the 1976–84 period. Although black average wages in the West were higher than in any other region, they still were lower than white wages even though black educational attainment was higher. In addition, although the differences were not statistically significant, blacks earned a lower rate of return on their schooling investments in the West than they did in any other region. Blacks thus experienced a greater amount of discriminatory treatment in the West than they did in any of the other regions.

In the Midwest, in terms of unemployment, blacks appear to have borne the brunt of the recession that occurred during the period. They also faced a significant amount of wage discrimination, which was both absolutely and relatively greater than blacks suffered in the South, the usual suspect in these matters.

In the South both black and white wages were relatively low and so was the educational attainment of both groups. Still, additional schooling paid off more for both blacks and whites than in any other region. Moreover, blacks also enjoyed higher rates of return to additional years of work experience than elsewhere. Nevertheless, blacks faced a substantial amount of wage discrimination as well.

Finally, the black average wage in the Northeast was only a few pennies higher than that in the South and both the wage and educational gaps were widest there. Nearly half of the wage gap, however, was attributable to differential treatment.

To the extent that these patterns continue up to the present it means that policies designed to improve racial equity in labor markets (and thereby labor market efficiency)[15] will need different emphases in different regions. In all regions of the country antidiscrimination laws must be strengthened and enforced. The West and South though will require particular attention. Programs aimed at narrowing any black-white education and training gaps are also needed in all regions, but especially in the Northeast and South. Insofar as blacks in the Midwest are more vulnerable than whites to the ravages of the business cycle some added, race-specific countercyclical protection must be afforded them.

NOTES

1. The employment/population ratio is a measure of the probability of being employed (and *not employed*). It is therefore perhaps a superior statistic for assessing a group's labor market situation than either the labor force participation rate or the unemployment rate. The latter two by ignoring discouraged workers tend to understate the problem. The employment/ratio is clearer and simpler—you are either employed or not employed, period.

2. The differences in the Midwest black unemployment rate and the black unemployment rates in the other three regions were statistically significant at the .10 level in both 1982 and 1989. There were no significant differences, however, in the unemployment rates among the other three regions taken together in either year. On the other hand, none of the regional differences in the black labor force participation rates were significant in 1982, while in 1989 all were significant. The white unemployment rate differences were statistically significant among all regions in 1982 and, with the exception of the Midwest-South difference, in 1989 as well. In both years all of the white labor force participation rate differences except the Midwest-West and Northeast-South were significant.

3. There is a substantial and well-known body of empirical research that has established the existence of racial, sexual and ethnic discrimination in U.S. labor markets. See, e.g., Otis D. Duncan. "Inheritance of Poverty or Inheritance of Race?" in D. P. Moynihan, ed., *On Understanding Poverty* (New York: Basic Books, 1968), 85–105; Anthony H. Pascal, ed., *Racial Discrimination in Economic Life* (Lexington, Mass.: D. C. Heath, 1972); Ronald L. Oaxaca, "Male-Female Wage Differential in Urban Labor Markets," *International Economic Review* 14 (October 1973): 693–709: Alan S. Blinder, "Wage Discrimination: Reduced Form and Structural Estimates," *Journal of Human Resources* 8 (Fall 1973): 436–55; Orley Ashenfelter and Albert Rees, eds., *Discrimination in Labor Markets* (Princeton, N. J.: Princeton University Press, 1974); James Gwartney and James Long, "The Relative Earnings of Blacks and Other Minorities," *Industrial and Labor Relations Review* 31 (April 1978): 336–46; Mary Corcoran and Greg J. Duncan, "Work History, Labor Force Attachment, and Earnings Differences Between the Races and Sexes," *Journal of Human Resources* 14 (Winter 1979): 3–20; William A. Darity, Jr. and Samuel L. Myers, Jr., "Changes in Black-White Income Inequality: A Decade of Progress?" *Review of Black Political Economy* 11 (Summer 1980): 355–79; Jeremiah Cotton, "A Comparative Analysis of Black-White and Mexican-American–White Male Wage Differentials," *Review of Black Political Economy* 13 (Spring 1985): 51–69.

4. See Nicholas M. Kiefer and Sharon P. Smith, "Union Impact and Wage Discrimination by Region," *Journal of Human Resources* 12 (Fall 1977): 521–34. The Census categorizes the four regions as "Northeast," consisting of Connecticut, Maine, Massachusetts, New Hampshire, Rhode Island, Vermont, New Jersey, New York and Pennsylvania; "North Central" or "Midwest," consisting of Illinois, Indiana, Iowa, Kansas, Michigan, Minnesota, Missouri, Nebraska, North Dakota, Ohio, South Dakota and Wisconsin; "South," consisting of Alabama, Arkansas, Delaware, District of Columbia, Florida, Georgia, Kentucky, Louisiana, Maryland, Mississippi, North Carolina, Oklahoma, South Carolina, Tennessee, Texas, Virginia, and West Virginia; "West," consisting of Alaska, Arizona, California, Colorado, Hawaii, Idaho, Montana, Nevada, New Mexico, Oregon, Utah, Washington, and Wyoming.

5. See Oaxaca, *op. cit.* and Blinder, *op. cit.* For a critique of their decomposition see Richard J. Butler, "Estimating Wage Discrimination in the Labor Market," *Journal of Human Resources* 17 (Fall 1982): 606–21; Jeremiah Cotton, "Discrimination and Favoritism in the U.S. Labor Market: A Cost/Benefit Analysis of Sex and Race," *The American Journal of Economics and Sociology* 47 (January 1988): 15–28; idem, "On the Decomposition of Wage Differentials," *Review of Economics and Statistics* 70 (May 1988): 236–43.

6. See Kiefer and Smith, *op. cit.*, p. 524, fn. 5.

7. Some decompositioners chose to combine the first term of (2) with the second term of (1) so that both weights are taken from the same (black) population. This, however, required the addition of a third term, called the "interaction" term:

$$(6.1) \quad \ln \overline{W}^W - \ln \overline{W}^B = \sum B^B (\overline{X}^W - \overline{X}^B) + \sum \overline{X}^B (B^W - B^B)$$

$$+ \sum (\overline{X}^W - \overline{X}^B)(B^W - B^B)$$

In form the interaction term is the difference in the productivity characteristics weighted by the difference in the regression coefficients (or vice-versa). And although this term has been variously interpreted, it is considered to be a measure of discrimination also. Stanley H. Masters read it as a measure of the relative magnitude of discrimination against blacks who have above-average or below-average educational and other productivity characteristics. Jones and Kelley saw it as the amount blacks would gain if they had the same productivity characteristics as whites and if those characteristics received the same rate of return as whites receive. See Stanley H. Masters, "The Effect of Educational Differences and Labor Market Discrimination on the Relative Earnings of Black Males," *Journal of Human Resources* 9 (Summer 1974): 342–60; F. L. Jones and J. Kelley, "Decomposing Differences Between Groups: A Cautionary Note on Measuring Discrimination," *Sociological Methods and Research* 12 (February 1984): 323–43. Both weights could also be taken from the white population, but in that case the interaction term would be negative.

8. These tests are designed to determine whether the different sets of structural coefficients estimated in two or more regression equations are equal in a statistical sense. If they are we can combine the samples from which the separate regressions are obtained and need estimate only one instead of several regressions (with the use perhaps of a dummy variable to take into account membership in one of the previous samples). If they are not equal then the model is correctly specified only by the use of separate regressions. See Gregory C. Chow, "Tests of Equality Between Sets of Coefficients in Two Linear Regressions," *Econometrica* 28 (July 1960): 591–605; and Franklin M. Fisher, "Tests of Equality Between Sets of Coefficients in Two Linear Regressions: An Expository Note," *Econometrica* 38 (March 1970): 361–66. The test statistic used was:

$$F_{k(r-1), (n-rk)} = \frac{(SSE_c - SSE_s)/k(r-1)}{(SSE_s)/n-rk}$$

where SSE_c is the residual sum of squares from the regression equation for the combined regional samples of either blacks or whites; SSE_s is the sum of the separate residual sums of squares from the regional samples: $SSE_{northeast} + SSE_{midwest} + SSE_{south} + SSE_{west}$; k is the number of independent variables; r is the number of regions; and n is the size of the combined samples. The results of the tests for the combined samples of blacks and whites separately and for the regions pair-wise are given below. In addition, tests were run *between* blacks and whites in each region. These results are not shown but are available from the author on request:

	Combined Samples	NE/MW Samples	NE/S Samples	NE/W Samples	MW/S Samples	MW/W Samples	S/W Samples
Blacks	1.64*	1.41*	1.36*	1.88*	1.96*	1.37*	2.10*
Whites	1.48*	1.36*	1.91*	1.33*	1.52*	1.29*	1.95*

* significant at the .05 level

9. The derivation of equation (3) takes as its point of departure the contention by Gary S. Becker in his seminal work on the economics of discrimination that in a perfectly competitive, nondiscriminatory labor market any differences in wages between black and white workers would be solely due to black-white differences in characteristics that directly determine productivity. Thus B*, the vector of coefficients that represent the nondiscriminatory, *ceteris paribus* rates of return to such productivity characteristics would be the same for both racial groups. The construction of an estimator of B* is based on three rather strong assumptions. The first states that labor market discrimination confers pecuniary benefits on whites and imposes pecuniary costs on blacks. Thus, $\sum B^W \overline{X} > \sum B^* \overline{X} > \sum B^B \overline{X}$. And hence in the absence of discrimination whites would receive lower average wages and blacks higher average wages. The second assumption maintains that in the absence of discrimination the prevailing wage structure, B*, will be some function of the market forces that currently determine the black and white wage structures, B^B and B^W. This assumption is simplified in (3) by specifying a linear relationship. The third assumption posits that B* will be closer to B^W than to B^B since whites make up

over 90 percent of the labor force. And indeed the proportions of blacks and whites in the labor force are the most plausible and convenient weights for the construction of the estimator of B* (see the subsequent text and the next footnote). And while there is certainly room for disagreement over the choice of weights, for as previously noted different decompositioners have employed different weights, I believe these weights, empirically based as they are, more nearly reflect the hypothesized nature of B*. See Gary S. Becker, *The Economics of Discrimination*, 2d ed. (Chicago: University of Chicago Press, 1971), and Cotton, "Discrimination and Favoritism . . . "

10. The average proportions of black and white male workers in the labor force used in this study were:

	Northeast	Midwest	South	West
Blacks	7.6%	6.6%	15.5%	4.5%
Whites	92.4%	93.4%	84.5%	95.5%

11. See, e.g., John D. Kasarda, "Urban Industrial Transition and the Underclass," *The Annals of the American Academy of Political and Social Sciences* 501 (January 1989): 26–47.

12. This latter portion of the wage difference is the residual. There is an ongoing debate over its interpretation. Those who are skeptical of the discrimination attribution argue that the residual is essentially the reflection of the failure to represent all of the relevant productivity-determining characteristics in the models. One suggested omitted characteristic is the differential cultural backgrounds of blacks and whites. Two of the principal adherents of this view are Thomas Sowell and Barry Chiswick. William Darity, Jr. and Rhonda Williams have provided the most cogent critique of this culturalogical approach. See, e.g., Thomas Sowell, *Race and Economics* (New York: McKay, 1975); Barry Chiswick, "The Earnings and Human Capital of American Jews," *Journal of Human Resources* 18 (Summer 1983): 313–36; William Darity, Jr. and Rhonda M. Williams, "Peddlers Forever?: Culture, Competition and Discrimination," *American Economic Review* 75 (May 1985): 256–61.

13. See Bart A. Landry, *The New Black Middle Class* (Berkeley, Calif.: University of California Press, 1988) and Jeremiah Cotton, "The Gap at the Top: Relative Occupational Earnings Disadvantages of the Black Middle Class," *The Review of Black Political Economy* 18 (Winter 1990): 21–38.

14. The greater relative discrimination in the West could also be due to the fact that blacks are not just one among several other large minority groups in the West (the largest of course being Mexican Americans), but are also the least preferred. It is clear from the work done in sociology in the late 1960s by Emory Bogardus and others that certain ethnic or racial groups are preferred over others. In studies conducted in 1946, 1956, and 1966, respondents were asked to rank "White Americans," "Irish," "American Indians," "Jews," "Chinese," "Japanese Americans," "Mexican-Americans," and "Negroes," as to which group they least objected to having social interaction with. Blacks were consistently ranked last. In another study of the attitudes of native white American adults towards blacks and Mexican Americans, there was considerably less prejudice expressed toward the former than the latter. See Emory Bogardus, "Comparing Racial Distance in Ethiopia, South Africa and the United States," *Sociology and Social Research* 52 (1968): 130–56; and Alphonso Pinkney, "Prejudice Toward Mexican and Negro Americans," *Phylon* (Winter 1963): 349–61.

15. Markets in the neoclassical lexicon are assumed to operate inefficiently when discrimination results in a factor of production receiving compensation that is either greater or less than the value of its marginal product. This is precisely the situation that is modeled in equation (3).

7

BLACK-WHITE WAGE DIFFERENTIAL: THE RELATIVE IMPORTANCE OF HUMAN CAPITAL AND LABOR MARKET STRUCTURE

Kwabena Gyimah-Brempong and Rudy Fichtenbaum

This article uses the decomposition analysis developed by Neumark and the 1987 CPS data to investigate the relative importance of human capital and labor market structure in explaining the observed wage differential between white males and blacks (both male and female). We find that labor market structure, as opposed to differences in human capital, explains a relatively large portion of the wage gap between white males and blacks. In addition to blacks and whites being paid different wages for the same work, they are also given unequal opportunities. This means that narrowing the human capital gap between the races will not be enough to close the wage gap, as argued by human capital theorists. It is equally important to pursue policies that provide access to higher paying jobs and industries for blacks.

This paper uses a wage decomposition methodology developed by Neumark and Cotton and 1987 Current Population Survey (CPS) data to investigate the relative importance of productivity characteristics and labor market structure in explaining the wage gap between blacks and whites.[1] By labor market structure, we mean labor market conditions that affect the wage structure but are neither the traditional productivity characteristics nor personal characteristics of the worker. We measure such labor market structure as consisting of industry classification, regional distribution of the work force, part-time and part-year employment status, unemployment rate, and the probability of employment.[2]

There is a debate over the relative importance of human capital in explaining the observed black-white (male-female) wage gap. Subscribers to the "human capital school" believe that blacks earn less than whites because they tend to be less educated and possess less of other productivity attributes than whites.[3] According to this school, elimination of this "human capital gap" could drastically reduce, if not eliminate, the observed black-wage differential. Paglin and Rufolo argue that even when males and females have the same amount of college education, differences in majors explain practically all the wage gap.[4] By implication, if whites and blacks tend to major in different subjects, then the black-white wage differential can be explained by the differences in college major. To allow for this possibility, we treat occupational classification as a manifestation of college major and treat college major as a human capital variable.[5] Other researchers point to the wage differential between blacks and whites with similar education and productivity characteristics and argue that differences in human capital endowments cannot explain all, or a large part of the black-white wage gap.[6]

The importance of labor market structure relative to human capital in explaining the black-white wage gap needs to be investigated in light of recent developments in the position of blacks in the labor market. There is no doubt that the black-white wage gap widened substantially in the 1980s.[7] This widening of the wage gap occurred in spite of the fact that the education gap between blacks and whites narrowed during the 1980s. The widening of the wage gap at the time when the education gap narrowed suggests that differences in educational attainment explain only part of the black-white wage gap. As Darity and Darity and Myers have argued, other factors may be more important in explaining the wage gap than differences in human capital.

The relative importance of productivity characteristics in explaining the black-white wage differential has policy implications. If productivity enhancing factors are the major cause of the black-white wage differential, then policies should be designed to increase black productivity characteristics. However, if the wage differential is mainly due to the structure of the labor market, hence labor market discrimination, then policy should emphasize the elimination of discrimination while narrowing the human capital gap.

Previous research on the black-white wage gap has used the decomposition analysis developed by Oaxaca and Blinder (hereafter referred to as Oaxaca decomposition) to decompose the wage differential into two components—differences in productivity characteristics and discrimination (coefficients).[8] Nord finds that college education decreases the wage gap between the sexes and argues that this gain from education is even more impressive for black females, contrary to the general assertion that returns to education are higher for men than for women.[9] Blau and Beller find that the male-female earnings gap declined between 1971 and 1981 and that changes in both endowments and returns to endowments are responsible for the closing of the gap.[10] Freeman finds that the black-white wage gap decreased between 1965 and 1976 and attributes most of the black gains to the effects of government antibias efforts.[11] Kamalich and Polacheck on the other hand, find no wage discrimination against either blacks or females in their study.[12]

Oaxaca decomposition generally uses the white wage structure as the reference wage structure. This implies that the white wage will be the equilibrium wage in the absence of discrimination. It is unlikely that the elimination of discrimination will leave the white wage structure unchanged if discrimination existed to begin with. In a competitive labor market, elimination of discrimination will result in an equilibrium wage structure that lies between the relatively high white wage structure and the relatively low black wage structure. This discrimination-free wage can be estimated if it is assumed that elimination of discrimination does not change the supplies of labor of the various races.[13]

Our approach to investigating the relative importance of productivity characteristics and labor market structure in explaining the black-white wage differential is as follows: We estimate a discrimination-free wage structure and use the coefficient estimates to conduct a decomposition analysis using Neumark's approach. We further investigate the proportion of the wage differential that is due to differences in endowments of productivity characteristics and the returns to these characteristics as opposed to "endowments" and returns to labor market structure.

The next section introduces the decomposition analysis employed in this study and describes the data used for the empirical analysis. This is followed by a discussion of the statistical results.

MODEL AND DATA

A. Model

We assume that the wage structure for a worker is determined by a vector of productivity characteristics, labor market structure, and personal characteristics. The wage equation can be written as:

(1) $ln\ W^j = X^{j\prime}\ \beta^j + e_j, \quad j =$ white, black

where W is the wage rate, X' is a vector of variables reflecting productivity, labor market structure, and personal characteristics, e_i is a stochastic error term, β is a vector of coefficients to be estimated and ln is the natural log operator.[14]

Neumark has shown that the log wage differential can be decomposed into an endowment effect, a white treatment effect, and a black treatment effect.[15] Formally,

$$(2) \quad \overline{ln\,W^w} - \overline{ln\,W^b} = (\overline{X^w} - \overline{X^b})'\beta* + \overline{X^w}(\beta^w - \beta*) + \overline{X^b}(\beta* - \beta^b)$$

where W^w, W^b, X^w, X^b, are the means of white wage, black wage, white and black endowments of wage explanatory variables, β^w and β^b are the coefficient estimates of white and black wage equations, and $\beta*$ is the discrimination-free wage coefficient vector. The first term on the right hand side is the endowment effect—wage differential due to differences in productivity, personal, or structural characteristics—while the second and third expressions are the white treatment advantage (if positive) and black treatment disadvantage (if positive) respectively. The sum of the second and third expressions on the right hand side constitute the crude measure of discrimination. While $\beta*$ is generally not known, Neumark and Cotton have shown that, if it is assumed that the elimination of discrimination does not change the supplies of labor of either whites or blacks, then $\beta*$ can be estimated from the data.[16]

B. Data

The data for this study comes form the Current Population Survey (CPS) 1987, March Supplement. The CPS data provides information on wages, education, location, and personal characteristics. In addition, it provides information on occupation and industrial concentration of workers. The variables used to estimate the wage equation are derived from the human capital model of wage determination. The variables in the X vector include the following:

(a) **College:** This was measured as dummy variables for high school graduation and for each of 1–6 years of college education. The base for comparison is nongraduation from high school. We measure this variable in this way so we can interpret the differences in coefficients of the dummy variables as the marginal returns to an additional year of post high school education.

(b) **Experience:** Years of potential work experience measured as age–years of school–6. We also included the square of this variable.[17]

(c) **Part-time:** Dummy variable which equals 1 if the worker worked less than 35 hours a week in the same period, zero otherwise.

(d) **Part year:** Dummy variable which equals 1 if the worker worked part of the year, zero otherwise.

(e) **Division:** Dummy variables for U.S. Census divisions of Middle Atlantic, East North Central, West North Central, South Atlantic, East South Central, West South Central, Mountain, and Pacific with New England as the reference division.

(f) **Employ2, Employ3:** Dummy variables which equal 1 if the worker changed employers once (twice) during the year, zero otherwise. These variables are intended to proxy job tenure to capture the impact of firm-specific training on the earning profiles of workers.[18]

(g) **Lambda:** Sample selectivity bias variable. This variable is included to account for the possibility that individuals in our sample were not randomly selected from the general adult population since the sample is made up of only those with a positive wage, hence only those employed. Lamba is calculated using Heckman's approach and is defined as: $-\phi(\hat{Y}W_i)/\Phi(\hat{Y}W_i)$ where $\phi(.)$ is the predicted probability that individual i is employed obtained from a probit regression and $\Phi(.)$ is the cumulative probability of employment from the probit function.[19]

(h) **Marital status:** Dummy variables for separated, divorced, widowed, never married, with married as the reference group.

(i) **Child:** Number of unmarried children under eighteen years old who live at home.

(j) **Industry:** Dummy variables for U.S. Census 2-digit industrial classification.

(k) **Occupation:** Dummy variables for U.S. Census 2-digit occupational classifications.

(m) **UR:** Unemployment rate in the state of residence of the worker. This variable is intended to capture the strength of demand in the labor market.

Our measure of college education differs from the way it has been measured in the literature and perhaps needs some explanation. We measure college education in dummy variable form because of our interest in the role of human capital, hence education, in narrowing the wage gap between the races. The usual way of measuring education—years of education—cannot adequately account for changing marginal returns to education since by measuring education as a continuous variable in a log-linear equation, we implicitly assume that the marginal returns to education change with only income. By measuring education in the dummy variable form, we are able to interpret differences in the coefficients of the dummy variables as the marginal returns to additional years of education.

In labor market studies, job tenure and its square are usually included as determinants of wages to account for the impact of firm-specific training on earnings. The CPS data does not provide information on job tenure or firm-specific training. We therefore use EMPLOY2 and EM-PLOY3 to proxy job tenure. We assume that these variables are negatively correlated with job tenure and will therefore have a negative impact on the wage rate, all things being equal. Our proxy for work experience may not correctly reflect the true work experience of part-time or part-year workers. The return to work experience for part-time (part-year) workers may be different from that of full time workers. To allow for different returns to experience for part time (part year) workers, we include interaction terms between the part time variable and EXPER and EXPERSQ.

The variables in the X vector are the variables that are traditionally used to estimate wage equations in the labor economics literature. We therefore neither spend time and space to defend their inclusion, nor indicate the expected signs of the coefficients for space consideration. However, since our study focuses on the relative importance of human capital and labor market structure in explaining the observed wage differential between blacks and whites, we have to provide an indication as to which variables are considered human capital variables and which ones are considered as labor market structure variables in this study. The human capital variables are: education, work experience and its square, occupational type, and the number of times a worker has changed jobs in the last year (EMPLOY2, EMPLOY3). The labor market structure variables are: unemployment rate, temporary and part year employment status, selectivity bias variable, industrial classification and region of residence. Appendix A provides definitions and classifications of all the variables in the X vector.

The sample used for the analysis consists of civilian workers who earned at least $1.00 or at most $99.00 per hour in wages in either full time or part time work, were not self-employed, and reported their sex and race. If any variable used in the wage equation is not reported by a worker, that observation is considered a missing observation. Because of incomplete data and hence missing observations, we were left with a total of 67,899 observations, of which 32,599 were white males, 2,950 were black males, 3,536 were black females and 28,814 were white females.[20]

The means of the log of wages for white males, black males, white females, and black females are 2.1909, 1.9612, 1.80, and 1.7534, implying geometric means of $8.94, $7.11, $6.05, and $5.77 respectively. There are relatively large differences in average wages when the sample is stratified by gender and race. While the proportion of white males with college education exceeds that of black males for every level of college education, black males tend to have more job experience than white males. White males are less likely than blacks to be part-time workers. While only about 30 percent of the sample lives in the South, about 60 percent of blacks in the sample are located in the South, indicating an overrepresentation of southern blacks in the sample.

DECOMPOSITION RESULTS

To obtain β^*, we pooled the sample and estimated a wage equation for a combined black males, white males, and black females samples as well as separate estimates for black males, black females, white females, and white males. The dependent variable in these wage equations is the log of hourly wage. In the pooled sample, we adjusted for sex and race. Coefficient estimates, together with the means of the variables are presented in Table 1, panel A. Column 2 presents estimates for the white male sample, column 3 presents estimates for the black male sample, column 4 presents the estimates for the black female sample, while column 5 presents the estimates for white females.[21]

In general, the coefficients have the expected signs and are significantly different from zero at reasonable levels of confidence. All the coefficients for the education and experience variables are positive and significantly different from zero as expected. For white and black males, the returns to education increase with the level of education. However, there is a discontinuity in the rate of return to education at four years of college education. For black females, there appears to be no significant gain to additional years of education until the attainment of a bachelor's degree, at which point we observe a discontinuity similar to those of black and white males. We also note that the returns to education for whites exceed those of their black counterparts—a finding that contradicts Nord's results. The return to work experience for males is about

TABLE 1
Coefficient Estimates of Wage: 1987

A. With Lambda

Variable	Male White	Male Black	Female Black	Female White
CONSTANT	1.4059 (30.775)*	1.7089 (11.547)	1.8069 (5.281)	1.2218 (10.468)
HIGHGRAD	.2283 (16.682)	.1229 (3.079)	.0845 (1.416)	.1748 (3.95)
COLLEGE1	.2884 (15.426)	.2003 (3.126)	.1522 (1.857)	.2589 (4.843)
COLLEGE2	.3324 (18.597)	.2147 (3.771)	.0978 (1.998)	.3056 (5.351)
COLLEGE3	.3531 (15.438)	.1998 (2.793)	.1282 (1.225)	.3586 (6.154)
COLLEGE4	.5218 (27.147)	.3144 (4.564)	.3030 (2.609)	.4326 (7.158)
COLLEGE5	.4999 (18.090)	.3744 (3.498)	.3696 (2.734)	.5241 (7.395)
COLLEGE6	.6631 (29.842)	.5183 (5.886)	.4746 (3.712)	.6096 (8.280)
EXPER	.0333 (19.608)	.0368 (6.906)	.0146 (2.478)	.0246 (10.048)
EXPERSQ	.0005 (11.359)	-.0006 (5.096)	-.0001 (0.939)	-.0005 (6.414)
WIDOW	-.0431 (0.771)	-.1307 (1.080)	-.0072 (0.123)	.0453 (1.502)
DIVORCE	-.1040 (6.041)	-.0715 (1.511)	-.0087 (0.282)	.0703 (2.153)
SEPARATED	-.0744 (2.587)	-.0954 (1.581)	-.0289 (0.663)	-.0507 (1.788)
NEVMARR	.2221 (13.073)	-.1700 (2.735)	-.0131 (.0395)	-.0003 (0.011)
EMPLOY2	-.1593 (13.781)	-.2321 (5.966)	.0074 (0.224)	-.1230 (9.315)
EMPLOY3	-.1407 (7.735)	.0185 (0.313)	-.1792 (3.007)	-.1480 (6.445)

TABLE 1 (continued)

Variable	Male White	Male Black	Female Black	Female White
CHILDREN	.0012 (0.303)	-.0109 (1.031)	-.0030 (0.323)	-.0284 (5.921)
PARTTIME	.0313 (1.511)	.1223 (2.029)	-.0155 (0.320)	.0087 (0.423)
PARTYR	-.0545 (5.924)	-.0780 (2.888)	-.1030 (4.617)	-.1063 (10.714)
LAMBDA	.1173 (1.260)	.0335 (0.156)	-.3818 (2.053)	.1667 (1.151)
UR	-.0024 (0.721)	.0060 (0.573)	.0346 (3.519)	-.0080 (1.600)
DIV2+	.06222 (3.764)	-.0633 (0.825)	-.0953 (1.311)	.0524 (2.292)
DIV3	.0299 (1.389)	-.1198 (1.392)	-.2506 (3.139)	-.0035 (0.146)
DIV4	-.1170 (6.473)	-.1147 (1.172)	-.2143 (2.407)	-.1498 (6.741)
DIV5	-.0407 (2.465)	-.2086 (2.838)	-.3390 (4.402)	-.0578 (2.969)
DIV6	-.1112 (4.084)	-.4064 (4.294)	-.5123 (5.663)	-.1616 (4.974)
DIV7	-.0852 (3.503)	-.2892 (2.975)	-.4595 (4.881)	-.0859 (2.935)
DIV8	-.0682 (3.290)	-.2491 (2.283)	-.4362 (4.220)	-.0949 (3.826)
DIV9	.0906 (4.672)	-.0120 (0.139)	-.1281 (1.580)	.0642 (2.810)
PARTTIME* EXPER	-.0232 (7.037)	-.0193 (2.386)	-.0024 (0.414)	-.0080 (3.302)
PARTTIME* EXPERSQ	.0004 (5.216)	.0003 (1.477)	.00001 (0.087)	.0001 (2.034)
lnWAGEHR	2.1909	1.9622	1.7534	1.999
N	32,599	2,950	3,536	28,814
$\bar{R}^2$	.3157	.3126	.3176	.2045
F	269.558	24.997	30.893	133.250

TABLE 1 (continued)

Variable	Male White	Male Black	Female Black	Female White
B. Without Lambda				
CONSTANT	1.4201 (31.974)*	1.7185 (11.436)	1.5129 (4.765)	1.3304 (19.356)
HIGHGRAD	.2195 (18.235)	.1191 (3.759)	.1957 (6.526)	.1273 (7.944)
COLLEGE1	.2793 (16.006)	.1946 (3.702)	.3005 (6.746)	.2024 (9.748)
COLLEGE2	.3213 (20.227)	.2094 (4.581)	.2899 (7.139)	.2441 (12.162)
COLLEGE3	.3435 (15.844)	.1936 (3.007)	.3206 (5.889)	.2985 (11.514)
COLLEGE4	.5077 (31.351)	.3072 (6.017)	.5307 (11.061)	.3673 (17.649)
COLLEGE5	.4872 (18.736)	.3700 (3.581)	.5932 (7.174)	.4506 (14.625)
COLLEGE6	.6503 (32.292)	.5104 (7.050)	.7104 (10.760)	.5305 (20.039)
EXPER	.0319 (24.225)	.0362 (9.654)	.0247 (6.934)	.0025 (13.708)
EXPERSQ	-.0005 (16.973)	-.0006 (8.140)	-.0004 (4.825)	-.0004 (11.122)
WIDOW	-.0238 (0.439)	-.1231 (1.111)	-.0684 (1.321)	.0305 (1.118)
DIVORCE	-.0941 (6.033)	-.0684 (1.592)	.00150 (0.050)	.0365 (2.545)
SEPARATED	-.0677 (2.389)	-.0909 (1.716)	-.0806 (2.207)	-.0572 (2.058)
NEVMARR	-.2056 (17.275)	-.1618 (4.883)	-.0567 (2.158)	-.0279 (2.088)
EMPLOY2	-.1595 (13.795)	-.2323 (5.973)	.0073 (0.218)	-.1231 (9.320)
EMPLOY3	-.1405 (7.726)	.0185 (0.312)	-.1776 (2.979)	-.1483 (6.456)
CHILDREN	.0016 (0.429)	-.0108 (1.023)	-.0037 (0.393)	-.0283 (5.911)

TABLE 1 (continued)

Variable	Male White	Male Black	Female Black	Female White
PARTTIME	.0306	.1234	.0073	.0085
	(1.481)	(2.061)	(0.152)	(0.413)
PARTYR	-.0573	-.0778	-.1063	-.1062
	(5.924)	(2.884)	(4.776)	(10.704)
UR	-.0013	.0065	.0258	-.0045
	(0.404)	(0.644)	(2.880)	(1.131)
DIV2	.0650	-.0616	-.0649	.0664
	(3.899)	(0.811)	(0.911)	(3.434)
DIV3	.0272	-.1176	-.0318	-.0068
	(1.354)	(1.384)	(2.920)	(0.288)
DIV4	-.1203	-.1168	-.2121	-.1603
	(6.718)	(1.206)	(2.381)	(7.903)
DIV5	0.0393	-.2100	-.2658	-.0640
	(2.384)	(2.878)	(3.845)	(3.420)
DIV6	-.1094	-.4079	-.4608	-.1659
	(4.024)	(4.332)	(5.279)	(5.141)
DIV7	-.0858	-.2882	-.3969	-.0926
	(3.525)	(2.972)	(4.430)	(3.232)
DIV8	-.0686	-.2499	-.3761	-.1014
	(3.3090	(2.293)	(3.776)	(4.197)
DIV9	.0912	-.0117	-.1089	.0669
	(4.700)	(0.135)	(1.351)	(2.943)
PARTTIME* EXPER	-.0233	-.0194	-.0019	-.0080
	(7.092)	(2.412)	(0.335)	(3.336)
PARTTIME* EXPERSQ	.0004	.0003	.00001	.0001
	(5.274)	(1.499)	(0.065)	(2.089)
lnWAGEHR	2.1909	1.9622	1.7534	1.7999
N	32,599	2.950	3,536	28,814
$\bar{R}^2$	.3157	.3128	.3171	.2045
F	274.418	25.409	30.841	135.647

Dependent Variable = lnWAGEHR

*Absolute value of "t" statistics in parentheses

+Division is indexed as follows: DIV2 = Middle Atlantic, DIV3 = East North Central, DIV4 = West North Central, DIV5 = South Atlantic, DIV6 = East South Central, DIV7 = West South Central, DIV8 = Mountain and DIV9 = Pacific. New England is the reference division.

three times that of black females. Changing employers once or twice in a year has a negative and significant effect on wages.

While not being married has a negative and statistically significant effect on the wages of males (black and white) and white females, marital status has no significant effect on the wages of black females. Except for white females, the presence of children at home has no significant effect on wages while part-time employment status has a positive and marginally significant effect on the wages of males but no significant effect on black female wages. Part-year employment has a negative and significant effect on wages. The part-time and experience interaction term has a negative and significant coefficient in the male and white female equations while it is insignificant in the black female equation. The coefficient of the interaction between part-time and EXPERSQ is positive and significant in the male and white female equations but insignificant in the black female equation. The coefficients of the part-time and experience interaction terms suggests that while part-time status depresses male wages, it has no significant impact on black female wages.

Black wages are lower in every census division than they are in New England, the reference region. This negative divisional effect on black wages is particularly large in the Southern census divisions (DIV5-DIV7). In these divisions, the coefficients of the census divisional dummy variables are two to five times as large for black males and black females respectively as for white males. If one considers the fact that more than 50 percent of blacks (male and female) in the sample are located in the South, this large wage differential in the South may, in part, make a large contribution to explaining the overall wage differential between blacks and whites in the sample. Lambda and the unemployment rate are significant only in the black female wage equation.

Changing employers twice or three times during the year depresses wages in our study. It is also possible that the structure of the labor market makes it hard for workers who lose their jobs to find high wage jobs. Using a time series data and a job search model, Topel finds that young people who change jobs more often had higher earnings growth than those who did not change jobs.[22] This appears to contradict our results. However, the two results need not be contradictory. In Topel's study, one can conceive of workers changing jobs because they had a better offer or the promise of steeper income profile than their current jobs promise. If on the other hand, most job changes are due to involuntary separation, workers may not find comparable jobs or higher paying jobs than their previous jobs. We do not believe the labor market in 1986 was robust enough for workers to have twice moved into higher paying jobs in the same year. The only way to resolve the apparent contradiction between our results and that of Topel is to provide the reason for job separation in our sample. Unfortunately, our data do not provide that information.

The coefficient of LAMBDA in the black female wage equation is negative and significantly different from zero while it is insignificant in the other equations. Given the positive truncation of the sample, the negative coefficient of LAMBDA implies positive selectivity. The implication of this positive selectivity is that the estimated coefficients of the independent variables may overestimate the marginal effects of these variables on the log of wages in the female equation if one does not adjust for the effects of selectivity.[23] This interpretation of the results is confirmed by comparing the coefficient estimates of females with those presented in Table 1-B. In Table 1-B where we do not correct for sample selectivity bias, the returns to education and work experience are higher for black females than for white females. The reverse is true in Table 1-A where we adjust for sample selectivity bias.

In addition to the issue of the marginal contribution of the regressors to the log of wages in the presence of selectivity bias, there is a debate in the literature on the robustness of Heckman's two-stage procedure used here.[24] In light of the debate about the robustness of Heckman's procedure, we estimated the wage equation without correction for selectivity bias and compare it to the results presented in Table 1-A. Coefficient estimates for these truncated wage equations are presented in Table 1-B. As in Table 1-A, column 2 presents estimates for white males, column 3 the estimates for black males, column 4 the estimates for black females, while column 5 presents the estimates for white females. In general, the coefficient estimates are very similar in terms of signs and magnitudes to those presented in Table 1-A. However, as indicated above, the coefficients of the female equations differ from those of the equations that include LAMBDA as a regressor. The coefficient estimates in Table 1-B also seem to be a little more precise than those presented in Table 1-A. However, Wald tests to test the hypothesis that Lambda does not contribute to explaining the variation in wages produced F statistics of 4.771, 1.02, 4.66, and 3.89 for the white male, black male, black female, and white female wage equations respectively. We therefore reject the null hypothesis for the white male, black female, and white female wage equations but not for the black male equation. Failure to correct for selectivity bias could result in misspecification of the white male, black female, and white female wage equations but not the black male wage equation.

We used the coefficient estimates to conduct a decomposition analysis of the white male-black male, white female-black female, and white male-black female wage differentials. The results are presented in panel A of Table 2. Panel A (i) presents the decomposition of the white male-black male wage differential, (ii) presents the decomposition of the white female-black female wage gap, while (iii) presents the decomposition of the white male-black female wage differential. From Table 2-A, we see that 64.46 percent, 144.17 percent, and 63.97 percent of the white male-black male, white female-black female, and the white male-black female wage differentials respectively are attributable to differences in endowments of characteristics while 35.54 percent, -44.17 percent, and 36.03 percent respectively are attributable to differences in returns to those characteristics. Of the 35.54 percent of the white male-black male wage differential attributable to discrimination, about 3.02 percent is due to favorable white male treatment while 32.52 percent is due to unfavorable treatment of black males. For the component of the white female-black female wage differential attributable to discrimination, -4.12 percent is due to unfavorable treatment of white females while -40.05 percent is due to unfavorable treatment of black females. This appears to indicate that white females are the victims of labor market discrimination. In the case of the white male-black female wage differential due to discrimination, 3.51 percent can be attributed to favorable treatment of white males while 32.52 percent is attributable to unfavorable treatment of black women. It is clear from Table 2-A that the major source of discrimination is unfavorable treatment of blacks rather than favorable treatment of whites in the labor market. These calculations indicate that a large part of the white male-black male/female wage differential can be attributed to discrimination against blacks.

For comparability, we used the estimated coefficients in Table 1-B to decompose the black-white wage differential. The results of this decomposition exercise are presented in panel B of Table 2. In general, the results in Table 2-B parallels those presented in Table 2-A. About 32 percent, -48.60 percent, and 36 percent of the white male-black male, white female-black female, and white male-black female wage differentials respectively is attributable to differences in returns to endowments

TABLE 2
Decomposition of Black-White Wage Differential, 1987

A. With Lambda

i. White Male-Black Male
   Wage Differential

a. ln Wage Differential	.2297
b. % Attributable to Endowments	64.46
c. % Attributable to White Treatment	3.02
d. % Attributable to Black Treatment	32.52
e. Gross Wage Differential (2) + (3) + (4)	100.00%
f. % Due to Discrimination (3) + (4)	35.54

ii. White Female-Black Female
    Wage Differential

a. ln Wage Differential	.0466
b. % Attributable to Endowments	144.17
c. % Attributable to White Treatment	−4.12
d. % Attributable to Black Treatment	−40.05
e. Gross Wage Differential (2) + (3) + (4)	100.00
f. % Due to Discrimination (3) + (4)	−44.17

iii. White Male-Black Female
     Wage Differential

a. ln Wage Differential	.4376
b. % Attributable to Endowments	63.97
c. % Attributable to White Male Treatment	3.51
d. % Attributable to Black Female Treatment	32.52
e. Gross Wage Differential (2) + (3) + (4)	100.00%
f. % Due to Discrimination (3) + (4)	36.03

B. Without Lambda

i. White Male-Black Male
   Wage Differential

a. ln Wage Differential	.2297
b. % Attributable to Endowments	68.45

TABLE 2 (continued)

c.	% Attributable to White Treatment	2.62
d.	% Attributable to Black Treatment	28.95
e.	Gross Wage Differential (2) + (3) + (4)	100.00
f.	% Due to Discrimination (3) + (4)	31.57

ii. White Female-Black Female
Wage Differential

a.	ln Wage Differential	.0466
b.	% Attributable to Endowments	148.60
c.	% Attributable to White Treatment	–5.30
d.	% Attributable to Black Treatment	–43.30
e.	Gross Wage Differential (2) + (3) + (4)	100.00
f.	% Due to Discrimination (3) + (4)	–48.60

iii. White Male-Black Female
Wage Differential

a.	ln Wage Differential	.4376
b.	% Attributable to Endowments	63.58
c.	% Attributable to White Male Treatment	3.57
d.	% Attributable to Black Female Treatment	32.85
e.	Gross Wage Differential (2) + (3) + (4)	100.00
f.	% Due to Discrimination (3) + (4)	36.42

of characteristics. This compares to about 36 percent for both white male-black male and white male-black female wage gap and -44.17 percent for the white female-black female wage gap respectively presented in Table 2-A. This implies that the inclusion or exclusion of Lambda in the wage equation makes little qualitative difference in our basic conclusion—a significantly large part of the white male-black male (white male-black female) wage differential is due to discrimination in the labor market.

Our analysis of the black-white wage differential so far has been conducted in terms of differences in endowments of "characteristics" and differences in returns to these endowments. The vector of characteristics includes the traditional productivity enhancing characteristics and personal characteristics, as well as factors relating to the structure of the labor market. Proponents of human capital theory argue that the wage gap can be attributed almost entirely to differences in endowments of productivity characteristics. There are reasons to believe that there is more to explaining the black-white wage differential than differences in productivity characteristics. Suppose workers in the same occupation and industry are paid equally but workers in different industries are paid differently even though they belong to the same occupation. Suppose blacks are employed in lower paid industries than their comparably qualified white counterparts because of discrimination. Obviously, the resulting wage differential between blacks and whites is not due to differences in endowments of productivity characteristics; it is due to the "structure" of the labor market that makes it possible to discriminate against blacks in entry to higher wage industries.

What is the relative importance of labor market structure in explaining the black-white wage differential? To investigate this issue, we decompose the wage differentials into three components—due to productivity characteristics, due to labor market structure, and due to other characteristics. In line with Neumark's decomposition analysis, each of these components is further subdivided into differences due to endowments and differences due to returns to these endowments. If human capital theory explains most of the wage differential, we expect most of the wage gap to be explained by differences in endowments of human capital; otherwise we expect a large part of the wage gap to be explained by variables representing labor market structure and other factors. The results of this decomposition analysis are presented in Table 3-A. Panel A-(i) presents the decomposition of the white male-black male wage differential, A-(ii) presents the decomposition of the white male-black female wage differential, A-(iii) presents the decomposition for white male-white female wage differential, A-(iv) presents the decomposition of the white female-black female wage differential, while A-(v) presents the decomposition for the black male-black female wage differential.

From Table 3-A, we find that -55.84 percent of the white male-black male wage gap can be attributed to human capital effects. This implies that if labor market structure and other characteristics, except endowments of human capital and the returns to these endowments were equal across the races, black male wages would *exceed* white male wages by an amount that is 56 percent of the white male-black male wage gap ($.71). The human capital effect of -55.84 percent is further subdivided into about 52 percent endowment effect and -108 percent treatment ef-

TABLE 3
Relative Importance of Human Capital and Labor Market Structure in
Explaining Wage Differential

A. With Lambda

i. White Male-Black Male Wage Differential

ln Wage Differential		.2297
% Due to Human Capital		−55.84
Endowments	51.69	
Treatment	−107.53	
(i) White	−8.30	
(ii) Black	−99.23	
% Due to Structure		149.67
Characteristics	2.66	
Treatment	147.01	
(i) White	10.26	
(ii) Black	136.75	
% Due to Other		6.18
Characteristics	10.11	
Treatment	−3.93	
(i) White	1.07	
(ii) Black	−5.00	
Gross Wage Differential		100.00%

ii. White Male-Black Female Wage Differential

ln Wage Differential		.4376
% Due to Human Capital		−5.73
Endowment	34.08	
Treatment	−39.81	
(i) White M	−2.14	
(ii) Black F	−37.67	
% Due to Structure		117.99
Endowment	21.59	
Treatment	96.40	
(i) White M	5.86	
(ii) Black F	90.54	

TABLE 3 (continued)

% Due to Other		−12.25
Endowment	8.30	
Treatment	−20.55	
(i) White M	−0.21	
(ii) Black F	−20.35	
Gross Wage Differential		100.00

iii. White Male-White Female Wage Differential

ln Wage Differential		.3910
% Due to Human Capital		103.59
Endowment	31.77	
Treatment	71.82	
(i) White M	49.90	
(ii) White F	21.92	
% Due to Structure		9.17
Endowment	−5.60	
Treatment	14.77	
(i) White M	−4.35	
(ii) White F	19.12	
% Due to Other		−12.77
Endowment	1.00	
Treatment	−13.76	
(i) White M	−8.65	
(ii) White F	−5.11	
Gross Wage Differential		100.00

iv. White Female-Black Female Wage Differential

ln Wage Differential		.0466
% Due to Human Capital		−923.34
Endowment	133.96	
Treatment	−1057.30	

TABLE 3 (continued)

% Due to Structure		1031.29
Endowment	−6.95	
Treatment	1038.24	
% Due to Other		-7.95
Endowment	17.16	
Treatment	−25.11	
Gross Wage Differential		100.00

v. Black Male-Black Female Wage Differential

ln Wage Differential			.2079
% Due to Human Capital			49.63
Endowment		11.53	
Treatment		38.10	
(i) Black M	16.56		
(ii) Black F	21.54		
% Due to Structure			82.99
Endowment		43.55	
Treatment		39.44	
(i) Black M	20.34		
(ii) Black F	19.11		
% Due to Other			−32.61
Endowment		4.49	
Treatment		−37.10	
(i) Black M	−15.65		
(ii) Black F	−21.45		
Gross Wage Differential			100.00

B. Without Lambda

i.   White Male-Black Male Wage Differential

ln Wage Differential	.2297

TABLE 3 (continued)

% Due to Human Capital			−55.84
Endowment Effect		51.04	
Treatment Effect		−106.62	
(i) White M	−7.76		
(ii) Black M	−98.85		
% Due to Structure			148.49
Endowment Effect		8.03	
Treatment Effect		140.46	
(i) White M	9.11		
(ii) Black M	131.34		
% Due to Other			7.08
Endowment Effect		9.35	
Treatment Effect		−2.27	
(i) White M	1.27		
(ii) Black M	−3.54		
Gross Wage Differential			100.00%

ii. White Male-Black Female Wage Differential

In Wage Differential			.4376
% Due to Human Capital			17.32
Endowment Effect		34.09	
Treatment Effect		−16.77	
(i) White M	−1.44		
(ii) Black F	−15.32		
% Due to Structure			88.95
Endowment Effect		21.12	
Treatment Effect		67.83	
(i) White M	3.86		
(ii) Black F	63.97		

TABLE 3 (continued)

% Due to Other		−6.28
Endowment Effect	8.37	
Treatment Effect	−14.65	
(i) White M	1.15	
(ii) Black F	−15.80	
Gross Wage Differential		100.00

iii. White Male-White Female Wage Differential

ln Wage Differential		.3910
% Due to Human Capital		89.88
Endowment Effect	32.36	
Treatment Effect	57.52	
(i) White M	27.63	
(ii) White F	29.89	
% Due to Structure		18.76
Endowment	23.33	
Treatment Effect	−4.57	
(i) White M	−1.62	
(ii) White F	−2.95	
% Due to Other		−8.63
Endowment	.85	
Treatment	−9.48	
(i) White M	−5.61	
(ii) White F	−3.87	
Gross Wage Differential		100.00

iv. White Female-Black Female Wage Differential

ln Wage Differential		.0466
% Due to Human Capital		−591.62
Endowment	129.12	

Table 3 (continued)

Treatment		−720.44	
(i) White F	9.92		
(ii) Black F	−730.66		
% Due to Structure			678.17
Endowment		−.63	
Treatment		678.80	
(i) White F	−10.29		
(ii) Black F	689.10		
% Due to Other			13.46
Endowment		20.11	
Treatment Effect		−6.65	
(i) White F	−4.93		
(ii) Black F	−1.72		
Gross Wage Differential			100.00
v. Black Male-Black Female Wage Differential			
ln Wage Differential			.2079
% Due to Human Capital			97.85
Endowment		9.44	
Treatment		88.41	
(i) Black M	35.19		
(ii) Black F	53.23		
% Due to Structure			23.19
Endowment		31.00	
Treatment		7.81	
(i) Black M	2.27		
(ii) Black F	−10.08		
% Due to Other			−21.04
Endowment		5.70	
Treatment		−26.74	
(i) Black M	−8.10		
(ii) Black F	−18.64		
Gross Wage Differential			100.00

fect. We interpret this as follows: If human capital endowment was the only factor that differed between white males and black males, the wage gap would be 52 percent more than the observed wage differential. On the other hand, if returns to human capital characteristics was the only factor that differed between white males and black males in the labor market, black male wages would *exceed* white male wages by 108 percent of the observed wage gap ($1.36). Our results show that while white males possess larger endowments of human capital, black males receive higher returns to their endowments of human capital and that this higher treatment effect overwhelms the higher endowments white males possess.

Labor market structure contributes about 150 percent—divided into 2.66 percent for endowments and 147 percent for treatment effect—of the white male-black male wage gap while other factors contribute an additional 6.18 percent. The treatment effect is further subdivided into 10.26 percent favorable white male treatment and 136.75 percent unfavorable black male treatment. The labor market structure effect of 150 percent indicates that if all other factors except labor market structure were equalized across the races, the white male-black male wage gap would be 50 percent more than the observed wage differential. In looking at the labor market structure effects, one sees that both endowments and treatment are positive although the treatment effect is about 50 times the endowment effects. This means that white males not only have better endowments of labor market structure, they are paid even more for the same jobs than black males when human capital is held constant.

The positive labor market structure effect is large enough to overwhelm the negative human capital effect. The labor market structural effect is the most important factor in explaining the observed wage gap between white males and black males. Indeed, virtually all the white male-black male wage gap is explained by the higher returns white males receive for their endowment of labor market structural characteristics. From Table 3-A (i), we see that practically all the white male-black male wage gap is accounted for by labor market structural variables. Human capital plays a relatively small role in explaining the white male-black male wage differential. In fact, the contribution of human capital to the wage differential is in favor of black males. This, of course, is contrary to the results obtained by the proponents of human capital theory.

Except for differences in magnitude, the decomposition of the white male-black female wage differential follows the same pattern as that of the white male-black male wage differential. Of the white male-black female log wage differential of .4376, −5.73 percent is attributable to human capital effects subdivided into 34.08 percent endowment effect and -39.81 percent treatment effect while 117.99 percent is attributable to labor market structure effects. The labor market structural effect is further subdivided into 21.59 percent endowment effects and 96.40 percent treatment effect. Other characteristics account for -12.25 percent of the wage differential. As in the white male-black male wage differential, white males have larger endowments of human capital than black females (accounting for 34.08 percent of the wage gap) but returns to black female human capital endowments are higher than those of white males (accounting for -39.81 percent of the wage gap) and this returns differential is large enough to swamp the male advantage in endowments of human capital. Again, as in the white male-black male wage differential, the black female advantage in human capital effects (sum of endowments and returns to endowments) is completely swamped by the white male advantage in labor market structure (both endowments and returns to endowments of about 117.99 percent of the wage gap). This large labor market structural effect accounts for virtually all of the white male-black female wage gap.

From Table 3-A, we can conclude that the entire wage gap between white males and blacks can be attributed to higher endowments of labor market characteristics possessed by white males and the even higher returns to these endowments that white males enjoy over their black counterparts. As seen by our calculations, if all factors except human capital were equalized across the races, blacks would earn more than white males even though white males have larger endowments of human capital. This is inconsistent with human capital theory. We can conclude from our calculations that labor market structure is more important than human capital in explaining the white male-black male/female wage gap.

We note that the effects of human capital in explaining the white male-black male (female) wage differential may be an upper bound for the effects of human capital since we included occupational classification and job changes as part of the vector of variables to reflect the "quality" of education. Even after the "overestimation" of human capital effects, the proportion of the black-white wage gap that is attributable to differences in human capital is relatively small as compared to the proportion that is attributable to labor market structure.

This article focuses on the white male-black male (female) wage differential. Also included is a brief analysis of the white male-white female, white female-black female, and black male-black female wage differential respectively to provide a more complete picture of the relative importance of labor market structure in explaining the observed wage differentials. (iii), (iv), and (v) of Table 3-A show that the observed log wage differentials between white males and white females, white females and black females, and between black males and black females are .3910, .0466, and .2079. Of these differentials, 27.17 percent, 144.18 percent, and 55.05 percent are due to differences in endowments of characteristics, while 72.83 percent, –44.18 percent and 44.95 percent of the white male-white female, white female-black female, and black male-black female wage differentials respectively are due to differences in treatment effect.

When one turns to the analysis of the relative importance of human capital and labor market structure in explaining the wage differentials, we see that 103.59 percent, –923.34 percent, and 43.40 percent of the white male-white female, white female-black female, and black male-black female wage differentials respectively are explained by differences in human capital. With the exception of the white female-black female wage differential, it is clear from Table 3-A that most of the human capital effects stem from the favorable treatment given to males. 9.17 percent of the white male-white female wage differential, 1031.29 percent of the white female-black female wage differential, and 92.12 percent of the black male-black female wage differential is due to the effects of labor market structure. Other factors account for –12.77 percent, –7.95 percent, and –35.52 percent of the white male-white female, white female-black female, and black male-black female wage differentials respectively. An interesting observation from Table 3-A is that labor market structure explains a very large proportion of the white male-black male (female) wage differential but only a small proportion of the white male-white female wage differential. This may be further indication that a large portion of labor market discrimination against blacks may take the form of hiring practices that direct them to lower paying industries as well as paying them higher wages in the same industries.

For completeness, we used the coefficient estimates in Table 1-A to decompose the wage differential into the three components—due to human capital, due to labor market structure, and due to other characteristics. The results are presented in Table 3-B. The results in Table 3-B parallels those presented in Table 3-A above. The conclusion to be drawn is that whether one controls for selectivity bias or not, labor market structure is more important than human capital in explaining the white male-black male/female wage gap.

Some tentative conclusions regarding the sources of the white male-black male (female) wage differential can be drawn from our calculations. Contrary to the arguments of those who contend that differences in human capital explain all or a large proportion of the white-black wage gap, our calculations indicate that differences in human capital, at most, play a minor role. Indeed our calculations show that equalization of the endowments and returns to human capital across the races would actually increase the wage gap, all things equal. The most important factors explaining the wage differential are variables reflecting the structure of the labor market. This is more so in the case of the white male-black male/female wage differential than for the white male-white female wage differential. The implication of this conclusion is that decreasing the human capital gap between blacks and whites will not be sufficient to close the wage gap, as some researchers argue.

It is natural to ask what accounts for this large labor market structural effect. This article is not intended to investigate that issue. However, we may speculate as to why such a large proportion of the white male-black male/female wage differential in 1987 is attributable to labor market structural characteristics. Freeman has argued that the dramatic improvement in the labor market position of blacks in the 1960s and 1970s can be largely attributed to government antibias efforts during that period. He noted, "if title VII were repealed and equal employment efforts ended, the rate of black advancement would fall."[25] In the 1980s, the Reagan administration reduced all government antibias efforts. One may conjecture that such a reduction may have led to increased discrimination against blacks in the labor market. While our data cannot be used to provide any definitive answers, the fact that the white male-black wage differential widened during a period when the education gap between the two races narrowed may suggest that the reduction in antibias efforts may have caused discrimination against blacks to increase. It may not be surprising that we find labor market structure to be a more important contributor to explaining the wage gap than differences in endowments of human capital.

Almost all the proportion of the wage differential attributable to labor market structure is due to returns to the "endowments" of labor market structural characteristics. Since differential returns to endowments are the measure of discrimination used in the literature, we can conclude that blacks earn less than whites with similar human capital endowments not only because they (blacks) are more likely to be employed in low wage industries or regions of the country, be part time or part year workers or

have more frequent spells of unemployment than their white counterparts; they are also more likely to be paid less in these situations than
white males, given the endowments of human capital. Labor market discrimination against blacks not only takes the form of lower returns to
some characteristics, it also takes the form of denying blacks access to
the most "desirable" industries. If blacks could find employment in high
wage industries, they would be paid relatively well compared to their
white counterparts. The problem for blacks is that access to employment
in such industries and other such opportunities are denied them.

Our results offer a sharp contrast to results of research that find differences in endowments of human capital as the major factor in explaining
the black-white wage differential. They are, however, consistent with the
findings of research that cast doubts on the efficacy of the human capital
model and point to other factors as more important in explaining the
black-white wage gap. The results are consistent with the results obtained by Freeman. They are also consistent with O'Neil's finding that,
at least in the 1980s, differences in educational attainment were not the
major cause of the widening wage gap between white and black college
graduates.

Previous researchers have partitioned the wage differential into aggregate characteristics (endowments) effects and treatment (returns) effect.
This approach does not make it possible to identify the contribution of
endowments (and returns) of human capital relative to that of labor market structural characteristics (and returns) in explaining the wage gap. By
disaggregating the determinants of the wage differential into various components, we are able to attribute the wage differential to various subgroups of arguments of the wage equation.

Bulow and Summers have argued that in an economy with high cost of
monitoring workers, employers will prevent labor from shirking through
wage differentiation not related to differences in labor productivity. In a
dual labor market, wage differentials between groups can be explained in
terms of group differences that are unrelated to differences in labor productivity.[26] They suggest that supervision and monitoring in the primary
sector is more costly than supervision in the secondary sector, hence
workers in the primary sector will be paid more than the value of their
marginal product while workers in the secondary sector will, at best, be
paid the value of their marginal product. In our sample, white males are
concentrated in industries and occupations that are classified as being in
the primary labor market while blacks are concentrated in the secondary
labor market.

This efficiency wage explanation of the white male-black wage differential does not, however, explain why blacks are concentrated in the secondary labor market. Bulow and Summers, however, argue that labor market segmentation occurs because blacks and whites have different labor market separation rates. Blacks, who generally have higher labor market separation rates than whites, are concentrated in secondary market. Higher separation rates may be caused by a number of factors such as liquidity constraints and therefore inability to accept low starting wages and rising wage profiles; it could also result from discrimination in hiring. Studies have shown that minorities tend to have higher labor market separation rates than white males.[27] Our results are consistent with Bulow and Summer's formulation, especially if one recognizes that, on the average, white males in our sample earn more than what the equilibrium wage would be in the absence of labor market discrimination while blacks earn less than what the equilibrium wage would be.

Some researchers have attributed the white male-black wage differential to differences in life cycle labor force participation among the various groups.[28] At first glance, our results seem to be at variance with the results of such studies. However, if one argues that differences in life cycle labor participation determine the sectoral allocation in the labor force, then one can reconcile our results with the results of life cycle labor participation models. The life cycle labor participation may explain why blacks are concentrated in the secondary labor market, and the differences in the structure of the two labor markets explain the observed wage differential. The problem with this reasoning is that life cycle labor participation models do not explain why blacks (black males in particular) will choose lower lifetime labor market participation and hence post school investment than their white counterparts.

CONCLUSION

This article used the 1987 Current Population Survey data and a discrimination-free wage structure to investigate the relative importance of human capital in explaining the black-white wage differential. Disaggregating the sample by gender and race, we find that wage discrimination against black men accounts for a substantial portion of the wage differential between white males and black males. Black women also face substantial wage discrimination compared to white males. This means that it is necessary to treat black males and black females as separate groups in decomposition analysis, else one may reach faulty conclusions.

The major conclusion is that differences in education and on-the-job training do not explain a large part of the wage differential between blacks and whites. Rather, the results of the study indicate that labor market structure, due in large part to institutional racism, is the major factor in explaining the black-white wage gap. One may also bear in mind that the fact that only about half the variance in log wages is explained by the wage equation, as is usually the case, indicates that there is a lot to the white male-black male/female wage differential that cannot be explained by differences in human capital.

The public policy implication from our results is that while human capital formation by blacks may play a role in narrowing the black-white wage gap, it is not the most important factor in closing the wage gap. Thus, programs designed to increase education and on-the-job training for blacks will not eliminate the white male-black wage gap by itself. Of more importance is the enforcement of policies designed to increase the accessibility of blacks to higher-wage industries. Furthermore, our results suggest that policies designed to improve the functioning of the labor market for all races and for all people with different endowments of human capital are critical to diminishing the wage gap. To narrow the wage gap, it may be necessary to pursue policies that ensure equal access to employment in all industries and regions, as well as stability of employment for all races and sexes, given their endowments of human capital. This can be achieved by vigorous enforcement of laws prohibiting employment discrimination, and by strengthening existing legislation.

ACKNOWLEDGMENTS

We thank two anonymous referees and the editor of *The Review* for helpful comments. We alone are, however, responsible for any remaining errors.

NOTES

1. David Neumark, "Employers' Discriminatory Behavior and the Estimation of Wage Discrimination," *Journal of Human Resources,* 23 (2), (1988), pp. 279–95, and Jeremiah Cotton, "On the Decomposition of Wage Differentials," *Review of Economics and Statistics,* 70, (1988), pp. 263–43.
2. While some may question the inclusion of part-time and part-year employment as measures of labor market structure variables, the CPS data indicate that workers mostly find themselves in these conditions for "economic reasons" and not because

they so desire. It is therefore reasonable to consider these variables as reflecting the structure of labor market conditions.

3. For example, James P. Smith and F. Welch, "Inequality: Race Differences in the Distribution of Earnings," *International Economic Review*, 20 (2), (June 1979), pp. 515–526, and R. F. Kamalich and S. W. Polachek, "Discrimination: Fact or Fiction? An Examination Using Alternative Approach," *Southern Economic Journal*, 49 (2), (1982), pp. 450–461.

4. M. Paglin and A. M. Rufolo, "Heterogeneous Capital, Occupational Choice, and Male-Female Wage Differential," *Journal of Labor Economics*, 8 (1), pt. 1, (1990), pp. 123–144.

5. We use occupational classification to measure differences in college majors for a lack of a better measure of college major in our data. One can assume a high correlation between college major and occupation.

6. For example, see William A. Darity Jr., "The Human Capital Approach to Black-White Earnings Inequality: Some Unsettled Questions," *Journal of Human Resources*, 17 (1), (1982), pp. 72–93, William Darity Jr. and Samuel L. Myers Jr., "Changes in Black-White Income Inequality, 1968–1978: A Decade of Progress?" *The Review of Black Political Economy*, 10 (Summer 1980), pp. 354–379, Paula England, "The Failure of Human Capital to Explain Occupational Sex Segregation," *Journal of Human Resources*, 17 (3), (Summer 1982), pp. 356–370, and D. Kiefer and P. Philips, "Doubts Regarding the Human Capital Theory of Racial Inequality," *Industrial Relations*, 27 (2), (Spring 1988), pp. 251–260.

7. June O'Neil, "The Role of Human Capital in Earnings Differences Between Black and White Men," *Journal of Economic Perspectives*, 4 (4), (Fall 1990), pp. 25–46.

8. See R. Oaxaca, "Male-Female Wage Differentials in Urban Labor Markets," *International Economic Review*, 14 (3), (1973), pp. 693–709, and Alan Blinder, "Wage Discrimination: Reduced Form and Structural Estimates," *Journal of Human Resources*, 8 (4), (1973), pp. 436–455.

9. S. Nord, "Productivity and the Role of College in Narrowing the Male-Female Wage Differential in the US in 1980," *Applied Economics*, 19, (1987), pp. 51–67.

10. Francine D. Blau and H. Beller, "Trends in Earnings Differentials by Gender, 1971–1981," *Industrial and Labor Relations Review*, 4 (4), (July 1988), pp. 513–529.

11. R. B. Freeman, "Black Economic Progress After 1964: Who Has Gained and Why?", in S. Rosen, ed., *Studies in Labor Economics* (Chicago: University of Chicago Press, 1981), pp. 247–294.

12. Kamalich and Solomon Polachek, "Discrimination: Fact or Fiction?"

13. If one assumes that elimination of discrimination does not affect the supplies of different types of labor and the wage bill remains unchanged, then only the distribution of the wage bill among different classes of labor changes. We assume that the elimination of discrimination does not change the supplies of labor of any type.

14. We make a distinction between productivity and personal characteristics as well as labor market characteristics, which we call structure in this article.

15. We note that the Neumark methodology uses the discrimination-free wage structure, β^* as the reference wage. We also note that this decomposition methodology allows us to indicate whether wage discrimination is due to favorable treatment of whites, unfavorable treatment of blacks, or both.

16. Empirically, β^* can be estimated as $\beta^* = S_w\beta^w + S_b\beta^b$. Alternatively, it can be obtained by estimating a wage equation using pooled data for blacks and whites.

Neumark has shown that both approaches provide equivalent estimates of β*. We use the latter approach in our estimation of β*. For a full description of this methodology, see Cotton (1988) and Neumark (1988).

17. It is clear that this variable is not the best measure of job experience, especially for women, who are likely to lose some working experience in order to raise families. However, the CPS data does not provide any other variable that could be used for job experience.

18. While this is not the best variable to measure firm-specific experience, we note that there is no better variable in our sample to proxy firm or job-specific experience in our sample.

19. See J. Heckman, "Sample Selection Bias a Specification Error," *Econometrica*, 47, (1979), pp. 153–161.

20. We do not stress the white female-black female wage differential in this study since it has been suggested that white females are themselves discriminated against in the labor market. For more on discrimination against white females, see Michael D. Robinson and Phanindra V. Wunnava, "Measuring Direct Discrimination in Labor Markets Using a Frontier Approach: Evidence from CPS Female Earnings Data," *Southern Economic Journal*, 56 (1), (July 1989), pp. 212–218.

21. Because of space consideration, we do not report the coefficients of the occupation and industry classification.

22. R. Topel, "Job Mobility, Search, and Earnings Growth: A Reinterpretation of Human Capital Earnings Functions," *Research in Labor Economics*, 8, Part A, (1986), pp. 199–233.

23. McDonald and Moffit show that the adjustment factors is the sample labor participation rate for black females, in this case. See J. F. McDonald and R. A. Moffit, "The Uses of Tobit Analysis," *Review of Economics and Statistics*, 67 (2), (1980), pp. 318–321.

24. See, for example, William H. Greene, "Sample Selection Bias as a Specification Error: Comment," *Econometrica*, 49, (1981), pp. 795–798 and F. Nelson, "Efficiency of the Two-Step Estimator for Models with Endogenous Sample Selection," *Journal of Econometrics*, 24, (1984), pp. 181–196.

25. Freeman, "Black Economic Progress…"

26. J. I. Bulow and L. H. Summers, "A Theory of Labor Markets with Application to Industrial Policy, Discrimination, and Keynesian Unemployment," *Journal of Labor Economics*, 4 no. 3, pt 1, (1986), pp. 376–414.

27. See for example, S. Marston, "Employment Instability and High Unemployment Rates," *Brookings Papers on Economic Activity*, no. 1 (1976), pp. 169–203.

28. For example, see Solomon Polachek, "Differences in Expected Post-School Investment as a Determinant of Market Wage Differentials," *International Economic Review*, 16 (2), (June 1975).

APPENDIX A
Definition and Mean Values of Variables

Definition	Variable Label	Male Means	Male Means	Female Means	Female Means
Log of Hourly Wage Rate	(lnWGHR)	2.19	1.96	1.80	1.75
Human Capital					
High School	HIGHGRAD	0.37	0.43	0.42	0.44
1 Year College	COLLEGE1	0.07	0.06	0.10	0.08
2 Years College	COLLEGE2	0.11	0.10	0.12	0.12
3 Years College	COLLEGE3	0.04	0.04	0.05	0.05
4 Years College	COLLEGE4	0.15	0.09	0.14	0.09
5 Years College	COLLEGE5	0.03	0.01	0.03	0.02
6 or More Years of College	COLLEGE6	0.09	0.04	0.06	0.04
Work Experience	EXP	17.71	18.04	16.90	17.29
Professional		0.12	0.06	0.15	0.11
Technicians		0.03	0.02	0.03	0.02
Sales		0.11	0.05	0.13	0.10
Administrative Support		0.06	0.10	0.30	0.27
Private Household		0.00	0.00	0.01	0.04
Protective Services		0.03	0.05	0.01	0.01
Service Except Private & Protective		0.07	0.13	0.15	0.23
Farming, Fishing & Forestry		0.04	0.04	0.01	0.01
Precision Production and Craft		0.21	0.15	0.02	0.03
Machine Operators, Assemblers & Inspectors		0.08	0.12	0.07	0.11
Transportation and Material Moving		0.07	0.11	0.01	0.01
Handlers, Equipment Cleaners, Helpers & Laborers		0.07	0.12	0.02	0.03
Armed Forces, Currently Civilian		0.00	0.00	0.00	0.00
Mining		0.02	0.00	0.00	0.00
2 Employers Last Year	EMPLOY2	0.13	0.09	0.13	0.09
3 or More Employers Last Year	EMPLOY3	0.05	0.04	0.04	0.03
Market Structure					
Midwest	REGION2	0.25	0.17	0.25	0.16
South	REGION3	0.28	0.57	0.28	0.57
West	REGION4	0.22	0.09	0.22	0.08
Part Time Employment	PARTTIME	0.09	0.12	0.30	0.22
Part Year Employment	PARTYEAR	0.25	0.31	0.36	0.35
Construction		0.11	0.08	0.01	0.01
Durable Manufacturing		0.16	0.14	0.07	0.06
Nondurable Manufacturing		0.09	0.10	0.07	0.10

APPENDIX A (continued)

Definition	Variable Label	Male Means	Male Means	Female Means	Female Means
Transport		0.09	0.12	0.04	0.05
Wholesale		0.06	0.04	0.03	0.01
Retail		0.14	0.12	0.21	0.16
Finance		0.04	0.04	0.09	0.07
Business and Repair Services		0.06	0.07	0.05	0.05
Personal Services		0.02	0.03	0.05	0.08
Entertainment Services		0.01	0.01	0.01	0.01
Professional Services		0.12	0.14	0.32	0.32
Public Administration		0.06	0.07	0.04	0.07
Unemployment Rate	UR	6.85	7.05	6.77	6.98
Selectivity Bias	LAMBDA	0.15	0.29	0.41	0.45
Other					
Widowed	MAR2	0.01	0.01	0.03	0.04
Divorced	MAR3	0.07	0.08	0.11	0.13
Separated	MAR4	0.02	0.05	5.03	0.08
Never Married	MAR5	0.26	0.34	0.23	0.33
Number of Children	CHILDREN	0.84	0.82	0.80	0.98

III

OCCUPATIONAL CROWDING

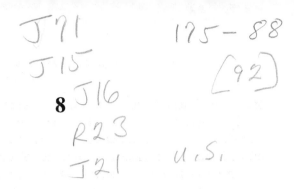

THE IMPACT OF CHANGES IN LOCAL LABOR MARKET CONDITIONS ON ESTIMATES OF OCCUPATIONAL SEGREGATION

Susanne Schmitz and Paul E. Gabriel*

Recent work by labor economists has suggested that differential labor market treatment of minorities (e.g., occupational segregation) may vary across local labor markets. This study assesses whether changing economic conditions in a local labor market affects the degree of occupational segregation by race and gender in the United States. Our empirical analysis finds evidence that the relative occupational structures of white women and black males are systematically related to changes in certain local labor market conditions.

INTRODUCTION

Occupational segregation refers to a situation where two groups of workers tend to work in a different set of occupations on the basis of nonproductivity factors such as race or sex. The numerous studies analyzing the existence and extent of occupational segregation against women and minorities implicitly assume all workers are participating in an aggregate labor market—since they group workers into a national data set. The empirical analyses of Hanushek, Hirsch and others cast doubt on the assumption of homogeneous aggregate labor markets.[1] Hence, past studies may have omitted an important consideration: the relationship between local labor market heterogeneity and the economic status of minorities and women.

This study investigates the possible impact that local labor market

*We are grateful to the two anonymous referees for their helpful comments on earlier versions of this paper.

conditions have on estimates of occupational segregation and expands previous empirical works in the area of labor market discrimination by: (1) accounting for different occupational structures across local labor markets; and (2) assessing the effect that local labor market conditions have on conventional estimates of occupational segregation against white women and black men.[2]

LITERATURE SUMMARY

Much of the empirical work that assesses the extent of occupational segregation of minorities and women compares the percentage of male (white) workers and the percentage of female (minority) workers in various occupations. Researchers such as Blau and Ferber, and Beller have noted that approximately two-thirds of all women (or men, or some combination of the two) would have to change jobs for the occupational distributions of the two groups to be the same.[3] On the other hand, estimates for minorities (for example blacks and Hispanics) suggest that 25 to 45 percent of the workers would have to change occupations to equalize the two distributions.[4]

Albelda examined trends in occupational segregation by race and sex over the period 1958–1981.[5] Using annual data from the Department of Labor for 29 occupations, she compares the occupational distributions for various gender-race subgroups, and finds that, holding race constant, the occupational distributions of all men and women have changed very little over the 24-year time span. The greatest convergence of distributions has been between that of nonwhite and white women. Occupational segregation between white and nonwhite men also declined during this time period. Differences in the occupational distributions between white men and nonwhite women was the largest in all years, ahead of that between white men and women. Based on her results, Albelda concludes that changes in occupational segregation by gender have been small, whereas improvements by race have been substantial.

Albelda also used regression analysis to evaluate the relative importance of structural changes, education and the business cycle in determining changes in occupational distributions. The variables, time (a vector of 1–24) and its square, are used to capture the effects of structural changes in the economy (e.g., affirmative action laws) on occupational segregation. Albelda speculates that with the advent of antidiscrimination legislation, occupational segregation should decline over time. Therefore, she hypothesizes the sign on the time coefficient to be negative. Secular movements in the general unemployment rate are used as proxies for cyclical variations. Albelda hypothesizes that during periods of low unemployment, women and nonwhites may gain access into occupations from which they have previously been excluded. This suggests that the general unemployment rate is positively related to the degree of occupational segregation.

Albelda's results for various race and gender subgroups suggest that, holding education and the business cycle constant, the similarity between the male and female occupational distributions is negatively correlated with time while the opposite is true for occupational comparisons by race. Hence, structural changes may have "impeded" occupational convergence by gender. With respect to education, Albelda finds that holding gender constant, educational attainment helped nonwhites gain access to traditionally white jobs. She also finds that fluctuations in unemployment affect the relative occupational distributions of women and nonwhites since the sign on the unemployment variable has the predicted sign in all equations.

Albelda's results suggest that differential occupational treatment of minorities is influenced over time by: (1) changes in relative educational attainment; (2) changes in labor market structure and; (3) fluctuations in the business cycle. However, at any given time, different geographical areas exhibit wide variations in these characteristics. It may therefore be of interest to examine the influence that such variables have on occupational segregation within the context of a local labor market. For the purpose of our study, a Standard Metropolitan Statistical Area (SMSA) is chosen to represent a local labor market.

METHODOLOGY

In this analysis we estimate occupational segregation against white females and black males within the context of a local labor market. Given our estimates we then measure whether any local change in occupational segregation has occurred over a specified period of time and finally, we analyze those factors that may explain the local changes in occupational segregation.

One well-established measure of occupational segregation is the index of dissimilarity.[6] The index is based on the absolute differences between the proportion of workers from the preferred group (i.e., white males) in a particular occupational category and the proportion of minority workers holding jobs in the same category. The index of dissimilarity is defined as:

(1) $S = \Sigma_i\, 1/2\, |\, PW_i - PM_i\, |$

where PW_i is the percentage of the white-male workforce in occupation i, and PM_i is the percentage of minority workforce in the same occupation. The index (S) gives the percentage of white-male (or minority workers who would have to shift between jobs to equalize occupational distributions between the two groups. S can range from zero to one hundred; a value of zero indicates that the distribution of the two groups of workers across occupational categories is identical, while a value of one hundred indicates total segregation. The principle objective here is to determine how local labor market conditions impact this index.

To assess how the occupational structure of minorities changes with concurrent changes in local labor market conditions, we apply the following strategy. First, the index of dissimilarity is calculated for each of the J SMSA's in time t (i.e., S_{jt}) and again for time t+n (i.e., $S_{j,\,t+n)}$, where n equals the number of periods forward, (here ten years). The change between the two yields:

(2) $\Delta S_j = S_{j,\,t+n} - S_{jt}$

If the change in the index is negative, this implies that the occupational distributions of the two groups have become more similar (a reduction in occupational segregation). An increase in the index implies that the two occupational distributions have become more dissimilar (an increase in occupational segregation). Next, we specify a 1×K vector of local labor market conditions (α_1, α_2, ..., α_K) for each SMSA. Changes over time in each local labor market condition in the jth SMSA can be expressed as:

(3) $\Delta\alpha_{1j}, \Delta\alpha_{2j}, ..., \Delta\alpha_{Kj}$ (k = 1, ..., K; j = 1, ..., J).

That is, $\Delta\alpha_{kj}$ represents the change in the kth labor market variable that has occurred during the specific time span in the jth SMSA.

To assess the direction of the relationship between changes in each local labor market variable and changes in the index of dissimilarity for each SMSA, we employ multiple regression analysis. In our specification, the change in the SMSA's index of dissimilarity is the dependent variable, while changes in each of the K labor market variables serve as the independent variables. Since each observation corresponds to an individual SMSA, the regression equation can be expressed as:

(4) $\Delta S_j = \gamma_0 + \gamma_1 \Delta \alpha_{1j} + \gamma_2 \Delta \alpha_{2j} + \ldots + \gamma_K \Delta \alpha_{Kj} + \varepsilon_j$

where $\gamma_0, \ldots, \gamma_K$ represent the coefficients to be estimated. Ordinary least square estimation of the coefficients in equation (4) provide estimates of the direction of the relationship between the change in the kth local labor market variable ($\Delta \alpha_K$) and the change in occupational segregation against the minority group. The testable hypotheses explored in this article are:

(5) $H_0 : \gamma_K = 0.$

A definitive list of local labor market variables that affect minority employment patterns relative to white males is difficult to compile. However, the following variables attempt to measure several factors that appear likely to influence the relative occupational distributions of black men and white women: a) the white-male unemployment rate; b) the unionization rate of the local labor market; c) the relative educational level of the minority group compared to that of white men; d) the relative labor force supply of the minority group; and e) the percentage of families below the poverty level. The white-male unemployment rate is proffered as the unemployment rate of the preferred group.[7] If discrimination exists in the labor market, a reduction in the white-male unemployment rate signals that competition for jobs has changed such that employers find it more difficult to hire the preferred group, *ceteris paribus*. Minority workers who might not have been hired or promoted prior to this change (due to discrimination) may now have job opportunities available to them that previously had been reserved only for the preferred group. If these workers now have more of the same job opportunities as the preferred group, we would expect their occupational distribution to become more similar to that of the preferred group, all else constant. Therefore, a reduction in the white-male unemployment rate may be associated with a reduction in the index of dissimilarity between the preferred and the minority group, implying that the two job distributions have become more similar.

On the other hand, if this unemployment rate rises, competition for jobs is expected to intensify so that employers may be able to fill their vacancies with workers from the preferred group, given the abundant supply of these workers. Employers may be less willing to employ or promote minority workers in this case. This would result in fewer occupational opportunities for minority workers, thereby increasing the difference in the occupational distributions of the two groups. Thus, the hypothesized sign on the coefficient for the white-male unemployment rate is positive.

A change in the unionization rate of a labor market has an indeterminate impact on the relative occupational distribution of the minority group. If minorities benefit more from union membership than their white-male counterparts, we would expect an increase in the unionization rate to provide job opportunities that are more similar to those of white males. This would cause the two job distributions to become more similar, thereby reducing the index of dissimilarity. On the other hand, if unions themselves are one of the discriminating agents, then an increase in the unionization rate might cause the two occupational distributions to become more dissimilar. Given these two possibilities, we therefore choose not to hypothesize *a priori* the direction of the relationship between a change in SMSA's unionization rate and the corresponding change in the index of dissimilarity.

On average, white men have attained higher educational levels than their comparable minority counterparts—this is especially true for the traditionally higher paying occupations such as professional, managerial and technical professions. If the educational levels of minorities were to rise and approach that of white men, it is reasonable to expect that the occupational distributions of minority workers should then become more similar to that of white men, *ceteris paribus*. To test this, we derive an index of educational dissimilarity between the two minority groups and white males. This index is computed in the same way as in equation (1) but now rather than occupational categories we employ educational categories. The six educational categories are defined as: 0–4 years elementary school; 5–8 years schooling; 9–11 years schooling; 12 years schooling (i.e., high school graduate); 1–3 years college; and 4 or more years of college.[8] Thus, we hypothesize that a decline in the educational index is associated with a decline in the index of dissimilarity. This implies an expected positive relationship between the change in the educational index and the change in the index of dissimilarity.[9]

A change in the percent of the local labor force comprised of the minority group (relative to that of white men) in an SMSA is offered as a proxy for a change in the relative supply of that group. Assuming discrimination exists in the labor market, an increase in the relative supply of the minority group would tend to "crowd" these workers into those occupations where minorities are already prevalent. If employers tend to exclude minority workers from certain jobs, then an increase in the relative supply of the minority group would tend to be associated with an increase in the index of dissimilarity, as more of the minority workers obtain jobs in those occupations in which they are overrepresented relative to white males. This argument parallels that of Becker for wage discrimination.[10] An increase in the relative supply of minority workers implies that these workers would encounter employers with greater "tastes" for discrimination against them. Applying this to occupational segregation, these workers may be denied access to jobs that are otherwise open to their white-male counterparts. Minority workers may then be crowded into certain occupations, suggesting that their occupational distribution would diverge further from that of white males.

The variable, percentage of families below the poverty level, gives a proxy for general economic conditions of the local labor market. As local labor market conditions deteriorate we expect more families to have income levels below the poverty line. The deteriorating conditions may allow employers to engage in discriminatory behavior against white women and black men, given the relative abundance of labor. Thus, the hypothesized sign on this coefficient is positive. This implies that as the percentage of families below the poverty level increases, we expect the occupational distribution of minorities to diverge from that of white males.

Table 1 summarizes the expected sign on the relationship between the proffered variables and the associated change in the index of dissimilarity.

DATA AND EMPIRICAL RESULTS

The data used in this study are drawn form the Public Use Samples of the 1970 and 1980 U.S. Censuses of Population and Housing. The census data provide comprehensive information on occupational patterns and allow us to draw adequate samples from various local labor markets (i.e., SMSA's). The SMSA's, which represent different local markets, were chosen from the largest 125 metropolitan areas with a population of 250,000 or more. To be included in this study, an SMSA had to have each demographic group represented by a sample size of 100 or more individuals. Using this criteria, 55 SMSA's were chosen.

The black male/white male and white female/white male indexes of dissimilarity, for each SMSA in 1970 and 1980, are shown in Table 2.[11] The indexes are calculated based on the 441 census detailed occupational

TABLE 1
Hypothesized Effects of Changes in Local Labor Market
Variables on the Index of Dissimilarity

(an increase in the) Local Labor Market Variable	Hypothesized Relationship to the index (S)
White male unemployment rate	+
Black male proportion of SMSA labor force	+
Female proportion of SMSA labor force	+
Percentage of the labor force unionized	?
Education dissimilarity index between white males and black males	+
Education dissimilarity index between white males and white females	+
Percentage of families in SMSA below the poverty level	+

categories for 1970 and on the 503 categories for 1980. The last entry shows the index for the United States as a whole. For black men relative to white men, the index ranged from 81.48 to 33.80 in 1970, whereas the range in 1980 was 63.38 to 32.20. Over the ten-year period the index fell in 54 of the SMSAs. Turning to white females, the index ranged from 83.32 to 60.58 in 1970, and 78.01 to 54.01 in 1980. In the decade between 1970 and 1980 the index of dissimilarity fell in all SMSAs.

When comparing the indexes of black males to that of white females, it can be seen that, on average, the index of white women exceeds that of black men.[12] This suggests that more workers (i.e., white women, white men or a combination of the two) would have to change jobs in order for white-female distribution to become more similar to that of white men, than would black men. On the basis of this index we cannot, however, make any qualitative judgments as to which group is "better" or "worse" off in terms of occupational structures or occupational segregation. There are numerous reasons as to why the occupational structures of white females may be more dissimilar to that of white males than black males relative to white males. A partial list of these reasons may include gender differences in tastes for certain jobs, tastes with respect to labor force attachment, levels and types of skills, and levels of job discrimination.

The OLS estimates of the parameters in equation (4) for black males

TABLE 2
1970 and 1980
Index of Dissimilarity
by SMSA

	1970 Black Male/ White Male	1980 Black Male/ White Male	1970 White Female/ White Male	1980 White Female/ White Male
Akron	64.55	62.17	73.76	69.25
Atlanta	57.71	43.29	71.73	61.89
Baltimore	51.17	44.18	70.78	61.93
Baton Rouge	74.07	55.00	81.09	71.63
Beaumont	71.52	54.32	83.32	78.01
Birmingham	60.12	48.79	79.74	71.02
Boston	53.73	47.05	68.58	60.41
Buffalo	57.31	50.88	71.33	66.20
Charleston	73.18	53.07	80.02	72.72
Charlotte	70.20	52.47	75.90	65.76
Chicago	42.50	36.54	67.73	59.34
Cincinnati	57.30	52.70	69.78	64.15
Cleveland	46.32	43.95	68.76	63.17
Columbia	72.90	60.50	77.63	64.84
Columbus	59.31	47.98	72.26	62.33
Dallas / Ft. Worth	58.81	48.06	69.40	61.15
Dayton	61.31	50.79	72.67	64.77
Detroit	46.96	38.18	70.52	63.54
Flint	50.58	50.09	71.12	64.31
Ft. Lauderdale	75.18	57.96	75.38	64.35
Gary	51.22	42.77	76.72	72.60
Greensboro	63.88	52.14	73.40	62.19
Hartford	68.83	62.05	70.39	64.26
Houston	55.89	46.56	74.39	64.74
Indianapolis	52.53	48.38	70.12	64.48
Jackson	81.48	61.21	83.18	70.76
Jacksonville	64.44	55.80	74.24	67.10
Kansas City	57.78	47.44	69.26	61.34
Louisville	57.84	49.05	69.60	64.73
LA / Long Beach	37.98	32.20	65.62	56.00
Memphis	60.94	53.97	73.48	66.63
Miami	59.30	48.83	67.74	59.13
Milwaukee	61.05	52.68	70.00	63.96
Mobile	69.58	55.55	79.49	72.51

TABLE 2 (continued)

	1970 Black Male/ White Male	1980 Black Male/ White Male	1970 White Female/ White Male	1980 White Female/ White Male
Nashville	63.34	51.80	72.28	63.56
Nassau / Suffolk	58.08	52.13	71.59	64.64
New Orleans	60.18	53.36	73.14	67.86
Newport News	70.35	54.75	78.48	70.84
New York	33.80	36.35	60.58	54.98
Newark	50.93	43.21	69.92	63.62
Norfolk	68.50	53.84	75.83	69.39
Orlando	73.63	63.38	74.66	66.37
Philadelphia	44.26	39.24	67.88	62.63
Pittsburgh	47.84	47.74	75.56	67.47
Richmond	65.33	58.41	76.94	68.26
Rochester	69.56	60.58	69.23	63.51
St. Louis	50.21	41.67	70.67	64.55
San Antonio	66.52	62.09	71.70	64.17
San Diego	64.32	54.68	70.31	58.39
San Francisco	49.83	42.36	67.82	55.65
Shreveport	73.93	62.15	78.83	69.68
Tampa / St. Petersburg	68.92	52.05	72.11	63.99
Toledo	65.48	56.55	72.16	66.35
Washington, D.C.	55.73	42.46	67.52	54.01
Wilmington	62.60	54.34	77.36	66.47
United States	41.06	34.21	67.78	61.02

are given in the first column of Table 3.[13] The estimates suggest that changes in the occupational segregation level of black males (as measured by the index of dissimilarity) are systematically related to changes in the white-male unemployment rate, the black-male portion of the local labor force, and the percentage of families below the poverty level. The positive sign on the white-male unemployment rate coefficient supports the notion that reduced employment prospects for white males is associated with increased differences in the occupational distributions of the two groups. The positive coefficient on the black-male portion of an SMSA's labor force indicated that an increase in the relative supply of minority workers adversely affects their relative occupational status.

Our proxy variable for general economic conditions in a local labor market, the percentage change in the proportion of families below the

TABLE 3
Estimated Aggregate Equation

Dependent Variable: Percentage Change in the Index of Dissimilarity between Black & White Males (column 1)
Percentage Change in the Index of Dissimilarity between White Males and White Females (column 2)

(Standard Error in Parentheses)

Exogenous Variable	Estimated Coefficient (1)	Estimated Coefficient (2)
Constant	−16.712* (1.720)	−15.794* (1.906)
%CHG IN WHITE MALE UNEMPLOYMENT RATE	0.030* (0.016)	0.017* (0.009)
%CHG IN BLACK MALE PROPORTION OF SMSA LABOR FORCE	0.145* (0.075)	
%CHG IN FEMALE PROPORTION OF SMSA LABOR FORCE		0.289* (0.170)
%CHG IN EDUCATION INDEX OF DISSIMILARITY W/WHITE MALES	0.025 (0.042)	-0.011 (0.027)
%CHG IN SMSA UNIONIZATION RATE	0.031 (0.040)	0.009 (0.018)
%CHG IN FAMILIES BELOW POVERTY LEVEL	0.077* (0.043)	0.002 (0.018)
R^2	0.25	0.26

*Significant at the 10% level.

poverty line, also has a positive coefficient. Thus, as the incidence of poverty rises in an SMSA, the occupational structures of black and white males diverge. This result again suggests that employers are perhaps better able to exclude black males from certain occupations as labor market conditions deteriorate.

The lack of significance of the educational index coefficient suggests that changes in the relative educational levels of black males are not associated with improvements in their occupational structures, as hypothesized previously. Although this proxy variable is imperfect, it appears that the acquisition of additional human capital by blacks does not reduce the observed occupational dissimilarities between black and white males in local labor markets. The SMSA unionization rate coefficient suggests that the occupational attainment of black males is not influenced by union activity in a local labor market.

Turning to white females, the estimated coefficients from equation (4) appear in column 2 of Table 3. At conventional levels, the coefficients on the following variables are significant and have the hypothesized sign: the percentage change in the white-male unemployment rate and the percentage change in the proportion of the labor force who are women. It appears that as the white-male unemployment rate rises, the occupational attainment of white women becomes more dissimilar to that of white men.

The coefficient on the educational index coefficient has the opposite sign of what is hypothesized, and is insignificant. As with black males, unionization has no apparent effect on the relative occupational attainment of white females; however, the incidence of poverty in a local labor market does not appear to influence the relative occupational attainment of white women.

SUMMARY

The purpose of this study was to develop a model that would test empirically whether changes in the relative occupational structures of white women and black men are systematically related to changing conditions in a local labor market. A comparison of the occupational distributions of white women and black men to white men was made through the use of the index of dissimilarity in both 1970 and 1980 for 55 SMSA's. We then presented an aggregate model that tested the direction of the hypothesized relationship between changes in measurable attributes of local labor markets and the relative race and gender occupational structures.

Our results provide some empirical evidence of systematic relationships between changing attributes of a local labor market and changes in the relative occupational attainment of white females and black males. The unemployment rate of preferred workers (i.e., white males) is directly related to differences in occupational distributions between white males and minority groups. For black males, the incidence of poverty in a labor market reduces their prospects for occupational attainment relative to white males. In addition, increases in the relative supply of black males and white females are associated with greater differences in their occupational distributions compared to white males. Finally, improvements in the relative educational levels of white women and black men and higher unionization rates in a local labor market do not appear to affect relative race and gender occupational structures. The substantial variation in occupational structures across local markets seems to warrant additional investigation into the role that labor market heterogeneity may play in explaining these differences.

NOTES

1. Eric Hanushek. "Alternative Models of Earnings Determination and Labor Market Structures," *Journal of Human Resources,* Volume 16 (1981), pp. 239–259; and Barry T. Hirsch, "Predicting Earnings Distributions Across Cities: The Human Capital Model vs. the National Distribution Hypothesis," *Journal of Human Resources,* Volume 13 (1978), pp. 366–384.

2. In this study, we focus our attention towards white females and black males. Black women are excluded from this analysis due to the interaction of race and gender bias but are worthy of further investigation. A topic for further research would be an investigation of how the relative occupational status of black women has changed relative to white women and black men, and the possible explanations for those changes.

3. Andrea H. Beller. "Changes in the Sex Composition of U.S. Occupations, 1960–1981." *Journal of Human Resources* Volume 20.2 (1985), pp. 233–250; Francine D. Blau and Marianne A. Ferber. *The Economics of Women, Men, and Work.* (Englewood Cliffs, N.J.: Prentice-Hall 1986).

4. Blau and Ferber as in note 3; Thomas A. Lyson, "Race and Sex Segregation in the Occupational Structures of Southern Employers." *Social Science Quarterly* Volume 66.2 (1985), pp. 281–295; Diane N. Westcott, "Blacks in the 1970's: Did They Scale the Job Ladder?" *Monthly Labor Review* Volume 105.6 (1982), pp. 29–38.

5. Randy P. Albelda, "Occupational Segregation by Race and Gender, 1958–1981." *Industrial and Labor Relations Review* Volume 39.3 (1986), pp. 404–411.

6. Otis Dudley Duncan and Beverly Duncan, "A Methodological Analysis of Segregation Indexes." *American Sociological Review* Volume 20 (1955), pp. 210–217; Paul W. Miller and Paul A. Volker. "On the Determination of Occupational Attainment and Mobility." *Journal of Human Resources* Volume 20 (1985), pp. 197–213.

7. In this analysis we assume employer discrimination against women and minorities. The "preferred" group therefore is white males.

8. This type of educational index of dissimilarity has been employed by Albelda (as in note 5) with similar educational categories.

9. See Albelda (p. 408 as in note 5) for a discussion of the relationship between the educational index and the index of dissimilarity.

10. Gary S. Becker. *The Economics of Discrimination.* (University of Chicago Press, 1971).

11. The data for the local labor market characteristics were obtained from: 1) U.S. Department of Commerce. Bureau of the Census. *1970 Census of Population: Vol. 1. Characteristics of the Population, General Social and Economic Characteristics. United States Summary.* (Washington: Government Printing Office 1973); 2) U.S. Department of Commerce. Bureau of the Census. *County and City Data Book 1972 (A Statistical Abstract Supplement).* (Washington: Government Printing Office, 1973); 3) U.S. Department of Commerce. Bureau of the Census. *State and Metropolitan Area Data Book 1982 (A Statistical Abstract Supplement).* (Washington: Government Printing Office, 1982); 4) U.S. Department of Commerce. Bureau of the Census. *1980 Census of Population: Vol. 1, Characteristics of the Population, General Social and Economic Characteristics. United States Summary.* (Washington: Government Printing Office 1983); and 5) Edward Kokkelenberg and Donna Sockell, "Union Membership in the United States, 1973–1981." *Industrial and Labor Relations Review* Volume 38.4 (1985) pp. 497–543.

12. This is consistent with findings by other researchers such as Albelda as in note 5 and Lyson as in note 4.

13. In defining the change in each local labor market characteristic, the percentage change (denoted as %CHG) in each variable is used. This is done to account for the relative magnitude of movements in variables.

J24
J15
9 J16

18 9- 203
[93]

U.S.

DO BLACK AND WHITE WOMEN HOLD DIFFERENT JOBS IN THE SAME OCCUPATION? A CRITICAL ANALYSIS OF THE CLERICAL AND SERVICE SECTORS

Augustin Kwasi Fosu

Employing 1960 and 1981 census data at the three-digit level, the study finds that black and white women were employed at different jobs in the predominantly female clerical and service occupations in both 1960 and 1981. However, there appears to be a slight reduction in black female job dissimilarity with white females between 1960 and 1981 in both occupations. Moreover, while employment of black women, relative to white women, in 1960 was observed to be generally skewed toward the low-paying, low-status jobs in clerical and service occupations, there was little evidence of this trend by 1981. The present results, then, complement previous findings at the more aggregative two-digit level of black female occupational advancement since the mid-1960s.

Available evidence points to significant occupational advancement of black women since the mid-1960s. For example, employing generally two-digit-level occupational classifications, Albelda finds a substantial occupational convergence of black women toward white women over the 1958–1981 period.[1] Fosu similarly observes a positive effect of post–1964 antidiscrimination measures on black female occupational mobility over the 1958–1981 period.[2] Fosu reports, for instance, that an index of occupational mobility of black women relative to white women, measured at the two-digit level, increased from 0.74 in 1960 to 0.95 in 1980 (Table 1),[3] suggesting virtual occupational equality between black and white women by 1981. However, does this parity exist at the more refined three-digit level? Using 1981 three-digit-level data for service and

TABLE 1
Duncan Index of Occupational Job Dissimilarity for Black Females Relative
to White Females, 1960 and 1981 (percent)*

	1960	1981
Service	32.1	28.4
Clerical	23.7	20.4

*For computation method and sources see text.

clerical occupations, Malveaux conjectures: "At the three-digit level, black women are segregated into 'typically black female' enclaves where wages are lower than those of white women."[4] Unfortunately, no statistical test is provided in support of this claim. If the hypothesis is true, however, and significant job reward differences exist between black and white females, then the usual aggregative two-digit-level measure of post–1964 occupational mobility of black women relative to white women may be overstating actual black female occupational advancement.

The present study examines, first, the basic hypothesis that black and white women were located in different jobs even in the same occupation over the 1958–1981 period for which black female occupational advancement has been observed. The hypothesis that wages have been lower in those jobs with higher concentrations of black females is then tested. The article will further attempt to shed light on the relationship between the socioeconomic status of a job within a given occupation, "occupational job," and black female concentration. Findings for 1981 are then compared with those for 1960, an earlier period pre-dating the antidiscrimination measures of the mid-1960s,[5] in order to investigate the extent to which occupational configuration at this relatively refined occupational level may or may not have complemented the observed occupational advancement at the more aggregative level over the 1958–1981 period. Specifically, the article attempts to answer the following questions. To what degree were black and white women located in different occupational jobs in 1960 and 1981? Did black women, relative to white women, tend to be concentrated in jobs with lower earnings or socioeconomic status in 1960, and how does the result compare with that for 1981? The empirical analysis is performed for the predominantly female occupations defined as Service and Clerical.[6]

THEORETICAL CONSIDERATIONS

Factors leading to unequal distributions of black and white women across jobs in a given occupation (occupational jobs) may be classified into human capital and institutional factors. To illustrate the effect of the former, suppose that occupational jobs have different human capital requirements (e.g., training and formal education), and that black and white women as groups differ in meeting such requirements. Then according to human capital theory, unequal distributions of the two groups across occupational jobs would result.[7] Furthermore, associated with the lower-paying jobs would be greater concentrations of that group with lower human capital.

Institutional factors may also lead to disparate distributions of black and white women across jobs in a given occupation. For example, the existence of institutional barriers, such as discrimination, preventing black women from entering certain jobs may result in their crowding into other more accessible jobs. This is akin to the "crowding hypothesis" usually used to explain occupational sex segregation.[8] Such crowding, in addition to resulting in unequal distributions of black and white females across occupational jobs, would lead to predominantly black female jobs having relatively low earnings.

Certain institutional factors, while possibly leading to disparate distributions of black and white women across occupational jobs, need not result in unequal inter-job earnings, however. Job preferences may simply vary between black and white females due to differences in socialization.[9] Thus, two jobs with identical human capital requirements may attract different proportions of the two groups. Differences in locational "preferences" (e.g., city versus non-city) between black and white women could also lead to their unequal distributions over two jobs with identical human capital requirements but with disparate optimal location vectors, so that earnings need not correlate with racial representation.

THE DATA AND EMPIRICAL EVIDENCE

A. Data

The data used here consists of two basic sets: (1) unpublished Bureau of Labor Statistics (BLS) data for 1981, derived from Current Population Surveys (conducted by the Census for the BLS), on proportions of black and white women in three-digit-level occupations, as well as female median earnings associated with these occupational jobs;[10] and (2) similar census data for 1960.[11] Also employed are data on the socioeconomic status of occupational jobs.[12] There are usable data for 43 clerical and 30 service occupational jobs for 1981, and 25 each in the case of 1960. However, matching the socioeconomic status to jobs in 1981 reduces the usable sample to 35 and 22 for Clerical and Service, respectively.

B. Independence Test—Race and Job

The first task is to statistically test if black and white women tend to be employed in different jobs in these two occupations. That is, we test the null hypothesis, H_0, versus the alternate hypothesis, H_1:

H_0: Race and job are independent

H_1: Race and job are dependent

For 1981, the chi-squared values are 359.1×10^3 and 606.7×10^3 for Clerical and Service, respectively, so that H_0 is soundly rejected.[13] Similarly for 1960, the respective chi-squared values are 92.02×10^3 and 322.21×10^3 for Clerical and Service and, once again, H_0 is easily refuted. Thus, it is inferable from these results that black and white females tend to be located in different occupational jobs in both Clerical and Service. This finding holds for 1981 as well as for 1960.

C. Occupational Job Distributions

To explain the degree to which the two groups might be located in different jobs in the same occupation, Table 1 reports the Duncan index of dissimilarity over occupational jobs for black females relative to white females for 1981 and 1960. This index is defined as:[14]

$$(1) \quad S^{ik} = (\sum_j | \lambda_{kj} - \lambda_{ij} |) / 2$$

where S^{ik} measures the (occupational job) dissimilarity of the ith group (black females) relative to the kth reference group (white females); $\lambda_{kj} =$ the share of the kth group's employment in occupational job j; and $\lambda_{ij} =$ the share of the ith group's employment in occupation j. The value of S^{ik} indicates the proportion of the workers in group i who must change jobs to achieve an occupational job distribution identical to that of workers in group k.

The results in Table 1 indicate that in 1960, roughly 32 percent of black female workers in Service would have had to change jobs in order to effect their equal distribution with white female workers in Service. For 1981, the proportion was slightly lower at 28 percent. In Clerical, the proportion was 24 percent in 1960 and 20 percent in 1981. While declines in the index between 1960 and 1981 are modest, these results suggest that the relative occupational mobility of black women at the three-digit level does not negate recent findings of their upward mobility at the more aggregative level. Nevertheless, the results still indicate that black and white women in the same occupation are generally located in different jobs.

D. Pay/Socioeconomic Status versus Black Female Concentration

The above results indicate only that black and white women are not equally distributed across jobs in Service or Clerical. However, they do not indicate the nature of this dissimilarity. We now test if there exists a special pattern to the above dependence between race and job. In particular, is there a tendency for black women, relative to white women, to be employed in low-paid occupational jobs, as Malveaux, for example, asserted for 1981?[15] The test consists of measuring the degree of association between black female concentration in a job, represented by the ratio of black women to all women, and the female median wage of the job. The correlation coefficient may be used to measure this relationship. Alternatively, regression analysis can be employed, although no causality from the independent variable(s) to the dependent variable is necessarily implied.

The latter method is chosen for the present analysis, mainly because it allows a more quantitative analysis, than in the case of correlation analysis, to be performed. For example, while the test of significance of the regression coefficient in the case of simple regression is equivalent to that of the correlation coefficient, regression analysis further permits a quantitative measure of the relationship.

E. Regression Results

Table 2 presents, for 1981, regression results of occupational job median pay for females, MDFPAY, versus black female concentration, measured as the proportion of females in the job who are black, PBFFEM. To control for possible obfuscation of the results by female concentration

TABLE 2
Pay versus Black Female Concentration, 1981

I. Regression Results--Coefficients (absolute t ratio in parentheses beneath coefficients) and Summary Statistics; Dependent Variable = Occupational Job Median Pay for Females (MDFPAY)

Eqn.	Const.	PBFFEM	PFEM	R^2	F	SEE	n
A. Clerical							
(1a)	219.03	93.80 (0.74)	--	.013	0.55	51.42	43
(2a)	291.98	51.44 (0.45)	-95.82*** (3.36)	.230	5.99	45.97	43
B. Service							
(1b)	194.06	-14.17 (0.24)	--	.002	0.06	53.98	30
(2b)	197.77	-14.30 (0.24)	- 5.88 (0.18)	.003	0.04	54.94	30

II. Variable Definitions, Sources, and Summary Statistics

Variable	Definitions and Sources	Mean and (Std. Dev.) Clerical	Service
MDFPAY	Median weekly pay for females in occupational job (source: BLS unpublished data)	232.02 (51.14)	191.00 (53.09)
PBFFEM	Proportion of females in occupational job who are black (source: ibid)	.138 (.063)	.216 (.172)
PFEM	Proportion of females in occupational job (source: ibid)	.700 (.250)	.627 (.307)

*** Statistically significant at the .01 level (2-tailed).

which may be correlated with black female concentration, the latter variable, measured as the proportion of females in the job, PFEM, is also included as a regressor in a separate equation. The results are reported separately for Clerical and Service. As these results indicate, the coefficient of the black female concentration variable is not statistically different from zero in any of the equations estimated, though it is negative in Service but positive in Clerical. Indeed, the magnitude of the t ratio in both the Clerical and Service regressions is quite small.[16] Thus, there ap-

TABLE 3
Socioeconomic Status versus Black Female Concentration, 1981

I. Regression Results--Coefficients (absolute t ratio in
    parentheses beneath coefficients) and Summary Statistics;
    Dependent Variable = Socioeconomic Status of Job (SESTA)

Eqn.	Const.	PBFFEM	PFEM	R^2	F	SEE	n
A. Clerical							
(1a)	76.03	−26.60 (0.99)	--	.029	0.99	10.33	35
(2a)	74.71	−25.82 (0.94)	1.71 (0.24)	.031	0.51	10.48	35
B. Service							
(1b)	41.15	−35.0[a] (1.65)	--	.120	2.72	13.27	22
(2b)	43.34	−37.13[a] (1.64)	−3.27 (0.33)	.125	1.35	13.58	22

II. Variable Definitions, Sources, and Summary Statistics

Variable	Definitions and Sources	Mean and (Std. Dev.) Clerical	Service
SESTA	Socioeconomic status of job (source: 1960 Pop. Census, Subject Report, Socioeconomic Status)	72.43 (10.33)	34.45 (13.81)
PBFFEM	Same as in Table 1.	.135 (.066)	.191 (.136)
PFFEM	Same as in Table 1.	.710 (.252)	.542 (.315)

[a]Marginally statistically significant (at the .2 level—2-tailed)

pears to be no evidence in favor of the hypothesis that black women, relative to white women, are segregated in jobs with low pay, in Clerical or Service, at least in the more recent 1981 period. It is interesting to note, however, that female concentration as a whole is strongly negatively associated with pay in Clerical, but not in Service.

There still remains the question of whether black female concentration might be negatively correlated with the broader BLS measure of socioeconomic status. The job pay variable is now replaced with the socioeconomic status index, and corresponding regression results are reported for 1981 in Table 3. While the coefficient of the black female concentration

TABLE 4
Pay versus Black Female Concentration, 1960

I. Regression Results--Coefficients (absolute t ratio in
    parentheses beneath coefficients) and Summary Statistics;
    Dependent Variable = Occupational Job Median Pay for
    Females (MDFPAY)

Eqn.	Const.	PBFFEM	PFEM	R^2	F	SEE	n
A. Clerical							
(1a)	3329.53	-8294.85**	--	.205	5.92	706.89	25
		(2.43)					
(2a)	3781.89	-10763.69**	-595.00	.264	3.95	695.83	25
		(2.81)	(1.33)				
B. Service							
(1b)	1759.54	-373.19	--	.011	0.25	605.68	25
		(0.50)					
(2b)	2033.67	-317.06	-628.04*	.145	1.87	575.70	25
		(0.45)	(1.86)				

II. Variable Definitions, Sources, and Summary Statistics

		Mean and (Std. Dev.)	
Variable	Definitions and Sources	Clerical	Service
MDFPAY	Median annual pay for females in occupational job (source: Occupational Characteristics, 1960 census)	2864.76 (775.98)	1680.20 (596.20)
PBFFEM	Proportion of females in occupational job who are black (source: ibid.)	.056 (.042)	.213 (.167)
PFEM	Proportion of females in occupational job (source: ibid.)	.528 (.363)	.455 (.348)

---

*Statistically significant at the .1 level (2-tailed).
**Statistically significant at the .05 level (2-tailed).

variable PBFFEM is now negative in both Clerical and Service, only that for Service appears statistically significant, and only marginally so.

A question now arises as to whether there was a negative association of the black female concentration variable with pay or socioeconomic status prior to the antidiscrimination measures of the mid-1960s, despite our finding to the contrary in the more recent period. Reported in Tables 4 and 5 are regression results for 1960 bearing on this question for pay

TABLE 5
Socioeconomic Status versus Black Female Concentration, 1960

I. Regressions Results--Coefficients (absolute t ratio in parentheses beneath coefficients) and Summary Statistics; Dependent Variable = Socioeconomic Status of Job (SESTA)

Eqn.	Const.	PBFFEM	PFEM	R^2	F	SEE	n
A. Clerical							
(1a)	77.15	−89.13* (1.74)	--	.116	3.03	10.61	25
(2a)	83.11	−121.65** (2.09)	−7.84 (1.16)	.167	2.21	10.54	25
B. Service							
(1b)	48.19	−53.95*** (3.14)	--	.300	9.84	16.42	25
(2b)	52.23	−53.12*** (3.10)	−9.25 (1.13)	.338	5.61	14.01	25

II. Variable Definitions, Sources, and Summary Statistics

		Mean and (Std. Dev.)	
Variable	Definitions and Sources	Clerical	Service
SESTA	Same as in Table 2.	72.16 (11.05)	36.72 (16.48)
PBFFEM	Same as in Table 3.	.056 (.042)	.213 (.167)
PFEM	Same as in Table 3.	.528 (.363)	.455 (.348)

*Statistically significant at the .1 level (2-tailed).
**Statistically significant at the .05 level (2-tailed).
***Statistically significant at the .01 level (2-tailed).

and socioeconomic status, respectively. In contrast to the 1981 findings, these results show the proportion of black women to be significantly negatively related to pay in Clerical, although not in Service. On the other hand, socioeconomic status is found to be negatively associated with black female concentration in both Clerical and Service.[17]

F. Sensitivity Measures

For purposes of comparison, Table 6 presents, for 1960 and 1981 and for Clerical and Service, summary results of sensitivity measures of association of black female concentration (PBFFEM) with pay (MDFPAY)

TABLE 6
Sensitivity of Pay and Socioeconomic Status to Black
Female Concentration,[a] 1960 and 1981

| | Pay | | Socioeconomic Status | |
	1960	1981	1960	1981
Clerical	-.210**	.047	-.094**	-.050
Service	-.040	-.016	-.308***	-.194[a]

[a] These sensitivity measures are elasticities at the means, computed as b(x/y), where b is the regression coefficient from the respective multiple regression model in tables 2-5, and x and y are the means for PBFEM and MDFPAY (or SESTA), respectively.

[a] Regression coefficient (marginally) statistically significant at the .2 level (2-tailed).

** Regression coefficient statistically significant at the .05 level (2-tailed).

*** Regression coefficient statistically significant at the .01 level (2-tailed).

and with socioeconomic status (SESTA), which are elasticity estimates at the means, based upon the regression and summary statistics of Tables 2–5. First, we note that the elasticity estimates for 1981 are quite small in magnitude, that is, in addition to the observation that the underlying regression coefficients are generally not statistically significant. Even the largest absolute elasticity, that of socioeconomic status in Service based on a marginally significant coefficient, suggests that an increase in black female concentration by 10 percent would be associated with only a 2 percent decrease in socioeconomic status.

Second, the sensitivity measures for 1960, whose underlying regression coefficients are generally statistically significant, appear larger in magnitude than those for 1981. This is true for both Clerical and Service as well as for pay and socioeconomic status. However, even these 1960 magnitudes are not that high. The largest magnitude of .3, for instance, suggests only a 3 percent decrease in socioeconomic status associated with a 10 percent increase in black female concentration. Similarly, the next larger magnitude of .2 predicts a relatively small proportionate decrease in pay to be related to a given percent increase in black female concentration in Clerical. The underlying regression coefficient of –10,763.69 suggests that a 1 *percentage point* rise in the proportion of black females would translate to a reduction in median annual pay of females of about $108 (1959 dollars). This represents 3.76 percent of the sample mean of the annual median female pay in Clerical.

Third, there appears to be a higher sensitivity of socioeconomic status to black female concentration in Service than in Clerical for both 1960 and 1981, suggesting that a negative association of job "status" with black female concentration is more relevant in Service than in Clerical. On the other hand, in the case of pay, Clerical exhibits a higher elasticity than Service for 1960; the underlying regression coefficients are not statistically significant for either Clerical or Service in 1981, however.[18]

DISCUSSION AND CONCLUSION

The present article has attempted to reveal the extent to which black and white females might be employed in different jobs even in the same occupation. In particular, we examined the degree to which black women were concentrated in low-paying or low-status jobs for 1960 and 1981 in order to evaluate recent findings of black female occupational mobility at the more aggregative occupational level over the 1958–1981 period. Two occupational groups, Clerical and Service, which contain the bulk of both black and white female workers, were analyzed.

Using 1981 unpublished BLS (Current Population Survey data collected by the Census for the BLS) and 1960 census data, the null hypothesis that black and white women were proportionately located in jobs in these occupations was rejected for both years. Using the Duncan index of dissimilarity, we observed that in 1960, roughly 32 percent of black female workers in Service would have had to change jobs in order to effect their equal distribution with white women. The proportion in 1981 was slightly lower at 28 percent. At 24 percent and 20 percent in 1960 and 1981, respectively, the proportion was smaller for Clerical although, as in the case of Service, there was a slight decrease between 1960 and 1981. In particular, these results are not at variance with recent findings at the more aggregative occupational level of an upward mobility of working black women over the 1958–1981 period.

For 1960, black female employment concentration was found to be negatively associated with female median occupational job pay in Clerical, and with socioeconomic status in both Clerical and Service. For the more recent 1981 period, however, there was generally no discernible evidence that black women, in relation to white women, were concentrated in low-paying occupations in either Clerical or Service. Nor was black female employment concentration correlated with socioeconomic status of jobs in Clerical. While there was some indication of a negative association in Service, this association appeared marginal. Again, these results do not contradict those at the more aggregative occupational level showing occupational advancement between 1958 and 1981.

The finding of a generally negative association of black female employment concentration with occupational pay and socioeconomic status in 1960, and of little or no such relationship in 1981, is consistent with both increasing relative school attainment of black women and the effectiveness of antidiscrimination measures of the mid-1960s.[19] Both of these factors would reduce occupational job barriers (human capital and institutional) that might be in existence prior to the mid-1960s. Medoff, for example, argues that observed occupational mobility of black males at the *two-digit* level between 1950 and 1980 is probably attributable to antidiscrimination measures of the 1960s.[20] Fosu, on the other hand, attributes slightly over 50 percent of such mobility of black women over the 1958–1981 period to these antidiscrimination programs, and the rest to pre-existing trends, cyclical conditions of the economy, education, and censoring supply factors.[21] It must be emphasized, however, that the association of racial employment concentration with occupational *job* pay and socioeconomic status appears to be rather small, even in 1960 when the correlation was generally statistically significant for Service and Clerical.

The present results indicate that while black female employment, relative to white females, might have been skewed toward low-paying, low-status jobs in Clerical and Service in 1960, there appeared to be little evidence of this by 1981.[22] The finding then seems to complement recent observations at the more aggregative occupational level, showing an increase in the occupational mobility of black women over the 1958–1981 period. However, the current finding, coupled with the observation here that race and occupational job classification are still dependent, suggests that factors other than pay and job "status" may explain the observed dependence between race and occupational job. One possible culprit, worthy of further investigation, is the set of institutional variables governing job "preference" that may not be independent of race.

ACKNOWLEDGMENTS

Grant support by the Research Committee and the School of Business Administration, Oakland University, is gratefully acknowledged. I wish to thank anonymous referees of the *Review* for helpful comments.

NOTES

1. Randy P. Albelda, "Occupational Segregation by Race and Gender, 1958–

1981," *Industrial and Labor Relations Review,* Vol. 39, No. 3 (April 1986), pp. 404–411.

2. A.K. Fosu, "Occupational Mobility of Black Women, 1958–1981: The Impact of Post-1964 Antidiscrimination Measures," *Industrial and Labor Relations Review,* Vol. 45, No. 2 (January 1992), pp. 281–294.

3. The index was computed using BLS data on occupational employment, with census data on median occupational earnings as weights. For details, see Fosu, *ibid.*

4. See p. 22, Julianne Malveaux, "The Economic Interests of Black and White Women: Are They Similar?" *The Review of Black Political Economy,* Vol. 14, No. 1 (Summer 1985), pp. 5–27.

5. Title VII of the Civil Rights Act of 1964 outlawed employment discrimination based upon race, sex and other defined attributes. Racial discrimination was probably the most blatant, however. "Affirmative Action" was established upon the creation in 1965 of the Office of Federal Contract-Compliance Programs (OFCCP) by Executive Order 11246 to monitor the hiring and promotion practices of federal contractors regarding blacks. The system of goals and timetables was required in 1968, and the program was extended to women as a class in 1972.

6. Over the 1960–1981 period, the proportion of black female workers in Service and Clerical has remained about two-thirds; for white females, the proportion has averaged approximately 55 percent. (Source: Bureau of Labor Statistics, *Labor Force Statistics Derived from the Current Population Survey, A DataBook, Vol. 1 (1982).)*

7. This conclusion assumes that black and white workers differ only by human capital. For details see, e.g., Solomon W. Polachek, "Occupational Segregation Among Women: Theory, Evidence, and a Prognosis," in Cynthia Lloyd et al., eds. *Women in the Labor Market* (New York: Columbia University Press, 1979), pp. 137–157.

8. See Janice F. Madden, *The Economics of Sex Discrimination* (Lexington, Mass.: Lexington Books, 1973), pp. 30–36; and Barbara Bergmann, "The Effect on White Incomes of Discrimination in Employment," *Journal of Political Economy* 79 (March–April, 1971), pp. 294–313.

9. See A.D. Brief and L.J. Aldag, "Male-Female Differences in Occupational Attitudes Within Minority Groups," *Journal of Vocational Behavior,* Vol. 6 (1975), pp. 305–314.

10. See, for example, J. Malveaux, *op. cit,* Tables 4 and 5. Note that published 1980 census data lack the 3-digit detail available from the CPS.

11. Source: *1960 U.S. Census of Population, Occupational Characteristics.*

12. Source: *1960 Population Census, Subject Reports, Socioeconomic Status.*

13. The chi-squared value are calculated using: $C^2 = \Sigma[(f_0 - f_t)^2/f_t]$, where f_0 is the observed frequency, and f_t is the expected frequency under H_0. In the case of Clerical, for instance, there are 43 occupational jobs, leading to a 2×43 contingency classification and 42 degrees of freedom.

14. See Gus Dudley Duncan and Beverly Duncan, "A Methodological Analysis of Segregation Indexes," *American Sociological Review* 20 (April 1955), pp. 210–217.

15. See J. Malveaux, *op. cit.*

16. A coefficient of -14, even if it were significant, suggests that a 1 percentage point increase in the proportion of black females would on average be associated with a decrease in the average median weekly pay of only 14 cents.

17. Also presented in the appendix (Table A.1) are the 1960–1981 pooled regression results based on the fixed-effects model. Note that these results are similar to and confirm the earlier results where the estimation was done separately for the two years.

18. Since the underlying regression coefficients are statistically indistinguishable

from zero, it seems reasonable to assume the elasticity estimates, which are also small in magnitude, to be insignificant.

19. For example, the median years of black female school attainment, relative to those of white women, have increased from .80 in 1960 to .98 in 1981. (Source: *Employment and Training Report of the President.*)

20. See Marshall H. Medoff, "Discrimination and the Occupational Progress of Blacks Since 1950," *American Journal of Economics and Sociology,* Vol. 44, No. 3 (July 1985), pp. 295–303.

21. Fosu, "Occupational Mobility of Black Women." For findings of a significant impact of post-1964 antidiscrimination measures on black female relative *earnings* see, for example, A.K. Fosu, "Explaining Post-1964 Earnings Gains by Black Women: Race or Sex?" *Review of Black Political Economy,* Vol. 15, No. 3 (Winter 1987), pp. 41–55; Charles Brown, "Black-White Earnings Ratios since the Civil Rights Act of 1964: The Importance of Labor Market Dropouts," *Quarterly Journal of Economics,* Vol. 99, No. 1 (February 1984), pp. 31–44; and Richard B. Freeman, "Changes in the Labor Market of Black Americans, 1948–1972," *Brookings Papers on Economic Activity,* 1 (1973), pp. 67–131. Heckman and Payner, p. 138, also find for South Carolina that "human capital stories, supply shift stories, and tight market stories do not account for the black breakthrough," and that there has been a "significant contribution of federal antidiscrimination programs" (James J. Heckman and Brook S. Payner, "Determining the Impact of Federal Antidiscrimination Policy on the Economic Status of Blacks: A Study of South Carolina," *American Economic Review,* Vol. 79, No. 1 [March, 1989], pp. 138–177).

22. It must be noted, nevertheless, that black women could still be receiving lower wages even in a high-paying occupational job. This would be so if black and white female employment differed by industry in the same occupational job classification, and black women were disproportionately employed in lower-paying industries. Although this problem cannot be ruled out entirely, available data on black female pay for 1960 (in jobs where there are significant numbers of black women) indicate no major differences between overall female pay and black female pay.

There have also been revisions in the census classification of occupations between 1960 and 1981, specifically in 1971 and 1972. Such changes could influence the comparison over time involving the chi-square test and the Duncan index of dissimilarity, especially if the job compositions of Clerical and Service changed. Fortunately, the revisions affected mostly the predominantly male managerial and administrative occupations (U.S. Bureau of Labor Statistics, *Employment and Earnings,* Washington, D.C.: GPO, 1979: 207). In addition, Jerry Jacobs finds that measures of occupational sex segregation over time were generally invariant to the various occupational classification systems (Jerry A. Jacobs, "Long-Term Trends in Occupational Segregation by Sex," *American Journal of Sociology,* Vol. 95, No. 1 [July 1989], pp. 160–173). It is expected, furthermore, that such changes in occupational classifications would affect women more as a group than black women in particular. Hence, the present results should not be appreciably changed by the reality of these revisions.

APPENDIX
1960 and 1981
Pooled Regressions[a]

TABLE A.1
Pay/Socioeconomic Status
Versus Black Female Concentration
(absolute values of the t ratio in parentheses)

	PBFFEM	PFEM	DPBFFEM	DPFEM	n	F
I. Dependent Variable = MDFPAY						
A. Clerical	−10763.64***	−595.00	11605.00***	−911.74	68	8.24
	(2.70)	(1.28)	(2.66)	(1.42)		
B. Service	−317.06	−628.03	88.22	534.00	55	9.44
	(0.34)	(1.41)	(0.07)	(0.84)		
II. Dependent Variable = SESTA						
A. Clerical	−121.65**	−7.84	95.83	9.55	60	1.09
	(2.10)	(1.16)	(1.50)	(0.97)		
B. Service	−53.12***	−9.26	15.99	5.98	47	2.89
	(3.15)	(1.14)	(0.56)	(0.47)		

III. Variable Definitions

Variable	Definition
MDFPAY	Median annualized pay for females in occupational job, 1960 and 1981, in 1960 dollars (1981 data converted using the CPI and assuming 50 weeks of work per year).
PBFFEM	Proportion of females in occupational job who are black (1960 and 1981).
PFEM	Proportion of females in occupational job (1960 and 1981).
DPBFFEM	D*PBFFEM, where D=1 if 1981, 0 if 1960.
DPFEM	D*PFEM, where D=1 if 1981, 0 if 1960.

[a] Also included in each regression, but not reported here, are a constant and a 1981 dummy variable, D, which equals 1 for 1981 and zero for 1960.
*** Statistically significant at the .01 level (2-tailed).
** Statistically significant at the .05 level (2-tailed).

10

LABOR MARKET SEGMENTATION: AFRICAN AMERICAN AND PUERTO RICAN LABOR IN NEW YORK CITY, 1960–1980

Andrés Torres

This study examines the determinants of wage differences between African Americans and Puerto Ricans in New York City. The empirical analysis, conducted on census data for 1960, 1970, and 1980, highlights two important patterns. Changes in returns to human capital have been more important for Puerto Ricans than for African Americans; and changes in group segmentation structure have had a positive effect for African Americans, a negative effect for Puerto Ricans. The results are suggestive of the notion that the two groups are pursuing different paths of economic mobility.

This article explores the effect of local labor market structure on interminority wage differentials by analyzing the determinants of earnings differentials between African American and Puerto Rican labor in New York City. Published data show that African Americans consistently report higher levels of family income, employment and wages.[1] An interest in examining the potential determinants of this persistent gap motivates this study.

The study seeks to ascertain the relative importance of individual (human capital) and structural (segmentation) factors in the determination of the relative status of individuals within these two groups, both of which have been subject to discrimination. The argument is extended to consider the role of political power in shaping wage differentials among minority groups in racially and ethnically diverse areas. Demographic trends indicate that U.S. urban labor markets will increasingly reflect this heterogeneity.

Segmentation theory posits a historically evolved stratification of the labor market. For labor *in general,* important determinants of labor market earnings lie in the characteristics of firms and their job structures, rather than the productivity attributes of workers. The factors influencing annual earnings differ substantially among segments and labor mobility among them is somewhat circumscribed.[2] In its theoretical discussion, this article assumes a tripartite structure of segmentation: independent primary, subordinate primary, and secondary segments.[3]

The independent primary segment is comprised largely of managerial, professional, and technical labor employed in large firms, who exercise considerable autonomy in their jobs. Access to this segment is determined by such factors as higher education, professional training and licensing, and labor force experience. Employees in the subordinate primary segment typically function within a regimented work environment and often belong to unions. Information networks, including family and community ties, facilitate access to jobs in this segment, in conjunction with human capital factors. Earnings levels are determined primarily through the formal wage bargaining process within the context of the management-union relation.

The secondary segment is comprised of workers employed in the marginal and/or highly competitive sectors of the economy and its workers are assumed to be a residual labor force. There are no major differences in the skill levels of secondary and subordinate primary workers. Generally, in the secondary segment are found contingent labor (housewives, part-time workers), new entrants (youth, immigrants) and workers vulnerable to discrimination (race, ethnic, gender). Large differences in human capital endowments and other measures of potential productivity are not expected to exist between secondary and subordinate primary workers. Earnings in the secondary segment are generally determined through an informal wage-setting process in which personal relations and employers' subjective preference play a conspicuous role.

Extension to the case of *minority labor* induces a consideration of the role of discrimination. Human capital endowments will lag for minority workers if access to schooling and professional training has been limited by institutional discrimination. The quality of a given level of human capital may also differ because of discrimination. This is the case, for example, if minority-dominated school districts receive lower per capita allocations of educational resources. These are indirect mechanisms by which discrimination inhibits minority access to preferred jobs. Access to independent primary jobs may be conditioned by direct discriminatory practices even in the instance of equally credentialed labor. Employers or professional associations may screen out qualified minority applicants because of a perceived interest in preserving the racial/ethnic homogeneity of a particular work setting. In the less preferred segments discrimination may affect access and wages, especially under conditions of high unemployment.

The assertion of political power has been a prominent response to these conditions. The Civil Rights Movement of the 1960s and its constituent strategies of affirmative action and equal opportunity are an example of the exercise of political power. Such strategies may be seen as an active adaptation to constrained opportunity inherent in labor market processes where discrimination has a direct or indirect influence. They also offer a way of transcending the limitations of traditional human capital approaches. In this context, minority labor exerts political power as a way of compensating for barriers in the labor market.

Aside from the employment and wage effects of civil rights legislation, political power enhances minority influence within the public sector through the electoral process. Government is a major employer; it also leverages job-creation resources in the private sector. This is manifested in a range of subsidy programs that support job training activities and minority entrepreneurship.

Finally, political power enters into the process of interethnic competition for employment and wage growth. In the absence of class solidarity, groups of labor may be forced to organize around specific self-interests. Racial/ethnic minorities may perceive themselves as confronting each other in a zero-sum game over employment opportunities. A feature or this competition is the interaction of political power and segmentation structure. By virtue of its impact on affirmative action policies, political power may enhance access to independent primary jobs, as well as facilitate promotions and earnings increases within this segment. It is likely to influence access to subordinate primary jobs by exploiting community ties, patronage relations and ethnically based information networks, especially in the public sector. Within this segment, promotions and wage increases likewise may be subject to these influences. Although least attractive, secondary jobs are preferred to unemployment and the political factor may mean the difference between labor force participation and exclusion.

A brief overview of the comparative experiences of African Americans and Puerto Ricans in New York highlights the differential development of political power in these two communities.

COMPARATIVE COMMUNITY STRUCTURES AND POLITICAL POWER

Racial/ethnic minorities similarly afflicted by poverty, discrimination, and low-wage employment may nevertheless exhibit a differential pattern of incorporation into a local economy. Dissimilar historical experiences will likely ensure a differential interaction between ethnic labor and changing economic conditions. A comparative historical examination of these communities highlights distinctive features accounting for such differential incorporation. A crucial feature that emerges in a review of the evolution of the African American and Puerto Rican communities in New York City is the comparatively greater development of *community structure* in the African American case. Community structure can be defined as the web of sociopolitical institutions, organizations and networks within a given ethnic population. An advanced community structure is necessary for the efficacious assertion of political power.

This greater development of community structure among blacks in New York is attributable to several factors: the earlier, more evenly paced immigration; a more concentrated residential pattern leading to a potentially greater electoral strength; more autonomous community institutions (political, social and religious).[4]

The prior incorporation of African American labor into the local economy appears to have conferred a relative advantage compared to Puerto Rican labor. It permitted the original black settlement to play an important role in the leadership and development of the burgeoning community. In contrast, the sheer size of the postwar migration of Puerto Ricans appears to have overwhelmed the pre-war community. Although vibrant Puerto Rican enclaves existed in the pre-war years, the earlier community was not sufficiently consolidated to provide leadership and influence to the newly arriving migration. The decline in the level of political activism among Puerto Ricans during the late 1940s and 1950s has been attributed in part to the imbalance between the size of the arriving population and that of the established community.[5]

Ironically, housing discrimination and the resulting segregation of the African American community may have facilitated a measure of political power as it increasingly concentrated African American constituencies into areas that assured electoral representation. Public housing projects also figure importantly, since they provide a fairly stable residential environment for a significant sector of the black community. By the early 1960s, about 40 percent of all public housing in New York City was occupied by blacks.[6]

These factors failed to lead to similarly agglomerative effects for Puerto Ricans. Although apparently less subject to housing discrimination than African Americans,[7] their later arrival and generally lower socio-economic conditions forced Puerto Ricans into an even more vulnerable position during the period of increasing housing shortages for low-income families.[8] Obliged to accept whatever affordable housing could be found, and lacking sufficient political power to compete with other groups (including whites) for public housing, the Puerto Rican community faced greater dispersal and fragmentation in residential patterns.[9]

Also related is the pattern of return migration and turnover within the Puerto Rican community.[10] Unlike European migrations, Puerto Ricans did not "burn their bridges" by leaving their homeland. U.S. citizenship, air transportation, and economic instability, both in the United States and Puerto Rico, promotes the flux of Puerto Ricans between the island and the continent. These factors also undermine the stability and long-term perspective that is essential to the development of U.S.-based political action. While a similar pattern of return migration has been observed for blacks who moved north, they appear to retain a longer uninterrupted residence in New York. In 1980, the percentage of New York City African Americans who lived in the same house five years earlier was 54 percent; the figure for Puerto Ricans was 42 percent.[11]

For minority groups, the successful exercise of political power is especially contingent upon a tradition of autonomous socio-political action. Otherwise these communities are thrust into a dependent relation with the dominant political interests. The Puerto Rican community has been hampered in this respect by being subject to the intervention and indirect control of the Puerto Rican government. Some analysts have argued that the Commonwealth government, which assumed responsibility for servicing and supporting the newly-arrived migrants, had a deterrent effect on the development of indigenous leadership and organizational infrastructure.[12] Religious institutions have had a different impact in the two communities, tending to foster indigenous organizations among African Americans,[13] in contrast to an apolitical and dependent tradition among Puerto Ricans.[14]

In summary, a comparative perspective suggests that the African American population has displayed a more developed community structure. This has enhanced the potential capacity of black labor to use political power in the competition for primary-type jobs and wage growth.

DATA, METHODS AND HYPOTHESIS

To explore some implications of the preceding argument this study employs a decomposition analysis on the results of a series of multiple regression procedures conducted on census data for 1960, 1970, and 1980.[15] Table 1 describes the variables entered in the regression equations. Mean values for selected variables are presented in Table 2.

The basic equation is an augmented human capital earnings function which includes a set each of human capital, demographic, and segmentation measures as independent variables. Logged hourly wage is entered as the dependent term.[16] Table 1 describes the principal variables.

Among the human capital variables are included schooling (EDUC), experience (LFEXP), language, or English-speaking ability (ENGLISH) and various interaction terms. Demographic factors encompass residential stability (MIGNONE, MIGNY), marital status (MARSP), head of household status (HH), and children (CHILDREN). Five terms were constructed to represent segmentation variables. The first four are INDPRM, INDPRMCR, SUBPRM, and SECOND, which represent the four labor market segments in descending hierarchy of preferred jobs: independent primary, independent primary craft, subordinate primary and secondary. INDPRMCR is a small segment but merits separate specification because of the unique influence exercised by craft unions. The fifth segmentation variable is GOVT, representing public sector employment.

The measures adopted to represent human capital and demographic variables are those customarily used in the literature.[17] The procedures used to construct the four segment location variables are based on a factor analysis of industry and occupation characteristics.[18] In the regression analysis, INDPRM is excluded to avoid the dummy trap; the coefficients on the other segment location variables are to be interpreted as differences with this segment. Since the theory posits INDPRM as the segment hosting the highest paid workers, we expect the signs on the other segment location variables to be negative, rising (in absolute value) from INDPRMCR to SUBPRM to SECOND.[19]

Government employment (GOVT) is treated as part of the set of seg-

TABLE 1
Table of Variable Definitions

LFEXP	Labor force experience. Calculated as AGE-EDIC-5.
LFEXPSQ	Labor force experience squared. Calculated as $(LFEXP)^2$.
EDUC	Schooling; highest grade completed.
EDUC*LFEX	Schooling and labor force experience interaction term.
EDUC*LFSQ	Schooling and labor force experience squared interaction term.
ENGLISH	English-speaking ability. For 1960: "Mother tongue is English" (asked of foreign-born); for 1970: "Mother tongue is English" (asked of all persons); for 1980: "Ability to speak English" (asked of all persons).
ENG*EXP	English-speaking ability and labor force experience interaction term.
ENG*EXPSQ	English-speaking ability and labor force experience squared interaction term. Note description of English for variations by year.
MIGNONE	Person resided in same house five years earlier.
MIGNY	Person resided in different house, same state five years earlier.
CHILDREN	Number of children ever born.
HH	Person is head of household.
MARSP	Married with spouse present.
MARPRE	Previously married (widowed, divorced, or separated).
SINGLE	Single, never married.
VETERAN	Person is a veteran.
YOTHER	Person had other source of income in addition to wage or salary; includes social security and public assistance, applies only to 1960.
PUBAST	Recipient of public assistance. In 1970 represents "not receiving public assistance." Note difference between PUBAST and YOTHER.
WORKDISI	Person has disability which limits ability to work; applies only to 1980.
GOVT	Person is government employee; includes all levels of government as well as public schools, hospitals, etc.
INDPRM	Located in independent primary segment.
INDPRMCR	Located in independent primary craft segment.
SUBPRM	Located in subordinate primary segment.
SECOND	Located in secondary segment.
LNWAGERT	Log of wage rate. Wage rate calculated as wage = total earnings from wage and salary / (hours worked x weeks worked).

TABLE 2
Selected Sample Characteristics

	BM		BF		PRM		PRF	
N	170		132		88		38	
Wage	$2.14	(1.09)	$1.79	(2.56)	$1.78	(0.92)	$1.44	(0.70)
LFEXP	22.0	(13.2)	22.1	(13.7)	19.30	(11.4)	21.3	(13.1)
EDUC	9.4	(3.5)	9.2	(3.5)	7.7	(3.2)	7.2	(4.2)
HH	0.78	(0.42)	0.25	(0.43)	0.81	(0.38)	0.21	(0.41)
GOVT	0.13	(0.34)	0.12	(0.33)	0.01	(0.12)	0.05	(0.23)
INSPRM	0.07		0.05		0.02		0.0	
INDPRMCR	0.08		0.02		0.09		0.0	
SUBPRM	0.30		0.30		0.22		0.29	
SECOND	0.5		0.63		0.67		0.71	

1970

	BM		BF		PRM		PRF	
N	324		286		143		72	
Wage	$2.84	(1.96)	$2.23	(1.82)	$2.58	(1.55)	$1.80	(1.42)
LFEXP	22.98	(1.40)	23.2	(14.4)	21.3	(12.4)	19.7	(13.4)
EDUC	10.5	(3.1)	10.8	(2.5)	8.8	(3.5)	9.5	(3.1)
HH	0.75	(0.43)	0.39	(0.48)	0.87	(0.33)	0.31	(0.46)
GOVT	0.23	(0.42)	0.28	(0.45)	0.17	(0.38	0.17	(0.38)
INDPRM	0.08		0.08		0.10		0.10	
INDPRMCR	0.11		0.01		0.10		0.01	
SUBPRM	0.31		0.51		0.25		0.33	
SECOND	0.50		0.40		0.55		0.56	

1980

	BM		BF		PRM		PRF	
N	326		428		123		74	
Wage	7.36	(7.04)	7.63	(9.46)	6.57	(6.52)	5.38	(4.40)
LFEXP	19.8	(13.8)	21.1	(14.1)	16.9	(12.7)	15.4	(12.5)
EDUC	11.8	(3.1)	12.1	(2.7)	10.5	(3.2)	11.4	(3.2)
HH	0.64	(0.48)	0.44	(0.50)	0.62	(0.49)	0.31	(0.47)
GOVT	0.28	(0.45)	0.33	(0.47)	0.15	(0.35)	0.23	(0.42)
INDPRM	0.11		0.13		0.18		0.08	
INDPRMCR	0.06		0.02		0.06		0.01	
SUBPRM	0.27		0.49		0.21		0.52	
SECOND	0.56		0.36		0.55		0.39	

Source: PUMS 1960, 1970 and 1980
Notes: See Table 1 for description of variables. LFEXP and EDUC are measured in years. Other variables are measured in percentages. For example in 1960 78% of black males were head of household (HH) and 55% were situated in the secondary segment (SECOND). Values in parentheses represent standard deviations.

mentation variables because it provides additional structural determinations of labor market processes that are not directly captured by the four segment location variables. The shares of public and private sector employment have varied over time, suggesting perhaps that the advantages attached to public employee status also may have varied. In addition, for those who are in nongoods producing industries, the algorithm assigning workers to segments ignores industry characteristics. The segment location of these workers is based strictly on occupational status. Inclusion of industry information for public employees supplies additional information relating to structural factors. The basic regression results are summarized in Table 3.

The objective of the present analysis is to separate intertemporal changes in the dependent variable, logged wage rate (LNWAGERT), into two components: that portion due to changes in the levels of the independent variables, and that portion due to changes in the regression coefficients.[20] The former captures the effects of compositional changes in human capital endowments and group segmentation structure. The latter measures the impact of changes in returns to human capital and segment location. For each race/gender group the results will indicate: (1) the comparative influence of compositional effects versus changes in returns to variables, (2) the relative importance of human capital and segmentation variables.

The specific issue addressed in this article is the presumed relationship between political power and the segmentation process in the determination of wages. Given a more developed base of political power for African Americans, we would expect to find that compared to Puerto Ricans this group derived greater positive effects from: (1) changes in segment distribution and (2) changes in returns to segment location. These two component sources of change reflect two distinct processes. The first component measures the extent to which the political factor may have facilitated a proportionately larger concentration in primary jobs for African Americans compared to Puerto Ricans; it is thus a measure of the effect on wages of group occupational mobility.[21] The second component measures the changes in returns to location given labor segments, the structural counterpart to changes in returns to human capital.

Since no attempt is made to measure directly the level of each group's political power, the regression equation does not explicitly include this variable. Our procedures indirectly test for the impact of this variable by attributing to it some of the difference in segmentation effects that we hypothesize will be found.

TABLE 3
LNWAGERT Regressions

		1960					
	VARIABLE	WM	WF	BM	BF	PRM	PRF
HK	LFEXP	1.29[a]	1.18[a]		1.07[a]		
	LFEXPSQ	−.77[a]	−.72[a]		−1.90[a]		
	EDUC	.52[a]	.45[a]		.42[c]		
	EDUC*LFEX	−.50[a]	.36[b]		−1.28[c]		
	EDUC*LFSQ				1.47[a]		
	ENGLISH						
	ENG*EXP						
	ENG*EXPSQ						
	ENG*EDUC		.36[a]				
DEMO	MIGNY	.05[a]	−.09[a]	.34[a]	.19[a]	.20[a]	
	MIGNONE	.06[a]	−.07[c]	.22[a]			
	CHILDREN	NA	−.50[a]	NA		NA	
	HH	.08[a]	.14[a]				
	MARSP					.94[b]	
	MARPRE	−.08[a]				.57[a]	
	SINGLE		.56[a]			.61[b]	
	VETERAN						
	YOTHER						
	PUBAST	NA	NA	NA	NA	NA	NA
SEG	INDPRMCR	.05[a]	−.05[a]	.23[a]	−.24[a]	.40[a]	
	SUBPRM	.03[b]		.20[a]		.32[a]	−.51[a]
	SECOND			.17[a]	−.22[b]	.44[a]	
	GOVT		.10[a]	.13[a]			
	$R^2/\bar{R}^2$	.14/.14	.13/.12	.14/.03	.21/.16	.28/.13	.33/−.08

For 1970 and 1980 data, see pages 68 and 69.
*For explanatory notes, see page 69.

Also, data limitations and resource constraints prevented the author from introducing controls for other potential determinants of earnings differentials. First, although we would normally expect compensating payments for undesirable working conditions, labor market segmentation may alter this relation. The job structure will be characterized by segments with low-wage/ poor working conditions versus those with highwage/favorable working conditions. If these conditions are accompanied by inter-segment immobility, the existence of negative compensat-

TABLE 3 (continued)

	1970				
WM	WF	BM	BF	PRM	PRF
.43[a]	.98[a]				
−.24[c]	−.52[a]				
.18[a]	.24[a]				
.36[a]			1.18[c]		1.79[c]
−.48[a]	−.37[b]		−1.27[a]		−1.43[a]
					.19[a]
			−.90[b]		
			.82[a]		
	.17[a]				
.03[a]	.04[a]				
NA	−.14[a]	NA		NA	−.24[a]
.19[a]		.12[a]	.19[a]	.17[c]	
.18[a]					
.06[a]			−.32[a]	−.27[a]	
.09[b]		.07[c]	−.27[a]		
−.10[a]					
NA	NA	NA	NA	NA	NA
.03[a]					
−.09[a]	−.08[a]				
−.10[a]	−.15[a]				
−.19[a]	−.24[a]		−.23[a]	−.12[a]	
	.05[a]	.09[a]	.14[a]		.24[a]
.31/.30	.18/.16	.15/.10	.14/.08	.18/.08	.40/.25

ing payments can be found. Thus some of the earnings differences in our sample may be due to this process.[22] Secondly, differential allocation across the occupational structure may arise from the optimizing behavior of individual workers who invest in training activities to enhance opportunities for promotions and career advancement.[23] Independently of any collective political efforts, this may partially account for the relatively favorable segment distribution of African Americans. Finally, the level of union membership may vary significantly between the two groups, leading to another source of earnings differences.[24]

Given these issues, results tending to confirm our hypothesis are to be construed as suggestive rather than conclusive.

TABLE 3 (continued)

	VARIABLE	WM	WF	BM	BF	PRM	PRF
			1980				
HK	LFEXP	$.81^a$	1.07^a	$.89^a$	$.86^a$	1.87^a	
	LFEXPSQ	$-.54^a$	$-.50^a$	$-.45^a$	$-.40^a$	-1.47^a	1.75^b
	EDUC	$.33^a$	$.38^a$	$.37^a$	$.45^a$	$.55^a$	$.56^b$
	EDUC*LFEX		$-.36^a$	$-.28^a$	$-.39^a$	$-.74^a$	
	EDUC*LFSQ						
	ENGLISH	$.05^a$					$.20^b$
	ENG*EXP	$-.33^a$		$-.38^c$			1.78^b
	ENG*EXPSQ	$.26^a$					-2.55^a
	ENG*EDUC						$.24^c$
DEMO	MIGNY			$-.08^a$	$-.06^c$		
	MIGNONE	$-.03^a$	$-.03^a$			1.24^c	
	CHILDREN	NA	$-.19^a$	NA		NA	
	HH	$.12^a$	$.08^a$	$.09^b$			
	MARSP	$.08^a$	$.10^a$			$.25^a$	
	MARPRE		$.06^a$			$.18^a$	$.24^b$
	VETERAN		$.04^a$	$.13^a$	$-.20^a$		
	PUBAST	$-.04^a$					
	YOTHER	NA	NA	NA	NA	NA	NA
	WORKDIS1						$-.23b$
SEG	INDPRMCR				$-.06^c$		
	SUBPRM	$.04^a$	$-.04^a$	$.13^a$			
	SECOND	$-.05^a$	$-.08^a$		$-.07^c$		$-.27^a$
	GOVT		$.04^a$			$.12^c$	$-.30^a$
	$R^2/\overline{R}^2$	.25/.24	.16/.15	.25/.21	.17/.13	.22/.06	.37/.14

Source: PUMS 1960, 1970, 1980. See text for description of data and procedures.
See Table 1 for definition of variables.
Notes: Values in columns represent parameter estimates (standardized regression coefficients). Where no value appears, coefficient is insignificant at alpha = .10 (one-tailed test). The letters accompanying each value signify: a = significant at 1%, b = significant at 5%, c = significant at 10%. NA signifies that variable was not entered into the regression equation.
Symbols at the top of each column are:
WM: White males
WF: White females
BM: Black males
BF: Black females
PRM: Puerto Rican males
PRF: Puerto Rican females
Additional symbols are:
HK: Vector of human capital variables
DEMO: Vector of demographic variables
SEG: Vector of segmentation variables

RESULTS

1960–1970: Changes in the levels of independent variables are much more important for females than males (see top of Table 4). For females changes in segment distribution had a greater positive impact (120% and 16% for African American and Puerto Rican females, respectively) than did increases in the levels of human capital skills. This was especially so for black females, who exhibited a sizable exodus from the secondary segment between 1960–1970. (Table 2 discloses that the proportion of black females located in the secondary segment declined from 63% to 40% during this period; for Puerto Rican women it fell from 71% to 56%). Changes in segment distribution had a negative impact for Puerto Rican males (–5) and were slightly positive (+1) for black males. Changes in segment returns (see "Effect of changes in regression coefficients" in Table 4) had a negative effect on predicted wage for both male groups, but much more so for Puerto Ricans (–139) than African Americans (–47). This result is in keeping with the reasoning that the political factor helped to shelter black males somewhat from the declining importance of segment returns in the 1960–1970 period. Changes in segment returns had a negative impact on wages for African American females, a slightly positive one for Puerto Rican females.

With regard to changes in the human capital regression coefficients, the data suggest that for all groups, except African American females, increases in the returns to human capital had greater positive influence than did changes in returns to segment location.

1970–1980: Only in the case of Puerto Rican females do changes in variable levels register a greater positive impact (a net positive effect of 70%: .97–.03 –.24) than changes in regression coefficients. For all groups, except Puerto Rican males, stocks of human capital levels contributed more to the increase in wages than did changes in the segmentation structure. For Puerto Rican males, changes in segment allocation had a slightly less negative effect (–5%) than did changes in human capital levels (–8%).

In assessing the influence of coefficient changes, we find that increases in returns to human capital variables are more important for most groups, especially Puerto Rican males, than changes to segment location returns. Puerto Rican females are an exception to this pattern.

1960–1980: Two broad conclusions emerge in assessing the entire period. First, changes in regression coefficients were more important for

TABLE 4
Percentage Decomposition of Changes in Mean Wage (Predicted LNWAGERT)

	1960–1970				1970–1980				1960–1980			
	BM	PRM	BF	PRF	BM	PRM	BF	PRF	BM	PRM	BF	PRF
Change in Mean Wage (Predicted LNWAGERT)	.6555	.4343	.081	.4573	.9707	.51	.5826	-.15	.6492	1.2795	2.598	.8419
	%	%	%	%	%	%	%	%	%	%	%	%
Effect of Changes in the means of independent variables												
Human Capital	1	-5	12	15	6	-8	4	97	1	-2	-4	13
Demographic	4	16	190	23	42	-12	4	-3	-20	-11	36	20
Segmentation	1	-5	120	16	-1	-5	1	-24	10	-2	3	-9
Effect of changes in regression coefficients												
Constant	54	372	1507	-147	-42	-265	-48	340	-9	-20	-35	-141
Human Capital	72	86	-1085	192	54	264	85	-429	142	156	62	191
Demographic	15	-224	-632	-24	22	81	24	-149	5	-30	30	19
Segmentation	-47	-139	-12	25	20	44	31	269	-28	-31	7	7
Total	100	100	100	100	100	100	100	100	100	100	100	100

Source: Regression estimates taken on PUMS 1960, 1970, and 1980.
Notes:(a) The figures in the top row represent the absolute value of the change in the mean predicted LNWAGERT.
(b) The figures in the columns headed by the percentage sign (%) represent the percentage of the total change in the mean predicted LNWAGERT contributed by each vector of variables (defined in the first column).

BM:	Black males
PRM:	Puerto Rican males
BF:	Black females
PRF:	Puerto Rican females

all groups. Second, within the component of changing regression coefficients, the vector of human capital variables is consistently greater in importance for all groups. With regard to variations in the levels of independent variables, the results suggest that changes in segment allocation have been more important for blacks, whereas the reverse holds for Puerto Rican females. In the case of Puerto Rican males neither component appears to exhibit much importance.

From the perspective of intergroup comparisons, the decomposition analysis highlights further important distinctions.[25] Changes in returns to human capital variables were proportionately greater for Puerto Ricans (156% for males, 191% for females) than African Americans (142% for males, 62% for females). Changes in the levels of human capital variables were proportionately more important for Puerto Rican females than for African American females (13% vs. –4%). Changes in the levels of the segmentation variables had a positive effect for African Americans, a negative one for Puerto Ricans.

CONCLUSION

The analysis indicates that changes in the levels of variables help to account for the increase in predicted wages for each intertemporal comparison. The influence of this component varies by race and gender and time period. Also, the results confirm the importance of increasing returns to human capital for all groups between 1960 and 1980.

Abstracting from the effects of demographic variables, the results highlight two important differential patterns that are of interest to our discussion. Changes in the returns to human capital were proportionately greater for Puerto Ricans than African Americans; and changes in group segmentation structure had a positive effect for African Americans, a negative one for Puerto Ricans. The latter result is consistent with the discussion on the link between political power and changing segmentation structure. The two groups appear to be pursuing different paths of economic advancement: African Americans relying on access to independent primary and subordinate primary occupations, Puerto Ricans relying on increasing returns to human capital. An alternate view might reason that increases in returns to human capital, which figure so importantly for Puerto Ricans, are also attributable to declines in discrimination resulting from politically based initiatives. Consequently, the political factor need not be linked exclusively to changes in the segmentation variable.[26] As noted earlier, additional controls need to be implemented before these interpretations can be treated as more than suggestive.

If there is validity in our argument regarding the importance of the political dimension for African American labor, it suggests that perhaps other minority groups need to pursue more actively this strategy for social mobility.

NOTES

The author has benefited from the valuable comments and criticisms of three anonymous referees. He is also grateful to Janis Barry, Frank Bonilla, David M. Gordon, and Edwin Mélendez for suggestions and advice, and to Paul Cooney for programming assistance. The author retains responsibility for all remaining errors.

1. Community Service Society, *Poverty in New York, 1980–1985* (New York: Community Service Society, 1987); U.S. Department of Labor, Bureau of Labor Statistics, *The Labor Force Experience of the Puerto Rican Worker* (Washington, D.C.: G.P.O., 1968); U.S. Department of Labor, Bureau of Labor Statistics, *A Socio-Economic Profile of Puerto Rican New Yorkers* (Washington, D.C.: G.P.O., 1975).

2. Paul Osterman, "An Empirical Study of Labor Market Segmentation, *Industrial and Labor Relations Review,* Volume 28 (1975), pp. 508–523; Michael Reich, "Segmented Labour: Time Series Hypothesis and Evidence," *Cambridge Journal of Economics,* Volume 8 (1984), pp. 63–81.

3. David M. Gordon, Richard Edwards and Michael Reich, *Segmented Work, Divided Workers* (Cambridge: Cambridge Univ. Press, 1982).

4. These factors are described at greater length in Andrés Torres, "Human Capital, Labor Segmentation and Inter-Minority Relative Status" (Ph.D. diss., New School for Social Research, 1988). Other sources alluding to African American community structure are P.K. Eisenger, "Black Employment in Municipal Jobs: The Impact of Black Political Power," *American Political Science Review,* Volume 76 (1982), pp. 380–392; Walter Stafford, *Closed Labor Markets* (New York: Community Service Society, 1985); Charles Abrams, "Recommendations and Report Summary," in Aaron Antonovsky and Lewis Lorwin (eds.), *Discrimination and Low Incomes (New York: New School for Social Research 1959).* Eisenger and Stafford analyze public sector employment; Abrams studies the private sector.

5. Angelo Falcón, "A History of Puerto Rican Politics in New York City," in James Jennings and Monte Rivera (eds.), *Puerto Rican Politics in Urban America* (Westport, Conn: Greenwood Press, 1984).

6. José R. Sánchez, "Residual Work and Residual Shelter: Housing Puerto Rican Labor in New York City from World War II to 1983," in Rachel G. Bratt, Chester Hartman and Ann Meyerson (eds.), *Critical Perspectives on Housing* (Philadelphia: Temple Univ. Press, 1986).

7. T.J. Rosenberg and R.W. Lake, "Toward a Racial Model of Residential Segregation and Succession: Puerto Ricans in N.Y.C., 1960–1970," *American Journal of Sociology,* Volume 81 (1976), pp. 1142–1150.

8. P. Jackson, "Paradoxes of Puerto Rican Segregation in New York," in C. Peach, V. Robinson and S. Smith, (eds.), *Ethnic Segregation in Cities* (London: Croom Helm, 1981).

9. Nathan Glazer and Daniel P. Moynihan, *Beyond the Melting Pot* (Cambridge: M.I.T. Press, 1963).

10. Oscar Lewis, *La Vida* (New York: Random House, 1966), Frank Bonilla and Ricardo Campos, "Evolving Patterns of Puerto Rican Migration," in Steve Sanderson (ed.), *The Americas in the International Division of Labor* (Chicago: Holmes and Meier, 1985).

11. U.S. Bureau of the Census, *Public Use Microdata Samples from the 1980 Census, Characteristics of Persons, Families and Households* (Washington, D.C., 1980).

12. Joseph Fitzpatrick, *Puerto Rican Americans* (Englewood Cliffs: Prentice-Hall 1971); James Jennings, *Puerto Rican Politics in New York City* (Washington D.C.: University Press of America, 1977).

13. Glazer and Moynihan, *Beyond the Melting Pot,* p. 80.

14. Antonio Stevens-Arroyo, "Puerto Rican Struggles in the Catholic Church," in Clara Rodríguez, Virginia Sánchez-Korrol and José Oscar Alers (eds.), *The Puerto Rican Struggle: Essays on Survival in the U.S.* (Maplewood, N.J.: Waterfront Press, 1984).

15. The reader is referred to Torres (1988) for a detailed description of the procedures used in constructing the samples and for a comparison that demonstrates general comparability between sample and population characteristics. The samples in this study were created from three Public Use Microdata Samples (PUMS): the 1960 PUMS 1 percent New York State File, the 1970 PUMS 1 percent County-Group 1960 File, and the 1980 5 percent "A" sample of the New York SMSA File. A random-sample generation procedure was adopted to select approximately 4,500 cases for each sample year, of which African Americans and Puerto Ricans constituted 7 percent and 3 percent, respectively in 1960, 14 percent and 5 percent in 1970, and 17 percent and 4 percent in 1980. The remaining cases represented whites. The sample for each year consists of wage and salary earners who reported a positive income. Persons receiving income from other sources as well as wage and salary were included.

16. Empirical tests of wage differentiation by labor market segment are subject to endogeneity bias if data on occupation and industry are used (as they are here) to construct the segment variables. Since a worker's choice of industry or occupation may be based on expected wages or other job characteristics, the resulting circularity creates the potential for bias in the results. Dickens and Lang offer a solution to this problem by modeling a two-segment labor market in which upward mobility is limited because of rationing of primary segment jobs. Their method permits a test of the hypothesis that the two segments are characterized by different wage-setting mechanisms. Resource limitations inhibited application of this procedure to the present work. William T. Dickens and Kevin Lang, "A Test of the Dual Labor Market," *American Economic Review,* Volume 75 (1985) pp. 792–805.

17. George Borjas, "The Earnings of Male Hispanic Immigrants in the U.S.," *Industrial Labor Relations Review,* Volume 35 (1982), pp. 343–353; Geoffrey Carliner, "Returns to Education for Blacks, Anglos, and Five Spanish Groups," *Journal of Human Resources,* Volume 11 (1976), pp. 172–184; Barry Chiswick, "An Analysis of the Earnings and Employment of Asian-American Men," *Journal of Labor Economics,* Volume 1 (1983), pp. 197–214.

18. A worker in a goods-producing industry is allocated to a segment on the basis of the core/periphery characteristic of the industry, and a set of occupational characteristics including skill requirements and the supervisory/nonsupervisory distinction. A worker in a non-goods producing industry is assigned to a segment strictly on the basis of occupational characteristics. Three-digit census categories of occupations and industries are used to classify segments. David M. Gordon, "Procedures for Allocating Jobs into Labor Segments," unpublished paper (New School for Social Research, 1986).

19. Since segment location is influenced partially by human capital variables, and vice versa, the results may be subject to multicollinearity problems, leading to large variances in the parameters. Resource limitations prevented further testing for robustness of the parameter estimates.

20. The approach used here is akin to that in Ronald L. Oaxaca, "Male-Female Wage Differentials in Urban Labor Markets," *International Economic Review*, Volume 14 (1973), pp. 693–709, in which intergroup differences in earnings for a given year are decomposed and an analysis conducted of the residual. More precisely, the method used in the present paper decomposes the *inter-temporal change in wage for each group separately*. It is drawn from David M. Gordon, "A Guide to Onerous Calculations," (unpublished paper, New School for Social Research, 1987). The calculations are based on the results of regressions taken on the wage equations of each decennial sample. The total value for a given vector is calculated as the sum of the change in explanatory power (R^2) accounted for by all the variables in that vector. The amount of each vector's contribution to total R^2 is then expressed as the percentage of explained variance ("percentage of the total change in the mean predicted LNWAGERT"; note b in Table 4) accounted for by each vector.

For example, in the case of Puerto Rican females during the 1960–1970 period (Table 4) changes in the level of human capital variables accounted for 15 percent of the increase (of $0.4573) in the mean wage. Changes in the levels of *all* variables contributed 54 percent (15% + 23% + 16%) of the total increase in LNWAGERT. These effects were accompanied by the changes in regression coefficients which exerted both positive (human capital, segmentation) and negative (constant, demographic) effects, summing to 46 percent. Comparing the sum of percentage change by the two components, it can be said that changing levels of independent variables had the dominant effect (54%) on the increase in LNWAGERT for Puerto Rican females during 1960–1970.

The discussion in the text focuses on comparisons of human capital and segmentation variables, abstracting from the demographic variables.

Note that the constant variable appears in Table 4, but not Table 3. The original set of regression procedures upon which this study is based generated two types of parameter estimates: first, the standardized regression coefficient ("beta"), reported in Table 3 and which is unaccompanied by an estimate for the constant variable (standardization forces the intercept to zero thus eliminating the constant); second, the absolute value of the parameter estimate ("b"), used to generate the predicted mean wage and appearing in Table 4. The regression procedure generates a constant value along with the "b's," which is why this value is shown in Table 4. To conserve space, Table 3 included only the "betas." A copy of the computer output reporting the "b's" is available from the author on request.

21. Since this model is unable to test for the importance of changes in the *demand* for labor, the significance of the entered variables may be overestimated. For example, the rise in subordinate primary jobs for black women during 1960–1970 (Table 2) may be due partially to shifts in labor demand from personal service to clerical and secretarial workers. The latter occupations are traditionally female jobs which underwent significant expansion during this period. This would counter the notion that the political factor was the driving force behind changes in segment distribution.

22. Randall K. Filer, "Male-Female Wage Differences: The Importance of Compensating Differentials," *Industrial and Labor Relations Review*, Volume 38, No. 3 (1985), pp. 426–437. The Public Use Microdata Sample (PUMS) used in this study does not provide information on working conditions or union status, measures that have been used in other efforts to estimate compensating payments. In a related

effort, Barry finds that women fail to receive compensating payments regardless of segment location. She attributes this pattern to gender inequality in bargaining power. Janis Barry, "Women Production Workers: Low Pay and Hazardous Work," *American Economic Review, Papers and Proceedings,* Volume 75, No. 2 (1985), pp. 262–265.

23. Solomon W. Polacheck, "Occupational Self-Selection: A Human Capital Approach to Sex Differences in Occupational Structure," *Review of Economics and Statistics,* Volume LXIII, No. 1 (1981), pp. 60–69.

24. To the author's knowledge there are no scholarly studies offering a comparative evaluation of union membership patterns among the two groups in the New York metropolitan area. While there is a greater representation of African Americans within the unionized public sector (Walter Stafford, *Employment Segmentation in New York City Municipal Agencies,* New York: Community Service Society, 1990), Puerto Ricans are highly represented within manufacturing, hotel, restaurant and building service industries in which unionization has been extensive. Surveys in the early postwar period estimated that more than half of Puerto Rican workers belonged to unions (Eddie Gonzalez and Lois Gray, "'Puerto Ricans, Politics, and Labor Activism," in *Puerto Rican Politics,* Jennings and Rivera, eds., pp. 117–127).

25. These interpretations abstract from the effects of demographic variables as well as the constant term.

26. However, I think it fair to say that the human capital tradition accords only slight importance to the political dimension in determining racial wage differentials. The primary concern is with examining the decision-making process that leads to differences in marketable skills, with negligible, if any, attention being paid to collective group behavior and agency in the political realm. For a representative statement on the human capital approach see: James P. Smith and Finis R. Welch, "Racial Discrimination, a Human Capital Perspective," in William Darity, ed., *Labor Economics: Modern Views* (Boston: Kluwer-Nijhoff, 1984).

Furthermore, this interpretation of the results would not be consistent with the argument made earlier; namely, that the political factor has not been so prominent within the Puerto Rican experience during the period examined. Another explanation for the rising returns to human capital for Puerto Ricans would stress rising English-language proficiency. Table 3 reports that this variable (ENGLISH) attained significance for Puerto Rican males in 1970 and for Puerto Rican females in 1980. Also, the variables measuring language interaction with education (ENG*EDUC) and labor force experience (ENG*EXP) were both significant for Puerto Rican females in 1980. Greater English language proficiency may have increased the quality of education and experience for this group, thus helping to raise returns to human capital.

IV

BLACK WOMEN IN
THE LABOR MARKET

11

RACIAL DIFFERENCES IN MARRIED FEMALE LABOR FORCE PARTICIPATION BEHAVIOR: AN ANALYSIS USING INTERRACIAL MARRIAGES

David A. Macpherson and James B. Stewart

Based on data from the 1980 census, three major findings emerge from this study. First, the labor force participation rate is higher for women in black-white interracial marriages than women in endogamous marriages. Second, the labor force participation rate of wives in interracial marriages, after adjusting for differences in observed personal characteristics, is approximately halfway between that of women in white homogeneous and black homogeneous marriages. Third, interracial marriages are more likely among women who are younger, Hispanic, foreign-born, more educated, previously married, and reside in the West.

INTRODUCTION

Empirical research consistently shows black married women have a higher labor force participation rate than white married women, even after adjusting for observed labor market characteristics.[1] Some researchers point to unobserved characteristics of black husbands such as their less stable employment as a possible explanation of this gap.[2] On the other hand, Reimers argues that "cultural" differences due to the historical experience of black women lie behind this gap.[3]

This analysis extends the existing literature by comparing the labor force participation rates of wives in black-white marriages with those in racially homogeneous (endogamous) marriages. Such an analysis is useful for two reasons. First, no other study has examined the economic behavior of partners in interracial marriages. This void is becoming more important because the number of black-white interracial marriages has been increasing steadily. The number of black-white married couples rose from 65,000 in 1970 to 218,000 in 1988.[4]

Second, this comparison sheds some light on the relative importance of unobserved characteristics of black husbands versus black wives. If the participation rates of black women in interracial marriages and white women in endogamous marriages are similar, after adjusting for differences in observed characteristics, then unobservables of black husbands such as their greater income instability may be important in explaining the black participation differential. On the other hand, if participation rates of black women in interracial and black women in endogamous marriages are similar, then unobservables of black women such as cultural differences are playing a role in the differential. Similar logic would apply for white women in interracial marriages.

PREVIOUS RESEARCH

Economic theories of marriage and household resource allocation have not examined interracial marriages. A variety of psychological and sociological literature does exist, however, on the topic.

The neoclassical model of marriage developed by Becker treats race as a trait that induces positive assortive mating.[5] In Becker's model individuals attempt to maximize gains in a marriage market through an optimal sorting process whereby "men differing in physical capital, education, or intelligence (aside from their wage rates), height, race, or many other traits will tend to marry women with like values of these traits."[6]

Sociologists and psychologists concur interracial marriages are superimposed on a prevailing pattern of endogamy.[7] Murstein argues that two distinct probabilities condition the likelihood of an interracial marriage: (a) the probability of an encounter conducive to the formation of a relationship, and (b) the probability that given such an encounter the probability that a marriage will result.[8] Herr found that the number of blacks in a county, the degree of residential segregation, and the proportion of blacks holding white collar jobs all affected the probability of encounters.[9] This finding is consistent with Becker's view that, in general, the gain to an individual from marrying versus staying single depends positively on incomes, human capital, and relative differences in wage rates. One issue that has been explored extensively is the extent to which deviation from the endogamous norm involves an exchange whereby the lower-caste person gives something extra to the relationship to compensate for the higher status of the partner.[10] Such a view suggests the most frequent observed interracial combination should be a white lower-class female and black upper-class male. In fact, the weight of the evidence suggests that socioeconomic status of partners in interracial marriages is roughly equivalent.[11]

Encounter probabilities appear to be increased by the combination of previous marriage and age. Previous research also suggests that partners in interracial marriages are older, in general, than their endogamous counterparts due primarily to differences in the number of times married.[12] Probabilities of interracial unions have also been found to differ between the native-born and foreign-born.

The work of Reimers provides a critical foundation for the present investigation. Reimers examines the extent to which married women's labor force participation rates vary across ethnic groups.[13] She undertakes a decomposition of differences that enables an assessment of the extent to which observed differences are due to differences in factor endowments or differences in participation equation coefficients. She finds that none of the gap between the labor force participation of black wives and U.S.-born white wives can be explained by race-related differences in characteristics. In fact, she reports that blacks would have an even higher participation rate if they had the white wives' labor market characteristics. The present study provides an opportunity to examine whether the findings of Reimers persist when the test group consists of partners in interracial rather than endogamous marriages.

ECONOMETRIC FRAMEWORK

The empirical analysis uses an extension of Oaxaca's method of decomposing gender wage differences into "explained" and "unexplained" components.[14] In Oaxaca's decomposition, the explained portion is the part of the wage gap due to gender-related differences in observed labor market characteristics. The unexplained part is the portion due to gender-related differences in wage equation coefficients. This study can not directly employ the Oaxaca decomposition since it analyzes a limited dependent variable (i.e., labor force participation behavior). Therefore, the investigation uses a version of the Oaxaca decomposition modified for use in the probit model.

The first step of the empirical analysis involves estimation of the following probit model of labor force participation:

(1) $\Pr(P_{ij} = 1 \mid X_{ij}) = \Phi(X_{ij}\beta_j)$

where X_{ij} is a k element vector of characteristics describing individual i with marital status j, $P_{ij} = 1$ indicates that individual i is in the labor force, β_j is a vector of parameters, and Φ is the standard normal cumulative density function. The model is estimated separately for wives in four types of households (j = 1..4); (1) white husbands/white wives; (2) black husbands/black wives; (3) black husbands/white wives; (4) white husbands/black wives.

The gap in labor force participation of wives in marriage type j and marriage type $\neq$ j is decomposed into two parts: unexplained (UNEXP) and explained (EXP). The unexplained component is the part of the gap that results from a given woman being more or less likely to be in the labor force. The explained component represents the difference in participation that can be attributed to observed differences in the characteristics of the women.

The unexplained portion of the participation gap between marriage types 1 and 2 is:

$$(2)\quad \text{UNEXP} = \left[(1/n_2)\sum_{i=1}^{n_2}\Phi(X_{i2}\hat{\beta}_2)\right] - \left[(1/n_2)\sum_{i=1}^{n_2}\Phi(X_{i2}\hat{\beta}_1)\right]$$

The corresponding explained portion of the gap is:

$$(3)\quad \text{EXP} = \left[(1/n_2)\sum_{i=1}^{n_2}\Phi(X_{i2}\hat{\beta}_1)\right] - \left[(1/n_1)\sum_{i=1}^{n_1}\Phi(X_{i1}\hat{\beta}_1)\right]$$

Following Even and Macpherson, the fraction of EXP due to changes in the kth explanatory variable is defined as[15]:

$$(4)\quad \text{EXP}_k = \text{EXP} * \left[\frac{(\overline{X}_2 - \overline{X}_{1k})\hat{\beta}_{1k}}{(\overline{X}_2 - \overline{X}_1)\hat{\beta}_1}\right]$$

An alternative method for the decomposition replaces X_{i2} with X_{i1} in (2), and β_1 with β_2 in (3) and (4).

DATA AND RESULTS

The data source for the analysis is the 1980 U.S. Census 5 percent A Sample. The sample is restricted to women who are 25 to 64 years old.

All interracial couples are included. However, only 5 percent of all endogamous black marriages and 0.4 percent of all endogamous white
marriages are included.

Table 1 presents summary sample statistics for each marriage type.
The labor force participation rate of women in interracial marriages (68.1
percent and 70.9 percent) is higher than those in endogamous white
marriages (57.8 percent) or in endogamous black marriages (67.3 percent). Simple pair-wise tests indicate all of the labor force participation
rates are significantly different from each other, at the 5 percent level, in
all but two cases. The participation rates of women in interracial marriages are not significantly different from each other as are the participation rates of black women married to white males and women in black
homogeneous marriages. Interracial marriages are more likely among
women who are younger, Hispanic, foreign-born, more educated, previously married, and reside in the West. The finding that younger women
are more likely to be in interracial marriages is in contrast to the findings
of earlier researchers.[16]

Table 2 contains the reduced form probit results obtained in the analysis of labor force participation. The determinants of labor force participation differ across the marriage types in four important dimensions. First,
the presence of a young child reduces labor force participation much
more for women in white endogamous marriages than for women in the
other marriage types. Partial derivatives, evaluated at the sample means,
indicate that an additional child reduces the labor force participation rate
of women in white endogamous marriages by 23 percentage points but
only 10–11 percentage points in the other marriage types. Second, the
earnings of males have a statistically significant effect on labor force
participation of wives only in endogamous households. Even in that subset of households, differences exist between endogamous white and endogamous black households. In the former case, increased earnings of
males depresses wives' labor force participation while the reverse is true
in all-black households. Third, asset income effects the labor force participation of wives only in endogamous white households. Lastly, black
women immigrants married to black men are more likely to be in the
labor force while white women immigrants married to black men are less
likely to be in the labor force.

Several interesting findings emerge from Table 3, which contains the
results of the decompositions of differences in the determinants of labor
force participation for white women in endogamous marriages relative to
(a) black women married to white men, (b) white women married to

TABLE 1
Means of Variables Among Married Women Aged 25–64,
by Type of Marriage[a]

Variables	White Male & White Female	White Male & Black Female	Black Male & White Female	Black Male & Black Female
Labor Force Participation Rate	57.8 (49.4)	68.1 (46.6)	70.9 (45.4)	67.3 (46.9)
# Children Age 0 to 5	0.3 (0.6)	0.4 (0.7)	0.5 (0.8)	0.3 (0.7)
# Children Age 6 to 13	0.5 (0.9)	0.6 (0.8)	0.6 (0.9)	0.7 (1.0)
# Children Age 14 to 17	0.3 (0.6)	0.2 (0.6)	0.2 (0.6)	0.4 (0.7)
Total # Children Ever Born to Woman	2.5 (1.7)	2.1 (1.8)	2.0 (1.8)	3.0 (2.5)
# Relatives Aged ≥ 18 Residing in Household	0.3 (0.7)	0.3 (0.7)	0.2 (0.5)	0.5 (0.9)
Age	42.8 (11.5)	38.4 (10.3)	35.8 (9.1)	41.4 (11.2)
Years of Schooling	12.2 (2.7)	12.5 (3.3)	12.7 (2.8)	11.4 (3.1)
Husband is Self–Employed (%)	15.8 (36.4)	9.8 (29.7)	6.9 (25.4)	5.3 (22.4)
Woman was Previously Married (%)	17.1 (37.6)	32.3 (46.8)	32.4 (46.8)	17.2 (37.7)
Husband's Earnings/1000	18.3 (14.7)	15.5 (13.6)	14.1 (11.4)	11.7 (9.5)
Woman's Asset Income/1000	1.3 (5.3)	0.6 (3.2)	0.3 (1.5)	0.2 (1.4)
Resides in Northeast	22.0 (41.4)	29.6 (45.7)	25.9 (43.8)	16.6 (37.2)
Resides in Midwest (%)	22.5 (41.7)	15.2 (36.0)	18.1 (38.5)	15.8 (36.5)
Resides in South (%)	37.7 (48.5)	30.5 (46.1)	27.3 (44.5)	59.5 (49.1)
Resides in West (%)	17.8 (38.3)	24.6 (43.1)	28.7 (45.3)	8.1 (27.3)
Woman is Immigrant (%)	5.8 (23.4)	12.7 (33.3)	17.1 (37.7)	4.0 (19.5)
Woman is Hispanic (%)	3.5 (18.3)	8.5 (27.9)	7.1 (25.7)	1.2 (10.9)
N	6958	1056	3599	6858

[a]Standard deviations are in parentheses.

TABLE 2
Reduced Form Probit Labor Force Participation Results
by Marriage Type[a]
(T-statistics are in Parentheses)

Variables	White Male & White Female	White Male & Black Female	Black Male & White Female	Black Male & Black Female
Constant	0.576 (1.75)	-1.747 (2.23)	0.216 (0.49)	-0.198 (0.61)
# Children Age 0 to 5	-0.587 (16.39)	-0.315 (4.31)	-0.347 (9.19)	-0.296 (9.6)
# Children Age 6 to 13	-0.166 (7.34)	-0.128 (2.13)	-0.118 (3.78)	-0.078 (3.79)
# Children Age 14 to 17	-0.008 (0.28)	-0.111 (1.27)	-0.029 (0.64)	-0.028 (1.05)
# Children Ever Born	0.003 (0.23)	-0.056 (1.67)	-0.017 (0.91)	-0.025 (2.74)
# Relatives Age ≥ 18	0.008 (0.30)	0. 057 (0.81)	0.097 (2.02)	0.011 (0.55)
Age	-0.015 (0.98)	0.009 (2.43)	-0.009 (0.38)	0.009 (0.59)
Age^2	-0.000 (1.36)	-0.001 (3.02)	-0.000 (1.01)	-0.000 (2.59)
Years of Schooling	0.089 (13.25)	0.093 (6.28)	0.109 (11.20)	0.095 (15.23)
Self-Employed Husband	-0.114 (2.63)	-0.344 (2.38)	-0.183 (2.02)	-0.150 (2.05)
Woman was Previously Married	0.110 (2.59)	0.065 (0.68)	0.162 (3.07)	0.161 (3.58)
Husband's Earnings/1000	-0.006 (5.21)	-0.005 (1.59)	-0.019 (1.30)	0.008 (4.42)
Woman's Asset Inc./1000	-0.011 (3.34)	-0.008 (0.55)	0.085 (1.16)	0.003 (0.22)
Resides in Midwest	0.083 (1.74)	0.089 (0.66)	-0.020 (0.32)	0.037 (0.62)
Resides in South	-0.038 (0.88)	0.238 (2.13)	0.020 (0.32)	0.246 (5.18)
Resides in West	0.030 (0.59)	0.091 (0.76)	0.002 (0.03)	-0.022 (0.31)
Woman is Immigrant	-0.120 (1.72)	0.162 (1.15)	-0.330 (5.36)	0.260 (2.84)
Woman is Hispanic	0.219 (2.37)	-0.359 (2.13)	-0.93 (1.02)	-0.051 (0.34)

[a]To calculate the partial derivative, evaluated at the sample means, of a unit change in an independent variable, multiply the coefficient by the appropriate constant of proportionality. The constants of proportionality are: White Male and White Female, .389; White Male and Black Female, .348; Black Male and White Female, .330; and Black Male and Black Female, .352.

TABLE 3
Decomposition of Differences in Labor Force Participation Rates Between
White Wives in Endogamous Marriages and Other Marriage Types

Variables	White Male & Black Female	Black Male & White Female	Black Male & Black Female
% of Participation Gap Explained by:			
# Children Age 0 to 5	–2.78	–4.42	–1.33
# Children Age 6 to 13	–0.28	–0.31	–0.82
# Children Age 14 to 17	0.02	0.02	–0.02
# Children Ever Born	–0.04	–0.04	0.05
# Relatives Aged ≥ 18	–0.01	–0.03	0.06
Age/Age^2	5.15	8.11	1.48
Years of Schooling	1.03	1.45	–2.05
Self–Employed Husband	0.23	0.34	0.37
Previously Married	0.56	0.57	0.00
Husband's Earnings/1000	0.55	0.84	1.24
Woman's Asset Inc./1000	0.25	0.36	0.37
Residence in Midwest	–0.20	–0.12	–0.17
Residence in South	0.09	0.13	–0.26
Residence in West	0.07	0.11	–0.09
Woman is Immigrant	–0.28	–0.46	0.07
Woman is Hispanic	0.37	0.27	–0.16
Total Explained	4.72	6.82	–1.27
Total Unexplained	5.52	6.30	10.74
Total Predicted Gap	10.24	13.12	9.47

black men, and (c) black women married to black men, respectively.[17]
First, differences in observed characteristics account for approximately
one-half of the participation gap for wives in interracial marriages. The
younger age and greater level of schooling of women in interracial marriages are the principal sources of their higher participation. Second,
consistent with earlier studies, black wives in endogamous marriages
would have a 1.3 percent higher labor force participation rate if they had
the same characteristics as white wives in endogamous marriages.

Lastly, the unexplained differences in participation are smaller for white male/black female (5.5 percent) and black male/white female (6.3 percent) couples than black male/female (10.7 percent) marriages. This finding is consistent with the hypothesis that unobserved characteristics of black men such as income instability may be partly responsible for the unexplained higher participation rate of black women in endogamous marriages. This interpretation must be viewed with some caution since a selectivity bias related to the decision to be a partner in an interracial marriage may exist. Furthermore, marriage-type related differences in unobserved labor market characteristics (such as actual labor market experience) may also be responsible for these findings.

CONCLUSION

Three major findings emerge from this study. First, the labor force participation rate is higher for women in black-white interracial marriages than women in endogamous marriages. Second, the labor force participation rate of wives in interracial marriages, after adjusting for differences in observed labor market characteristics, is approximately halfway between that of women in white homogeneous and black homogeneous marriages. Third, interracial marriages are more likely among women who are younger, Hispanic, foreign-born, more educated, previously married, and reside in the West. Further research needs to be directed at discovering the source of the unobservables that is causing the differences in participation rates across marriage types.

NOTES

1. See Mark R. Killingsworth and James J. Heckman, "Female Labor Supply," in Orley Ashenfelter and Richard Layard (eds.), *Handbook of Labor Economics* (Amsterdam: North-Holland, 1986) for a survey of such studies.
2. See Phyllis Wallace, *Black Women in the Labor Force* (Cambridge, MA: MIT Press, 1980). Income stability of black males also has a major role in some explanations of the rise in households headed by black females. For example, see George Gilder, *Wealth and Poverty* (New York: Basic Books, 1981) and Charles Murray, *Losing Ground: American Social Policy, 1950–1980* (New York: Basic Books, 1984).
3. Cordelia W. Reimers, "Cultural Differences in Labor Force Participation Among Married Women," *American Economic Review* 75 (1985), pp. 251–255.
4. See U.S. Bureau of the Census, *Statistical Abstract of the U.S.: 1990* (Washington, D.C.: GPO, 1990).
5. Gary Becker, "A Theory of Marriage: Part I," *Journal of Political Economy* 32 (1974), p. 44.
6. Becker (1974), p. 44.

7. See J. D. Bruce and H. Rodman, "Black-White Marriages in the United States: A Review of the Empirical Literature," in I. R. Stuart and L. E. Abt (eds.) *Interracial Marriage: Expectations and Realities* (New York: Grossman Publishers, 1973, pp. 147–159); J. H. Burma, "Interethnic Marriage in Los Angeles, 1940–1959," *Social Forces* 42 (1963); J. H. Burma, G. A. Gretser, and T. Seacrest, "A Comparison of the Occupational Status of Intramarrying and Intermarrying Couples: A Research Note," *Sociology and Social Research* 54 (1970), pp. 508–519; K. Davis "Intermarriage in Caste Societies." *American Anthropologist* 43 (1941), pp. 376–395; D. M. Heer, "Negro-White Marriage in the United States," *Journal of Marriage and the Family* 28 (1966), pp. 262–273; R. K. Merton, "Intermarriage and the Social Structure," *Psychiatry* 4 (1941), pp. 361–374; B. I. Murstein, "Empirical Tests of Role, Complementary Needs, and Homogamy Theories of Marital Choice," *Journal of Marriage and the Family* 29 (1967), pp. 689–696; B. I. Murstein, "A Theory of Marital Choice Applied to Interracial Marriage," in I. R. Stuart and L. E. Abt (eds.) *Interracial Marriage: Expectations and Realities* (New York: Grossman Publishers, 1973), pp. 17–36; E. Porterfield, *Black and White Mixed Marriages* (Chicago: Nelson Hall, 1978); J. R. Udry, K. E. Bauman, C. Chase, "Skin Color, Status, and Mate Selection," *American Journal of Sociology* 76 (1971), pp. 722–733; and J. R. Washington, *Marriage in Black and White* (Boston: Beacon Press, 1970).

8. Murstein (1967) and Murstein (1973).

9. Heer (1966).

10. See Merton (1941).

11. See Bruce and Rodman (1973). In addition, this study's data also indicate the socio-economic background of those in interracial marriages is quite similar. The difference in the educational attainment of the partners in interracial marriages ranges from almost 0 in black female/white male marriages to 0.5 more years of schooling for the male in white female/black male marriages.

12. See Bruce and Rodman (1973).

13. Reimers (1985).

14. Ronald Oaxaca, "Male-Female Wage Differentials in Urban Labor Markets," *International Economic Review* 14 (1973), pp. 693–709.

15. William E. Even and David A. Macpherson, "Plant Size and the Decline of Unionism." *Economics Letters* 32 (1990): pp. 392–398.

16. See Bruce and Rodman (1973).

17. Results using the alternative decomposition described earlier are similar to those presented. These and any other results not presented are available on request.

$J15$
$J31$
$J16$
$237-45$
$[95]$
$4,5,$

12

RESIDENTIAL LOCATION AND THE EARNINGS OF AFRICAN AMERICAN WOMEN

Emily Hoffnar and Michael Greene

In comparing the earnings of African American women to three reference groups—white women, African American men, and white men—three principal findings emerge. First, African American women residing in the suburbs are worse off than any other suburban group. Second, central city African American women are worse off than any other group of central city residents. Third, while central city residence imposes a statistically significant earnings penalty on men of both races, no such penalty is found for African American or white women. Therefore, African American women will enjoy no earnings advantage if they move to the suburbs. This finding underscores the importance of including women in studies of residential location and the socioeconomic status of African Americans. A narrow focus on male data to inform policy is clearly insufficient.

INTRODUCTION

Kain's seminal article on the spatial dimension of racial inequality has spawned a spirited debate over the extent to which residential location influences the socioeconomic well-being of whites and African Americans.[1] Indeed, much of the recent empirical literature on the spatial dimension of racial inequality can be viewed as responding to Kain's central hypothesis that residential segregation—coupled with the post-World War II suburbanization of employment—has had a pronounced negative impact on the socioeconomic status of African Americans. Subsequent research on the relationship between residential location and socioeconomic status has produced decidedly mixed results. While Danziger and Weinstein,[2] for instance, find that African American earnings are independent of residential location, more recent studies by Price and Mills, Reid, Sexton, and Hoffnar and Greene[3] suggest that (a) everything else being equal, central city residents earn significantly less than suburban males and (b) central city residence imposes a larger earnings penalty on African Americans than whites.

The purpose of this research note is to assess the impact of residential location on the earnings of African American women. Such an examination is warranted for at least two reasons. First, and perhaps most importantly, much of the extant literature is characterized by a singular focus on the role of residential location in the determination of male earnings. Sexton, Price and Mills, and Hoffnar and Greene,[4] for instance, evidence no concern for how (a) location and gender may interact to influence the earnings of women nor (b) whether this effect is different for African American than white women. This neglect results in an incomplete, and possibly misleading, depiction of the spatial dimension of earnings determination. Second, among the few studies that do examine the impact of residential location on the earnings of African American women, the dominant tendency has been to either compare the earnings of central city African American women either to suburban African American women[5] or to central city white women.[6] We contend that a thorough approach requires a comparison of African American females to white women, to African American males, and to the most frequently used reference group: white males. Thus, there are compelling reasons for revisiting the issue of the manner in which race and sex interact to determine individual earnings.

The remainder of this research note is organized as follows. The next section outlines the empirical model employed here, as well as discusses the data underlying our findings. The following section presents and discusses our empirical results, while the final section underscores the implications of our findings both for public policy activities and for future research concerning the socioeconomic status of African American females.

EMPIRICAL MODEL AND DATA

The primary purpose of this research note is to measure the impact of residential location on African American women relative to three reference groups: white men, African American men, and African American women. More formally, we estimate a baseline earnings model, which controls for sample selection:

(1) $Y_i = \beta X_i + \delta \lambda_i + \in_i$

where Y_i is the log of annual earnings for the ith individual, X_i is a vector of characteristics known to influence earnings (e.g., education), β is a vector of parameters to be estimated, λ_i is the inverse of the Mill's ratio controlling for potential sample selectivity bias emanating from the labor force participation decision,[7] and $\in$ is a stochastic disturbance term.

Equation (1) is estimated for a pooled sample of white males and females and African American males and females. The independent variables included in the X vector, defined in Table 1, are similar to those typically employed throughout the social science literature and, as a result, no attempt is made to justify their inclusion here.

We do note, however, that we follow the recent literature[8] in utilizing a string of dummy variables to capture the effect of residential location on individual earnings. In particular, the pooled model contains five residential dummy variables: the first one indicating whether the individual is an African American female residing in the central city; the second denoting whether the individual is an African American woman living in the suburbs; the third indicating whether the observation is a white female residing in the central city; the fourth indicating a suburban white female; and the fifth a white male residing in the central city. White suburban men serve as the reference group. While suburban white males serve as the primary reference group, the flexibility of the research design employed here also permits comparisons of the residential impact on the earnings of African American females with other specific reference groups (e.g., white females and African American males).

The principal data source is the 1990 Current Population Survey (CPS), March Annual Demographic File.[9] Coverage is restricted to those individuals aged 16-64 and who did not report themselves as being self-employed or in the military at the time of the survey. Data on metropolitan statistical area (MSA) unemployment rates—used as an explanatory variable for variation in labor demand—is drawn from the 1990 Census of Population and Housing Characteristics. This data from the Census was matched and subsequently merged with the individual microdata file from the CPS.

EMPIRICAL RESULTS

Coefficient estimates generated by estimating Equation (1) are shown in Table 2. Column 2 presents the parameter estimates from the ordinary least squares (OLS) estimation with no control for sample selection,

TABLE 1
Variable Definitions and Sample Means

Table 1: Variable Definitions and Sample Means		
Variable	Definition	Sample Mean
LNEARN	Log annual earnings	9.980
SOUTH	1 if resident of south, 0 otherwise	0.272
SCHOOL	highest grade attended	13.727
EXPER	experience = age-school-6	18.398
EXPERSQ	experience squared	471.63
MARRIED	1 if married, spouse present, 0 otherwise	0.581
KU6	children in family under 6 years old (truncated at 6)	0.256
K6TO18	children in family from 6 to 18 years old (truncated at 9)	0.476
URATE	MSA unemployment rate	6.070
OTHINC	Family income less individual's earned income	21,970
GOVT	1 if government worker, else 0	0.169
AAFCC	1 if African American female central city resident, else 0	0.049
AAFSUB	1 if African American female suburban resident, else 0	0.022
WFCC	1 if white female central city resident, else 0	0.123
WFSUB	1 if white female suburban resident, else 0	0.253
WMCC	1 if white male central city resident, else 0	0.151
AAMCC	1 if African American male central city resident, else 0	0.043
AAMSUB	1 if African American male suburban resident, else 0	0.020
λ	inverse Mills ratio from labor force probit	0.173E-06

while column 3 shows the corresponding results from the model which includes a control for selection into the labor force. The selection variable, LAMBDA, is significant—indicating the possibility of bias in the OLS estimation without selection control. The sample selection model also is somewhat better at explaining the variation in log earnings: the model which does not control for sample selection explains 28 percent of the variation in log earnings. Adding a sample selection variable increases the explained variation to 33 percent. Overall, the two models yield strikingly similar results, and we restrict our discussion to the selection model. Given the focus of this research, we shall confine our remarks to the parameters associated with the residential location variables, although we do note that each of the other independent variables (e.g., education), where significant, tend to have signs predicted by economic theory.

How do African American women fare relative to suburban members from each of the three reference groups? Insight into this issue is shed via inspection of the parameters associated with the variables AAFSUB (i.e., the binary variable indicating that the individual is an African American female reporting suburban residence) and AAFCC (African American female residing in the central city). Perusal of these coefficients indicates that, everything else being equal, African American women, regardless of residential location, earn significantly less than all three reference groups: suburban white males, suburban white females, and suburban African American males. For example, the coefficient associated with the variable AAFSUB indicates that African American females residing in the suburbs earn about 50 percent less than suburban white males. Suburban African American women also earn substantially less than suburban white females (WFSUB), who suffer a smaller earnings disadvantage—40 percent—relative to their white male counterparts. An F test reveals that the racial earnings gap among suburban women is statistically significant, with 99 percent confidence.[10] Clearly, African American women experience a racial earnings penalty: they earn less than white suburbanites, whether male or female. How do they fare relative to African American male suburbanites? An F test comparing the coefficient of AAFSUB (-0.498) to that of AAMSUB (-0.206) indicates that, after controlling for race, a gender earnings gap also exists.

So far, our results indicate that the situation for African American women residing in the suburbs is bleak: they earn less than other suburbanites of other race or gender. Results for central city African American women (AAFCC) show a similar pattern: their earnings lag significantly behind those of other central city residents: white women, African American men, and (the largest gap) central city white men. For example, comparison between coefficients of AAFCC (–.515) and the variable indicating white male central city residence, WMCC (–.089), indicates that among central city residents—and after controlling for many earnings-relevant characteristics—African American women earn about half of what comparable suburban white men earn. Similar, although smaller

TABLE 2
OLS Log Earnings Equations, Without and With Selection Control. 25078 Observations, (t statistics) *90%, **95%, ***99% Confidence

	OLS without selection $R^2 = 0.285$, F = 623.58	OLS with selection $R^2 = 0.328$, F = 720.80
	Table 2: OLS log earnings equations, without and with selection control. 25078 observations, (t statistics) *90%, **95%, ***99% confidence	
Constant	8.028*** (0.038)	8.027*** (0.037)
SOUTH	-0.072*** (0.010)	-0.072*** (0.010)
SCHOOL	0.114*** (0.002)	0.114*** (0.002)
EXPER	0.050*** (0.001)	0.050*** (0.001)
EXPERSQ	-0.001*** (0.000)	-0.001*** (0.000)
MARRIED	0.169*** (0.010)	0.169*** (0.009)
KU6	-0.020*** (0.008)	-0.020*** (0.008)
K6TO18	-0.040*** (0.005)	-0.040*** (0.005)
URATE	0.002 (0.004)	0.002 (0.003)
GOVT	0.054*** (0.012)	0.054*** (0.011)
AAFCC	-0.515*** (0.021)	-0.515*** (0.021)
AAFSUB	-0.498*** (0.030)	-0.498*** (0.029)
WFCC	-0.400*** (0.014)	-0.400*** (0.014)
WFSUB	-0.402*** (0.011)	-0.402*** (0.011)
WMCC	-0.089*** (0.013)	-0.089*** (0.013)
AAMCC	-0.308*** (0.022)	-0.308*** (0.022)
AAMSUB	-0.206*** (0.032)	-0.206*** (0.031)
λ		0.425*** (0.011)

in magnitude, results emerge when comparing central city African American women to the other two groups of central city residents: F tests confirm that these earnings differentials are statistically significant. In conclusion, the choice of reference group is not responsible for the bleak earnings outlook of African American women.

The research reported here indicates that central city African American women earn less than comparably skilled white males, white females, and African American males. This is true whether the reference groups are central city residents or suburbanites. Given this result, the question arises: would central city African American women be better off in the suburbs?

One finding emerging from the extant literature on the spatial dimension of male earnings determination is that, ceteris paribus, central city residents earn significantly less than suburbanites. Vroman and Greenfield, Price and Mills, and Sexton find that central city residence imposes an earnings penalty on the earnings of white and African American males, with the effect being more pronounced on the latter. Greene and Hoffnar[11] report similar results in their recent study of the impact of residential location on the earnings of white and Hispanic males. One might expect African American women to experience a central city earnings penalty. We find no such penalty: regardless of residential location, African American women earn approximately 50 percent less than suburban white males. This stands in contrast to the results for African American and white males. Among men, central city residents suffer a significant earnings disadvantage. Results in Table 2 show that white males suffer an 8.9 percent earnings penalty for central city residence: the coefficient of WMCC is -0.089. African American men also earn significantly less when they reside in the central city: the coefficients of AAMCC and AAMSUB are -0.308 and -0.206 respectively. While the coefficients of AAFCC are slightly larger in magnitude than the coefficients of AAFSUB in each regression, Wald tests indicate that, in each case, there is no statistically significant difference between the coefficients. Evidence therefore suggests that residential location has no impact on African American female earnings. Like their African American counterparts, white women also experience no significant earnings differential related to residential location.

CONCLUSIONS

This research note examines the impact of residential location on the earnings of African American women. African American women are compared to three reference groups: (1) white women, white males, and African American males. The results of this research are consistent with the hypotheses that, ceteris paribus, (a) African American women residing in the suburbs are worse off (i.e., have lower earnings) than other suburban groups, (b) the earnings of central city African American women are significantly below those of any other group of central city residents, and (c) African American—as well as white women—in the suburbs fare no better than those in the central city. One implication of these results is that efforts to raise the earnings of white and African American females by increasing their access to suburban labor markets (e.g., increased and better transportation from the central city to the suburbs) is unlikely to appreciably change their mean earnings; while—everything else being equal—relocation to the suburbs is predicted to raise the earnings of both white and African American males, such a change in residential status produces no significant increase in the earnings of white and African American females.

How can these results be explained? We believe our results suggest that "race and gender, not space" determines the relative economic status of African American females. That women, for instance, experience no significant earnings penalty associated with central city residence may reflect the possibility that occupational discrimination against females is relatively invariant across geographical areas. To the extent that this is true—a hypothesis that these authors is currently examining—one would not expect significant differences in the earnings of central city and suburban females. In contrast, males who gain access to suburban labor markets may experience substantial improvement in their occupational status, thereby giving rise to an earnings penalty associated with central city residence. Moreover, it seems equally clear that race continues to play an important role in shaping socioeconomic status: Regardless of residential location, African Americans earn significantly less than comparably skilled whites. With regard to African American females, problems of gender discrimination are undoubtedly compounded by racial discrimination, thereby ensuring that, regardless of residential location, they occupy the lowest positions in the labor market. We believe that the results of this study underscore the importance of directing future research toward explicating the manner in which race and gender interact to determine the relative economic status of African American women.

NOTES

1. See John F. Kain, "Housing segregation, Negro employment, and metropolitan decentralization," *Quarterly Journal of Economics,* 82, 2 (1968), 175–97; also see Duran Jr. Bell, "Residential location, economic performance, and public employment," in *Patterns of Racial Discrimination,* ed. G.M. Von Furstenburg, A.R. Horowitz, and B. Harrison (Lexington, Mass.: Lexington Books, 1974); Sheldon Danziger and Michael Weinstein, "Employment location and wage rates of poverty-area residents," *Journal of Urban Economics,* 3 (1976), 127–45; Emily Hoffnar, and Michael Greene, "Residential location and the earnings of white and Hispanic men," *Applied Economics Letters,* 1 (1994a), 127–31; Emily Hoffnar and Michael Greene (1994b), "The impact of central city residence on the earnings of white and African American males: a bivariate selectivity approach," unpublished manuscript. Richard Price and Edwin Mills, "Race and residence in earnings determination," *Journal of Urban Economics,* 18 (1985), 1–18. Clifford E. Reid, "The effect of residential location on the wages of black women and white women," *Journal of Urban Economics,* 18 (1985), 350–63; Edwin A. Sexton, "Residential location, workplace location, and black earnings," *Review of Regional Studies,* 17, 1 (1991), 11–20.
2. See Danziger and Weinstein (1976).
3. See Price and Mills (1985); Reid (1985); Sexton (1991); and Hoffnar and Greene (1994b).
4. See Price and Mills (1985); Sexton (1991); and Hoffnar and Greene (1994b).
5. See Bell (1974).
6. See Reid (1985).
7. See James Heckman, (1979) "Sample selection bias as a specification error," *Econometrica,* 47, 153–61. Labor force participation probit results, while not presented here, are available from the authors.
8. See Price and Mills, "Race and residence in earnings determination," *Journal of Urban Economics,* 19 (1985), 1–18; Edward Sexton, "Residential location, workplace location, and black earnings," *Review of Regional Studies,* 17, 1(1991), 11–20; Vroman and Greenfield, "Are blacks making it in the suburbs? Some evidence on intrametropolitan spatial segmentation," *Journal of Urban Economics,* 7, (1980), 155–67; and Hoffnar and Greene (1994b).
9. U.S. Department of Commerce, Bureau of the Census. *Current Population Survey: Annual Demographic File 1990* [Computer file]. 2nd release. Washington, DC: U.S. Department of Commerce, Bureau of the Census [producer], 1991. Ann Arbor, MI: Inter-university Consortium for Political and Social Research [distributor], 1991.
10. F tests are performed to test eight hypotheses (* indicates rejection of the hypothesis, with 99% confidence): AAFCC=AAFSUB, AAFSUB=WFSUB*, AAFCC=WFCC*, AAFSUB=AAMSUB*, AAFCC=AAMCC*, AAFCC=WMCC*, AAMCC=AAMSUB*, WFCC=WFSUB. Results hold for both models (with and without sample selection).
11. See Hoffnar and Greene (1994a).

V

STRUCTURAL UNEMPLOYMENT
AND JOB DISPLACEMENT

J31   J15   249 - 60
U.S.   J71   (92)

13

VACANCIES, UNEMPLOYMENT, AND BLACK AND WHITE WAGE EARNINGS: 1956–1983

Don Mar

Utilizing recent developments in the literature on vacancies and unemployment, the effects of changes in the vacancy to unemployment ratio on black and white wage earnings are examined. The primary result argues that black women's wage earnings are less sensitive to changes in the national vacancy to unemployment ratios than white earnings. Another way of interpreting this result is that black women are not experiencing wage gains when new jobs are created. This finding suggests that black women may not experience increases in earnings if the vacancy to unemployment ratio increases in the future.

Recent attention has been paid to incorporating vacancy rates as an important factor in macroeconomic theory and wage determination. Much of the focus has been on developing theoretical models of the business cycle and the effects of output shocks on wages and unemployment using vacancies as an explicit element of these models. In addition, vacancy rates have been used to empirically examine structural shifts in the macroeconomy, particularly long-run increases in unemployment rates.[1] However, there has been little empirical research on the effect of vacancies on black and white wages. In this article, I examine the effects of changes in the vacancy rate to unemployment rate ratio on wage earnings by race and gender.

Hansen originally presented a rigorous model of vacancies, unemployment, and wages in 1970.[2] However, the lack of vacancy rate data in the United States hampered new work in this area. Recently, Katherine Abraham's study of the Conference Board's help-wanted index found that an adjusted help-wanted index served as a usable proxy for vacancies.[3] The index is based on the number of help-wanted advertisements in newspapers in 51 large cities.[4] Abraham was able to make adjustments to the Conference Board's raw index for factors that could bias the index upward. Her empirical work centered on simultaneous increases in unemployment and vacancies over time that is indicative of structural unemployment—changes in the structure of the U.S. economy characterized by mismatches in worker skills and job skill requirements.

Blanchard and Diamond employ Abraham's adjusted help-wanted index to empirically test a simple macroeconomic model of vacancies and unemployment with the goal of distinguishing causes for movements in the vacancy-unemployment relationship (basically to distinguish movements along the "Beveridge Curve" from shifts of the curve itself) over the last three decades.[5] Although they were able to confirm Abraham's conclusion that the Beveridge Curve has moved out, they stopped short of examining the effects of this outward movement on wages.

Pissarides developed a theoretical model of the short-run dynamics of vacancies, unemployment, and wages.[6] Wages are positively related to the vacancy-unemployment ratio (henceforth called the v-u ratio). In Pissarides's model, vacancies and unemployment exist simultaneously in the economy with workers and firms both engaged in search for suitable worker-job matches. A suitable worker-job match yields a surplus determined by the productivity of a match. The division of this surplus between a worker and the firm depends on Nash bargains, with the relative bargaining strength of the worker depending on the worker's reservation wage, the firm's capital cost for idle capital, the productivity of the job, and finally the v-u ratio. Increases in the v-u ratio are assumed to increase the bargaining power of workers in the firm-worker bargain over wages. Thus, the v-u ratio is positively related to wages. However, Pissarides did not examine the wage to v-u ratio relationship empirically.

My study relies heavily on the model developed by Pissarides and the adjusted help-wanted index of Abraham. To briefly summarize the major conclusion, I find that black women's wage earnings are *not* sensitive to changes in the v-u ratio whereas white men and women's wage earnings are significantly related to the v-u ratio. The results for black men are mixed. Until the late 1970s and early 1980s the long-term trend was of decreasing v-u ratios.[7] However, since the early 1980s, this trend has reversed, with v-u ratios in the United States increasing.[8] This implies that black women's wage earnings will not experience increases in earnings if the v-u ratio continues to increase in the United States as expected.

I begin with a brief discussion of the data, particularly the adjusted help-wanted index and the v-u ratios for four demographic groups: black men, black women, white men, and white women. The data section is followed by econometric evidence on the relationship between wage earnings and v-u ratios for each of the four groups. Various tests of robustness will be applied to the major finding of less sensitivity to v-u ratios for black women. I end with a discussion of the results.

VACANCY RATE TO UNEMPLOYMENT RATE RATIOS

As mentioned earlier, empirical studies of the vacancy-unemployment relationship had been hampered until Abraham's careful study on the help-wanted index as a proxy for vacancies in the United States. Her study finds that the help-wanted index, normalized by the level of employment, has drifted upward due to declines in competition in the newspaper industry, changes in employer advertising practices, and changes in the occupational composition of employment. She is able to calculate adjustments for these factors to derive an adjusted, normalized help-wanted index as a proxy for the vacancy rate. She finds that this normalized, help-wanted index is highly correlated with the Minnesota vacancy rate index, which is the only reliable vacancy rate data available in the United States.

I employ Abraham's methodology to derive annual vacancy rate proxies for white men, white women, black men, and black women for the period 1955–1983.[9] I assume that the help-wanted index is a proxy for vacancies for all four groups, normalize the help-wanted index with the employment level of each group, and finally employ the adjustments given by Abraham to obtain vacancy measures for the four groups.

The adjusted, normalized help-wanted indices are then used to calculate proxy v-u ratios for the four groups (shown in Figure 1).[10] They show an increase in v-u ratio from the late 1950s until the late 1960s. From a peak in 1969, the proxy v-u ratio has a downward trend that appears to bottom out in the early 1980s.

The logarithm of median real wage earnings for full-time workers from 1956 to 1983 for the four groups are shown in Figure 2.[11] There is some apparent relationship between the v-u ratio and wage earnings with both wage earnings and v-u ratios increasing from the mid-1950s until the early 1970s. However, by the mid-1970s, wage earnings had flatted out while v-u ratios decreased.

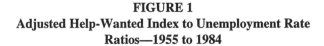

FIGURE 1
Adjusted Help-Wanted Index to Unemployment Rate
Ratios—1955 to 1984

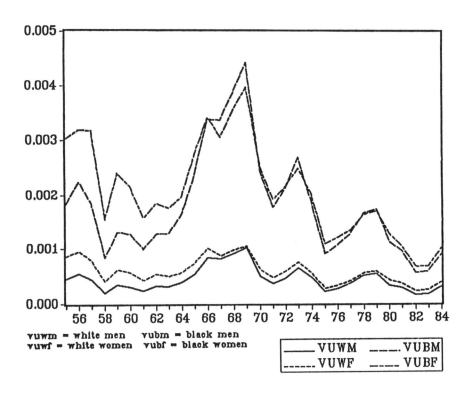

ECONOMETRIC TESTS

The basic model is suggested by both Pissarides and by Blanchard and Diamond where wages are assumed to be a function of the v-u ratio and job productivity.[12] Again, increases in the v-u ratio are assumed to increase the bargaining power of employees relative to firms, moving wages upward. The basic estimated equation is:

$$\text{lnwage}_t = b_0 + b_1 * vu_t + b_2 * ed_t + u_i$$

where: lnwage = natural log of median real wage earnings; vu = adjusted, normalized help-wanted index divided by the unemployment rate; and ed = median years of educational attainment of the labor force; u_i = random

FIGURE 2
Log of Real Wage Earnings for Full-Time
Workers—1956 to 1983

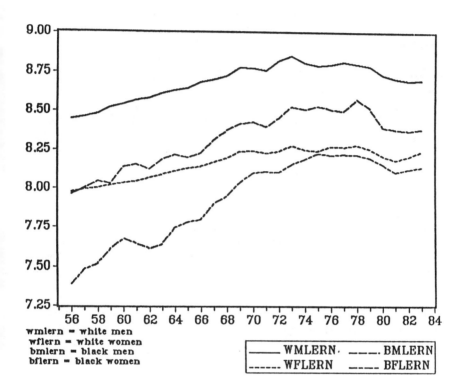

wmlern = white men
wflern = white women
bmlern = black men
bflern = black women

———— WMLERN·	— — —. BMLERN
------ WFLERN	— — — BFLERN

disturbance term; and t = time. The time period contained by the data is from 1956 to 1983. From the previous discussion, the expected sign of the vacancy-unemployment parameter should be positive. Higher vacancies relative to unemployment should increase the relative bargaining power of workers relative to employers. The educational attainment variable is intended to control for productivity changes in the labor force over time. Pissarides argues that the size of the surplus and thus the wage depends on the productivity of the job. Alternatively, human capital argues for an increase in wages with education so the expected sign of the education variable should be positive. Separate regressions are estimated for each of the four groups. The means of the independent variables are shown in Table 1.[13]

TABLE 1
Means of Independent and Dependent Variables

Variable	White Men	White Women	Black Men	Black Women
v–u ratio (*1000)	0.434	0.575	1.814	2.070
median years of education	12.329	12.454	10.600	11.371
log of real wage earnings	8.687	8.162	8.310	7.926

Data sources: vacancy proxies constructed as described in the text. Help–wanted index provided by the Conference Board. Employment data from Dept. of Labor, *Labor Force Statistics Derived from the Current Population Survey: 1948–1987*. Adjustments to the help–wanted index provided by Abraham, "Help–Wanted Advertising, Job Vacancies, and Unemployment," *Brookings Papers on Economic Activity*. Unemployment rates and median years of school completed by the labor force from *Employment and Training Report of the President*. Median wage and salary earnings from U.S. Bureau of the Census, *Current Population Reports, Series P–60*. Real earnings obtained by deflating by the CPI, *Statistical Abstract of the United States, 1990*.

Table 2 shows the results of the estimated equations and the regression statistics. Almost all the parameter estimates have the anticipated positive signs for both the v-u ratio and education parameters. The notable difference in the wage regressions across gender and race is the lack of statistical significance for the v-u ratio for black women. The parameter estimates on education are consistent with the Pissarides's model as well as human capital with wages increasing with education.

Elasticity estimates of the effects of changes in the vacancy-unemployment ratio based on the parameter estimates are of interest. The elasticity estimates are 0.068, 0.073, and 0.048 for white men, white women, and black men respectively. These estimates imply that wages for blacks are not as sensitive to changes in the vacancy-unemployment ratio as wages of white workers. In addition, the low elasticities are consistent with Pissarides's discussion of the sluggish adjustment of wages to changes in the v-u ratio.

The Durbin-Watson statistics for the simple regressions, however, indicate the presence of positive serial correlation in the estimates or model misspecification. Various methods were utilized to remove the serial correlation and adjust for the possible misspecification. The first method

TABLE 2
Regression Results on the Natural Log of Median
Real Wage Earnings: 1956–1983

Ind. Variable	White Men	White Women	Black Men	Black Women
v–u ratio	156.338***	127.896**	27.460**	–10.798
	(39.868)	(51.183)	(10.554)	(17.366)
education	0.317***	0.612***	0.103***	0.207***
	(0.026)	(0.078)	(0.006)	(0.012)
constant	4.706***	0.465	7.162***	5.594***
	(0.329)	(0.982)	(0.077)	(0.129)
Adjusted R^2	0.848	0.702	0.905	0.924
SEE	0.047	0.053	0.054	0.074
DW Statistic	0.358	0.366	0.811	0.442

Notes: Standard errors are included in the parentheses. DW statistic is the Durbin–Watson statistic; SEE is the standard error of the estimate. * means that the parameter estimate is statistically different from zero at the 0.05 level of significance; ** at the 0.01 level of significance; *** at the 0.001 level of significance. All tests are one–tail tests.

was to control for the serial correlation using the Cochrane-Orcutt technique. Table 3 gives results for the model adjusted for serial correlation using this technique.

The estimated parameters on the adjusted model show a different pattern from the original model. The parameters for the v-u ratios are positive and significant for white men and women, but not for black men. Again, the v-u ratio does not affect black women's wages. The signs and significance of the education variables are changed, with most of the parameters becoming nonsignificant. The estimated elasticities for white men and white women are smaller, with the elasticity for white men equal to 0.038 and for white women equal to 0.027.

I also employ alterantive specifications of the model to further test the robustness of the results. Smith and Welch argue that in addition to changes in education, location and EEOC programs have affected wages in the post-World War II period.[14] I controlled these factors using different specifications of the basic model. Location was controlled in the

TABLE 3
Regression Results on the Natural Log of Median Real Wage Earnings:
1956–1983. Estimated with autocorrelation coefficient

Ind. Variable	White Men	White Women	Black Men	Black Women
v–u ratio	88.889***	47.121*	21.037	5.475
	(23.959)	(23.385)	(13.511)	(13.927)
education	0.004	–0.013	0.091***	–0.027
	(0.064)	(0.107)	(0.017)	(0.083)
constant	8.700***	8.426***	7.313***	8.610***
	(1.000)	(1.376)	(0.195)	(1.086)
Adjusted R^2	0.968	0.956	0.927	0.973
SEE	0.020	0.019	0.045	0.041
Autocorr. coefficient	0.895***	0.917***	0.611**	0.919***
	(0.034)	(0.039)	(0.178)	(0.027)
DW Statistic	1.384	1.437	2.044	1.365

Notes: Standard errors are included in the parentheses. DW statistic is the Durbin–Watson statistic; SEE is the standard error of the estimate. * means that the parameter estimate is statistically different from zero at the 0.05 level of significance; ** at the 0.01 level of significance; *** at the 0.001 level of significance. All tests are one–tail tests.

black wage regressions using a variable for the percentage of blacks living in the South. The expected sign of the coefficient for this variable is negative. (See Table 4.) I also attempted to control for the impact of EEOC programs using a time dummy for years after 1965. The anticipated sign for the post-1965 dummy is positive as EEOC programs should assist black workers in obtaining higher wage jobs. As yet another alternative, I also used a time dummy covering only the years 1965–1974, as Smith and Welch argue that EEOC programs had only a limited impact on wages during these years. (See Table 5.) Finally, I employ the Ramsey RESET test of misspecification for the original Cochrane-Orcutt estimates and find the F-statistics to be insignificant for all four groups, indicating that omitted variables are not a likely problem.[15] In all cases, black women's earnings were still not statistically related to the v-u ratio.

TABLE 4
Regression Results on the Natural Log of Median Real Wage Earnings: 1956–1983

Ind. Variable	Black Men	Black Women
v–u ratio	30.381*	0.707
	(15.430)	(14.993)
education	0.131**	–0.017
	(0.040)	(0.084)
percentage of black pop. living in South	0.016	–0.012
	(0.015)	(0.014)
constant	5.970***	9.071***
	(1.243)	(1.208)
Adjusted R^2	0.928	0.973
SEE	0.045	0.041
Autocorrelation coefficient	0.581**	0.917***
	(0.181)	(0.034)
DW Statistic	2.075	1.353

Notes: Standard errors are included in the parentheses. DW statistic is the Durbin–Watson statistic; SEE is the standard error of the estimate. * means that the parameter estimate is statistically different from zero at the 0.05 level of significance; ** at the 0.01 level of significance; *** at the 0.001 level of significance. All tests are one–tail tests.

For black men, the regressions with additional variables finds the v-u ratio to be on the margin of statistical significance with estimates little changed from the original estimates without the Cochrane-Orcutt adjustment.

CONCLUSION

The results for all of the estimates show that the v-u ratios are indeed positively related to real wages for white men and women. The statistical significance of changes in the v-u ratio on black male workers' real wage

TABLE 5
Regression Results on the Natural Log of Median Real
Wage Earnings: 1956–1983

Ind. Variable	Black Men	Black Women	Black Men	Black Women
v–u ratio	27.294* (14.695)	4.935 (15.383)	27.609* (16.033)	9.134 (16.244)
education	0.107*** (0.024)	–0.032 (0.098)	0.087** (0.026)	–0.005 (0.098)
Post65	–0.060 (0.056)	0.004 (0.054)	—	—
Dummy 65–74	—	—	–0.041 (0.037)	–0.018 (0.039)
constant	7.175*** (0.248)	8.670*** (1.247)	7.362*** (0.298)	8.319*** (1.292)
Adjusted R^2	0.928	0.972	0.927	0.972
SEE	0.045	0.042	0.045	0.042
Autocorr. coefficient	0.617** (0.185)	0.919*** (0.027)	0.697*** (0.173)	0.917*** (0.030)
DW Statistic	2.137	1.368	2.140	1.332

Notes: Standard errors are included in the parentheses. DW statistic is the Durbin-Watson statistic; SEE is the standard error of the estimate. * means that the parameter estimate is statistically different from zero at the 0.05 level of significance; ** at the 0.01 level of significance; *** at the 0.001 level of significance. All tests are one-tail tests.

earnings is marginally significant given alternative specifications. There is no ambiguity with respect to the lack of effect on real wage earnings for black women.

The results of this study can be termed as being somewhat preliminary. A number of problems make the study less than definitive. One, the sample data period is extremely small. Two, the small sample size precludes better specification of the model. Nonetheless, the results of the regressions are generally robust with alternative specifications for black women.

If these results are confirmed with additional research, black women will not experience earnings increases like other workers as the v-u ratio improves in the future. Blanchard and Diamond have identified a *decrease* in the v-u ratio from 1952 to 1975 followed by an *increase* in the v-u ratio after 1975.[16]

The results also suggest another fruitful area of research with policy significance. Both Pissarides and Blanchard and Diamond argue that changes in the vacancy to unemployment ratios change the bargaining power of workers relative to employers. Given the relatively negligible effects of changes in the v-u ratio on black women's earnings, the results suggest that the process of wage bargains for black women are significantly different from white women. Additional research on the *process* of how blacks and whites differ in making wage bargains could be useful in understanding the wage determination process differences between blacks and whites. Finally, an upswing in the v-u ratio means that jobs are being created at a faster rate relative to job losses. Given the lack of sensitivity of black women's wages to the v-u ratio, black women may not be beneficiaries of this job creation. This would have a prominent impact on black women's economic well-being in the future.

NOTES

1. See, for example, K. Abraham and L. Katz, "Cyclical Unemployment: Sectoral Shifts or Aggregate Disturbances?" *Journal of Political Economy,* Vol. 94 no. 3 (June 1987), pp. 507–22 or O. Blanchard and P. Diamond, "The Beveridge Curve," *Brookings Papers on Economic Activity,* Vol. 1989 no. 1 (1989), pp. 1–76.
2. B. Hansen, "Excess Demand, Unemployment, Vacancies, and Wages," *Quarterly Journal of Economics,* Vol. 84 no. 1 (February, 1970), pp. 1–23.
3. K. Abraham, "Help-Wanted Advertising, Job Vacancies, and Unemployment," *Brookings Papers on Economic Activity,* Vol. 1987 no 1 (1987), pp. 207–244.
4. N. Preston, *The Help-Wanted Index: Technical Description and Behavioral Trends,* (New York: The Conference Board, 1977).
5. Blanchard and Diamond, (1989).
6. C. Pissarides, "Short-run Equilibrium Dynamics of Unemployment, Vacancies, and Real Wages," *American Economic Review,* Vol. 74 no. 4 (September 1985), pp. 676–690.
7. See, for example, Blanchard and Diamond (1989) or F. Schioppa, "A Cross Country Comparison of Sectoral Mismatch in the 1980s," in F. Schioppa, editor, *Mismatch and Labour Mobility,* (New York: Cambridge University Press, 1991).
8. Schioppa, (1991).
9. The adjustments to the help-wanted index are given in Abraham, 1987. Data was not available outside the 1956–1983 time period. Abraham only provided adjustments for the 1960–1985 period. I employed her estimate of an upward drift of 5.8 percent in the index from 1960–1965 to adjust the index from 1956–1959. In addition, the earnings data is only available from 1955–1983.

10. Help-Wanted Index provided by the Conference Board as unpublished data, (New York: Conference Board). Unemployment data and employment data from U.S. Department of Labor, *Labor Force Statistics derived from the Current Population Survey: 1948–1987*, (Washington, D.C.: USGPO, 1989); U.S. Department of Labor, *Employment and Earnings*, various months, (Washington, D.C.: USGPO); U.S. Department of Labor, *Employment and Training Report to the President*, various months, (Washington, D.C.: USGPO).

11. Nominal earnings given by the U.S. Bureau of the Census, *Current Population Survey Reports, Series P-60*," various years, (Washington, D.C.: USGPO). Real earnings were obtained using the CPI's from *Statistical Abstract of the United States: 1990*, (Washington, D.C.: USGPO).

12. Pissarides (1985) and Blanchard and Diamond (1989).

13. Note that the data on black wage earnings, unemployment, and education from 1956–1976 includes workers classified as "other" in the CPS reports. In addition, education data was interpolated for years that were missing in the *Employment and Training Report to the President.*

14. J. P. Smith and F. Welch, "Black Economic Progress after Myrdal," *The Journal of Economic Literature*, Vol. 27 no. 2 (June, 1989), pp. 519–564.

15. The Ramsey RESET procedure is a general test of specification error for omitted variables. Statistically significant F-statistics indicate a model is misspecified. See D. N. Gujarati, *Basic Econometrics*, 2nd Ed. (New York: McGraw-Hill, 1989), pp. 406–413 for a simple explanation of this test.

16. Blanchard and Diamond, (1989).

J 15
R 2 3   U. S.   261- 74
(95)

14

RACIAL DIFFERENCES IN THE UNEMPLOYMENT RESPONSE TO STRUCTURAL CHANGES IN LOCAL LABOR MARKETS

Thomas Hyclak and James B. Stewart

This analysis uses establishment-level data on job creation and destruction to examine the unemployment rate responses of black, Hispanic and white workers to shifts in demand across firms and industries during the period 1980–84. Black unemployment rates are significantly more responsive to differences in aggregate demand growth and wage flexibility than are white and Hispanic unemployment rates, and they are also more severely impacted by structural changes in labor demand than are white and Hispanic unemployment rates. Additional research using the measures and focus of the present analysis that cover other time periods can assist in developing a clearer picture of the contemporary dynamics of urban labor markets and can provide guidance for public policy.

INTRODUCTION

In recent years increasing attention has been devoted to the phenomenon of job displacement created, in part, by new patterns of intra- and international firm mobility.[1] Many of the early studies focused on the mid-1980s for two principal reasons. First, the effects of substantial volatility in traditional manufacturing industries that began in the 1970s were particularly evident during this time frame in the form of substantial employment losses. To illustrate, almost 11 million workers were displaced from their jobs because of plant closings or employment cutbacks between January, 1981 and January, 1985.[2] The second reason attention crystallized on job displacement during this period was that the availability of new data sets enabled detailed analysis of employment shifts. As an example, the Displaced Worker Survey (DWS) was implemented in 1984 as a supplement to the Current Population Survey (CPS) and constitutes the largest nationally representative database on displaced work-

ers. This database captures retrospective employment information for
five years, along with reasonably detailed information about the characteristics of the previous job and postdisplacement labor market experience in addition to standard CPS variables.

While studies examining job displacement have generated various critical insights about employment shifts, it is less clear how this phenomenon relates to what has been traditionally characterized as "structural
unemployment." Some analyses examining the relative number of job
vacancies and unemployed workers have concluded that deficient aggregate demand is the primary cause of unemployment rather than shifts in
demand across firms and industries.[3] To the extent that this is the case,
job training and other structural unemployment policies are not likely to
significantly affect unemployment levels.

However, recent work by Hyclak examining the problem of mismatch
unemployment in local labor markets found that changes in the structure
of labor market demand across industry by firm-size sectors had a highly
significant positive effect on male and female unemployment rates in a
sample of 30 large markets during the periods 1977 to 1980 and 1981 to
1984.[4] Hyclak's study illustrates the benefits that can be derived from
using establishment-level data on job creation and destruction to measure
changes in labor demand across sectors in the context of structural change.

This analysis extends Hyclak's work by disaggregating the unemployment effects across race. Specifically, the unemployment response of
blacks, whites and Hispanics to structural shifts in labor demand is compared for the period 1980–84. Disaggregating the unemployment response
is important because the available data from studies of job displacement
indicate that black and Hispanic workers have suffered disproportionate
employment losses compared to whites.

To illustrate, data from the 1984 DWS indicate that while blacks constituted 9 percent of the labor force, they constituted 12 percent of the
displaced workers. Hispanics comprised 5 percent of the workforce and 6
percent of displaced workers. In contrast, whites comprised 88 percent of
the total labor force, compared to 86 percent of displaced workers.[5] For
the period 1981 to January, 1986, blacks constituted 11.2 percent of
displaced workers, compared to 11.2 percent of the workforce in January, 1986. The comparable figures for whites were 86.5 percent and 86.0
percent, respectively.[6]

Although the data above do not suggest substantial overrepresentation
of blacks among displaced workers over the period 1981–86, blacks were

substantially overrepresented among those displaced workers who experienced postdisplacement adjustment difficulties. While, as noted above, blacks constituted 11.2 percent of displaced workers, they comprised 16.6 percent of those experiencing long-term postdisplacement unemployment. The comparable postdisplacement unemployment figure for whites was 81.2 percent (compared to 86.0 percent of displaced workers as indicated above).[7]

Our results indicate that black unemployment rates are significantly more responsive to differences in aggregate demand growth and wage flexibility than are white and Hispanic unemployment rates. Black unemployment rates are also more severely impacted by structural changes in labor demand than are white and Hispanic unemployment rates.

The remainder of the analysis proceeds as follows. The second section describes the measures used in this investigation to assess structural changes in the demand for labor. The empirical model is presented and the results of the estimations are contained in the third section. The implications of the study are presented in the concluding section.

STRUCTURAL CHANGES IN LABOR DEMAND

Structural changes in the demand for labor can be measured by employment shifts across sectors, using data on job creation and job destruction. Dunne, Roberts and Samuelson and Davis and Haltiwanger have analyzed such data for the U.S. manufacturing sector and have developed relevant measures of job turnover within and across sectors that are used to identify the extent of structural change in local labor markets.[8]

Our starting point is the recognition that the economy grows by a process of simultaneous job creation and Job Destruction. Gross Job Creation (GJC) refers to the change in employment at business establishments that are newly created or expanding. Gross Job Destruction (GJD) measures jobs lost due to establishment closings and contractions in employment at continuing job sites. Total employment turnover is defined as:

(1) $T_t = |GJC_t| + |GJD_t|$

which measures the total number of employment positions that have been reallocated across establishments during period t.

For a given period, T, GJC and GJD can be calculated in numbers of jobs or as a fraction of employment at the beginning of the period. Davis and Haltiwanger show that, on average, 20.5 percent of U.S. manufacturing jobs were reallocated across firms each year during the period from 1972 to 1986 by using this process of simultaneous job creation and destruction.[9]

Net job creation, or the change in employment in the economy during a given period (ΔL_t) is defined as the difference between the absolute values of GJC and GJD. Net job creation by U.S. manufacturing firms from 1972 to 1986 averaged –2.1 percent per year according to Davis and Haltiwanger.[10]

When similar establishments are grouped into sectors (e.g., industries or regions), total turnover of jobs across establishments can be partitioned into net job growth for the entire economy, job reallocations across firms within sectors and job reallocations across sectors, according to the following formula by Dunne, Roberts and Samuelson:[11]

$$(2) \quad T_t = L_t + |\Delta L_t| + (\Sigma_j |\Delta L_t|) - |\Delta L_t|) + \Sigma_j (T_t^J - |\Delta L_t^J|)$$

The first term on the right side of equation (2) is job turnover due to the net expansion or contraction of the economy. The second term measures job reallocations across sectors resulting from shifts in employment from declining to growing sectors of the economy. If all sectors are growing or declining, this term will be zero. The third term is a measure of the employment turnover generated by job shifts across establishments within sectors. Dunne, Roberts and Samuelson interpret the second term as a measure of structural changes in employment and the third term as a measure of frictional job turnover related to the entry, growth and exit of employers.[12]

We use equation (2) to compute indices of job turnover across and within sectors for each of the 30 metropolitan areas in the sample. Sectors are defined by one-digit industry level and by size of employer. Size is measured by three categories: 19 or fewer employees, 20 to 99 employees and 100+ employees. Thus, establishments in each area are allocated to one of 27 sectors. Both establishment size and industry are used to define sectors within the local labor market because of the strong empirical evidence of persistent industry[13] and size effects on wage levels.[14] This implies the existence of barriers to perfect mobility across industries and firms of different sizes that can be used to define the structure of the local labor market.

Table 1 presents data on the three components of total job turnover for

30 metropolitan areas for the four-year period 1980–84. These data are from the USELM 76/84 data base developed by Social and Scientific Systems Inc., from Dun and Bradstreet files under contract for the Office of Advocacy of the U.S. Small Business Administration.

A number of characteristics revealed by Table 1 are consistent with previous research. First, gross job turnover across establishments for these areas was fairly large. Second, most of the inter-establishment job turnover occurred within sectors rather than across sectors. On average, within sector turnover accounted for 83 percent of turnover in the 1980–84 period.

In general, across sector employment changes were higher for the older, industrial areas of the Northeast and Great Lakes regions. This is certainly what we might expect for a measure of structural change in employment.

UNEMPLOYMENT EFFECTS

Labor demand shifts across establishments within and across relevant sectors of the local labor market could be thought of as increasing the unemployment rate for a given level of aggregate labor demand. A greater fraction of jobs being reallocated across firms in a local labor market would raise the natural unemployment rate by increasing the rate of job separations. An increase in the rate of job reallocation across sectors could also raise the natural unemployment rate by lowering the job-finding rate of the unemployed. This would result if job reallocation across sectors led to a mismatch between the skills and job expectations of workers released from declining sectors and the job characteristics in expanding sectors.

We examine the empirical importance of such labor demand shifts by using the measures of job change within and across sectors reported in Table 1 as independent variables in a regression model of the local unemployment rate. The dependent variable in these regressions is the unemployment rates of white, black and Hispanic workers for the 30 metropolitan areas included in the annual *Geographic Profile of Employment and Unemployment* published by the Bureau of Labor Statistics. Since the USELM data used in Table 1 cover changes over the period 1980 to 1984, we use the average annual unemployment rate for the 1981 to 1984 periods in our regression analysis.

The analysis controls for cyclical determinants of unemployment and

TABLE 1
Components of Job Turnover as a Percentage
of Initial Employment 1980–1984

AREA	NET	ACROSS SECTORS	WITHIN SECTORS
Anaheim	17.6	0.01	76.79
Atlanta	18.7	0.14	61.46
Baltimore	5.2	4.94	61.86
Boston	12.4	0.35	57.05
Buffalo	-7.1	6.87	50.73
Chicago	2.1	5.24	60.56
Cincinnati	3.0	4.64	57.36
Cleveland	-0.8	12.30	55.70
Dallas	26.0	0.49	68.91
Denver	19.6	0.22	69.58
Detroit	-2.0	10.34	53.86
Houston	22.3	0.0	76.40
Indianapolis	-8.4	9.96	49.24
Kansas City	5.6	3.24	59.96
Los Angeles	6.5	1.63	71.77
Miami	3.0	5.77	70.63
Milwaukee	0.3	6.36	56.44
Minnesota	13.6	0.58	60.22
Nassau	12.7	2.48	61.32
New York	8.8	3.33	57.47
Newark	4.7	3.48	58.32
Philadelphia	8.1	3.03	63.77
Pittsburgh	-1.0	16.27	43.33

TABLE 1 (continued)

Riverside	15.9	2.90	76.90
St. Louis	-1.6	11.05	51.15
San Diego	20.0	0.02	75.38
San Francisco	15.6	0.81	62.19
San Jose	26.2	0.04	63.56
Seattle	5.7	4.77	64.43
Washington	20.4	0.48	70.52

Source: Authors' calculations from USELM 76/84 data base provided by U.S. Small Business Administration.

other factors related to the natural rate of unemployment. Previous research illustrates the importance of the interaction of nominal aggregate demand shifts and wage flexibility in explaining cyclical differences in unemployment across regions.[15] The average annual rate of change of Gross State Product for the state in which the metropolitan area is centered is used as an instrument for cyclical changes in the demand for labor in the local labor market.

As an indicator of wage flexibility we use the estimates of the responsiveness of manufacturing hourly earnings to the local unemployment rate over the 1984 to 1986 period reported in Hyclak and Johnes.[16] Data availability allowed the direct estimation of wage responsiveness coefficients for 16 of the metropolitan areas in the sample. Because of proximity we used the estimates for the New York metropolitan area as a proxy for the flexibility measures for the Newark and Nassau-Suffolk areas. State-wide estimates of wage flexibility are used for the Atlanta, Denver, Indianapolis, Kansas City, Miami, Seattle and California metropolitan areas.

Two demographic characteristics of the local labor force are included as controls for inter-urban differences in the natural rate of unemployment. These are the percentages of the white, black and Hispanic labor forces in 1980 that were female and that had some college education. Data for these variables were taken from the 1980 Census Reports.

Our analysis also controls for the effect on local unemployment of the generosity of the state unemployment insurance system. This generosity varies across states along three facets: (1) the fraction of the unemployed covered by insurance, (2) the fraction of wages replaced by insurance benefits, and (3) the fraction of the year during which a covered worker could potentially receive benefits. All three fractions can be calculated from data in the *Annual Report* of the Department of Labor. These three fractions are added together to form an index of average unemployment insurance generosity in the state in which each area is centered.

Again, we use the value of this index for 1980 in our regressions in order to minimize simultaneous equations biases. Thus our model can be written as:

$$U_{iJ} = a_0 + a_1 (\% \, \Delta \, GSP)_J + a_2 (WAGE \, FLEX)_J$$

$$+ a_3 (ACROSS)_J + a_4 (WITHIN)_J$$

$$+ a_5 (\% \, FEMALE)_{iJ} + a_6 (\% \, COLLEGE)_{iJ}$$

$$+ a_7 (UNEM \, INS)_J + e_{iJ}$$

where U_{iJ} is the average unemployment rate over the 1981 to 1984 period for the ith race group in the Jth urban area; $(\% \Delta \, GSP)_J$ is the average annual rate of growth of aggregate demand over the 1981 to 1984 period in the state in which the Jth urban area is centered; $(WAGE \, FLEX)_J$ is an index of wage flexibility in the Jth urban labor market; $(ACROSS)_J$ is the fraction of 1980 jobs that were reallocated across industry and firm-size sectors between 1980 and 1984 in the Jth area; $(WITHIN)_J$ is the fraction of 1980 jobs that were reallocated among firms within industry by firm-size sectors between 1980 and 1984 in the Jth area; $(\% \, FEMALE)_{iJ}$ is the percentage of the 1980 labor force that was female for the ith race group and Jth area; $(\% \, COLLEGE)_{iJ}$ is the percentage of the 1980 labor force with some college education for the ith race group and Jth area; $(UNEM \, INS)_J$ is our index of unemployment insurance generosity for the state in which the Jth area is centered; and e_{iJ} is a random error term.

Table 2 reports descriptive statistics and OLS regression results from estimating our model on a pooled sample for all three racial groups, adding separate constant terms for blacks and Hispanics to our basic model. Data limitations posed by the sample size for the Current Population Survey in each area restrict our sample to 30 observations for black rates and just 10 observations on the average unemployment rate for Hispanic workers over the 1981 to 1984 period. Thus, the results in Table 2 are drawn from a pooled sample of 63 observations.

The results in Table 2 illustrate significantly lower average unemployment rates in urban labor markets located in states with more rapid rates of growth in Gross State Product and in those areas with greater wage flexibility. This is consistent with our expectations based on the results reported by Hyclak and Johnes.[17] Average unemployment rates were significantly higher for Hispanic and black workers, controlling for the other unemployment determinants included in our model.

Our measure of structural change in labor demand across industry and firm-size segments of the labor market is shown to have a statistically positive relationship with the average unemployment rate across areas and racial groups. A one standard deviation increase in the value for ACROSS would raise the mean predicted unemployment rate average by slightly more than two percentage points, indicating that the effect of this variable is quantitatively important as well as statistically significant. Shifts in employment among firms within industry by size categories is also positively related to the unemployment level, although the estimated coefficient on this variable is only marginally greater than its standard error.

For the full sample the fraction of the labor force that is female has a significantly negative relationship to the unemployment rate average. This is consistent with the observation that male and female unemployment rates became more equal during the decade of the 1980s. The fraction of the 1980 workforce with some college education is unrelated to the average unemployment rate over the 1981 to 1984 period in this sample of white, black and Hispanic workers in 30 metropolitan areas.

Finally, the extent of "generosity" of the unemployment insurance system in the state in which each metropolitan area is centered has a marginally significant positive relationship to the level of unemployment in this sample.

The results reported in Table 2 allow only for different intercepts for each racial group. We also carry out Chow-type tests of the null hypothesis of common slope coefficients for each racial group. The resulting F statistics are $F(8,39) = 22.05$ for black workers, and $F(8,39) = 1.30$ for Hispanics. Thus, we can reject the null hypothesis for blacks but not for Hispanics at the .05 significant level. Table 3, then, reports regression results estimated for a sample of black unemployment rates across 23 urban areas and for a sample combining data on white workers across 30 areas, with data on Hispanics for 10 areas.

Some key differences can be seen in these results. Black unemploy-

TABLE 2
Regression Estimates, Pooled Sample

	MEAN	STANDARD DEVIATION	COEFFICIENT
Constant	-----	-----	14.32
% GSP	8.76	1.45	-0.59 (0.25)
WAGE FLEX	0.65	0.29	-3.79 (1.18)
ACROSS	3.85	4.17	0.49 (0.12)
WITHIN	63.08	8.60	0.07 (0.05)
% FEMALE	43.70	5.02	-0.26 (0.08)
% COLLEGE	31.36	10.24	0.03 (0.05)
UNEM INS	1.24	0.17	2.87 (1.91)
BLACK	0.36	0.48	12.01 (1.09)
HISPANIC	0.16	0.36	5.29 (1.31)
R^2			.84
SEE			2.36
N			63

Heteroskedasticity-resistant standard errors in parentheses. The mean and standard deviation of the dependent variable are 11.36 and 5.84.

TABLE 3
Regression Estimates, Separate Samples

	BLACKS	WHITES AND HISPANICS
Constant	44.15 (8.68)	0.29 (7.29)
% GSP	-1.37 (0.34)	-0.08 (0.17)
WAGE FLEX	-5.96 (1.36)	-1.77 (0.68)
ACROSS	0.52 (0.21)	0.32 (0.10)
WITHIN	0.05 (0.08)	0.11 (0.05)
% FEMALE	-0.32 (0.06)	0.03 (0.13)
% COLLEGE	-0.07 (0.09)	-0.06 (0.05)
UNEM INS	0.18 (2.27)	6.12 (2.07)
HISPANIC	-----	3.60 (1.17)
R^2	.76	.67
SEE	2.59	1.58
N	23	40

Heteroskedasticity-resistant standard errors in parentheses.

ment rates are significantly more responsive to differences in aggregate demand growth and wage flexibility than are white and Hispanic unemployment rates. Black unemployment rates are also more severely impacted by structural changes in labor demand than are white and Hispanic unemployment rates. These results suggest that the cyclical and structural causes of unemployment during the first half of the 1980s were more important for black workers in the urban labor markets in our sample.

White/Hispanic unemployment during the 1981 to 1984 period seems to be more closely related to frictional factors across this sample of large metropolitan areas. Educational characteristics, unemployment insurance and job shifts within sectors are the most significant determinants of inter-urban unemployment rate differences for these workers. Of course, these results are based on small samples.

CONCLUSION

This analysis has focused on the extent to which the shifts in demand across firms and industries are a primary cause of observed levels of unemployment and, in particular, whether unemployment rate responses to demand shifts differ across racial groups. Although survey data indicate that black and Hispanic workers suffered disproportionately high rates of displacement and longer spells of unemployment following displacement during the mid-1980s, previous analyses have not examined whether the forces affecting unemployment levels differ across racial groups.

Using establishment-level data on job creation and destruction to measure changes in labor demand across sectors in the context of structural change, the following conclusions were derived from the present analysis: (1) black unemployment rates are significantly more responsive to differences in aggregate demand growth and wage flexibility than are white and Hispanic unemployment rates, and (2) black unemployment rates are also more severely impacted by structural changes in labor demand than are white and Hispanic unemployment rates.

The results underscore the usefulness of employing data on establishment job creation and destruction to examine patterns of structural change. Establishment size and industry may be important characteristics that influence the structure and functioning of labor markets. Further research using the measures and focus of the present analysis that cover other time periods can assist in developing a clearer picture of the contemporary dynamics of urban labor markets. Generating such additional information about the dynamics of the labor market adjustment process can guide the development of more effective interventions targeted at particular problem areas/groups.

NOTES

1. See, for example, the various essays in John Addison, (ed.), *Job Displacement, Consequences and Implications for Policy* (Detroit: Wayne State University Press, 1991); Francis W. Horvath, "The Pulse of Economic Change: Dislocated Workers of 1981–1985." *Monthly Labor Review,* (June, 1987); Louis Jacobson, Robert LaLonde and Daniel Sullivan, *The Costs of Worker Dislocation* (Kalamazoo, MI: W.E. Upjohn Institute for Employment Research, 1993); Duane Leigh, *Does Training Work for Displaced Workers, A Survey of Existing Evidence* (Kalamazoo, MI: W.E. Upjohn Institute for Employment Research, 1990); and Adam Seitchik and Jeffrey Zornitsky, *From One Job to the Next, Worker Adjustment in a Changing Labor Market* (Kalamazoo, MI: W.E. Upjohn Institute for Employment Research, 1989).

2. Francis W. Horvath, "The Pulse of Economic Change: Dislocated Workers of 1981–1985." *Monthly Labor Review,* (June, 1987).

3. See for example, Katherine Abraham, "Structural/Frictional v. Deficient Demand Unemployment: Some New Evidence," *American Economic Review,* vol. 73, no. 4 (1983): 708–24.

4. Thomas Hyclak, "Mismatch Unemployment in Local Labor Markets," (unpublished, 1994).

5. Reported in Louis Jacobson, Robert LaLonde and Daniel Sullivan, *The Costs of Worker Dislocation* (Kalamazoo, MI: W.E. Upjohn Institute for Employment Research, 1993), p. 21.

6. Reported in Adam Seitchik, "Who Are Displaced Workers?" in Seitchik and Zornitsky, *From One Job to the Next,* p. 62.

7. Ibid., p. 77.

8. Timothy Dunne, Mark Roberts and Larry Samuelson, "Plant Turnover and Gross Employment Flows in the U.S. Manufacturing Sector," *Journal of Labor Economics,* vol. 7, no. 1 (1989): 48–71; Stephen Davis and John Haltiwanger, "Gross Job Creation and Destruction: Microeconomic Evidence and Macroeconomic Implications," *NBER Macroeconomics Annual,* vol. 5 (1990): 123–86; Stephen Davis and John Haltiwanger, "Gross Job Creation, Gross Job Destruction, and Employment Reallocation," *Quarterly Journal of Economics,* vol. 152, no. 3 (1992): 819–63.

9. Davis and Haltiwanger (1990).

10. Davis and Haltiwanger (1992).

11. Dunne, Roberts and Samuelson (1989).

12. Alan Krueger and Lawrence Summers, "Efficiency Wages and the Interindustry Wage Structure," *Econometrica,* vol. 56 (1988): 259–93.

13. Charles Brown and James Medoff, "The Employer Size Wage Effect," *Journal of Political Economy,* vol. 97, no. 5 (1989): 1027–59.

14. Thomas Hyclak and Geraint Johnes, "Wage Rigidity and Cyclical Unemployment," *Proceedings of the Forty-Fifth Annual Meeting* (Madison: Industrial Relations Research Association, 1993), pp. 524–30.

15. Thomas Hyclak and Geraint Johnes, *Wage Flexibility and Unemployment Dynamics in Regional Labor Markets* (Kalamazoo, MI: W.E. Upjohn Institute, 1992).
16. Hyclak and Johnes (1993).

RISING BLACK UNEMPLOYMENT:
CHANGES IN JOB STABILITY
OR IN EMPLOYABILITY?

M. V. Lee Badgett

This article analyzes the effects of changes in flows into and out of
unemployment on the growing gap between black and white unemployment rates in the 1970s and 1980s. Current Population Survey
data show that black workers' unemployment inflows increased, suggesting that job instability increased. Declining employment opportunities were also implicated, as black workers left unemployment for a
job less often in 1987 than in 1971. White women's situation improved considerably, with lower inflows and higher employment probabilities. Although the effects of declining federal equal employment
opportunity (EEO) pressure cannot be detected, these findings are consistent with increasing racial discrimination.

INTRODUCTION

Current political debates over affirmative action policies in the United
States raise the question of whether black workers have made economic
progress at the expense of white workers. Economists' research on racial
differences in wages and incomes has shown that the period of rising
relative black incomes ended sometime in the 1970s and fell far short of
equality.[1] For black men, the 1970s and 1980s were a time of falling
labor force participation and employment.[2] This article focuses on another labor market measure of blacks' economic situation that also shows
a pessimistic pattern: black workers' official unemployment rate *increased*
relative to white workers' rate throughout the 1970s, and blacks' relative
position failed to improve despite the long business cycle upswing of the
1980s (Figures 1a and 1b). Through the 1970s and 1980s, then, evidence

is mixed as to the improvement of black workers' position relative to white workers and as to the sources of any improvement or regression. The analysis here attempts to sort out factors influencing racial differences in unemployment, including antidiscrimination policies, skill mismatches, and job instability.

While the influence of micro-level effects on the unemployment rate cannot be easily or directly measured given available data, such pressures can be translated into macro-level measurements. If these forces—skill mismatches, affirmative action policy, or job instability—have had a major effect on unemployment differentials, then the effects should be evident in the time series and cross-section patterns of the relative probabilities of entering and leaving unemployment. While the analysis of the time series patterns does not constitute a formal statistical test of each specific hypothesis—some of which obviously interact—the analysis does provide a plausibility check as well as identification of changes that need explaining. In this paper, time series measures are constructed for these two components of the unemployment rate in the 1970s and 1980s, as are more detailed cross-sectional measures for 1971 and 1987. In addition to looking for broad changes in the flows in and out of unemployment, the relative contribution of changes in the two flows to the growing unemployment gap can be assessed.

POSSIBLE EXPLANATIONS

Little recent work focusing on racial unemployment differences exists.[3] This paper's approach of using labor market transitions to look at race and gender differences in unemployment is not a new method. But most past studies focus on cross-section results that make longer term changes in labor market forces difficult to detect, or the studies were conducted before the deterioration in black worker's labor force experience was apparent. Older studies[4] often concluded that black workers' higher unemployment rates were due to greater job turnover, largely as a result of holding unstable jobs or jobs that have high quit rates regardless of race. This pattern depends on the reference points, however, especially with regard to gender. For instance, Marston finds that racial differences in women's unemployment rates result from black women's lower probability of moving into employment from either unemployment or from being out of the labor force.[5] Juhn's more recent comparison of black and white men shows that the same pattern was true for black men relative to white men over the 1970s and 1980s, but he does not calculate this pattern's effect on unemployment rate differences.[6]

FIGURE 1a
Unemployment Rates, 1972–1990

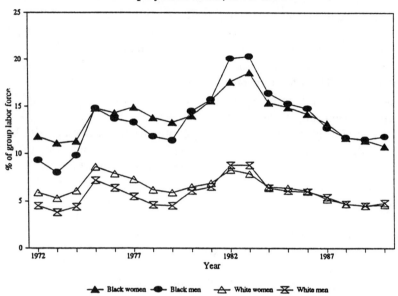

—▲— Black women —●— Black men —△— White women —✕— White men

FIGURE 1b
Unemployment Ratios, 1972–1990

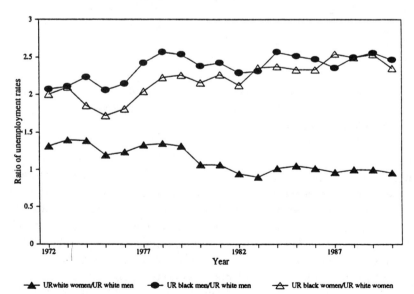

—▲— URwhite women/UR white men   —●— UR black men/UR white men   —△— UR black women/UR white women

The potential influence of policy and economic change on labor market transitions focuses attention on several possible explanations for black workers' deteriorating unemployment situation, most of which are derived from studies of wage and employment differences. First, the skill mismatch hypothesis blames the decline of manufacturing industries in urban areas for declining employment opportunities among lower-skilled black men.[7] The literature on dislocated workers suggests that such an explanation may also be applicable to black women, even though they have not been employed in manufacturing to the extent that black men have been.[8] With fewer appropriate job opportunities, unemployed black workers may remain unemployed longer. A previous study supports this hypothesis emphasizing the loss of employment opportunities for less-skilled workers, finding that most of the increase in black workers' unemployment between 1971 and 1987 came from higher unemployment for less-educated women and for blue collar men.[9] And Juhn shows that the decline in black men's employment to population ratio (which he calls labor force participation) was concentrated among less-educated black men.[10]

While a mismatch between skills supplied and demanded might lead to a lower probability of leaving unemployment for all less-skilled workers, reasons for a disproportionate impact on blacks are less clear. Thus, a second explanation is related to the impact of federal EEO policy. To the extent that EEO laws and affirmative action, the strong form of EEO policy, significantly increased the demand for black workers, we would expect to see an increasing probability of employment (i.e., increasing flows out of unemployment) for black workers during the period of heaviest enforcement in the 1970s. By the same argument, less effective enforcement of affirmative action policies in the 1980s would have resulted in a relative decline in movements out of unemployment if employers returned to discriminatory practices.[11]

The effect of antidiscrimination policies on relative wage levels could result in the opposite effect, however. If the increase in black relative wages reflects a decline in discrimination and leads black workers to raise their reservation wages, then unemployment durations might actually increase. But recent studies demonstrate that the trend toward higher relative black male earnings was reversed in the late 1970s and 1980s.[12] By the late 1980s, the racial differential in male earnings had returned to the level of the early 1970s. Thus, a more empirically based hypothesis would focus on the effects of black workers' higher wage expectations based on the growth of relative wages in the late 1960s and early 1970s.

This duration-increasing effect also results from the Bulow and Summers dual labor market model of affirmative action.[13] In their model, increasing black workers' access to efficiency wage-paying primary sector jobs would increase queuing for those jobs, lengthening unemployment spells.

To a lesser extent, white women have had rising relative wages relative to white men[14] and have also benefitted somewhat from affirmative action,[15] providing a point of comparison to assess the EEO/affirmative action hypotheses. In other words, white women's flows in and out of unemployment should demonstrate effects of policy similar to the effect on black workers, providing a point of comparison to assess the EEO effect.

A third set of hypotheses is related to unemployment inflows through job turnover. Affirmative action policies might reduce flows into unemployment from job loss by discouraging employers from discharging black workers for fear of discrimination lawsuits. Also, in a dual labor market model, the inflow rate into unemployment would fall as blacks enter more stable and desirable primary sector jobs. But Dickens and Lang report that the proportion of primary sector jobs in the U.S. economy fell during the 1980s.[16] This suggests that more jobs were being created in the high-turnover secondary sector in the 1980s, and that the inflow rate would rise for black workers who must increasingly hold jobs in that sector.

Most of the previous explanations focus on the role of labor demand in creating unemployment. Of course, in the absence of downwardly flexible wages, an increase in the supply of labor might also push up the unemployment rate. In the most general terms, the fastest growing groups of workers would have the slowest absorption, possibly resulting in longer unemployment spells and higher inflow rates for new labor force entrants and reentrants. Between 1972 and 1987, the black female labor force grew by 67 percent, the fastest rate of growth of the four race-gender groups analyzed here, while the white female labor force grew by 56 percent.[17] On the face of it, this racial difference in women's labor supply growth might be thought to explain why black women's unemployment rose more than white women's. However, this aggregate supply growth differential cannot account for all of the unemployment growth differential since employment growth diverged even more dramatically: black women's employment grew by only 30 percent, while white women's employment grew by 57 percent, motivating this article's analysis of possible differences in labor demand.

Men's declining labor supply makes their increasing unemployment all the more puzzling in a simple measurement sense. If men, especially black men, are more likely to leave the labor force when unemployed, then their unemployment rate should *fall*. Labor force participation has been falling steadily among men in the two decades under consideration. From 1972 to 1990, the labor force participation rate of black men aged 20 years and over fell from 78.5 percent of the population to 70.1 percent. The decline over the same period for comparable white men was from 82.0 percent to 78.3 percent. If some of those leaving the labor force are discouraged workers—the hidden unemployed—then the official unemployment rate underestimates the severity of employment problems. Thus this paper's findings could be considered as a lower bound on the estimate of the effect of declining employment opportunities on black men's labor market position.

Finally, co-worker discrimination models, e.g., Shulman's job competition model,[18] and some job matching models suggest that, aside from their correlation across the business cycle, flows in and out of unemployment are not independent. In a job competition model, unemployed white workers win out in competition for jobs because their employed white counterparts pressure employers to hire white applicants. Thus their outflow rate will exceed black workers' flows out of unemployment. And since more stable primary sector jobs should be more attractive (holding wages equal) and generate more competition, white workers' inflows into unemployment should also be lower. Some job matching models predict that faster separations lead to faster job finding, i.e., higher inflows lead to higher outflows. Although Blanchard and Diamond do not find evidence of such "thick markets" in their estimation of an aggregate matching function, they do not reject the possibility that their data simply cannot pick up such an effect.[19] These two models suggest that changes in flows in and out of unemployment will be related.

Table 1 summarizes the hypotheses and their predictions for changes in flows in and out of unemployment in the 1970s and 1980s.

METHOD

This paper compares the effects of changing flows into and out of unemployment on the ratio of the black unemployment rate to the white unemployment rate. The Current Population Survey (CPS) collects data on workers' employment status and on the duration of unemployment for currently unemployed workers. Comparisons of the stock of unemployed workers across months permits the calculation of estimates of workers'

TABLE 1
Effect of Hypotheses on Black/White Ratio of Flows
In and Out of Unemployment

Hypothesis	Effect on inflows 1970's	1980's	Effect on outflows 1970's	1980's
Skill Mismatch			-	-
EEO/Affirmative Action				
Employment	-	-	+	-
Wages			-	?
Dual labor market/ job turnover	-	+		
Labor Supply	+	+	-	-(women)
			+	+
Job competition	+	+	-	-

net flows in and out of unemployment.[20] These measures differ from the gross flow data from the CPS but capture some of the same movements between labor force states.

The CPS is conducted monthly and asks unemployed workers how long they have been on layoff or looking for work. Those who have been unemployed for less than 5 weeks are counted as newly unemployed in the current month and make up the net inflow of workers into unemployment in month t. To get the net inflow rate (f), the number of newly unemployed (u^{0-4}) in group i at time t is divided by the labor force (n) of that group at time t:

$$(1) \quad f_{it} = u_{it}^{0-4}/n_{it}$$

This measure excludes any workers who became unemployed during the month but left unemployment before the survey date. Thus few movements from one job to another with little or no unemployment in between are accounted for, making f a conservative measure of unemployment inflows or job turnover.

The probability of leaving unemployment combines the probability that an unemployed person will get a job with the probability that she or he will leave the labor force. (The resulting difficulty in interpretation of changes in this measure will be discussed below.) Subtracting off the newly unemployed from the current stock of unemployed workers leaves the number of workers who were also unemployed in the previous month. Dividing this number by the previous month's stock of unemployed gives an estimate of the probability of remaining unemployed. The probability of *leaving* unemployment will be one minus the probability of remaining unemployed:

(2) $p_{it} = 1 - (u_{it} - u_{it}^{0-4})/u_{i,t-1}$

Given these relationships, the unemployment rate (r) can be expressed in terms of the inflows, the growth rate of the labor force (g) and the previous month's unemployment rate:[21]

(3) $r_{it} = f_{it} + [(1 - p_{it})/1 + g_{it})] * r_{i,t-1}$.

In a steady state, flows into and out of unemployment are equal, resulting in an unchanging steady state unemployment rate, r*:

(4) $r_{it}* = f_{it}/p_{it}$.

Equations (3) and (4) allow two different simulations of unemployment rates under different sets of assumptions about the behavior of inflows (f) and outflows (p): a dynamic simulation using different monthly values in equation (3) and a steady state simulation using equation (4).

NET FLOW ESTIMATES—TIME SERIES

The outflow probability, p, and the inflow rate, f, for white workers and for "black and other" workers were calculated using published monthly data from *Employment and Earnings*.[22] Figures 2 and 4 chart annual averages of the monthly values of f and p from 1970 through 1990 by race and gender group.

According to Figure 2, the inflow rate for black workers is far higher than that for white workers, regardless of gender. Men have lower inflow rates than do women within racial groups. Average inflows into unemployment rose steadily for black women in the 1970s through 1983, followed by a steady decline to levels in 1990 that were below the 1970 inflow rate. Black men have yet to recover from their inflow rate's steep increase of the mid-1970s through early 1980s. White men's inflow rate trended upward slightly but eventually dropped to levels comparable to the early 1970s. The gradual decline of white women's inflow rate was interrupted only by the 1974–75 and 1982–83 recessions.

Figure 3 charts the ratio of the black to white inflow rates by sex. Inflows for both black men and women rose relative to their white counterparts from 1974 through most of the 1980s. This pattern casts doubt on the hypothesis that affirmative action either increased access to stable

FIGURE 2
Monthly Unemployment Inflow Rate
Annual Average

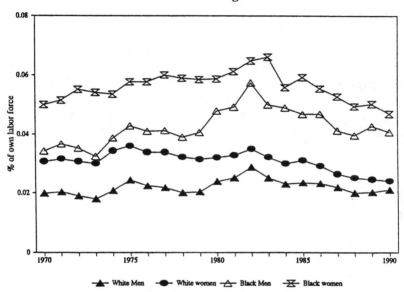

FIGURE 3
Ratio of Inflow Rates
Compared by Sex and to White Men

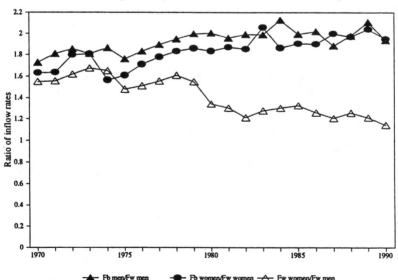

primary sector jobs or led to fewer discharges of black workers. Both the relative and absolute decline in white women's inflows indicate aggregate-level improvements, possibly resulting from antidiscrimination policy. And in the 1980s, when affirmative action enforcement was relatively low, the relative flow measures unexpectedly stabilized for black workers and continued to improve for white women.

Figure 4 shows that, as a whole, women are more likely than men to leave unemployment since this probability measure combines the probability of leaving the labor force with the probability of getting a job. Within gender groups, white workers are more likely than black workers to leave unemployment in a given month, but the difference narrows during downswings. As the outflow probability varied over the business cycle, both the peaks and troughs were lower in the late 1970s and early 1980s than they were in the early 1970s for all groups. This absolute drop for all four groups suggests that other general economic forces were more important in determining the length of an unemployment spell. (By 1989, the outflows for all groups had at least recovered to their 1979 levels but not to 1970 levels.)

Figure 5 plots the ratios of the outflow probabilities. The stability of the ratio throughout the 1970s, the period of heaviest EEO/affirmative action enforcement, implies that affirmative action had little or no effect on the relative demand for black workers at an aggregate level. Black workers' probability of leaving unemployment fluctuated around 90 percent of white workers' probability for the past two decades. White women had a period of higher outflows relative to white men in the mid-1980s, i.e., *after* EEO and affirmative action pressure dropped off. Increasing reservation wages or queuing for primary sector jobs could have resulted in the apparent lengthening of unemployment durations implied by Figure 4, however, but only if those hypotheses are applied to all workers.

The relative flows, both in and out of unemployment, were changing over the last two decades, but the temporal flow patterns provide little support for the simple EEO/affirmative action hypotheses that changes in enforcement would have hurt black workers in the 1980s, not in the 1970s as we observed. To sort out the potential influence of the other hypotheses on changes in the unemployment rates and in the racial differential, two different methods will be used. The first panel of Table 2 presents the simulated steady state unemployment rates using equation (4), and the second panel presents the results of the dynamic simulations using equation (3). The reference points, 1971 and 1987, were chosen for comparability with the cross-section data taken from March of 1971 and

FIGURE 4
Monthly Unemployment Outflow Probabilities
Annual Average

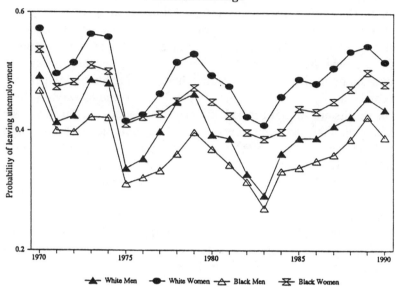

FIGURE 5
Ratio of Outflow Probabilities
Compared by Sex and to White Men

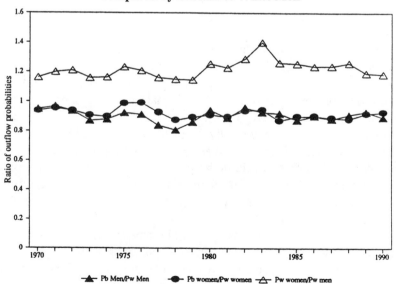

1987 (two similar points on the seasonal and business cycles). In each panel, the first row presents either the implied steady state unemployment rate or the actual unemployment rate (in the dynamic simulation panels). The second row holds inflows constant at their average 1971 level and calculates the unemployment rate with varying levels of the outflow probability. The third row reverses the procedure, holding the outflow probability constant and allowing the inflow rate to vary. The seventh column gives the percentage change in the unemployment ratio that can be attributed to the change in the flow allowed to vary.

The results are similar for both kinds of simulations. In the steady state simulations, changes in outflows and inflows both account for roughly half of the increase in the black female unemployment rate (.9 percentage points): allowing only the outflow probability to change (it decreases) raises the rate from 10.9 percent to 11.3 percent, and allowing the inflow rate to rise (while holding outflows constant) increases the rate from 10.9 percent to 11.4 percent. For white women, the increase in the outflow probability only reduces the unemployment rate by .2 percentage points, while the fall in the inflow rate pushes the unemployment rate down from 6.5 percent to 5.3 percent, or 80 percent of its total drop. The only difference in the dynamic simulations is that the influence of changing outflow probabilities is clearly stronger than the influence of changes in the inflow rate for black women. But even if falling outflow probabilities contribute more to the increase in unemployment among black women, the growing ratio of black to white women's unemployment rates—from 1.7 to 2.3—is clearly driven by the divergence of their inflow rates in both simulations.

The results for male workers are similar: rising inflow rates account for more of the increase in the unemployment rate in all simulations. For black men, both rising inflows and falling outflows contributed a substantial part of the increase in the black male unemployment rate. The outflow probability changed so little for white men that the change in the inflow rate accounted for virtually all of the increase in the white male unemployment rate. The racial *divergence* in outflow probabilities, however, played an important role in the increase of men's racial unemployment ratio from 1.9 to 2.1. The relative increase in black male inflows does contribute up to 33 percent of the increase in the ratio if we use the dynamic simulations, however.

In summary, the time series data argue against the EEO/affirmative action hypotheses implying that changes in policy drove the racial wedge between white unemployment and black unemployment. First, the outflow probability patterns suggest that an affirmative action-induced in-

TABLE 2
Simulated Average Annual Unemployment Rates

	Black & Other		White		Ratios		% chg.*
	1971	1987	1971	1987	1971	1987	in rat.
Women:							
Average inflow rate (f_t)	.051	.053	.032	.026	1.6	2.0	
Average outflow prob. (p_t)	.466	.451	.495	.511	.9	.9	
Steady state simulations							
unemp. rate (f_t/p_t)	10.9	11.8	6.1	5.1	1.7	2.3	
inflows constant (t_{71}/p_t)	10.9	11.3	6.5	6.3	1.7	1.8	16.7
outflows constant (f_t/p_{71})	10.9	11.4	6.5	5.3	1.7	2.2	83.3
Dynamic simulations							
Actual unemp. rate	10.8	11.7	6.3	5.2	1.7	2.3	
inflows constant** (t_{71}/p_t)	10.7	11.5	6.3	6.2	1.7	1.8	16.7
outflows constant** (f_t/p_{71})	10.9	11.2	6.4	5.4	1.7	2.1	66.7
Men:							
Average inflow rate (f_t)	.037	.041	.020	.022	1.9	1.9	
Average outflow prob. (p_t)	.399	.365	.414	.417	1.0	0.9	
Steady state simulations							
Unemp. rate (f_t/p_t)	9.3	11.2	4.8	5.3	1.9	2.1	
inflows constant (f_{71}/p_t)	9.3	10.1	4.8	4.8	1.9	2.1	100.0
outflows constant (f_t/p_{71})	9.3	10.3	4.8	5.3	1.9	1.9	0.0
Dynamic simulations							
Actual unemp. rate	9.1	11.5	4.9	5.4	1.9	2.1	
inflows constant** (f_{71}/p_t)	9.2	10.0	5.0	5.0	1.8	2.0	66.6
outflows constant** (f_t/p_{71})	9.4	10.4	5.0	5.3	1.9	2.0	33.3

*Gives percentage of the change in ratio of unemployment rates accounted for by the simulation. Totals will not necessarily add up to 100%.
**Simulations calculated from monthly CPS data using equation (3) from text using either constant inflows (f_{71}) or constant outflows (p_{71}):

$$r_t = f_t + [(1 - p_t)/(1 + g_t)] * r_{t-1}$$

Source: *Employment and Earnings*, various issues.

crease in labor demand was not visible at the macro-level for black workers and white women. Second, the patterns are consistent with an increase in the reservation wage or increased queuing for *all* groups in the 1970s and early 1980s. And third, relative inflow rate patterns in Figure 3 show that any effect of EEO/affirmative action on discharges or on access to more stable jobs went to white women and not to black men and women. The time series data do support the declining primary sector argument in that inflows rose for all groups (except for white women) in the 1970s and failed to return to 1970s levels for men by the late 1980s.

Finally, the simulations suggest that most of the divergence in unemployment rates by race within gender groups stems from a racial divergence in one flow: inflows for women, and outflows for men. Thus, the explanations for rising relative black unemployment must clearly be consistent with these changes and the different patterns by gender.

NET FLOWS—CROSS-SECTION DATA

A more detailed breakdown of the flow measures is necessary to assess more directly the hypotheses concerned with skill mismatches, increased job instability, job competition, and thick markets. CPS data from March of 1971 and of 1987 are used in these cross-sectional comparisons.

The detailed cross-section data also have the advantage of allowing the separation of black workers from the "black and other" group. The last two columns of Table 3 reveal a much larger inflow increase for black workers once they are separated from other racial groups—a 1.2 percentage point increase for black women and a one percentage point increase for black men. White women's inflow rate shows a slightly larger decrease and white men's a larger increase when comparing March data than in the annual averages of Table 2.

Divergence of inflow rates caused most of the widening gap between black women and white women. For black women, increases in job quits and in reentrants both account for approximately one half of the inflow rate increase.[23] Small declines in newly unemployed job losers and reentrants account for the fall in white women's inflow rate. Although differences in outflow probabilities pushed black men's unemployment up relative to white men's, rising inflow rates increased both groups' unemployment rates. Both black men and white men experienced close to a .5 percentage point increase in the inflow rate of job losers. Rising inflows from black male new entrants pushed black men's rate up even more.

Cross-tabulations of inflows by education (also in Table 3), reveal that the total inflow rate (in the last two columns) for the group of workers with less than 12 years of education rose in all race-gender groups. High school graduates' inflows increased for all groups except for white women. College graduates' inflow rates improved or at least showed virtually no deterioration. Unemployed reentrants and new entrants account for most of the increase in inflows in the lowest education category for all four race-gender groups. Higher job loss rates among men pushed up the inflow rate at all education levels. Quits increased among non-college

Rising Black Unemployment   289

TABLE 3
Detailed Inflow Rates for March 1971 and 1987

	Job Losers		Job Leavers		Re-entrants		New Entrants		Total	
	1971	1987	1971	1987	1971	1987	1971	1987	1971	1987
Black:										
Women	.014	.013	.004	.011	.019	.025	.008	.008	.045	.057
Men	.015	.020	.003	.004	.009	.008	.005	.010	.032	.042
White:										
Women	.008	.007	.005	.005	.011	.008	.004	.004	.028	.024
Men	.008	.012	.002	.003	.005	.004	.002	.002	.017	.021
By education:										
Black women:										
< 12	.019	.009	.007	.011	.019	.037	.012	.026	.057	.083
12 yrs.	.009	.020	.001	.018	.022	.022	.003	.003	.035	.063
Some Col.	.011	.010	.000	.006	.019	.029	.000	.004	.030	.049
Col Grad	.005	.002	.004	.005	.006	.003	.011	.000	.026	.010
Black men:										
< 12	.017	.024	.002	.007	.009	.016	.007	.029	.035	.076
12 yrs.	.014	.020	.006	.002	.005	.004	.000	.002	.024	.028
Some Col.	.009	.021	.004	.004	.022	.010	.008	.003	.043	.039
Col Grad	.000	.005	.000	.004	.008	.000	.000	.000	.008	.009
White women:										
< 12	.011	.015	.006	.009	.012	.021	.010	.002	.039	.047
12 yrs.	.008	.009	.005	.005	.010	.007	.001	.000	.034	.021
Some Col.	.005	.004	.005	.006	.016	.009	.003	.000	.029	.019
Col Grad	.002	.003	.004	.002	.004	.003	.000	.000	.010	.008
White men:										
< 12	.012	.019	.003	.006	.007	.012	.004	.009	.026	.047
12 yrs.	.008	.015	.002	.003	.002	.002	.000	.000	.012	.020
Some Col.	.007	.010	.004	.002	.008	.004	.002	.004	.021	.017
Col Grad	.002	.003	.001	.001	.002	.002	.000	.002	.005	.005

Note: "Black" does *not* include "& other"
Souce: Calculated from CPS tapes using equation (1): $f_{ijt} = u_{ijt}^{0-4}/n_{ijt}$ where n_{ij} is the labor force for race i and (where appropriate) education subgroup j.

graduate black women and in the non-high school graduates of other race-gender groups.

The increased unemployment among less-educated new entrants suggests that they are less likely to move from school or other non-labor market activities into a job, indicating a drop in job opportunities for low-skilled new workers. The importance of both job loss (for men) and quits (for black women) suggests that the quality of jobs held by less-educated workers decreased, i.e., that more of those workers had secondary sector jobs or lost primary sector jobs in 1987.

The increase in black female reentrants, which accounts for a large part of the divergence of black and white women's inflow rates, is harder to interpret. If much of the reentrant inflow into unemployment is made up of workers who lost their last jobs, then job instability may be significantly higher than indicated by the inflow rates of job losers. If rising reentrant flows indicate an increase in unemployed black workers' propensity to leave the labor force, then the outflow probability measurement overestimates the probability of leaving unemployment for a job (discussed further below). Rising inflows of black entrants might be the result of a growing labor supply, but the supply of white women also grew rapidly without an increase in these flows, further suggesting differential labor demand shifts.

Overall, the detailed inflows provide evidence of decreasing job stability for less-educated workers, but they could also reflect diminished employment opportunities for those same workers. Outflow probabilities should also reflect this skill pattern if skill mismatches are an important source of unemployment. Because of data limitations, the level of detail available for inflow rates is not possible for the outflow probabilities. By using the steady state assumption, however, outflow probabilities can be estimated for the education subgroups using equation (4). Table 4 gives the implied outflow values, which provide weak support for the hypothesis that employment opportunities are declining for less-skilled workers: of those workers with no more than a high school degree, only black female high school graduates and white men have a higher outflow probability in 1987. Curiously, outflows fall for all groups' college graduates, perhaps because unemployed college graduates are queuing for the smaller number of stable jobs implied by the rising inflow rates.

Separating the outflow measure into the probability of leaving unemployment for a job from leaving the labor force requires additional data. In spite of the well-known problems with the gross flow data from the CPS, these data are the only data available that both match the measurements considered earlier in terms of definition, sample, and time period and provide a way to split the outflow probability into its two components. Unfortunately, this can only be done at a highly aggregated level.

If reporting errors in these data have not changed significantly between 1971 and 1987, then the transition probabilities in Table 5 suggest that employment opportunities have fallen for black women and men but have risen for white women. This means that relatively constant outflow probabilities disguise an important shift in the measure's two components. For black workers, the probability of leaving unemployment for a

TABLE 4
Estimated Steady State Outflow Probabilities by Education Group

	Black		White	
	1971	1987	1971	1987
WOMEN:				
< 12	.471	.417	.429	.392
12 yrs.	.357	.406	.444	.389
Some Col	.370	.386	.460	.452
Col Grad	.481	.196	.385	.381
MEN:				
< 12	.376	.351	.325	.373
12 yrs.	.296	.246	.273	.303
Some Col	.336	.336	.368	.327
Col Grad	1.000	.180	.238	.208

Note: Probabilities calculated by solving equation (4) using group unemployment rates from Table 1 as steady state rate and inflow rates from Table 3.

job fell by 36 percent, while the probability of an unemployed white woman finding a job rose by 69 percent. Thus, black women's declining probability of leaving unemployment, identified previously as a major reason for their rising unemployment rate, was clearly dominated by the fall in movements from unemployment to employment when comparing March 1971 and March 1987. Similarly, the divergence in outflows between black and white men that drove their unemployment rates apart was due to black men's declining flows into employment.

Neither of the labor force participation trends that are clear in stock data for the black population—increasing participation for black women and decreasing participation for black men—are evident in the flow data. According to Table 5, the probability of moving from unemployment to not in labor force rose for black women and fell for white women. DeBoer and Seeborg[24] find that *declining* movements in and out of the labor force account for much of the fall of the total female unemployment rate relative to the male rate. The findings of this study suggest that the DeBoer and Seeborg result reflects the high proportion of white women in the female labor force and may not be true of black women. Further research will be necessary to reveal the reasons for the apparent rise in black women's movements into and out of the labor force.

Overall, the more detailed data support both the declining low-skill employment opportunities hypothesis and the increasing job instability

TABLE 5
Transition Probabilities* from Gross Flow Data

	U to E 1971	U to E 1987	U to N 1971	U to N 1987
Black & Other				
Women	.208	.132	.303	.331
Men	.295	.189	.197	.178
White				
Women	.199	.255	.300	.255
Men	.293	.289	.144	.130

Source: Author's calculations from unadjusted, unpublished gross flows data from the Bureau of Labor Statistics.
*Probability that a person in state i (U or E) in February will be in state j (U, E, or N) in March, where U is unemployment, E is employment, and N is not in labor force.

hypothesis. Further research with detailed micro-level data will be necessary both to clearly establish a skill-biased pattern in movements from unemployment into employment and to control for other factors determining job stability, however.

PUTTING THE PIECES TOGETHER

As noted earlier, EEO and affirmative action had little discernable impact on racial differences in macro-level unemployment components, either when policy enforcement was at its peak or when it dropped off dramatically during the Reagan administration. Taken alone, the declining employment opportunities hypothesis has support when applied to black men, whose unemployment gap rose because flows out of unemployment declined relative to white men. That hypothesis cannot completely explain the relative deterioration of black women's unemployment rate, though, recalling the simulations in Table 2 that pointed to the importance of diverging inflow rates in explaining the rise in black women's unemployment rate relative to white women's. The job instability argument can account for much of the increase in absolute unemployment levels of men and in the relative rates of black women, but it cannot explain the disproportionate impact of those forces on black workers.

The job competition and job matching hypotheses provide a way of relating changes in the two flows. The "thick markets" variant of job matching models predicts faster job finding when job turnover rates are higher. The average inflow rate for all workers was 2.7 percent in both 1971 and 1987, and the average outflow probabilities were .447 in 1971 and .445 in 1987. In other words, workers as a whole were entering and leaving unemployment at about the same rate in both years. If jobs had been strictly segregated by race, then we would expect black workers' higher inflows to result in faster outflows. Jobs are not completely segregated, of course, but as this article clearly shows, the distribution of the flows shifted dramatically across race and gender groups as those for whom turnover increased the most—black men and women—also faced *lower* job finding rates.

The job competition hypothesis can account for the combination of patterns: As unemployment rose after the oil shock in the mid-1970s, white workers competed more fiercely and successfully (given their employed white allies) for jobs and were therefore able to find work more easily than black workers. Those jobs with lower turnover probabilities were the most desirable to white workers, who were disproportionately hired into those jobs. According to this hypothesis, new job creation and higher turnover of black workers would create opportunities for other workers, which apparently went to white women. Both macroeconomic conditions and EEO policy would be important to this argument, interacting to influence both the incentives for and constraints on firms' and workers' actions. While antidiscrimination policy was not effective in raising black workers' relative probability of leaving unemployment (see Figures 4 and 5), the decline in enforcement when primary sector employment was shrinking may have altered black workers' access to primary sector jobs, affecting the underlying components of unemployment outflows and inflows.

These results suggest at least two directions for future empirical work. One direction is to search for evidence of mechanisms by which white workers can exert influence over firms' hiring decisions, resulting in hiring practices that favor white workers in both the private and public sectors. The importance of social networks, the role of unions, and white workers' legal challenges to affirmative action plans are all possible suspects. A second important direction would be to consider how gender interacts with race in discrimination, i.e., in the non-productivity-based ordering of the queue of unemployed workers. For instance, white women's increasing contribution to family incomes may reduce white male discrimination against white women, who could be wives or daughters, more rapidly than against black men or women.[25]

Future research could help flesh out the deficiencies in the design and enforcement of past antidiscrimination policy, as persistent racial differentials in flows from unemployment into jobs highlights a continuing need for firm-level policies aimed at promoting racial equality. Promoting stabilizing policies such as on-the-job or formal training in what have traditionally been secondary jobs—including the burgeoning category of part-time, temporary, and contractual employment—would contribute to reducing unemployment, particularly for black workers. But race neutral policies designed to stabilize employment will help black workers only if their access to new and more attractive jobs is maintained. To make a dent in the historically stubborn unemployment differential, access must be thought of in terms of quality as well as quantity of jobs.

NOTES

I would like to thank Bill Dickens, Clair Brown, Michael Reich, and Jonathan Leonard for many helpful comments on the dissertation chapter upon which this paper is based. Also, Kathy O'Regan, Mary King, Libby Bishop, Mark Carey, Suzanne Meehan, Rhonda Williams, and Gary Burtless made useful suggestions on previous versions. I also thank LaDonna Mason for her research assistance.
1. See John Bound and Richard B. Freeman "Black Economic Progress: Erosion of the Post-1965 Gains in the 1980's?" in *The Question of Discrimination,* Steven Shulman and William Darity, Jr., (eds.), (Middletown, CT: Wesleyan University Press, 1989); John H. Donohue and James Heckman, "Continuous Versus Episodic Change: The Impact of Civil Rights Policy on the Economic Status of Blacks," *Journal of Economic Literature,* XXIX (December 1991).
2. Gerald D. Jaynes, "The Labor Market Status of Black Americans: 1939–1985," *The Journal of Economic Perspectives,* 4 (4) (1990), 9–24.
3. Some recent work does examine racial differences in male teenage unemployment rates, e.g., Harry J. Holzer, "Black Youth Nonemployment: Duration and Job Search," in *The Black Youth Employment Crisis,* Richard B. Freeman and Harry J. Holzer (eds.), (Chicago: The University of Chicago Press, 1986).
4. Robert Hall, "Turnover in the Labor Force," *Brookings Papers on Economic Activity,* 3 (1972); Stephen T. Marston, "Employment Instability and High Unemployment Rates," *Brookings Papers on Economic Activity,* 1 (1976); Clair Vickery, "The Impact of Turnover on Group Unemployment Rates," *Review of Economics and Statistics,* 59 (November 1977).
5. Marston, op. cit.
6. Chinhui Juhn, "Decline of Male Labor Market Participation: The Role of Declining Market Opportunities," *The Quarterly Journal of Economics* (February 1992), 79–121.
7. John Kasarda, "Urban Industrial Transition and the Underclass," *Annals of the American Academy of Political and Social Science* (January 1989); John Bound and Harry Holzer, "Industrial Shifts, Skills Levels, and the Labor Market for White and Black Males," NBER Working Paper No. 3715, (1991).
8. Lori G. Kletzer, "Job Displacement, 1979–86: How Blacks Fared Relative to Whites," *Monthly Labor Review* (July 1991).

9. M. V. Lee Badgett, "Racial Differences in Unemployment Rates and Employment Opportunities," (Ph.D. dissertation, Berkeley: University of California, 1990).
10. Juhn, op. cit.
11. Jonathan Leonard, "The Impact of Affirmative Action Regulation and Equal Employment Law on Black Employment," *Journal of Economic Perspectives,* 4 (Fall 1990).
12. See Bound and Freeman, op. cit.; Donohue and Heckman, op. cit.
13. Jeremy I. Bulow and Lawrence H. Summers, "A Theory of Dual Labor Markets with Application to Industrial Policy, Discrimination, and Keynesian Unemployment," *Journal of Labor Economics,* 4 (1986).
14. Francine D. Blau and Andrea H. Beller, "Black-White Earnings Over the 1970's and 1980's: Gender Differences in Trends," NBER Working Paper No. 3736 (June 1991).
15. Jonathan Leonard, "Women and Affirmative Action," *Journal of Economic Perspectives,* 3 (Winter 1989).
16. William T. Dickens and Kevin Lang, "Why It Matters What We Trade: A Case for Active Policy," in *The Dynamics of Trade and Employment,* Laura D. Tyson, William T. Dickens, and John Zysman (eds.) (Cambridge, MA: Ballinger Publishing Co., 1988).
17. Labor force percentages and labor force participation rates are from *Economic Report of the President* (Washington: United States Government Printing Office, 1991).
18. Steven Shulman, "Competition and Racial Discrimination: The Employment Effects of Reagan's Labor Market Policies," *Review of Radical Political Economics,* 16 (4) (1984); Shulman, "Racial Inequality and White Employment: An Interpretation and Test of the Bargaining Power Hypothesis," *The Review of Black Political Economy,* 18 (Winter 1990), 5–20.
19. Olivier Jean Blanchard and Peter Diamond, "The Beveridge Curve," *Brookings Papers on Economic Activity,* 1 (1989).
20. These measurements were created and used most extensively by Michael R. Darby, John Haltiwanger, and Mark Plant, "Unemployment Rate Dynamics and Persistent Unemployment Under Rational Expectations," *American Economic Review,* 75 (4) (1985).
21. For derivation of equations (3) and (4), see Darby, et al., op. cit., or Badgett, op. cit.
22. Separate data on black workers was not published until 1983. The distinction between "black" and "black and other" has become more important in recent years. In March 1971, for instance, blacks made up 90% of the black and other group. By March 1987, however, blacks were only 78.2% of black and other. Unless otherwise noted, "black" will actually refer to the "black and other" group.
23. If reentrants are less committed to the labor force, they may also be less committed to employment, suggesting that the rise in reentrant unemployment and in quits might be related.
24. Larry DeBoer and Michael C. Seeborg, "The Unemployment Rates of Men and Women: A Transition Probability Analysis," *Industrial and Labor Relations Review,* 42 (3) (1989).
25. For a broader discussion of this hypothesis, see M. V. Lee Badgett and Rhonda M. Williams, "The Changing Contours of Discrimination: Race, Gender, and Structural Economic Change," in *Understanding American Economic Decline,* David Adler and Michael Bernstein (eds.) (Cambridge: Cambridge University Press, forthcoming, 1994).

VI

SECTORAL ANALYSES

THE DEMOGRAPHICS OF TRADE-AFFECTED SERVICES AND MANUFACTURING WORKERS (1987–1990): A COMPARATIVE ANALYSIS

Bartholomew Armah

Using input-output data for 1987 and 1990, this study identifies the demographic characteristics of trade-affected workers in U.S. manufacturing and service industries. Trade-affected workers are defined as employees in industries that experienced a change (positive or negative) in net total (direct and indirect) trade-related employment between 1987 and 1990. For the period 1987–1990, three industry categories were examined: (a) industries that experienced an increase in positive net trade-related employment; (b) industries that experienced a decline in positive net trade-related employment; and (c) industries that suffered net trade-related employment losses in both years yet experienced an improvement over the period. The study finds that, while manufacturing industry workers in the most favorably affected industry group (i.e., group "a") were more likely to be highly skilled (i.e., scientists & engineers), highly educated (i.e., over four years of college education), unionized, married and white males, corresponding service sector workers were predominantly unskilled (laborers), less educated, non-unionized, young (i.e., aged 16–24) and male (black and white). Furthermore, the service sector was associated with greater mean trade-related employment and output gains and lower mean employment and output losses than was the manufacturing sector.

INTRODUCTION

Although trade liberalization policies are motivated by a desire to raise world incomes, they are also associated with adjustment pressures. Within the context of current U.S. initiatives to liberalize world trade in goods and services (e.g., North American Free Trade Agreement, Uruguay Round of the General Agreement on Trade and Tariffs), this exercise seeks to reveal those groups most likely to be favorably or unfavorably affected by a policy of trade liberalization. Despite its obvious importance, few studies[1] have focused on this issue, particularly as it relates to the service sector. The current study estimates trade-related employment *and* output trends in the manufacturing and services industries during the 1987–1990 period. It is based on the most recent input-output data (i.e., 1987 and 1990) available. The latter is disaggregated to 228 sectors and comprises 80 service and 115 manufacturing sectors. The study also compares the demographic characteristics of manufacturing and service sector workers at risk of trade-related employment displacements, using input-output and Current Population Studies (CPS) data. Service and manufacturing industries are classified on the basis of their trade-related employment performance between 1987 and 1990. Three industry categories were identified: (a) industries that experienced an increase in positive net trade-related employment between 1987 and 1990; (b) industries that experienced a decrease in positive net trade-related employment between 1987 and 1990; and (c) industries that suffered net trade-related employment losses in both years, yet experienced an improvement between the two reference years.

TRADE AND DOMESTIC EMPLOYMENT

In the extended Heckscher-Ohlin-Samuelson (H-O-S) model of comparative advantage, trade patterns are explained by variations in national resources and human capital among economies. Hence, the relative abundance of capital (both human and physical) in the U.S. suggests a comparative advantage in products that are both physical and human capital-intensive. Despite the intangible nature of services, most scholars[2] are of the opinion that the theory of comparative advantage is equally applicable in predicting the pattern of service trade. While the determinants of service sector comparative advantage remains an empirical issue, it is generally conceded that skill-intensity, or knowledge, is a critical component of most service activities.[3] To the extent that these conditions hold true, we should expect international trade in goods and services to disproportionately benefit skilled workers in the services and manufacturing industries.[4] The corresponding effect of trade on various demographic groups will depend on their level of human capital endowments and their ability to translate such endowments into employment in skill-intensive industries.

It should be noted, however, that differences in factor endowments alone do not explain trade patterns. Improved access to information and the presence of scale economies can also lower unit costs and thus enhance international competitiveness.[5] Alternatively, excessive trade barriers—particularly in the service sector, which faces higher tariff and nontariff barriers than does manufacturing—tend to undermine international competitiveness and alter the predicted incidence of trade adjustment pressures on various groups within in the service sector.[6] Thus, in the context of current regulatory regimes, skill-intensive U.S. service industries may not necessarily be internationally competitive. Indeed, while empirical studies[7] on the determinants of service trade confirm the importance of skill intensity as a source of comparative advantage, they find that service sector comparative advantage is also influenced by differences in physical capital-intensity and by disparities in scale economies. In a study of four service industry categories, Sapir[8] reports that comparative advantage in transportation services is determined by physical capital. Scale economies was identified as an important factor for "other" services, while human capital was isolated as a key determinant of comparative advantage in insurance services. However, the relative size of the insurance industry's professional and technical staff was reported to have no influence on that sector's competitiveness.

The factor endowments theory also fails to adequately explain the post WW II growth in manufacturing intra-industry goods trade[9] since the latter is characterized by exchange among similarly endowed countries. This trend is largely attributed to scale economies in manufacturing production,[10] a phenomenon that is at odds with the underlying assumption of constant returns to scale embedded in orthodox trade theory.[11] Krugman, Dixit and Norman,[12] and Lancaster[13] show that even if countries are the same in every respect (i.e., tastes, technologies, and factor endowments) intra-industry trade will occur in order to exploit the benefits of increasing returns to scale, and, in fact, the more similar trading partners are, the more trade will occur. Thus, within the context of manufacturing intra-industry trade, it is conceivable that displaced workers will be comprised of skilled workers in high-tech manufacturing industries if market distortions or other relevant factors reduce the competitiveness of such industries.

METHOD

Trade-affected industries are identified by using an input-output model to estimate the net (exports less imports) total (i.e., direct and indirect) labor inputs required to satisfy the change in export and import levels between 1987 and 1990. For each industry and reference year, the total job creating effects of exports[14] were subtracted from the total job displacing effects of imports[15] to arrive at the net total trade-related employment estimates. Subtracting the 1987 net trade-related employment estimates from corresponding estimates for 1990 yields the change in net trade-related employment between 1987 and 1990. The labor displacing (creating) impact of imports (exports) is defined as the direct and indirect sectoral labor inputs required to satisfy the sectoral change in import (export) levels between 1987 and 1990. Services and manufacturing industries were subsequently classified based on their net total trade-related employment performance between 1987 and 1990.

The direct effects of trade comprise the employment and output effects in the industry directly impacted by a change in exports or imports (e.g., an increase in the foreign demand for the services of U.S. engineering consultants). The indirect impact reflects the ripple effect on related industries. For instance, U.S. engineering consultants may require the services of lawyers to work out the legal complexities associated with doing business abroad; sophisticated computer software may be required to successfully undertake the consulting task; and airline services may be required to transport the consultants to the foreign location. Such activities will invariably affect the level of output and employment in the industries doing business directly or indirectly with the engineering consulting firm. These indirect effects are captured by the input-output model.

The Model

The following model draws heavily on Young et al.,[16] Miyazawa,[17] and Kim and Turrubiate.[18] The balance equation in the input-output system states that for any sector, gross domestic output (X) is the sum of intermediate goods demand (AX) and final demand (F), minus imports (M):

(1) $X = AX + F{-}M$

where A is a square matrix of total (domestic plus imported) intermediate input coefficients. The elements of the A matrix (a_{ij}) indicate the level of the ith commodity used in the production of each unit of the jth commodity. Denoting by Am a matrix of imported input-output coefficients, total Imports (M) are disaggregated into their final (Mf) and intermediate (Am) use components to allow for the possibility of substitution between domestic and imported inputs.[19] Since the amount of intermediate imports (Am) needed depends on the level of output (X):

(2) $M = Mf + AmX$

Substituting terms, the solution for X is:

(3) $X = (1 - A + Am)^{-1} (F - Mf)$

Let EX_t represent the export component of final demand (F_t) in time 't', and designate Mf_t as final import demand in the corresponding time period. The total (direct plus intermediate) effect of a hypothetical change in exports on domestic employment in time 't' is:

(4) $XE_t = L_t(1 - A_t + Am_t)^{-1}\Delta EX_t$

where:

L_t is a vector of sectoral labor output coefficients in year 't'.

ΔEX_t is a vector representing a hypothetical change in sectoral exports in year 't'. Note that these changes are assumed to equal the sectoral change in exports between 1987 and 1990, expressed in 1987 dollars.

The impact of a change in imports on employment is:

(5) $ME_t = L_t(1 - A_t + Am^t)^{-1} \Delta Mf_t$

where:

ME_t represents potential domestic employment shifts due to a hypothetical change in imports.

ΔMf_t is a hypothetical change in sectoral final imports in year 't'. Again, these changes are assumed to equal sectoral changes in imports between 1987 and 1990, expressed in 1987 dollars.

Net trade-related employment in time 't' (N_t) is:

(6) $N_t = XE_t - ME_t$

The shift in net trade-related employment between 1987 and 1990 (ΔN) is:

(7) $\Delta N = N_{1990} - N_{1987}$

where:

N_{1987} is total net trade-related employment in 1987.

N_{1990} is total net trade-related employment in 1990.

DATA SOURCES

The input-output model used in the study is based on the Office of Employment Projection's 1987 and 1990 228-sector input-output tables, which cover a total of 115 manufacturing and 80 service industries. The I-O tables provide information on inter-industry technical coefficients and final demands, including exports and imports. The output measures follow the definition and conventions used by the Bureau of Economic Analysis (BEA) in its input-output tables published every five years. These industry output measures are based on producers' value and include both primary and secondary products and services. Note that the service industry includes "margin industries"—trade and transportation industries—which are defined in terms of distribution costs incurred in the distribution process. Both the 1990 and 1987 tables are expressed in 1987 dollars and have been adjusted by the Bureau of Labor Statistics (BLS) to reflect the 1987 Standard Industrial Classification (SIC) revision. Three-digit (SIC) services and manufacturing employment data from the March Current Population Survey (CPS) for the period 1987–1990, were used to identify the characteristics of workers employed in the four industry groups. The data set is restricted to full-time manufacturing and service sector employees aged 16 years or older. CPS industrial classifications are based on Census Industry Classifications, while I-O classification combine industries as defined in the Standard Industry Classification (SIC). Thus, CPS and I-O classification do not necessarily coincide. Since Census Industry Classifications also provide SIC code equivalents, reconciliation of the two schemes was achieved by matching industry classifications that were common to both. In cases where there was no discernable match between the two classification schemes, the relevant industries were omitted from the analysis.

Employment output ratios are combined with the 1987 and 1990 input-output tables to estimate trade-related employment. The employment data is derived from 1987 and 1990 wage and salary employment statistics obtained from the Office of Employment Projections. The ratios are estimated by dividing wage and salary employment per sector by the total output of the corresponding sector.

RESULTS

Trade-related employment estimates and the demographic characteristics of the three industry groups are provided below. The trade-related employment figures below are measured in "person years" since sectoral employment output ratios are based on yearly estimates. Within the manufacturing sector, a fourth group of industries was identified (i.e., indus-

tries that experienced an increase in negative net trade-related employment levels between 1987 and 1990); however, since no corresponding
category was identified among service industries, the latter category is
not discussed. Nonetheless, trade-related employment figures for this industry category are provided in the appendix.

Positive Trade-related Employment (Positive Trend)

A comparison of Tables 1 and 2 reveals that services and manufacturing industries that enjoyed positive shifts in net trade-related employment between 1987 and 1990 experienced a similar trend in trade-related
output. Although manufacturing industries generated relatively greater
total levels of trade-related employment than did service industries in
both years (e.g., 1,216.9 versus 696.5 person-years in 1990), mean employment levels were significantly higher in the services sector (e.g.,116.08
versus 76.05 person-years in 1990). Furthermore, between 1987 and 1990,
the service sector recorded larger trade-related employment (281.7 person-years versus 221.38 person-years) shifts than did the manufacturing
sector. As a whole, service industries in this category created approximately 60 more trade-related employment opportunities than did manufacturing industries. Percentage shifts in trade-related employment (67.9
percent versus 18.19 percent) and output (73.9 percent versus 48.2 percent) were also relatively higher in services than they were in manufacturing.

Among services and manufacturing industries the greatest increase
occurred in air transportation (230 person hours) (see Table 1), and pe-
troleum refining (91 person hours) (see Table 2) respectively. Air transportation generated higher levels of trade-related employment in both
years than did any of the manufacturing industries. This finding is noteworthy, particularly since goods are generally perceived to be more trad-
able than services.

Demographics

Manufacturing industry workers in this industry group comprised a
higher percentage of black and white union members, scientists and engineers, married couples, highly educated blacks (i.e., blacks with more
than four years of college education) and white males (71.5 percent) than
did manufacturing workers in the other industry categories. On the other

hand, both black and white service sector workers in this group were less skilled, less educated, less unionized, younger (i.e., aged 16–24) and more likely to be male than were service workers in the other industry groups (see Tables 7 and 8).

Positive Net Trade-related Employment (Negative Trend)

Tables 3 and 4 indicate that within this category, service industries also fared better than did manufacturing industries in the sense that they experienced a smaller mean decline in trade-related job and output creation. In the service sector, mean trade-related employment and output levels declined 5.14 person-years and $11.59m respectively, compared to corresponding figures of 6.69 person-years and $27.2m in the manufacturing sector. Overall, the manufacturing sector created approximately 174.2 fewer trade-related job opportunities in 1990 than it did in 1987, while output declined by approximately $709m. Corresponding employment and output estimates for the services sector were -102.8 person-years and -$231.82m respectively. Engineering and architectural services, however, accounted for the greatest employment decline (45.2 person-years) in trade related employment among all industries in this category. It was closely followed by industrial machinery nec., (44.4 person-years). To the extent that trade-related employment declines were correlated with output losses, this category of industries appears to have experienced a decline in international competitiveness.

Demographics

Manufacturing industries that experienced a decline in positive net trade-related employment were more likely to employ black females and unskilled (i.e., laborers) and less educated (i.e., high school graduates) black and white workers than were other manufacturing industries. However, the corresponding service sector workforce was more educated (i.e., completed four or more years of college education), more skilled (i.e., scientists, engineers and managers) and more feminized than were workers in the other service industry categories (see Tables 7 and 8).

TABLE 1
Positive Net Trade-Related Service Employment (Positive Trend)
(Person-Years)

Industry	Employment			Output[1]	
	1987	1990	Change	1987	Change
Air Transport	235.60	465.60	230.0000	$1.96	$2.43
Computer & Data Processing Services	78.40	96.70	18.3000	$1.11	$0.44
Gas utilities including combined services	49.90	54.19	4.2900	$1.04	$0.05
Retail Trade except Eating & Drinking	30.60	57.20	26.6000	$0.58	$0.64
Miscellaneous Equipment Rental & Leasing	13.90	15.13	1.2300	$0.10	$0.02
Miscellaneous Repair Shops	6.40	7.70	1.3000	$0.05	$0.01
Total	414.80	696.52	281.7200	4.84	3.59
Mean	69.13	116.09	46.9533	0.81	0.60

[1] Output change between 1990 and 1987, measured in billions of dollars.

TABLE 2
Positive Net Trade-Related Manufacturing Employment (Positive Trend)
(Person-Years)

Industry	Employment			Output[1]		
	1987	1990	Change	1987	1990	Change
Petroleum Refining	100.0000	191.300	91.30	$2.850		$2.80000
Rubber products and plastic hose footwear	237.4000	294.400	57.00	$1.230		$0.40000
Luggage, handbags, and leather products, nec	171.0000	196.000	25.00	$0.920		$0.23000
Footwear, except rubber and plastic	210.0000	229.700	19.70	$0.590		$0.10000
Pulp, paper, and paperboard mills	233.0000	246.400	13.40	$2.380		$0.30000
Motor vehicle parts and accessories	6.3000	14.800	8.50	$0.060		$0.09000
Medical instruments and supplies	16.0000	17.800	1.80	$0.080		$0.02000
Preserved fruits and vegetables	8.0000	9.400	1.40	$0.070		$0.02000
Telephone and telegraph apparatus	5.0000	6.000	1.00	$0.030		$0.01000
Aircraft	2.9000	3.700	0.80	$0.020		$0.01000
Boat building and repairing	0.5000	1.000	0.50	$0.003		$0.00300
Miscellaneous textile goods	3.5000	3.800	0.30	$0.023		$0.00400
Electrical equipment and supplies, nec	1.0000	1.300	0.30	$0.005		$0.00400
Dairy products	0.8000	1.100	0.30	$0.008		$0.00300
Ammunition and ordnance, except small arms	0.1500	0.220	0.07	$0.001		$0.00030
Printing trade service	0.0002	0.005	0.01	$0.000		$0.00002
Total	995.5502	1,216.930	221.38	$8.270		$3.99000
Mean	62.2219	76.058	13.84	$0.517		$0.2494

[1] Output change between 1990 and 1987, measured in billions of dollars.

TABLE 3
Positive Net Trade-Related Services Employment (Negative Trend)
(Person-Years)

Industry	Employment 1987	Employment 1990	Change	Output Change[1]
Trucking and warehousing	413.50	400.90	-12.60	$203.00
Engineering & Architectural Services	119.50	74.30	-45.20	-$189.00
Management & Public Relations	68.80	47.85	-20.95	-$109.00
Depository Institutions	38.40	26.92	-11.48	-$119.00
Legal Services	17.40	16.38	-1.02	$8.10
Colleges and Universities	12.30	9.73	-2.57	-$9.30
Passenger Transport Arrangements	11.80	8.68	-3.12	-$4.00
Research and Testing Services	7.20	4.18	-3.02	-$6.40
Motion Pictures	4.70	4.37	-0.33	-$1.60
Miscellaneous transportation services	2.70	2.30	-0.40	-$1.30
Services to buildings	2.50	1.92	-0.58	-$0.10
Business services nec	2.46	1.86	-0.60	-$1.40
Personnel supply services	2.39	1.92	-0.47	-$0.25
Insurance agents, brokers and services	0.70	0.49	-0.21	-$0.78
Pipelines except natural gas	0.50	0.46	-0.04	-$0.94
Automobile parking, repair and services	0.39	0.32	-0.07	-$0.41
Detective guards and security services	0.33	0.28	-0.05	-$0.04
Amusement and recreational services nec.	0.07	0.06	-0.01	-$0.35
Photocopy, commercial art, photofinishing	0.05	0.03	-0.02	-$0.05
Total	705.69	602.95	-102.74	$-232.82
Mean	35.28	30.15	-5.14	$-11.64

[1] Output change between 1990 and 1987, measured in millions of dollars.

TABLE 4
Positive Net Trade-Related Manufacturing Employment (Negative Trend)
(Person-Years)

Industry	Employment			Output[1]
	1987	1990	Change	Change
Industrial machinery, nec	83.40	39.00	-44.400	-$161.10
Meat products	270.20	240.30	-29.900	-$155.00
Agricultural chemicals	50.00	29.10	-20.900	-$153.00
Household furniture	24.20	12.80	-11.400	-$44.20
Metalworking machinery	31.10	6.20	-24.900	-$25.30
Apparel	53.00	46.50	-6.500	-$36.50
Office and accounting machines	16.50	10.60	-5.900	-$20.00
Glass and glass products	24.60	20.10	-4.500	-$24.90
Grain mill products and fats and oils	26.30	22.00	-4.300	-$16.70
Toys and sporting goods	17.00	13.30	-3.700	-$9.17
Household appliances	17.60	14.10	-3.500	-$11.60
Search and navigation equipment	7.00	3.50	-3.500	-$19.30
Motor vehicles and car bodies	12.50	10.00	-2.500	-$31.40
Stone, clay, and misc., mineral products	1.70	0.30	-1.400	-$9.06
Storage batteries and engine electrical parts	15.50	14.10	-1.400	-$6.20
Household audio and video equipment	33.30	32.20	-1.100	$16.70
Jewelry, silverware, and plated ware	20.20	19.10	-1.100	-$2.10
Alcoholic beverages	3.00	2.10	-0.900	-$4.50
Photographic equipment and supplies	8.00	7.30	-0.700	$4.60
Mining and oil field machinery	2.50	2.00	-0.500	-$1.90
Ship building and repairing	3.60	3.10	-0.500	-$0.20
X-ray and other electromedical apparatus	5.00	4.60	-0.400	$1.02
Veneer and plywood	0.90	0.70	-0.200	-$0.87
Office and misc. furniture and fixtures	4.14	4.10	-0.040	$1.70
Partitions and fixtures	0.05	0.04	-0.011	-$0.03
Guided missiles and space vehicles	0.01	0.003	-0.004	-$0.02
Total	731.30	557.14	-174.160	-$709.03
Mean	28.13	21.43	-6.699	-$27.27

[1] Output change between 1990 and 1987, measured in millions of dollars.

TABLE 5
Negative Net Trade-Related Service Employment (Positive Trend)
(Person-Years)

Industry	Employment			Output[1]
	1987	1990	Change	Change
Wholesale trade	-1159.20	-704.50	454.70	$8,500.000
Real Estate	-341.30	-268.36	72.94	$4,000.000
Water Transportation	-191.50	-180.75	10.75	-$42.800
Railroad transportation	-53.70	-48.50	5.20	-$11.860
Eating & drinking places	-44.60	-37.60	7.00	$46.400
Communications except broadcasting	-41.20	-34.60	6.60	$4.900
Insurance carriers	-33.80	-32.10	1.70	-$30.100
Security and commodity brokers	-31.10	-23.80	7.30	$42.300
Hotels and other lodging places	-2.20	-1.60	0.60	$2.700
U.S. postal services	-1.70	-1.27	0.43	$0.644
Accounting Auditing and services	-1.00	-0.82	0.18	$1.120
Water and sanitation incl. combined services	-0.18	-0.15	0.03	$0.168
Electrical repair shops	-0.11	-0.09	0.02	$0.082
Automotive rentals without drivers	-0.07	-0.06	0.01	$0.106
Offices of health practitioners	-0.01	-0.01	0.00	$0.020
Health services, not elsewhere specified	-0.01	-0.01	0.00	$0.004
Total	-1,901.68	-1,334.22	567.46	$12,513.684
Mean	-111.86	-78.48	33.38	$736.099

[1] Output change between 1990 and 1987, measured in millions of dollars.

TABLE 6
Negative Net Trade-Related Manufacturing Employment (Positive Trend)
(Person-Years)

Industry	Employment			Output[1]		
	1987	1990	Change	1987	1990	Change
Knitting mills	-0.2500	-0.09000	0.16	-$1.080	-$0.4000	-$1.700
Forgings	-0.0700	-0.06000	0.01	-$0.420	-$0.3970	$0.019
Miscellaneous food and kindred products	-0.6000	-0.50000	0.10	-$4.670	-$3.8000	$0.870
Miscellaneous chemical products	-55.0600	-54.15000	0.91	-$470.200	-$498.4000	-$28.200
Plumbing and nonelectrical heating equipment	-2.9000	-2.40000	0.50	-$14.160	-$13.2000	$0.960
Industrial chemicals	-2265.3000	-1842.50000	422.80	-$32,600.000	-$27,400.0000	$5,200.000
Paperboard containers and boxes	-2.1000	-1.30000	0.80	-$15.500	-$10.7000	$4.800
Metal cans and shipping containers	-0.2400	-0.22000	0.02	-$1.990	-$1.9950	-$0.008
Mobile homes	-0.0002	-0.00002	0.00	-$0.001	-$0.0001	$0.001
Miscellaneous plastic products nec.	-2613.0000	-2443.70000	169.30	-$22,380.000	-$22,100.0000	$280.000
Converted paper products except containers	-30.0000	-29.50000	0.50	-$234.000	-$271.6000	-$37.600
Nonferrous foundries	-0.2000	-0.05000	0.15	-$253.900	-$253.4000	$0.500
Drugs	-26.2000	-24.30000	1.90	-$214.800	-$216.4000	-$1.600
Fabricated structural metal products	-7.8000	-7.70000	0.10	-$51.860	-$53.9000	-$2.040
Cement, concrete, gypsum, & plaster products	-1.9000	-1.60000	0.30	-$12.700	-$11.0000	$1.700
Automotive stampings	-1.2400	-1.00000	0.24	-$8.800	-$7.3000	$1.500
Semiconductors and related devices	-160.0000	-152.30000	7.70	-$681.900	-$860.2000	-$178.300
Miscellaneous electronic components	-95.8000	-93.80000	2.00	-$510.100	-$609.8000	-$99.700
Engines and turbines	-5.8000	-4.00000	1.80	-$32.900	-$24.5000	$8.400

[1] Output is measured in millions of dollars.

TABLE 6 (continued)

Industry	Employment			Output[1]		
	1987	1990	Change	1987	1990	Change
Stampings except automotive	-1.40	-1.00	0.40	-$7.90	-$5.40	$2.50
Special industry machinery	-225.00	-190.00	35.00	-$1,178.50	-$1,120.00	$58.50
Sawmills and planning mills	-15.00	-10.20	4.80	-$64.30	-$44.60	$19.70
Periodicals	-1.60	-1.40	0.20	-$9.29	-$8.50	$0.79
Railroad equipment	-1.00	-0.60	0.40	-$3.45	-$3.30	$0.15
Material handling machinery and equipment	-6.40	-6.00	0.40	-$30.99	-$32.80	-$1.81
Aircraft and missile parts and equipment	-85.00	-71.00	14.00	-$422.40	-$394.30	$28.10
Miscellaneous petroleum and coal products	-24.00	-17.30	6.70	-$317.80	-$234.40	$83.40
Logging	-77.80	-70.00	7.80	-$369.60	-$327.70	$41.90
Measuring and controlling devices; watches	-52.30	-46.30	6.00	-$255.90	-$252.80	$3.10
Plastics materials and synthetics	-1404.50	-1261.70	142.80	-$16,540.00	-$15,400.00	$1,140.00
Total	-7,162.46	-6,334.67	827.79	-$74,702.11	-$68,170.79	$6,526.15
Mean	-238.75	-211.16	27.59	-$2,490.07	-$2,272.36	$217.54

[1] Output is measured in millions of dollars.

*Negative Net Trade-related Employment (Positive Trend): Trade-related
Employment*

Tables 5 and 6 show that unlike the other industry categories, manufacturing industries in this industry group experienced a larger total increase in trade-related employment, between 1987 and 1990, than did
service industries (827.79 person-years versus 567.46 person-years). However, corresponding gains in trade-related output levels were significantly
lower for manufacturing ($6.5bn versus $12.5bn in services). On the
other hand, mean employment and output shifts were higher among service industries. Mean trade-related employment and output increased by
33.38 person-years and $736m respectively in the services sector, com-
pared to 27.59 person-years and $217m in the manufacturing sector (see
Tables 5 and 6). For both sectors, net trade-related employment losses in
both years were associated with corresponding trade-related output losses.
Hence, trade-related employment displacements among this category of
industries may have resulted from limited international competitiveness
although these industries experienced an improvement over the period.

Demographics

Relative to other manufacturing industries, manufacturing workers in
this industry group were more likely to be managers, black males, college graduates (i.e., completed four years of college education) and young
(i.e., in the 25 to 35 age bracket). Service sector workers in this category
were relatively more unionized than were those in other service industries (see Tables 7 and 8).

DISCUSSION AND CONCLUSIONS

A comparison of the services and manufacturing sector using 1987 and
1990 input-output data reveals that the manufacturing sector created fewer
net total trade-related employment and output opportunities per industry
than did the services sector. On average, service industries also accounted
for fewer trade-related employment and output losses than did the manufacturing sector. There is some evidence of higher manufacturing sector
productivity levels among industries that experienced an increase in positive net trade-related employment since output grew more than twice
(2.65) the rate of employment growth. The corresponding ratio for services was only 1.08. The effects of trade on the service and manufactur-

TABLE 7
Distribution of Employment by Service Industry Category

Demographic Characteristic	Positive Employment				Negative Employment	
	Positive Trend		Negative Trend		Positive Trend	
	White	Black	White	Black	White	Black
Male	62.3 (71.5)	56.9 (61.6)	55.8 (70.9)	45.0 (56.4)	60.4 (69.8)	52.8 (62.0)
Female	37.7 (28.5)	43.1 (38.4)	44.1 (29.1)	54.9 (43.6)	39.6 (30.2)	47.2 (38.0)
Married	63.3 (70.8)	45.5 (59.5)	65.0 (70.6)	47.3 (56.7)	64.5 (69.7)	47.1 (57.5)
25 to 35 yrs of age	33.7 (31.6)	37.9 (31.6)	34.8 (33.0)	39.3 (34.6)	34.1 (34.6)	37.3 (36.1)
16 to 24 yrs of age	18.0 (9.8)	21.5 (8.1)	11.4 (11.3)	13.8 (12.9)	14.1 (11.3)	14.7 (8.6)
Resides in northcentral[1]	26.0 (40.8)	17.6 (42.2)	24.7 (36.0)	16.6 (21.6)	26.5 (31.2)	17.0 (21.4)
Resides in northeast	25.4 (25.5)	21.2 (15.6)	28.5 (24.6)	27.4 (12.9)	25.8 (28.4)	20.7 (20.1)
Resides in west	15.3 (11.6)	6.6 (2.3)	15.4 (11.2)	7.2 (2.0)	16.4 (9.7)	7.0 (2.2)
Resides in south	33.3 (22.1)	54.5 (39.9)	31.3 (28.2)	48.8 (63.5)	31.3 (30.7)	55.3 (56.3)
Union member	1.8 (7.8)	3.1 (11.0)	2.0 (5.8)	3.8 (7.1)	3.7 (3.9)	8.0 (7.1)
Work experience	19.0 (21.7)	17.2 (21.5)	19.0 (21.7)	18.0 (20.6)	19.7 (20.6)	19.1 (20.7)
4yrs of college	12.5 (12.7)	9.3 (7.3)	18.7 (9.7)	13.3 (4.8)	15.6 (13.6)	9.0 (7.4)

TABLE 7 (continued)

Demographic Characteristic	Positive Employment				Negative Employment	
	Positive Trend		Negative Trend		Positive Trend	
	White	Black	White	Black	White	Black
Post-college education	4.7 (6.8)	2.6 (2.3)	21.5 (4.6)	8.5 (1.7)	7.3 (7.8)	3.0 (1.2)
4 yrs of high school	46.8 (45.0)	47.4 (50.0)	30.6 (46.9)	38.3 (50.8)	39.7 (44.9)	46.0 (50.6)
Manager	8.0 (12.5)	5.0 (3.0)	21.5 (11.4)	11.6 (2.4)	18.7 (14.6)	11.0 (3.2)
Scientist/engineer	1.8 (5.5)	1.0 (2.6)	6.8 (4.6)	2.9 (1.5)	1.8 (4.6)	1.5 (0.9)
Laborer	6.1 (4.3)	13.5 (4.4)	1.7 (5.3)	3.4 (10.4)	3.3 (4.5)	6.4 (9.2)

Source: Current Population Survey: 1987–1990 Annual Averages.
Note: Estimates for manufacturing sector are in brackets. Numbers may not sum to 100 percent due to rounding.
[1] The percentages only include persons in sample who reside in either of the four regions.

ing sectors also varied by region of impact. Within the manufacturing sector, the highest concentration of white workers (40.8 percent) was in industries with positive employment trends (i.e., increasing net positive employment) located in the northcentral region. On the other hand, blacks (56.3 percent) were concentrated in southern industries, which experienced a decline in net positive employment. Unlike the manufacturing sector, the highest concentration of both black and white service workers was found in southern industries. However, while blacks were more likely to be employed in southern industries that suffered net negative employment (55.3 percent), white southern workers were more likely to be employed in industries that enjoyed an increase positive employment (33.3 percent) between 1987 and 1990. (See Tables 7 and 8.)

To the extent that manufacturing and services activities tend to be inextricably linked, the favorable performance of service industries may be due to their support role in satisfying export demand initially generated within the manufacturing sector. For example, an increase in foreign demand for U.S. computers will tend to generate indirect employment and output benefits in related service industries such as shipping, telecommunications and insurance services. Since direct exports of services occur on a lesser scale than do goods exports, it is likely that a higher share of service sector trade-related employment is indirectly generated by manufacturing trade. In other words, the bulk of service sector trade-related employment may result from service activities linked directly or indirectly to manufacturing exports.

The study also reveals marked differences in the skill levels of trade-effected services and manufacturing industries. While internationally competitive manufacturing industries tend to be human capital-intensive, corresponding service sector industries exhibit relatively low levels of human capital intensity. This finding is at odds with the extended H-O-S model of comparative advantage since the U.S. is blessed with an abundance of both human and physical capital. Unlike manufacturing industries, the most human capital-intensive service industries experienced a decline in positive net trade-related employment. Indeed, service industries with declining positive net trade-related employment were more skill-intensive (as measured by the share of scientists and engineers in the labor force) than were manufacturing industries in the same category. On the other hand, trade-enhanced (i.e., the most favorably affected) service industries used laborers more intensively than did corresponding manufacturing industries. Thus, unlike the manufacturing sector, skilled and highly educated service workers face fewer trade-related employment opportunities than do unskilled and less educated service workers.

However, not all categories of skilled and educated manufacturing workers were immune from trade-related employment pressures. Managers and workers with no more than four years of college education were more likely to be employed in manufacturing industries that suffered trade-related employment losses in 1987 and 1990, even though displacements were considerably lower in 1990. It is conceivable that the latter workers may be victims of less competitive U.S. industries engaged in intra-industry manufacturing trade. On the other hand, the less favorable effects of trade on skilled service workers may be attributable to trade barriers disproportionately targeted at high-tech U.S. service industries. An alternative explanation is that, unlike the manufacturing sector, human capital-intensity may not be a decisive determinant of service sector comparative advantage after all; the importance of a service as an input in a manufactured export, as opposed to the skill level of the service provider, may ultimately dictate the level of trade-related employment and output generated in that service sector. In either case further research aimed at identifying the factors shaping service sector comparative advantage will provide policymakers with a framework for predicting the effects of service trade liberalization on various groups in the domestic economy.

TABLE 8
Characteristics of Trade-Affected Workers by Industry Category

	PP		PN		NP	
	Service	Manuf.¹	Service	Manuf.	Service	Manuf
	male	white male	-	-	-	Black male
	-	-	female	black female	-	white female
	-	married	married	-	-	-
	teenager	-	young	-	-	young
	-	union member	-	-	union member	-
	high school graduate	black post-college	4yr college	high school graduate	-	4yr. college
	-	-	post-college	-	-	-
	-	-	-	-	-	-
	laborer	-	manager	laborer	-	manager
	-	scientist/engineer	scientist/engineer	-	-	-
	South (White)	Northcentral (White)	-	South (Black)	South (Black)	-

¹ Manufacturing
PP—Positive net trade-related employment with a positive trend
PN—Positive net trade-related employment with a negative trend
NP—Negative net trade-related employment with a positive trend

Negative Net Trade-Related Employment (Negative Trend)
(Person-Years)

Industry	Employment 1987	Employment 1990	Change	Output[1] Change
Nonferrous rolling & drawing	-24.30	-60.00	-35.70	-$332.00
Blast furnaces and basic steel products	-507.00	-540.30	-33.30	-$929.80
Computer equipment	-6.30	-30.00	-23.70	-$240.70
Weaving, finishing, yarn, and thread mills	-247.50	-263.70	-16.20	-$160.20
Electric lighting and wiring equipment	-2.00	-10.50	-8.50	-$51.90
Refrigeration and service industry machinery	-18.60	-25.40	-6.80	-$56.20
Tires and inner tubes	-100.00	-106.70	-6.70	-$128.00
Miscellaneous fabricated metal products	-119.00	-124.00	-5.00	-$101.00
Screw machine products, bolts, rivets, etc.,	-1.10	-4.10	-3.00	-$14.60
Soap, cleaners, and toilet goods	-8.00	-10.60	-2.60	-$32.20
Miscellaneous primary and secondary metals	-1.50	-4.00	-2.50	-$26.30
Electrical industrial apparatus	-3.00	-4.30	-1.30	-$10.50
Wood containers and miscellaneous wood products	-18.80	-20.00	-1.20	-$8.40
Miscellaneous fabricated textile products	-3.40	-4.60	-1.20	-$5.97
Paints and allied products	-1.20	-2.30	-1.10	-$11.05
Manufactured products, nec	-7.10	-8.20	-1.10	-$8.50
Sugar and confectionery products	-2.40	-3.20	-0.80	-$8.30
Electric distribution equipment	-2.00	-2.60	-0.60	-$5.80
Millwork and structural wood members, nec	-1.10	-1.70	-0.60	-$2.70
Books	-2.00	-2.30	-0.30	-$4.70

APPENDIX (continued)

Industry	Employment			Output[1]
	1987	1990	Change	Change
Farm and garden machinery	-7.40	-7.600	-0.20	-$9.20
Miscellaneous transportation equipment	-0.60	-0.800	-0.20	-$1.40
Carpets and rugs	-0.20	-0.400	-0.20	-$1.00
Blankbooks and bookbinding	-0.20	-0.300	-0.10	-$0.49
Miscellaneous publishing	-0.07	-0.200	-0.13	-$0.55
Broadcasting and communications equipment	-0.50	-0.600	-0.10	-$1.30
Construction machinery	-10.00	-10.100	-0.10	-$13.00
Small arms and small arms ammunition	-0.06	-0.150	-0.09	-$0.40
Tobacco products	-0.25	-0.290	-0.04	-$0.49
Aircraft and missile engines	-0.84	-0.870	-0.03	-$0.78
Greeting card publishing	-0.02	-0.025	-0.01	-$0.06
Total	-1,096.44	-1,249.840	-153.40	-$2,167.49
Mean	-34.26	-39.060	-4.79	-$67.73

[1] Output change between 1990 and 1987, measured in millions of dollars.

NOTES

This is a revised version of a paper presented at the Western Economic Association Internationale 69th Annual Conference, Vancouver, British Columbia, June 29–July 3, 1994.

1. With the notable exception of A. Sapir and Ernst Lutz, "Trade in Services: Economic Determinants and Development-Related Issues." *World Bank Staff Working Paper* 480, (1981); Nicholas Oulton, *International Trade in Services and the Comparative Advantage of E. C. Countries.* Trade Policy Research Center (London, 1984); and B. Armah, "Impact of Trade on Service Sector Employment: Implications for Women and Minorities," *Contemporary Economic Policy*, vol. XII, no. 1, (January 1994), the author is not aware of any other studies on service sector international trade. With the exception of Armah (1994), these studies do not identify at-risk service sector workers. Studies aimed at identifying the characteristics of trade-affected manufacturing sector workers include B. Armah, "Trade Sensitive Manufacturing Industries: Some New Insights," *The Review of Black Political Economy* 21 (Fall 1992), 37–54; M.C. Aho and J.A. Orr, "The Growth of Trade Sensitive Employment: Who are the Affected Workers?", *Monthly Labor Review* 104 (Feb. 1981), 29–35; and Robert Z. Lawrence, "Minority Employment and U.S. Trade" in *Foreign Trade Policy and Black Economic Advancement,* Proceedings of a Roundtable. (Washington D.C.: Joint Center for Political Studies, May 1980).

2. For a discussion of this issue see Deardorff, "Comparative Advantage and International Trade and Investment in Services" in Robert Stern (ed.), *Trade and Investment in Services: Canada/U.S. Perspectives,* (University of Toronto Press, Toronto, 1985); Brian Hindley and Alisdair Smith, "Comparative Advantage and Trade in Services," *The World Economy* 7 (1984): 369–390; and B. Herman and B. van Holst, *Towards a Theory of International Trade in Services,* (Rotterdam: Netherlands Economic Institute,1981).

3. See Murray Gibbs, "Services, Development and TNC's," *The CTC Reporter,* (Spring, 1986); and Jacques Nusbaumer, *Services in the Global Market,* (Boston/ Dordrech/Lancaster: Kluwer Academic Publishers, 1987).

4. See M.C. Aho and J.A. Orr, "The Growth of Trade Sensitive Employment: Who are the Affected Workers?"; and B. Armah, "Trade Sensitive Manufacturing Industries: Some New Insights."

5. See Irving Kravis, "The Current Case for Import Limitations," in *Commission on International Trade and Investment Policy: US Policy in an Interdependent World,* (Washington D.C. Government Printing Office, 1971); and Bela Balassa, *Trade Liberalization Among Industrial Countries: Objectives and Alternatives,* (McGraw-Hill, New York, 1967).

6. Rachel McCulloch, "Services and the Uruguay Round," *The World Economy,* vol. 13, no. 3, (Sept. 1990), 329–48.

7. A. Sapir and Ernst Lutz, "Trade in Services: Economic Determinants and Development-Related Issues;" Nicholas Oulton, *International Trade in Services and the Comparative Advantage of E.C. Countries.*

8. Andre Sapir, "Trade in Services: Policy Issues For The Eighties," *Columbia Journal of World Business,* (Fall 1982), 77–83.

9. According to Herbert G. Grubel and Peter J. Lloyd, *Intra-industry Trade: The Theory and Measurement of International Trade in Differentiated Products,* (New York: John Wiley,1975), the share of manufacturing intraindustry trade in all trade is more than 50 percent and increasing rapidly.

10. Paul R. Krugman, "Increasing Returns, Monopolistic Competition and International Trade," *Journal of International Economics,* vol., 9, (1979): 469–79.

11. This theory also assumes product homogeneity and perfect competition, which are not characteristic features of manufacturing trade.

12. A. Dixit and Victor Norman, "Product Differentiation and Intraindustry Trade," in Gene Grossman (ed.) *Imperfect Competition and International Trade,* (MIT Press, 1992).

13. K. Lancaster, "Intra-industry Trade Under Perfect Monopolistic Competition," *Journal of International Economics,* vol.10, (1980): 151–75.

14. It must be noted, however, that the initial decline in employment caused by adverse domestic effects of shifts in demand may be offset by corresponding increases in exports in the long run. Increases in imports can induce domestic exports by increasing incomes in the foreign country. Furthermore, under a system of flexible exchange rates, increased imports may result in a depreciation of the foreign exchange value of the currency of the importing country and thereby stimulate exports. The magnitude of this effect, however, depends on the foreign elasticity of demand for domestic exports.

15. Increases in imports are assumed to result from a shift in demand away from domestic products, as opposed to increases in aggregate domestic demand, which do not necessarily reduce output and employment except in the sense that they reduce the level of employment and output that could have been achieved in the absence of a demand for imports.

16. K. Young, A. Lawson, and J. Duncan, "Trade Ripples across U.S. Industries," (Washington, D.C.: U.S. Department of Commerce, Office of Business Analysis January, 1986).

17. Ken Miyazawa, *Input-Output Analysis and the Structure of Income Distribution,* (Berlin: Springer-Verlag, 1976).

18. Kwan S. Kim and Gerardo Turrubiate, "Structures of Foreign Trade and Income Distribution: The Case of Mexico," *Journal of Development Economics,* 16 (1984): 263–78.

19. Ibid.

AN ESTIMATE OF BLACK GROSS JOB LOSSES DUE TO REDUCED DEFENSE EXPENDITURES

Roger C. Williams

The reduction in defense expenditures, due to the end of the cold war, is estimated to have a disproportionately heavy impact on black gross job losses. Several solutions are discussed with the hope that if they are successful, the negative social behavior that is often associated with increased joblessness can be ameliorated.

INTRODUCTION

In a recent article in the *Journal of Economic Perspectives* entitled "Converting Resources from Military to Non-Military Uses," the authors, J. Brauer and J. Marlin, estimated the impact of defense expenditure reductions, due to the end of the cold war, on aggregate gross job losses in each state, covering the years 1991–96. Combining their estimates, as well as estimates cited in their review of other studies, the forecasted range of private sector defense industry gross job losses is between 530,000 and 920,000; for active duty military personnel cuts the forecasted range is between 207,000 and 400,000; and for civilian Department of Defense (DoD) personnel the forecasted range is between 100,000 and 130,000.[1]

This study extends the work of Brauer and Marlin by extracting, from their state-by-state estimates of job losses, a forecast of the number of these job losses that will be borne by the defense-employed black population in each state. This exercise is important because compared to their numbers in the general population and labor force, blacks are perhaps underrepresented in private sector defense employment but they are disproportionately overrepresented in the armed services and DoD civilian employment. Thus, a priori, on balance, one would expect the gross job losses from defense cutbacks to fall disproportionately harder on blacks. Since many young military-age blacks, as a group, already experience difficulty in obtaining employment in the private sector, some have forecast difficult times for the near-term black employment outlook.

The results of this research show that across the nation, blacks can expect to lose 158,000 military and defense-related jobs between 1991 and 1996. This accounts for 12 percent of total defense-related job losses, which compares to a 9.2 percent representation of blacks in the nationwide civilian labor force. However, this does not tell the whole story because the job losses are not uniformly spread out over the entire country. Instead they tend to disproportionately affect the employment of blacks in some states far more than in some others. The details of the state by state impact are to be found in the analysis section but next we provide some background material in the literature survey.

SURVEY OF THE LITERATURE

This survey of the literature is divided into two parts. In the first section, some of the main issues that affect total job losses due to defense cutbacks are discussed. In the second part, some of the primary issues that affect black defense-related employment specifically are presented.

Although the estimates of Brauer and Marlin do not include the multiplier effects of gross job losses, they cite one study that suggests that the military base closing multiplier is 1.2, the civilian DoD multiplier is 1.8 and the military industry multiplier is 2.5. Also their estimates do not take into account the reemployment some retrenched military workers will undoubtedly find. Factoring in reemployed workers reduces the gross job loss numbers. The authors cite one estimate, by the Office of Technology Assessment (OTA), of 250,000 net jobs lost per year between 1992 and 1995.[2] A recent report by the Defense Conversion Commission (DCC) indicates that, computer simulations of the effects on the entire economy will be that, the 1995 unemployment rate could be as much as a 0.5 percentage point higher than it would have been had 1992 spending levels been maintained; and that the cutbacks will reduce the annual GDP growth rate by between 0.25 and 0.5 percentage points over the next few years.[3]

In the report of the DCC, the authors stress that it is important to distinguish between job losses and unemployment. They argue that as the number of jobs in the defense sector decline, new jobs are being created in the sectors of the economy that are growing. For workers who do not find new work immediately, job losses result in a temporary period of unemployment that typically lasts several months. Thus, the concept of job losses tends to overstate the employment effects of the defense cuts because it does not account for the ability of the economy to absorb unemployed workers.[4] This idea is supported in a report published by the OTA.[5] The authors indicate that the number of defense positions eliminated will be larger than the number of defense workers who will actually be displaced. Perhaps as much as 75 percent of the decline in DoD military personnel will come from attrition as the armed forces simply accept fewer new enlistees. DoD expects to handle much of the decline in its civilian personnel through natural attrition and a hiring freeze. In the private sector defense industry, some of the people whose positions are lost may never actually be laid off but will take up a new job in the same company, as the company replaces military customers with civilian customers. Thus, the overall results suggested by several studies is that the cutbacks are unlikely to result in a macroeconomic catastrophe, although some states and regions within states, that are particularly defense industry dependent, will suffer disproportionately.

With respect to blacks in the armed forces the immediate short-term future outlook is not good. Before this future is discussed, it is important to place blacks in the armed forces in some historical perspective.

Historically blacks have served in all the major armed conflicts in which this country has been involved. For instance some 5,000 blacks served in the Revolutionary War, fighting in almost every battle from Bunker Hill to Yorktown; 220,000 fought in the Civil War; 437,710 served in World War I, more than one million served in World War II and 275,827 served during the Vietnam conflict.[6]

In 1973, as the Vietnam conflict came to an end, the Nixon administration decided to replace the Selective Service System with an all-volunteer military. The result was that many young blacks began to view the military as an institution that provided a long-term career with benefits such as housing, health care, education, travel, a chance for advancement based on merit and a pension at retirement.[7]

Thus, black enlisted personnel went from 14 percent in 1973 to 22.3 percent by 1989. Black officers increased from 2.5 percent in 1973 to 6.7 percent by 1989. For black females the percent of enlisted personnel went from 15.7 percent in 1973 to 32.8 percent by 1989. The percent of black female officers went from 3.5 percent in 1973 to 12.9 percent by 1989. Black DoD civilian employment went from 11.8 percent in 1973 to 14.6 percent in 1989.[8]

The above increases caused a few concerns. The first is a concern by some segments of the population that the military has too many blacks. That is, large numbers of blacks might discourage whites from joining. This leads to the second related issue some have raised, that large numbers of blacks could mean a lower quality force. Both these issues are discussed in Smith.[9] He concludes that these issues are of concern to only a minority of the white population.[10] Third, the numerical increases may be partly due to the perception by many young blacks that the military is an institution that is a meritocracy and is relatively free of racial bias. Not everyone has agreed with this perception. For instance, Butler wrote, "Black enlisted men are not equally distributed throughout the enlisted grade structure of the Army. The higher the grade, the smaller the percentage of blacks in grade."[11] He continues, "In all grades, overall, blacks take more time (from the time they entered service) to make their current grade(s) than whites. This holds true even when universalistic controls (Armed Forces Qualifying Test, Education and Occupation) are considered."[12] He attributed this to institutional racism.[13] Nevertheless the numbers increased steadily throughout the 1980s.

Due to the end of the cold war it appears that this relatively rapid growth in black military and civilian DoD accession is about to slow down considerably. According to OTA, the army and to a lesser extent the air force will bear the brunt of the military reductions. The army and the air force bore the burden of the defense of Europe during the cold war. Now that the Soviet threat has significantly decreased, their missions are radically reduced. The historical missions of the Marine Corps and the navy are thought to be a better match for the kinds of regional conflict that the United States may encounter in the future. Thus, army reductions will account for one-half of all armed service cuts. Of the estimated 100,000 DoD-wide all services involuntary separations, from fiscal years 1990–95, two-thirds will come from the army. Because the army is the service with the smallest percentage of skilled jobs, the lowest levels of aptitude, and the highest concentration of minorities, the transition problems faced by its separatees may be somewhat greater than is implied by the aggregate levels of skills in all the services. The army has a larger share of combat, service and supply positions than either the air force or the navy. Skills in combat occupations are generally the least transferrable to the private sector, and service and supply jobs tend to be rather low skilled. In addition blacks in the military tend to have lower Armed Forces Qualifying Test (AFQT) and Armed Services Vocational Aptitude Battery (ASVAB) test scores. To the extent that test scores predict service performance, and to the extent service performance is the basis for deciding which soldiers shall be involuntarily separated, black service members could be disproportionately affected. Thus blacks make up 31 percent of the army but they could account for a larger percentage of those denied reenlistment.[14]

Reduced access to military careers could represent a significant reduction in economic opportunity to blacks. The military is a very important employer of blacks. Of all blacks between the ages of 18 and 29, 4.1 percent are serving in the military, compared to 2.4 percent for whites. Of all jobs held by blacks in this age group, 7.1 percent are in the military compared to 2.4 percent for whites. Among black men aged 18 to 29, 7.2 percent are serving in the military, accounting for 10.6 percent of that group's employment. Further, less than 43 percent of young black males actually qualify for the military compared to 85 percent of young white males. Thus about one-quarter of the qualified employed black male population between the ages of 18 and 29 is serving in the military.[15]

The bottom line to this is that if the overall entry rate into the military decreases by 20 percent, the percent of blacks in the military could decrease by 36 percent in the long run. Without military training and experience, many young black men could find it harder to get a civilian job. Because there is evidence that black veterans enjoy higher post-service job status than white veterans, the situation could reach a crisis.[16]

METHODOLOGY AND RESULTS

The method by which the following estimates were obtained is straightforward. The data were obtained from sources that are available to the public; or are estimates based on reasonable assumptions. The estimates used for the defense reductions in the categories of military personnel, DoD civilian and private sector defense firm personnel were the same as those that Brauer and Marlin used. These were 17.5 percent military reductions, 11.6 percent DoD civilian reductions and 25.6 percent private sector defense reductions. Although there are higher and lower estimates located in different sources and based on different scenarios, for the percent personnel reductions in each category, Brauer and Marlin appear to have chosen just about the average of all the published defense cut scenarios. Hence using their numbers makes for easy comparison and they are reasonable.[17]

As a whole blacks make up 9.2 percent of the civilian labor force in the nation. Yet there are 33 states in which the percentage of blacks in the civilian labor force falls below this percentage. The states in which blacks are significantly higher than this percentage are mostly southern states such as Georgia, Louisiana, Mississippi, North Carolina, South Carolina, Virginia and the District of Columbia (D.C.).[18]

By contrast blacks constitute 12.7 percent of defense employment. This figure is a weighted average that includes 26.9 percent of the armed forces, 14.6 percent of the DoD civilian work force and an estimated 9.2 percent of private sector defense employment. There are only three states (Alabama, Maryland and Mississippi) and D.C. in which the percentage of blacks employed in defense-related institutions is less than those that comprise the civilian labor force. This illustrates the disproportionate reliance on defense employment by the black community as a whole. Also note that the states in which this 12.7 percent figure is significantly exceeded are located in the south.[19]

Table 1 is based on the estimates of defense employee reductions, performed by Brauer and Marlin, along with the assumption that their estimates would be applied proportionately to the black defense employed population in each state.

States with relatively high absolute numbers of black job losses are California (18,900), Virginia (14,500), Texas (11,800), New York (8,700), Georgia (9,100), North Carolina (8,400), Maryland (7,800), and Florida (7,600). These estimates are for gross job losses and they do not include multiplier effects.[20]

A deeper analysis of Table 1 reveals that the percentage breakdown yielded a slightly different mix of states. For instance, states that will experience a high percentage of black military and defense-related job losses are: D.C. (39), South Carolina (29), Mississippi (28), Georgia (28), Louisiana (28), Maryland (24), Alabama (22) and Virginia (22).

It is important to note that there are some obvious limitations to any estimate of this kind. This study has the limited objective of extracting from the state by state overall gross job losses estimated by Brauer and Marlin, an estimate of the state-by-state black gross job losses. However, there are other issues that should be mentioned. First, the impact on black-owned firms that rely on defense subcontracting in any significant way, directly or indirectly, has not been taken explicitly and separately into account; employees of black-owned firms are part of the private sector defense employment. A separate study on black-owned firms needs to be performed. Second, the focus has not been on specific communities within states. Generally speaking, blacks are not uniformly distributed

TABLE 1
Estimates of Defense Employee Reductions

State	Estimated Defense Employee Decrease 1991–96	Estimated Black Employee Decrease 1991–96	State	Estimated Defense Employee Decrease 1991–96	Estimated Black Employee Decrease 1991–96
AL	18,074	4,035	MT	2,215	76
AK	7,052	865	NE	6,205	419
AZ	17,105	1,048	NV	4,115	381
AR	7,656	1,082	NH	4,668	116
CA	184,409	18,908	NJ	30,103	4,575
CO	19,239	1,713	NM	8,174	553
CT	21,477	1,815	NY	55,974	8,764
DE	3,176	532	NC	31,367	8,423
D.C.	9,572	3,729	ND	3,291	205
FL	52,611	7,618	OH	36,749	3,799
GA	32,591	9,112	OK	15,767	2,073
HI	14,967	1,967	OR	5,187	128
ID	2,721	76	PA	38,534	3,939
IL	34,428	4,717	RI	4,495	288
IN	20,006	1,700	SC	19,683	5,710
IA	5,638	120	SD	2,649	109
KS	14,092	1,547	TN	13,277	2,575
KY	14,369	1,896	TX	80,854	11,817
LA	16,510	4,686	UT	9,035	461
ME	6,402	346	VT	1,657	16
MD	32,860	7,802	VA	67,204	14,554
MA	30,531	1,739	WA	31,627	2,449
MI	23,318	2,862	WV	2,773	114
MN	12,341	282	WI	11,051	515
MS	12,465	3,447	WY	1,889	95
MO	25,859	2,186	Nation	1,128,013	157,984

across most states, as this analysis assumes. Thus more intrastate regional and local analyses needs to be done. This applies particularly to the issue of military bases that are scheduled to be closed down. See Brauer and Marlin[21] for more on this issue. Third, accurate rather than estimated data on black DoD civilian and black private sector defense firm employment, broken down by individual states, would sharpen these estimates. Fourth, the projected cuts were forecast before newly elected

President Clinton had a chance to have any significant input. As of this writing, there are indications that he intends to try and persuade Congress to authorize deeper cuts than the consensus forecasts of Brauer and Marlin and others. If deeper cuts do in fact occur, the general conclusions of this study still hold, the magnitudes of the forecasted job losses would obviously be greater. Finally although the cold war has ended, there are still numerous situations throughout the world that potentially could end up requiring United States armed forces intervention. If any of these situations are perceived in the near future to warrant military force for a protracted period of time, this could slow the rate of projected reductions.

SOLUTIONS

The solutions section to the defense cutback problem is divided into two sections. The first part is based on programs that the government has implemented to lessen the impact of military downsizing. The second part is based more on a suggestion for increased black self-help.

One of the most important assistance programs for dislocated workers from private sector defense firms, is the Economic Dislocation and Worker Adjustment Assistance Act (EDWAA), which is also referred to as Title III of the Job Training Partnership Act (JTPA). EDWAA funding in 1993 was $567 million. EDWAA is designed to help dislocated workers through five basic services: (1) Rapid response assistance, which is designed to provide workers and employers information about programs available to workers, as soon as a plant closure or a substantial layoff is announced; (2) Basic readjustment services, which provides for assisting retrenched workers with career counseling, labor market information and relocation assistance; (3) Retraining services, which consists of basic and remedial education and entrepreneurial training; (4) Supportive services, which includes child care assistance and commuting assistance; (5) Needs-related payments, which is designed to make payments to eligible workers after they have exhausted their unemployment compensation benefits.[22]

For DoD civilian personnel who lose their jobs, the DoD has established a Priority Placement Program (PPP), a worldwide referral program. The skills of employees, scheduled to lose their jobs, are matched with vacant positions at other DoD locations, where the employee has indicated a willingness to work and is eligible to register. Generally, PPP registrants whose qualifications match job requirements must be given a job offer. In addition, DoD maintains local Reemployment Priority Lists, which provide priority consideration for hiring eligible separated employees over outside applicants for open positions.[23] The National Defense Authorization Act for Fiscal Year 1991 gave the DoD and the armed services the task of increasing the number of transition assistance programs and employment assistance centers for military personnel leaving active duty. The Act provides for pre-separation counseling, employment assistance, and benefits such as health care and in some cases military family housing and DoD schools.[24]

Because the armed services expect to enlist, from 1993–97, about 100,000 fewer high school graduates than in the mid-1980s, many of them black, the Department of Labor's Secretary Commission on Achieving Necessary Skills (SCANS) program could prove important. SCANS brings together schools and employers in a realistic examination of the skills and competencies needed in the work place and determines how the schools can ensure that students graduate with them. SCANS is now being implemented across the country through a series of community coalitions.[25]

What blacks can do for themselves is to note that the hardest hit states, on a percentage basis as previously mentioned, also happen to be states that have at least one and in most cases several Historically Black Colleges and or Universities (HBCUs). For instance, Mississippi has 10, Georgia has 12, South Carolina has 8, Louisiana has 4, Maryland has 5, Alabama has 11, Virginia has 6, Delaware has 1, and the District of Columbia has 2.[26] These institutions perhaps could develop aggressive local and nationwide fund-raising plans, recruiting and marketing strategies in order to ready themselves to increase their share of training and educating the 18 to 29 age group, that will have reduced opportunities to join the army and the other services.[27]

However, I am not suggesting that going to college is a substitute for military training; I am suggesting it is a positive alternative to the projected reduced opportunities for military training.

It is important that these institutions also emphasize training in entrepreneurship and business formation. Perhaps more could develop small business incubation programs. The point here is that HBCUs should not only train their graduates to be employees, but also to be employers. Finally, these institutions could find themselves overwhelmed by the potential sharp increase in enrollment if careful planning and coordination is not done.

CONCLUSION

I conclude this study with hope that all the solutions outlined in the previous section come to a successful fruition so that the adverse employment effects of defense expenditure reductions on currently employed as well as the next generation of young blacks, are minimized. To the extent that these solutions are not successful, we can expect to see a rise in the negative social behavior that is often associated with joblessness.

NOTES

1. John Brauer and John Tepper Marlin, "Converting Resources from Military to Non-Military Uses," *Journal of Economic Perspectives* 6 (4) (Fall 1992), 147.
2. Brauer and Marlin (1992), 147.
3. Defense Conversion Commission (DCC). *Adjusting to the Drawdown.* Report. (Washington, D.C.: Defense Budget Project, August 1991), 12.
4. Defense Conversion Commission Report (1991), 40.
5. Office of Technology Assessment (OTA). *After the Cold War: Living With Lower Defense Spending.* (Washington, D.C.: Government Printing Office, February 1992), 60.
6. Department of Defense, Office of the Deputy Assistant Secretary of Defense for Civilian Personnel Policy and Equal Opportunity. *Black Americans in Defense of Our Nation.* (Government Printing Office, 1991), 10–28.
7. *Black Americans in Defense of Our Nation* (1991), 88.
8. *Black Americans in Defense of Our Nation* (1991), 286.
9. A. Wade Smith, "Public Consciousness of Blacks in the Military," *Journal of Political and Military Sociology,* 11 (Fall 1983), 299.
10. Ibid.
11. John S. Butler, *Inequality in the Military: The Black Experience,* (Saratoga, CA: Century Twenty One, 1980), 103–104.
12. Ibid.
13. Ibid.
14. OTA Report (1992), 137.
15. OTA Report (1992), 138.
16. OTA Report (1992), 138.
17. For instance C.P. Schmidt and S. Kosiak in their report, *Potential Impact of Defense Spending Reductions on the Defense Industrial Labor Force by State*; (Washington, D.C., 1992), listed three budget decline options between fiscal years 1991–97: The first option was based on that proposed by former President Bush—24 percent total defense employment cuts between 1991–96; the second was called the Medium Cut Option, 27 percent, and the third was designated the Deep Cut Option, 29 percent. In the report by the OTA, *After the Cold War: Living With Lower Defense Spending* (1992), the authors present two budget cut scenarios between 1991–95: They average 19 percent for military personnel; 10 percent for DoD civilians; and 25 percent for defense industry employment. The report by the DCC *Adjusting to the Drawdown* (1991) estimates between 1991–97 a 25 percent military personnel reduction and a 20 percent reduction in DoD civilian personnel.

18. See, *Employment Status by Race and Sex for U.S. States* (Population Division of the U.S. Census, Washington, D.C., 1992).

19. The private sector defense firm component of these estimates assumes that the percent of blacks who work for private sector defense firms in each state, is equal to the percent of blacks in each state's civilian labor force. This assumption was made because I was unable to obtain a source of actual figures for this component of the estimates. Over 53 percent of the occupations in these firms are in professional, technical, engineering, scientific and administrative support positions. Since these are positions in which blacks tend to be underrepresented, this component of the estimates are probably higher than the situation is in reality.

The DoD civilian component of the estimate uses 14.6 percent as the aggregate percentage of blacks who work for the DoD as civilians, according to the DoD publication *Black Americans in Defense of Our Nation* (1991). Because I was unable to obtain a source that provided an actual state-by-state percentage breakdown, I assumed that this 14.6 percent figure was the same across each state. This probably overestimates the real figure in some states and underestimates it in others.

20. This is consistent with the analysis of Brauer and Marlin (1992).

21. Brauer and Marlin (1992), 154.

22. Defense Conversion Commission Report (1991), 63–64.

23. Defense Conversion Commission Report (1991), 61.

24. Defense Conversion Commission Report (1991), 55.

25. Defense Conversion Commission Report (1991), 53.

26. In Mississippi the HBCUs are: Alcorn State University, Coahoma Junior College, Jackson State University, Mary Holmes College, Mississippi Valley State University, Natchez Junior College, Prentiss Norman Industrial Institute, Rust College, Tougaloo College and Utica Junior College; Georgia has Albany State College, Atlanta Junior College, Atlanta University, Clark College, Fort Valley State College, Interdenominational Theological Center, Morehouse College, Morehouse School of Medicine, Morris Brown College, Paine College, Savannah State College and Spelman College; South Carolina has Allen University, Benedict College, Claflin College, Clinton Junior College, Denmark Technical College, Morris College, South Carolina State College and Voorhees College; Louisiana has Dillard University, Grambling State University, The Southern University System and Xavier University; Alabama has Alabama A&M University, Alabama State University, Concordia College, Lawson State Community College, Miles College, Oakwood College, S.D. Bishop State Junior College, Selma University, Stillman College, Talladega College and Tuskegee University; Maryland has Bowie State College, Coppin State College, Morgan State University, Sojourner-Douglass College and University of Maryland Eastern Shore; Virginia has Hampton University, Norfolk State University, Saint Paul's College, Virginia Seminary, Virginia State University and Virginia Union University; Delaware has Delaware State College; The District of Columbia has Howard University and the University of the District of Columbia.

27. The largest percentage of new armed service recruits come from the southern states (40.4 percent). See the OTA Report (1992), 130–131.

RACE AND REHIRING IN THE
HIGH-TECH INDUSTRY

Don Mar and Paul M. Ong

Previous research reveals that economic dislocation generates racial inequality because minorities suffer greater consequences from job displacement—longer unemployment duration and greater downward mobility. These outcomes, however, are conditional on being permanently laid off. This article examines the factors, including race, that influence whether or not a worker becomes displaced. More specifically, the article analyzes the probability of being rehired after an initial layoff using administrative data collected on workers laid off after the severe 1985 sectoral recession in Silicon Valley's semiconductor industry. The results from logit regressions show that, after controlling for observable worker and firm characteristics, black workers are less likely to be rehired than other workers.

INTRODUCTION

Racial economic inequality is not just a static difference but is a disparity that is reproduced through the very process of economic change. There is considerable literature on disproportionate racial effects of economic dislocation, with the majority of studies arguing that minorities are more adversely impacted by job displacement. After job displacement, minorities are found to suffer longer spells of unemployment, be less likely to find new work, and when reemployed, receive lower wages.[1]

Perhaps as important as the racial disparities in post-displacement outcomes are the racial differences in who is permanently laid off and who is returned to the same job after an initial layoff. This article examines the role of race in the rehiring process among workers in a nonunion, high-technology industry. We define rehiring as returning to work with the same employer after a temporary layoff. Although the effects of rehiring and permanent layoffs on wages have been documented,[2] there is little in the literature concerning the rehiring process itself, let alone the impact of racial differences.

The case study is based on the semiconductor industry. This high-technology industry, which is centered in Silicon Valley, is important because it epitomizes the new high-wage sector. Semiconductors, along with computers and aerospace, are seen as the modern motor of growth and prosperity in the United States. Race plays an important role in Silicon Valley's semiconductor industry in terms of occupational segregation. Minorities are generally well represented, but they are concentrated in lower paying production jobs.[3] Given the importance of the high-tech sector as a source of high-paying manufacturing jobs, investigation of the role of race in the rehiring process in this industry has implications for minority incomes and unemployment.

DETERMINANTS OF REHIRING

For this article, rehiring is defined as the process that determines whether a layoff is temporary or permanent. Although temporary layoffs and permanent layoffs are conceptually distinct—the former is a brief disruption to employment with the firm/employee contract being maintained while the latter is a permanent severance of the firm/employee contract—in practice the *ex ante* distinction is blurred *ex post*. Even when a firm's initial intention is to rehire a worker, a temporary layoff becomes permanent when production levels fail to justify recalling the worker, or when the worker finds permanent employment elsewhere. Despite this problematic nature, the rehiring of temporarily furloughed workers is not a random process. We expect employees are more willing to wait to be rehired if opportunity wages elsewhere are lower, and also expect firms to rehire workers who are the most productive, particularly if the firm has sunken investments in the requisite training.

Existing rehiring studies focus on the unionized sector and the use of seniority as the primary criteria for rehiring. Most union contracts include provisions granting members with more seniority greater protection against layoff and higher priority in being recalled.[4] The role of seniority is well documented in empirical work explaining layoffs but not rehires.[5]

Abraham and Medoff find that seniority is often used as a criteria for layoff even in the nonunion sector, though with less frequency than in the unionized sector.[6] This is not surprising as several theories can account for the role of seniority in determining layoffs. Human capital theory argues that employee-firm attachment should be stronger in the presence of specific human capital acquired during the worker's tenure with the firm.[7] Internal labor market theory argues that the acquisition of specific skills by workers on the job combined with institutional work rules make seniority a major criterion for determining layoffs.[8] According to implicit contract theory, lower wages are accepted by workers early in their careers in exchange for greater employment stability and higher wages in the future.[9] Finally, Abraham and Farber believe that length of tenure is an indicator of the quality of a worker/firm job match.[10] Thus, seniority should play an important role in personnel practices in nonunion firms.

In one of the few empirical studies directly concerned with rehiring, Santiago, using longitudinal data collected from a unionized firm, finds that employees's wage level, along with seniority, are positively correlated with the probability of being rehired.[11] Santiago argues that in addition to specific human capital, Lazear's shirking argument relating wages to worker reliability is also important in the rehiring process.[12] However, Santiago does not include race in his analysis of rehiring.

Firm characteristics, in particular degree of firm economic recovery, firm size, and firm use of layoff, are also important. Firm characteristics have largely been ignored due to the lack of available data. At a minimum, one should include the degree of firm economic recovery as this is directly tied to the probability of a worker being recalled. Larger firms may utilize a greater division of work that induces more investments in job-specific human capital, which in turn increases the likelihood of rehiring trained senior workers. From an institutional perspective, larger firms are more likely to have formalized employment practices with personnel departments and written policies governing rehiring practices, even in the absence of unions. Firms may also vary with regards to idiosyncratic preferences on security of employment. Some employers may rely more heavily on using temporary layoffs with the risk of losing some valued workers, while other employers may choose to hoard workers, leading to a larger wage bill but fewer losses of valued workers.

DATA AND EMPIRICAL ANALYSIS

This article utilizes logit analyses to examine the roles of race, individual productivity characteristics, and firm characteristics in the rehiring process. This study is limited to the nonunionized, semiconductor industry (SIC 3674) in Northern California's Silicon Valley. The analyses are based on a sample of workers obtained from administrative files maintained by California's Employment Development Department who were laid off in 1985 due to the industry-wide recession and were claimants in California's unemployment insurance (UI) program.[13] During the recession, nearly half of the total labor force suffered at least one spell of unemployment, and nearly half of those workers laid off were never rehired by their firms as companies downsized their labor force during the subsequent recovery.[14]

The UI records provided basic demographic data (ethnicity, age, sex, and occupation). This information is combined with information from two other sources: 1) quarterly earnings reports for individual workers, which were filed by firms in accordance with the unemployment and disability insurance programs, and 2) firm records from California's 202 program, which provided data on firm size and industrial classification. These data sets allow the inclusion of firm characteristics such as past employment practices, layoff rates, employment growth rates, and firm size into the analysis.

Persons included in the sample met the following three criteria: 1) the person lived within reasonable commuting distance of the Silicon Valley;[15] 2) the individual was at least 18 years old at the time of layoff; and 3) the person was reemployed in 1987. The final sample contains 1,692 persons from 47 different firms. Although the data set contains some unique information, it also has limitations. The data does not contain information on educational attainment, seniority past 4 years, and workers who did not file for UI.

For the purposes of this study, rehired is defined as being reemployed by the same employer within two years of the initial layoff. The year 1987 is used as the cutoff date for being classified as rehired, as the chances of being recalled were negligible after that time. About half of the group initially laid off in 1985 went back to work for the original firm in the quarter following the first layoff. By 1987, 61 percent of the entire sample had been rehired. However, the rehire rates did differ by race. Only 43 percent of black workers were rehired as compared to 60 percent of white workers, 65 percent of Hispanic workers, and 64 percent of "other" workers.[16]

To examine the importance of race in the rehiring process, the following logit probability function is estimated with the probability of being rehired as the dependent variable:

$$P(R = 1) = a + M*B + X*C + Y*D$$

where R equals 1 if the worker was rehired within 2 years of the 1985 layoff; a is the intercept term; M is a vector of race dummies; B is a vector of logit coefficients on the race dummies; C is a vector of logit coefficients on individual worker characteristics X; and D is a vector of logit coefficients on firm characteristics Y. A description of the relevant variables are presented in Table 1, and the associated summary statistics are listed in Table 2.

The three race variables are dummy variables for black, Hispanic, and Asian workers (BLACK, HISPANIC, and OTHER variables). Previous studies have only examined differences in reemployment by black and nonblack workers. The existence of any racial differences indicates differential treatment of workers based on race, ceteris paribus. No dummy variable is included for non-Hispanic whites who are used as the base reference group. Thus, the racial dummies should be interpreted as increasing or decreasing the probability of being rehired relative to non-Hispanic whites.

Individual characteristics include years of seniority (YEAR2, YEAR3, and YEAR4 dummy variables), age (AGE and AGESQ), occupation (ENGINEER, WHITE-COLLAR, OTHER PRODUCTION and ASSEMBLER), wage prior to layoff (LNWAGE84), and gender (MALE). Given the earlier discussion, the coefficients for the seniority variables are expected to be positive and to increase with the number of years of service. The base reference group is workers with a year or less of seniority. As older workers are generally considered to be more diligent workers, the shirking model predicts that age is positively correlated with the probability of being rehired. Since the magnitude of the relationship may decline with age, the expected coefficient for squared age variable is negative. The four dummy occupational variables are included to control for differences by occupation as previous studies argue that reemployment varies by occupational category.[17] The base reference group are managerial occupations. If earnings, as argued by Santiago, are reflective of worker reliability beyond those related to occupation and seniority, earnings should have a positive impact on the probability of being rehired. Earnings before layoff also serves as a proxy for educational attainment as data on educational attainment is not available for the sample. Finally, inclusion of the gender variable captures any differential treatment based on gender.[18]

Firm characteristics include the number of employees at the firm in

TABLE 1
Definition of Regression Variables

Variable	Definition
LNWAGE84	Log of average quarterly earnings in 1984
BLACK	Equal to 1 if person is black
HISPANIC	Equal to 1 if person is Hispanic
OTHER	Equal to 1 if person is other minority
AGE	Equal to age of person
AGESQ	Equal to square of the age of the person
MALE	Equal to 1 if person is male
ENGINEER	Equal to 1 for engineering and scientific occupations
WHITE COLLAR	Equal to 1 for other white collar occupations (non-managerial)
ASSEMBLER	Equal to 1 for assembly occupations
OTHER PROD	Equal to 1 for other production occupations
FIRMSIZE	Log of the number of employee in 1984 firm
YEAR2	Equal to 1 if person has two years of seniority
YEAR3	Equal to 1 if person has three years of seniority
YEAR4	Equal to 1 if person has three years of seniority
LAYOFFS	Layoff rate as annual percentage of laid off employees to total employees in 1985.
TAX	Firm unemployment insurance tax in 1985, on a scale of 22 to 45. Higher numbers indicate a higher tax.
GROWTH	Growth (or decrease) rate as annual percentage of employment size change in 1985.

1985 (FIRMSIZE), each firm's unemployment tax rate assessed by the state unemployment administration (TAX), the percent of a firm's work force that was laid off in 1985 (LAYOFFS), and the two-year growth trend of a firm's work force (GROWTH).[19] Larger firms are more likely to provide more on-the-job training and to have formal personnel practices.[20] The TAX variable serves as a measure of past employment practices. Although the tax rate is not perfectly experience rated, a higher rate does indicate that a firm had more layoffs in the past (pre-1985). A high rate would indicate a firm had very low turnover costs and/or less investment in firm specific human capital. As a result, firms with higher unemployment tax rates would be less likely to rehire workers for their negligible amounts of specific human capital. Higher unemployment tax rates should be negatively related to rehiring. The percent of employees laid off and two-year change in employment size are treated as accounting variables that are

TABLE 2
Means of Regression Variables.
Semiconductor Workers Laid Off in 1985

Variable	Mean	Standard Deviation
REHIRED	0.613	0.487
LNWAGE84	8.656	0.474
BLACK	0.029	0.168
HISPANIC	0.207	0.405
OTHER	0.175	0.080
AGE	36.162	9.559
AGESQ	1399.030	768.272
MALE	0.413	0.492
ENGINEER	0.137	0.344
WHITE COLLAR	0.092	0.289
ASSEMBLER	0.524	0.500
OTHER PROD	0.188	0.391
FIRMSIZE	8.059	1.024
YEAR2	0.183	0.387
YEAR3	0.131	0.338
YEAR4	0.464	0.499
LAYOFFS	0.694	0.184
TAX	29.955	4.792
GROWTH	0.737	0.271
TOTAL OBSERVATIONS	1692	

mathematically tied to the probability of being rehired. Increasing the size of the layoff population would lower an individual's chances of being rehired because there are more job competitors, while a more robust employment trend would increase the chances because there are more positions. If the queue of laid-off workers waiting to be rehired remained intact, then the two variables should have exactly offsetting effects. The impact of a one percent increase in the layoff rate on the rehire probability would be neutralized by a one percent increase in the two-year employment trend. However, there is no reason to believe that this was the case. For example, if workers saw the two-year trend as a signal of the firm's long-term prospects, the employment trend would alter their willingness to return or to stay with the firm. Moreover, firms that recovered fully might be more willing to keep their old work force intact, while weaker firms might seek to shake out their work force as they reposition themselves in the product market. In both cases, the impacts may not be of the same magnitude—that is, the absolute value of the coefficient for GROWTH would be larger than the coefficient for LAYOFFS.[21]

RESULTS

Table 3 shows the effects of changes in the variables on the probability of being rehired. Two different models were estimated to examine the stability of the logit coefficients. The first column is the basic model, containing all the variables. The second model omitted the firm variables. Separate logit regressions were not done by race due to the small sample of black workers.

There are differences in rehiring by race. The coefficients for black workers are significant in both models, indicating that black workers were 19 percent less likely to be rehired. There may have been a preference for hiring "other" (primarily Asian) workers but the coefficient is only significant in the second model. In addition, the coefficients for Hispanic workers are not significant.

The occupational variables are not significant in either model 1 or model 2. Gender differences are significant only at the 10 percent level of significance, with men being slightly less likely to be rehired. The age variables are not significantly related to rehiring. As seniority is correlated with age, multicollinearity effects could be responsible for the lack of significance of the age variables. However, the age variables are still not significant in logits excluding the seniority variables.

The wage variable coefficient is significant at the 5 percent probability level in model 2 and at the 11 percent level in model 1. A 10 percent increase in the log of the wage increases the probability of being rehired by approximately 7 percent. All the seniority dummies are significant with the expected positive signs and values showing that the probability of being rehired rises with seniority. Each additional year of seniority increases the probability of being rehired by approximately 5-6 percent. Finally, all the firm characteristic coefficients are significant. The firm size and the two-year employment trend are positively related to being rehired, while the UI tax rate and layoff rates are negatively related to being rehired.

As minority workers are generally overrepresented in blue collar production jobs, separate logits were estimated for blue-collar and white-collar workers in order to test for differences in the rehiring process by class of worker. Table 4 reports the logit results for subsamples of white-collar and blue-collar workers.

Black workers were less likely to be rehired in both types of jobs. Although the parameter estimates are not significant at the 5 percent level of significance, they are significant at the 7 percent level in both the

TABLE 3
Changes in the Probability of Being Rehired.
Semiconductor Workers Laid Off in 1985

Variable	Model 1		Model 2	
LWAGE84	0.049		0.066	*
BLACK	-0.186	*	-0.206	**
HISPANIC	0.047		0.035	
OTHER	0.064		0.073	*
AGE	0.015		0.010	
AGESQ	0.003		0.006	
MALE	-0.042		-0.050	
ENGINEER	-0.070		-0.040	
WHITE COLLAR	0.013		0.065	
ASSEMBLER	-0.003		0.042	
OTHER PROD	0.044		0.094	
YEAR2	0.112	**	0.101	**
YEAR3	0.182	***	0.170	***
YEAR4	0.300	***	0.280	***
FIRMSIZE	0.034	**	---	
LAYOFFS	-0.018	***	---	
TAX	-0.024	*	---	
GROWTH	0.027	***	---	
-2 Log Likelihood	2001.34		2070.45	

*, **, and *** indicates logit coefficients significant at p<.05, p<.01, and p<.001 respectively. For continuous variables, logit coefficients are evaluated given a 10% increase in the variables' mean value. For dichotomous variables, logit coefficients are evaluated with the variable equal to 1.

blue collar and white collar logits. Black workers were 25 percent less likely to be rehired for white collar jobs and 16 percent less likely to be rehired for blue collar jobs. Asian workers were significantly more likely to be hired for blue-collar production jobs. The parameter estimates for Hispanic workers are positive but not significantly different from zero.

The results by occupational subsample also finds that race still has an important effect on rehiring after controlling for observable individual and firm characteristics. More specifically, black workers were much less likely to be rehired than workers of other ethnic groups, particularly for white-collar jobs.

TABLE 4
Change in Probability of Beging Rehired.
Rehired Workers in the Semiconductor Industry;
Blue-Collar versus White Collar Samples

Variable	White Collar		Blue Collar	
LWAGE84	0.145	*	0.012	
BLACK	-0.252		-0.165	
HISPANIC	0.003		0.053	
OTHER	-0.009		0.102	*
AGE	-0.154		0.071	
AGESQ	0.008	*	-0.023	
MALE	-0.062		-0.036	
ENGINEER	-0.059		---	
WHITE COLLAR	0.036		---	
ASSEMBLER	---		-0.047	
YEAR2	-0.012		0.167	***
YEAR3	0.121		0.200	***
YEAR4	0.258	***	0.325	***
FIRMSIZE	0.039		0.028	
LAYOFFS	-0.018		-0.020	**
TAX	-0.020		-0.029	*
GROWTH	0.036	***	0.022	***
-2 Log Likelihood	566.78		1418.25	

*, **, and *** indicates coefficients significant at p<.05, p<.01, and p<.001 respectively. For continuous variables, logit coefficients are evaluated give a 10% increase in the variables' mean value. For dichotomous variables, logit coefficients are evaluated with the variable equal to 1.

CONCLUSION

The 1985 experience in the semiconductor industry is illustrative of the role of race in job displacement in a high-wage industry. Following the 1985 industry recession, employment levels in California's Silicon Valley never reached the pre-recession level of employment. Rehiring mitigates the wage effects of an economic downturn. However, the rehiring process is clearly a nonrandom process in the nonunion semiconductor industry, with race influencing who returned to his or her employers and who became displaced.

The results of this analysis may be influenced by unobserved characteristics correlated with race. In addition, these results may not be generalizable to other industries. Nonetheless, we feel the results do contribute to the literature on differential effects of job displacement on racial groups. Given the current restructuring of the U.S. economy, black workers, at least in the semiconductor industry bear a greater burden of this restructuring.

NOTES

This research was partially supported by grants from the Institute of Industrial Relations and the Academic Senate at UCLA, and from the Associate Provost's Office of Affirmative Action and the Research and Professional Development Committee at San Francisco State University. Technical support was provided by the staff of the Employment Data and Research Unit of California's Employment Development Department. This is a revised version of a paper presented at the Western Economic Association International, San Francisco, July 12, 1992.

1. See P. Ong, "Race and Post-Displacement Earnings Among High-Tech Workers," *Industrial Relations*, 30 (3) (Fall 1991), 456–468 for the wage effects of displacement. For other effects of displacement by race see, D. Hammermesh, "What Do We Know About Worker Displacement in the U.S.?," *Industrial Relations*, 28 (1) (Winter 1989), 51–60; T. Moore, "Racial Differences in Postdisplacement Joblessness," *Social Science Quarterly*, 73 (3) (Sept. 1992), 674–689; Lori Kletzer, "Job Displacement, 1979–86: How Blacks Fared Relative to Whites," *Monthly Labor Review*, 114 (7) (July 1991), 17–25. Only Ruhm disagrees with these studies, finding little difference by race in unemployment duration after displacement when compared with nondisplaced workers (C. Ruhm, "Displacement Induced Joblessness," *Review of Economics and Statistics*, 73 (3) (Aug. 1991), 517–522.

2. See M. Podgursky and P. Swaim, "Job Displacement and Earnings Loss: Evidence from the Displaced Worker Survey." *Industrial and Labor Relations Review*, 41 (1) (Oct. 1987), 17–29; Hammermesh, (1989); and P. Ong and D. Mar, "Post-Layoff Earnings Among Semiconductor Workers," *Industrial and Labor Relations Review*, 45 (2) (Jan. 1992), 366–379.

3. See, Ong (1991). For example, in 1980, 4% of all high-tech workers in the Silicon Valley were black, 14% were Hispanic, and 15% were Asian, which is close to the racial distribution of the region's total labor force. However, approximately half of all minority jobs were concentrated in production jobs as compared to 29% of non-Hispanic white workers.

4. See J. Medoff, "Layoffs and Alternatives under Trade Unions in U.S. Manufacturing," *American Economic Review*, 69 (3) (June 1979), 380–95; R. Freeman, "The Effect of Unionism on Worker Attachment to Firms," *Journal of Labor Research*, (Spring 1980), 29–61; K. Abraham and J. Medoff, "Length of Service and Layoffs in Union and Nonunion Work Groups," *Industrial and Labor Relations Review*, 37 (1) (Oct. 1984), 87–97.

5. See F. Blau and L. Kahn, "Unionism, Seniority, and Turnover," *Industrial Relations*, 22 (4) (Fall 1983), 362–73 and R. Freeman, "The Exit-Voice Tradeoff in the Labor Market: Unionism, Job Tenure, Quits, and Separations," *Quarterly Journal of Economics*, 94 (4) (June 1980), 643–73.

6. See Abraham and Medoff (1984).

7. See, W. Oi, "Labor as a Quasi-fixed Factor," *Journal of Political Economy*, 70 (6) (Dec. 1962), 538–55 and D. Parsons, "Specific Human Capital: An Application to Quit Rates and Layoff Rates," *Journal of Political Economy*, 80 (6) (Nov./Dec. 1972), 1120–43.

8. P. Doeringer and M. Piore, *Internal Labor Markets and Manpower Analysis*, (Lexington, MA: Heath Lexington, 1971).

9. See C. Azariadis, "Implicit Contracts and Underemployment Equilibria," *Journal of Political Economy*, 83 (6) (Dec. 1975), 1183–1202.

10. See, K. Abraham and H. Farber, "Returns to Seniority in Union and Nonunion Jobs: A New Look at the Evidence," *Industrial and Labor Relations Review*, 41 (1) (Oct. 1988), 3–19.

11. See, C. Santiago, "Rehiring, Seniority, and Labor Force Adjustment," *Journal of Labor Economics*, 5 (4) (Oct. 1987), 18–35.

12. See, E. Lazear, "Agency, Earnings Profiles, Productivity, and Hours Restrictions," *American Economic Review*, 71 (4) (Sept. 1981), 606–20.

13. To ensure confidentiality, the analysis does not identify individual firms or workers. The raw data set is kept by the Employment Development Department, and all empirical work was done at the department's research office in Sacramento, California.

14. See, P. Ong and D. Mar, *Silicon Valley's Displaced Semiconductor Workers: Recession in 1985,* (Sacramento, CA: California Employment Development Department, 1989).

15. For computational reasons, the Silicon Valley is defined as an area comprised of the counties of San Francisco, Alameda, San Mateo, Santa Clara, Santz Cruz, and San Benito.

16. This category consists primarily of workers categorized as "Asian" in the EDD files.

17. See, Kletzer (1991).

18. See, J. Keller, "The Division of Labor in Electronics," in *Women, Men, and the International Division of Labor,* edited by June Nash and Maria Patricia Fernandez-Kelly, (Albany, NY: SUNY Press, 1983), 346–373 for a discussion of gender differences in the industry.

19. GROWTH and LAYOFFS are not simple mathematical complements. Both variables are not only affected by changes in the overall size of a firm's labor force, but also by the extent that a firm restructures its market strategies and production methods. Consequently, two firms with identical levels of net growth can have very different levels of layoffs.

20. See, for example, D. Angel, "New Firm Formation in the Semiconductor Industry: Elements of a Flexible Manufacturing System," *Regional Studies,* 24 (3) (June 1990), 211–221 and R. Oakey, *High Technology Small Firms: Innovation and Regional Development in Britain and the USA,* (London: Frances Pinter, 1984).

21. There is no evidence of any compensating wage differential for layoffs. The correlation between wages and layoffs was negative and not statistically significant.

J15
J45   U.S.   34 9-56
(94)

19

THE EFFECT OF PUBLIC SECTOR EMPLOYMENT ON THE EARNINGS OF WHITE AND AFRICAN AMERICAN MALES: A SAMPLE SELECTIVITY APPROACH

Michael Greene and Emily Hoffnar

This research note uses a sample selection model to measure the earnings premium (or penalty) to public sector employment. A model correcting for both labor force participation and sectoral choice is estimated for both white and African American males. Results indicate that African American males are no better off in the public than in the private sector. Moreover, white males employed in the public sector earn significantly less than their private sector counterparts.

INTRODUCTION

Selectivity bias is a well-known problem involved in the estimation of wage equations.[1] In particular, earnings information is available only for those individuals who participate in the labor force and, as a result, estimation of such equations via ordinary least squares (OLS) provides biased parameter coefficients if the error terms in the wage and labor supply equations are correlated.

This issue of sample selectivity bias is particularly problematic as regards analyses of the public-private earnings differential amongst white and African American males. Specifically, such analyses must contend with an additional source of sample selectivity bias—namely, that individuals may choose to enter that sector (public versus private) which provides them with the greatest net advantage. To the extent that the variables which affect sectoral choice are correlated with those factors which determine earnings, the earnings equation will not be independent of the sectoral selection process and, as a result, estimates of the public-private earnings differential will be biased. Viewed somewhat differently, analyses of public-private earnings differentials should, at minimum, simultaneously control for potential sample selectivity bias emanating from both the labor force participation and the sectoral choice process. With the exception of the recent study by Choudhury,[2] based on aggregate data from the Current Population Survey and limited to males and females without racial breakdowns, we are unaware of any analyses of the public-private earnings differential which simultaneously mitigate against sample selection bias from the labor supply decision and the sectoral choice process. Early work by Smith[3] on government wage differentials, for instance, published prior to advances in selection research, do not correct for sample selectivity bias. Blank[4] does estimate the determinants of sectoral choice using single equation probit estimates but fails to incorporate the results into earnings regressions. Elsewhere, Belman and Heywood[5] use a sample selectivity approach to estimate government wage differentials among civilian males; however, their estimated wage equations control for sectoral choice but ignore potential bias emanating from the labor supply decision. And while Choudhury,[6] as mentioned above, does control for both sources of sample selectivity bias, she provides limited insight into how (a) the public-private differential might vary by race and (b) the earnings premium might differ by sector of public employment (e.g., federal versus state).

The purpose of this research note is to use a model correcting for double-sample selectivity bias to determine the extent to which, if any, public sector employment raises the earnings of white and African American males. Moreover, the results reported below provide (a) evidence concerning whether the public sector earnings premium varies by sector of employment and (b) a comparison between unadjusted and adjusted (i.e., corrected for double sample selectivity) estimates of the public-private earnings differential for each group.

EMPIRICAL MODEL

Our goal is to estimate earnings equations which permit testing the hypothesis that, everything else being equal, public sector males earn more than private sector males. In undertaking this endeavor, we mitigate against the two aforementioned sources of sample selectivity bias. The basic equation to be estimated may be expressed as:

(1) $Y_i = X_i\beta + \varepsilon_{il}$

where Y_i is the log earnings of the ith individual, X_i is a vector of characteristics either known or believed to influence earnings determination, β is a vector of parameters, and ε is a stochastic error term. Estimation problems arise because (a) information on earnings is available only for those who select into the labor force and (b) individuals choose the sector of employment which provides them with the greatest net advantage. To illustrate, consider the issue of sample selectivity bias due to the fact that earnings information is available only for those individuals who select into the labor force. More specifically, define an indicator variable, S_i, such that earnings information is available if and only if $S_i = 1$.

Let S_i be modelled as:

(2) $\quad S_i = K_i A + \varepsilon_{i2}$

where K_i represents the determinants of labor force participation, A is a vector of parameters to be estimated, and ε_{i2} is an error term. Joint normality is assumed for ε_{i1} and ε_{i2}.

While the unconditional population mean of $\varepsilon_{i1} = 0$, the conditional sample mean from the censored sample, $[E(\varepsilon_{i1}/S_i =1)]$, may not be. Heckman and Lee[7] have shown that this problem of missing data on the dependent variable (i.e. earnings information only being available for individuals who enter the labor force) can be transformed into one of specification bias due to the omission from eq (1) of an explanatory variable. Moreover, the omitted variable can be represented by the ratio of the density of the standard normal ($\phi(K_i A)$) to the distribution function ($\Phi(K_i A)$) and is typically referred to as the inverse of the Mills' ratio. A probit equation (1 = in the labor force; else = 0) can be used to compute the Mills' ratio for each individual to be included in the basic regression model as an additional explanatory variable:

(3) $\quad Y_i = X_i \beta + \dfrac{\delta 12}{\delta 2} \lambda_{i1} + v_i$

where v_i is the standard normal error term, λ_i is the inverse of the Mills' ratio computed from the labor force participation probit equation, δ_{12} is the covariance between ε_{i1} and ε_{i2}, and δ_2 is the standard error of ε_{i2}. Applying a similar line of reasoning to the second potential source of sample selectivity bias, eq. (3) can be modified such that:

(4) $\quad Y_i = X_i \beta + \dfrac{\delta 12}{\delta 2} \lambda_{i1} + \dfrac{\delta 13}{\delta 3} \lambda_{i2} + v_i$

where λ_{i2} is computed from a probit equation predicting sector of employment (i.e. coded as 1 if in the public sector, 0 if in private sector). Estimation of (4) by ordinary least squares controls for double sample selectivity bias and provides unbiased estimates of the population parameters. The t-statistics on the coefficients of λ_{i1} and λ_{i2} provide a statistical test of the significance of each source of sample selectivity bias.

ESTIMATION RESULTS

Data for this study are extracted from the 1990 Current Population Survey (CPS), March Annual Demographic File.[8] Coverage is restricted to white and African American males between the ages of sixteen and sixty-four and who did not report themselves as being in the military or self-employed at the time of the survey. We note that the probit equation predicting sectoral labor force participation for each group is based on a sample of both labor force participants and nonparticipants, while the second sample selection correction variable (λ_{i2}) is generated via estimation of a univariate probit from a sample of both private and public sector workers among each group.

Equation (4) is separately estimated for pooled samples of all African American and white males. The sample sizes for whites and African Americans are 14,485 and 1,675, respectively. The dependent variable in our earnings regression is the natural log of annual earnings. Independent variables include an experience proxy—defined as "age-schooling-6" and its square (EXPER^2); number of years of education completed (SCHOOL); the number of children under age six residing in the household (KU6); dummy variables identifying whether the individual is "married, spouse present (MARRIED)," resides in a city (CITY) or suburb (SUBURB), reports working less than thirty-five hours per week (PTIME). The dummy variable SOUTH is included to identify whether or not the individual reports residing in the southern region of the United States. These explanatory variables are similar to those typically used throughout the social science literature analyzing socioeconomic outcomes and, as a result, no attempt is made to justify their inclusion here. However, some discussion is warranted concerning the manner in which we attempt to identify whether public sector employment increases the earnings of white and African American men.

To ascertain whether each group receives an earnings premium (or penalty) associated with public sector employment, we include three binary variables identifying each individual's sector of employment. The first one is coded as one if the individual reports being employed in the federal sector (FEDERAL), while the other two identify whether the respondent reports being employed in the state (STATE) or local (LOCAL) level of public sector employment. The omitted category (i.e., the reference group) is those individuals employed in the private sector. Thus, each of the estimated coefficients associated with the binary public sector variables permits one to identify how males within each of these public sectors fare relative to comparable males within the private sector. Positive and statistically significant parameter estimates would be consistent with the hypothesis that, everything else being equal, males within the public sector earn significantly more than their private sector counterparts.

Table 1 shows the results generated via estimation of equations (1) and (4) for separate samples of white and African American males. In order to conserve space, we report neither the univariate probit estimates for sector choice nor labor force participation, although these results are available from the authors upon request. For purposes of comparison, the table presents both unadjusted OLS results and adjusted regression results which incorporate double selectivity bias correction. Columns (1) and (2) present the results for African American males; comparable results for white men are found in columns (3) and (4).

Inspection of Table 1 reveals that, with few exceptions, each of the coefficients tend to have the anticipated sign and are significantly different from zero. Additional years of schooling, experience, and being "married, spouse present" significantly increase male earnings, while part-time employment and southern residence tend to have negative effects on earnings. This pattern generally holds for both the adjusted and unadjusted parameters, as well as for both white and African American males.

Of particular concern here, however, is whether white and African American males experience an earnings premium for public sector employment. The unadjusted OLS estimates suggest that, relative to their private sector counterparts, African American males earn significantly more in the federal and local levels of public sector employment. The coefficient associated with the variable Federal in the unadjusted results (column (1)) indicates that African American males employed by the federal government earn about 17 percent more than those employed in the private sector. In contrast, we find strong evidence that white males fare better in the private than in the public sector: While the unadjusted OLS coefficient associated with the variable FEDERAL is insignificant, those associated with the variables State and Local are negative and

TABLE 1
Unadjusted and Selection Adjusted OLS Earnings Equations
*** 99% confidence, ** 95%, * 90%, (standard errors)

	AFRICAN AMERICAN SAMPLE, 1675 OBSERVATIONS		WHITE SAMPLE, 14485 OBSERVATIONS	
	UNADJUSTED	ADJUSTED	UNADJUSTED	ADJUSTED
Constant	8.07*** (0.119)	7.53*** (0.302)	8.07*** (0.034)	7.82*** (0.057)
SOUTH	-0.058* (0.033)	-0.037 (0.044)	-0.049*** (0.011)	-0.032*** (0.012)
SCHOOL	0.086*** (0.008)	0.128*** (0.026)	0.102*** (0.002)	0.130*** (0.005)
EXPER	0.039*** (0.005)	0.043*** (0.006)	0.051*** (0.002)	0.054*** (0.002)
EXPER^2	-0.0005*** (0.0001)	-0.0005*** (0.0001)	-0.001*** (0.000)	-0.001*** (0.000)
PTIME	-1.07*** (0.064)	-1.06*** (0.064)	-1.20*** (0.022)	-1.19*** (0.023)
MARRIED	0.226*** (0.037)	0.276*** (0.046)	0.236*** (0.013)	0.249*** (0.016)
KIDSU6	0.0002 (0.028)	-0.010 (0.028)	0.039*** (0.009)	0.039*** (0.009)
CITY	0.080* (0.046)	0.083 (0.059)	0.008 (0.015)	-0.014 (0.015)
SUBURB	0.198*** (0.051)	0.186*** (0.052)	0.070*** (0.013)	0.022 (0.015)
FEDERAL	0.174*** (0.067)	-0.631 (0.707)	0.008 (0.026)	-1.186*** (0.187)
STATE	0.003 (0.075)	-0.805 (0.714)	-0.150*** (0.027)	-1.336*** (0.186)
LOCAL	0.090* (0.051)	-0.729 (0.716)	-0.079*** (0.019)	-1.285*** (0.188)
λ_1		1.121** (0.554)		-0.243 (0.236)
λ_2		0.471 (0.413)		0.662*** (0.102)

strongly significant. Column (3) indicates that white males employed in state and local government earn 15 percent and 8 percent less, respectively, than comparable white men employed in the private sector.

Does controlling for double sample selectivity bias significantly alter the above results? Insight into the issue can be gained by contrasting the unadjusted and unadjusted coefficients associated with the public sector variables (e.g., contrasting columns (1) and (2) for African American males and (3) and (4) for white men). Columns (2) and (4) reveals that λ_1 (i.e., the Mills' ratio computed from the labor force participation function) is statistically significant in the African American earnings function, while λ_2 (i.e., the Mills' ratio computed from the sector choice equation) is significant in the white male earnings function. These results suggest that for (a) African American males the covariance between earnings and participation is strong and, therefore, critical to take account of earnings analysis and (b) the covariance between the error terms in the earnings equation and the sectoral choice equation is strong for white males. Particularly important is the fact that correction for sample selectivity bias substantially changes the findings regarding the impact of public sector employment on African American male earnings: After correction for both sources of sample selectivity bias, we find no evidence that African American men are better off in the public than the private sector. Equally important, correction for double sample selectivity bias increases the magnitude of the negative effect of public sector on the earnings of white males (as well as the size of t-statistics); moreover, the adjusted parameter associated with the variable Federal is now significantly negative, whereas in the unadjusted estimation the effect of federal sector employment on the earnings of white men was found to be statistically trivial.

CONCLUSION

This research note examines the hypothesis that, everything else being equal, males in the public sector earn significantly more than their private sector counterparts. A pooled model correcting for double sample selectivity bias is separately estimated for white and African American males. Our results suggest that, after adjusting for potential sample selectivity bias emanating from the participation and sectoral choice processes, African American males are no better off in the public than in the private sector. Moreover, the evidence reported above provides strong support for the hypothesis that, ceteris paribus, white males employed in the public sector earn significantly less than their private sector counterparts. That African Americans—in contrast to whites—do not appear to experience an earnings premium associated with private sector employment is an intriguing finding. One possible explanation—which we intend to explore in future research—is that earnings declines for African Americans employed in the private sector during the 1980s may have culminated in the eradication of any earnings premium associated with private sector employment. At a more general level, this study underscores the fact that failure to adequately control for sample selectivity bias may produce misleading estimates of the public-private earnings differential.

NOTES

1. See J. Heckman, "Sample Selection Bias as a Specification Error," *Econometrica,* 47, (1979): 153–61.
2. See S. Choudhury, "New Evidence on Public Wage Differentials," *Applied Economics,* 26 (1994): 259–266.
3. See S.P. Smith, "Government Wage Differentials," *Journal of Urban Economics,* 4 (1977): 248–271 and S.P. Smith, *Equal Pay in Public Sector: Fact or Fantasy?* Industrial Relations Section, Princeton University, Princeton, N.J. (1977).
4. See R.M. Blank, "An Analysis of Workers' Choice Between Employment in the Public and Private Sectors," *Industrial and Labor Relations Review,* 38 (1985): 211–224.
5. See D. Belman and J.S. Heywood, "Government Wage Differentials: A Sample Selection Approach," *Applied Economics,* 21 (1989): 427–438.
6. See Choudhury (1994).
7. See Heckman (1979); L.F. Lee, "Unionism and Wage Rates: A Simultaneous Equations Model with Qualitative and Limited Dependent Variables," *International Economic Review,* 19 (1978): 415–433; and L.F. Lee, "Identification and Estimation in Binary Choice Models with Limited (Censored) Dependent Variables," *Econometrica,* 47 (1979): 977–996.
8. See *Current Population Survey: Annual Demographic File. 1990* [Computer file]. 2nd release. Washington, DC: U.S. Department of Commerce, Bureau of the Census, 1991. Ann Arbor, MI: Inter-university Consortium for Political and Social Research, [distributor], (1991).

VII

STRATEGIES TO INCREASE EMPLOYMENT

THE IMPACT OF TARGETED PARTNERSHIP GRANTS
ON MINORITY EMPLOYMENT

Maurice Y. Mongkuo and William J. Pammer, Jr.

This paper assesses the relative impact of the major design components of the Urban Development Action Grant (UDAG) targeted partnership development initiative on minority employment in the Pittsburgh, Pennsylvania Primary Metropolitan Statistical Area (PMSA).
Data are drawn from records obtained from the Department of Housing and Urban Development of completed UDAG projects between
1978 and 1988 for the Pittsburgh PMSA. The results suggest that
targeting geographic projects by leveraging private investment in a
central city does not yield a significant increase in minority employment. Moreover, the geographic emphasis of UDAG projects do not
exhibit an ability to increase minority employment. These findings
support the benefit capitalization and ecological fallacy arguments,
which propose that the benefits of targeted partnerships (i.e., employment) is shifted away from the original beneficiaries. The paper concludes by discussing the implications of these findings and directions
for future research.

THE EFFECT OF TARGETED PARTNERSHIP GRANTS ON
MINORITY EMPLOYMENT

Over the past two decades, the federal government has targeted public
dollars to declining communities with the objective of improving economic opportunities for local residents. A primary example is the Urban
Development Action Grant (UDAG) program. This program is based on
the principle of geographic targeting through public-private partnerships
to directly assist people, places, or firms with special needs. In effect, the
program is designed to encourage private investment by using public
funds to reduce the risk of investing in distressed areas and, in turn,

stimulate job creation among socially disadvantaged residents.

The targeting approach of job creation, however, has been the subject of major controversy. While state and local officials, as well as some private entities, have applauded this approach as a viable tool for countering economic decline in local areas, others have argued that the approach is an ineffective and inequitable means of providing government assistance to low income and minority persons in distressed areas. In particular, critics argue that a geographic targeting grant program, such UDAG, may have its benefits diverted from the intended beneficiaries through ecological fallacy or through the process of benefit capitalization.[1] Ecological fallacy refers to a skewing of eligibility such that eventually ineligible individuals become beneficiaries by their place of residence, while some intended beneficiaries are excluded for the same reason.[2] Benefit capitalization, on the other hand, is a shifting of benefits (i.e., employment and wealth) from the original beneficiaries to the owners of land and skilled labor pool; a shifting that may sometimes involve the actual removal of the intended beneficiaries from the target area.[3]

The purpose of this study is to test these two propositions by assessing the impact of using UDAG to leverage private investment with the intent of providing economic benefits (i.e., jobs and income) to minority persons residing in the Pittsburgh Primary Metropolitan Statistical Area. (PMSA). The Pittsburgh PMSA is considered to be the most appropriate site for this study for two reasons. First, in the 1970s and early 1980s, the area's primary industry, steel, suffered a major decline, which led to the loss of many jobs in primary metals, electric machinery, and transportation industries. These economic changes in the local economy established the Pittsburgh PMSA as a distressed area, and thus, a prime recipient of UDAG funds. Second, similar to most older urban centers, a majority of minorities in the Pittsburgh PMSA reside in the depressed areas of the central city. Since a major objective of the UDAG program is to reduce the jobless rate among minority persons residing in distressed local areas, we might expect a positive association between the level of private investment leveraged by UDAG projects and the number of new permanent minority jobs while controlling for location and the type of economic activity funded by UDAG. Conversely, no significant relationship may suggest evidence of ecological fallacy or benefit capitalization.

While UDAG is a small program compared to many other recent federal geographic targeting initiatives, it is indicative of a number of current trends in federal policies toward local jurisdictions; that is, targeting distressed places through the reliance on discretionary funding and capital subsidies to promote private investment with the hope of enhancing economic opportunities for the disadvantaged. The argument that federal spending must be curbed invariably has many urban areas concerned, particularly those areas who have relied heavily on targeted partnership grants. Therefore, the concern for the design and distribution of federal assistance to localities takes on an added significance. This state of uncertainty urgently demands a constructive policy opinion not only on the design and implementation of the nation's redistributive development policy, but on addressing the influence of capital subsidies targeted specifically to an urban constituency.

THE ECONOMIC IMPLICATIONS OF GEOGRAPHIC TARGETED PARTNERSHIP GRANT PROGRAMS

Most targeted partnership grant programs, such as UDAG, are designed to create jobs for poor and unskilled residents in central cities. These grants also have eligibility criteria based not on income but on residence in areas with income below the poverty threshold. Given these criteria, it can be argued that the program benefit will reach targeted groups given the segregated nature of contemporary American urban centers. Historically, this segregation can be attributed to economic and social forces, which for more than half of the nation's two centuries, have been effective in sorting out different income strata into different neighborhoods. The economic and social forces include: the existence of a land allocation system based on individual bidding for homesteads or apartments in which individuals with higher income and particular tastes (supported by sufficient income) can outbid others for sites they consider prime, the institution of zoning and other government policies that prohibit mixed land use, and the prevalence of self-segregation or involuntary exclusion by different social groups based on class, racial, ethnic or lifestyle standards.[4]

From a policy standpoint, the residential pattern may make it easier for the government to provide assistance to selected population subgroups by targeting resources to their neighborhoods. However, Taeuber and Taeuber have observed that very few districts are large enough to be considered completely segregated, even in income and racial terms.[5] This phenomenon is attributed to the dynamics involved in the selection of a residential location. For instance, as neighborhoods change it is unlikely that all residents collectively move from their location. Thus, the prevalence of market or social forces that ensure uniformity of new residents into a particular neighborhood may not necessarily imply that all residents will share the same characteristics. Under the most reasonable system of boundary-drawing, service or eligibility districts will encompass residents with a variety of income and other characteristics. To attribute individual characteristics (such as presumed income eligibility) on the basis of the area of residence is to commit what is popularly referred to in the statistical literature as the "ecological fallacy."[6] Thus, a targeted partnership program that defines eligibility in terms of residence in a poor district may, by default, make eligible many nonpoor residents, while at the same time excluding poor persons.

A second implication of targeted programs is a possible shift of benefits from the intended beneficiaries (i.e., minority persons) to skilled workers and owners of capital. By making an investment in distressed areas more attractive through capital subsidies, a targeted grant program may increase the amount some investors would be willing to invest in the site. To the extent that market competition allows these private investors to make their desire effective, they will bid away the use of land from prior users, and, in the process, raise the effective rent or property value in the area. If the previous residents do not have ownership rights either to property or businesses, it is highly unlikely that they will benefit from the increased value.

Moreover, if minorities lack sufficient job skills and training they may also be excluded from employment opportunities offered by targeted grants. The injection of capital subsidies into a distressed area and the resultant increase in competition may enhance the need for more effective production in goods and services compelling investors to hire available skilled labor. This phenomenon seems natural since employment opportunities will gravitate toward individuals with skill levels that are consumerate with effective competition in the marketplace. Unfortunately, this trend may inadvertently diminish employment opportunities for unskilled minorities. In the Pittsburgh PMSA, as in many other urban centers in the United States, where a majority of the minority population not only reside in the geographically targeted central cities, but also are underrepresented in terms of ownership of plants and businesses, the occurrence of benefit capitalization resulting from a targeted grant program may inadvertently cause further economic hardship and despair.

The significance of this discussion is that the ultimate users (i.e., minority residents) of space in the targeted area are, in many cases, not the initial owners of land, and many are unskilled tenants as well who may be excluded from employment opportunities. Thus, while a targeted partnership grant program may show positive benefits based on land value criteria (i.e., increase in property values and assessment), it may leave a majority of initial residents worse off, since they do not own investment property or possess employable skills. Consequently, as one scholar asserts: "[This phenomenon] suggests that when we talk of 'place' we may really be referring to a particular set of people—the owners of land and [skilled labor]" who may benefit from targeted partnerships.[7]

A THEORETICAL FRAMEWORK FOR UNDERSTANDING THE IMPACT OF TARGETED PARTNERSHIPS ON MINORITY EMPLOYMENT

The implications of our discussion lead us to question empirically the real impact of targeted partnerships on minority employment. It is hypothesized that perhaps it may be unrealistic to expect a targeted action grant investment to be a powerful job creation mechanism for low-skill residents in geographically targeted areas. From an empirical standpoint then, leveraging private investment through the use of UDAG funding may not be a significant determinant of the variation in minority employment in distressed areas. In particular, we expect that perhaps for every increase in the ratio of private to UDAG dollars per capital project there may be an increase in the number of permanent jobs among minorities. However, the increase will not be significant to suggest that private dollars alleviate unemployment among minorities in distressed areas.

Could perhaps the level of public dollars contribute to a significant increase in minority employment? Since the UDAG program provides a government subsidy to induce private development in high risk areas, it may be logical to assume that as public sector contributions increase so do opportunities for minority employment since these subsidies are reducing the risk of the private sector. In fact, some research has indicated that communities may provide the highest possible subsidy in order to maximize the possibility of success.[8] Of course, a fundamental question raised earlier was whether or not targeting programs benefit eligible groups. Therefore, a significant, positive association between UDAG contributions and minority employment implies that minorities are benefiting from targeting programs, while an indirect relationship implies the opposite.

To further assess the impact of UDAG grants on minority employment it is important to consider other features of UDAG programs designed to address employment. As a targeted program, UDAG was intended to help those areas in major urban centers suffering the greatest degree of economic distress.[9] Indeed, Rich has found that older, central cities have been the most successful in getting their action grant programs funded.[10] However, Stephenson has argued that despite the ability of central cities to attract targeting grants, there is no a priori reason to suppose that these programs will prove effective in providing jobs since minority individuals who are adversely affected by urban decline lack specific skills and job experience to be employed on a permanent basis.[11] It is expected that the regional emphasis of a target grant, whether central city or suburban, will not produce a noticeable increase in minority employment.

If job training is sufficiently lacking, then it only stands to reason that targeted investment in both commercial and industrial development will not yield a significant increase in minority employment as well. The literature laments this argument, and even goes so far as to argue that simple job training for those citizens who are most negatively affected might prove more efficacious.[12] While from a normative standpoint this proposition appears logical, it remains an empirical question that we intend to test. A final aspect of UDAG projects worth exploring is the UDAG stipulation of mandatory minority participation in these projects. Since many UDAG projects are capital projects, the federal government requires that a specific percentage (at least 10 percent) of the total contract amount be set-aside for minority contractors. It is hypothesized therefore that an actual increase in minority participation may yield an increase in minority employment since minority firms may be more prone to hire minority employees than majority firms.[13]

DATA AND METHODS

Data for this study were obtained from records of the UDAG program located in the regional HUD office in Pittsburgh, Pennsylvania. The primary data sources included: (1) The Semi-Annual Progress Report (SPR); (2) the Consolidated Annual Report to Congress on Community Development Programs; (3) the UDAG Data Book, and (4) Housing and Urban Development UDAG project files. The units of analysis for this study are completed UDAG projects undertaken in the Pittsburgh PMSA from the time of program inception in 1978 to 1988. A list of all UDAG Projects undertaken during this time frame was obtained form the HUD regional office in downtown Pittsburgh. The list contained a total of 75 projects in the Pittsburgh PMSA. A sample of 44 completed projects was selected from the total list. A UDAG project is considered complete when a final audit has been completed and the Department of Housing and Urban Development (HUD) decides that expectations, such as jobs and taxes, have been met or best efforts were made.[14]

The primary dependent variable is minority employment. Operationally, this variable is defined as the proportion of new permanent jobs created per UDAG project.[15] As noted earlier, one objective of this research is to assess the relative effect of leveraging private investment on minority employment. The leveraging variable is measured as the ratio of private dollars spent to UDAG dollars awarded per project.[16] Another concern was the impact of public sector contributions on minority employment. The rationale was that larger contributions may yield higher levels of minority employment since public sector contributions reduce the risks to the private sector for investing in distressed areas. The public sector contribution measure is operationally defined as the ratio of public dollars per minority job.[17]

To understand more fully the impact of targeted partnerships, the geographic targeting and type of investment emphasized by UDAG were identified as important variables in the analysis. To quantify the relative effects of these variables they were treated as dummy variables (1/0). In particular, geographic targeting was measured as a location variable where 1 = central city and 0 = non central city.[18] Two measures of type of investment—commercial and industrial—were included in the analysis to follow. Both measures were measured as dummy variables, where commercial activity is 1 = yes and 0 = no, and industrial activity is 1 = yes and 0 = no.[19] Finally, it was assumed that the proportion of minority vendor participation on UDAG projects may influence minority employment. This variable was operationalized as the percent of total contract dollar awarded to minority firms for each UDAG project.[20]

Multiple regression was used in an attempt to sort out the effects that each characteristic of a UDAG project has on minority employment. The model is of the general form:

MINORITY = $a + b_1$ (LEVER) + b_2 (PUBLIC) + b_3 (MBE) + b_4 (COM) + b_5 (IND) + b_6 (CENTRAL) + e_i where,
MINORITY: Percent of minority employment for UDAG projects;
LEVER: Leverage ratio of private dollars to UDAG monies;
PUBLIC: Ratio of UDAG dollars to minority jobs;
MBE: Percent of actual minority contractor participation per UDAG project;

COM: Commercial project;
IND: Industrial project, and;
CENTRAL: Central city target.

RESULTS

Table 1 contains the regression results. As expected the regression results confirm our hypothesis that leveraging private investment through the use of UDAG funding is not a significant determinant of minority employment. Although the standardized beta weight (Beta = .15) suggests that leveraging increases minority employment, the relationship is not statistically significant to imply that this variable has a profound ability to increase job opportunities for minorities. A similar relationship is found between the actual percent of minority firm participation and minority employment as well (Beta = .17).

The measure of public commitment emerges as a significant predictor of minority employment (Beta = –.49). However, contrary to what was expected, the sign of the relationship suggests that despite more UDAG dollars per minority job, less permanent job opportunities exist for minorities. This finding supports the benefit capitalization argument discussed earlier in this paper, which implied that the beneficiaries do not receive the employment benefits from more public spending. The results also confirm the ecological fallacy argument. In particular, the central city measure reveals a very weak, indirect relationship with minority employment suggesting that the more the central city is targeted for assistance, the less likely minority employment will increase. Finally, neither the commercial nor industrial activity variables exhibit a significant impact on minority employment.

DISCUSSION AND CONCLUSION

This study has demonstrated that targeting geographic projects by leveraging private investment in distressed or declining areas, in this case areas located in the Pittsburgh PMSA, has no significant impact on alleviating periodic or chronic unemployment of minority residents. Perhaps this phenomenon is attributed partly to investors' orientation toward urban development. For instance, Barnekov and Rich observe that developers and business individuals will organize for self-protection to ensure that their interests are accounted for in redevelopment efforts. As a result, to guarantee their competitive standing in the market they may use

TABLE 1
Regression Model Explaining Minority Employment
Among UDAG Projects

Independent Variables	Beta[a]
Private Investment Leverage Variable	.15
UDAG Contribution Measure	- .49***
Central City Concentration[b]	.10
Investment in Commercial Development[c]	.03
Investiment in Industrial Development[d]	.08
Minority Firm Participation in UDAG Projects	.17
	$R^2 = .31$
	$N = 44$
	$F = 3.72$
	$p < .05$

[a]The standardized beta is reported since it corrects for the differences in the units of measurement among the independent variables.
[b]This variable represents regional concentration of targeting grants, where 1 = central city and 0 = suburb.
[c]This measure is a dummy code 1/0, where 1 = yes and 0 = no.
[d]This measure is a dummy code 1/0, where 1 = yes and 0 = no.
***$p < .001$

targeting partnerships to initiate development only to resort to more skilled labor, which, in some cases, may exclude minority residents with marginal or no specific job skills. Hence, in the end, market forces may dictate where the benefits go regardless of the urban problem or condition to be addressed.

Another consideration is that much of the UDAG projects under investigation were dedicated to capital projects that were technology intensive, which required skilled labor, and, in some cases, required no labor because of robotics. As a consequence, the emphasis on high technology produces a residual population consisting mostly of minorities unable to take advantage of emerging economic opportunities.

Future research, however, should investigate further the observations outlined in this study. Similar research should be pursued using UDAG data from other cities, particularly older central cities who have relied heavily on UDAG grants. This approach could yield a more complete profile of the effect of UDAG projects on minority employment. Moreover, future research should be extended to other geographic targeting programs, such as enterprise zones, to develop a better understanding of their net effect on minority employment, and the extent to which they generate benefits to disadvantaged groups.

In effect, the results presented here suggest a profound philosophical conflict of government. While on the one hand government offers a redistributive development policy, it also appears to compound the economic plight of minority residents through leveraging grants such as UDAG. Hence, the very problems it seeks to rectify are only perpetuated by its action. Nevertheless, the issue of minority employment might be sustained if local decision makers not only be sensitive to the type of economic activity, but tie targeting to job training and upgrading skill levels of the targeted groups in order for them to take advantage of new economic opportunities.

NOTES

1. Matthew Edel, "Land Values and the Cost of Urban Congestion: Measurement and Distribution," in I. Sachs, *Political Economy of Environment: Problems and Methods* (Paris: Mouton, 1972); Robert Levine, *The Poor Ye Need Not Have With You: Lessons From the War on Poverty* (Cambridge: MIT Press, 1970).

2. Julian L. Simon, *Basic Research Methods in Social Sciences* (New York: Random House, 1958; Karl E. Taeuber and A. F. Taeuber, *Negroes in Cities* (Chicago, IL.: Aldine, 1965); Matthew Edel, "Land Values and the Cost of Urban Congestion: Measurement and Distribution," in I. Sachs, *Political Economy of Environment: Problems and Methods* (Paris: Mouton, 1972).

3. Matthew Edel, "Land Values and the Cost of Urban Congestion: Measurement and Distribution," in I. Sachs, *Political Economy of Environment: Problems and Methods* (Paris: Mouton, 1972); Charles M. Eastman, "Hypotheses Concerning Market Effects on Neighborhood Development Program," *Urban Affairs Quarterly* 7 (March 1972), 287–300; Henry George, *Progress and Poverty* (New York: Modern Library, 1938); Frederick Engel, *The Housing Question* (New York: International Publishers, n.d.); Herbert Mohring, "Land Values and the Measurement of Highway Benefits," *Journal of Political Finance* 69 (June 1961), 236–49; W. E. Oates, *Fiscal Federalism* (New York: Harcourt Brace Jovanovich, 1972).

4. Matthew Edel, "People versus Places in Urban Impact Analysis," in Norman J. Glickman, *The Urban Impact of Federal Policies* (Baltimore: John Hopkins University Press, 1980).

5. Karl E. Taeuber and A. F. Taeuber, *Negroes in Cities* (Chicago, IL.: Aldine, 1965).

6. Julian L. Simon, *Basic Research Methods in the Social Sciences* (New York: Random House, 1958).

7. Matthew Edel, "People versus Places in Urban Impact Analysis," in Norman J. Glickman, *The Urban Impact of Federal Policies* (Baltimore: Johns Hopkins University Press, 1980).
8. Peter K. Eisinger, *The Rise of the Entrepreneurial State: State and Local Economic Development in the United States* (Madison: The University of Wisconsin Press, 1988).
9. U.S. House of Representatives, *Authorization Hearings for the Department of Housing and Urban Development Before the Subcommittee on Community Development* (Washington, D.C.: U.S. Government Printing Office, April 1977).
10. M. Rich, "Hitting the Target: The Distributional Impacts of the Urban Development Action Grant Program" *Urban Affairs Quarterly,* 17 (Winter 1982), 285–301.
11. Max O. Stephenson, "The Policy and Premises of Urban Development Action Grant Program Implementation: A Comparative Analysis of the Carter and Reagan Presidencies." *Journal of Urban Affairs,* 9 (Winter 1987), 19–35.
12. Pat Choate, *Retooling the American Workforce* (Washington, D.C.: Northeast-Midwest Institute, 1982); National Commission on Excellence in Education, *A Nation at Risk: The Imperative for Educational Reform* (Washington, D.C.: USGPO, 1983); Jermone M. Rosmow and Robert Zager, *Training—The Competitive Edge* (San Francisco: Josey Bass, 1988); Commission on the Skills of the American Workforce, *America's Choice: High Skills or Low Wages!* (Rochester, New York: National Center on Education and the Economy, 1990).
13. Nancy McCrea, *Minority Enterprise Development* (Washington, D.C.: The National Council for Urban Economic Development, 1989).
14. U.S. Comptroller General, *Report to the Congress of the United States: Insights into Major Urban Development Action Grant Issues* (Washington, D.C.: U.S. Government Printing Office, 1984).
15. Mean and median comparisons were performed on the minority employment variable, and the measure was subsequently logged yielding a mean of .568 and a standard deviation of .617.
16. The leveraging variable was also logged after conducting a mean and median comparison. The logged measure yielded a mean of .5420 and a standard deviation of .709.
17. The mean and standard deviation for the public sector contribution measure was 5.420 and 5.266, respectively.
18. The mean and standard deviation for the geographic targeting variable were .455 and .504, respectively.
19. The dummy code for the commercial activity variable yielded a mean of .386 and a standard deviation of .492. The industrial activity measure had a mean of .3182 and a standard deviation of .471.
20. The minority participation variable had a mean of 4.159 and a standard deviation of 4.885.

21

RACE, JOB TRAINING, AND ECONOMIC DEVELOPMENT: BARRIERS TO RACIAL EQUITY IN PROGRAM PLANNING

Joan Fitzgerald and Wendy Patton

This article examines barriers to implementing government programs designed to redress racial economic exclusion. The authors review the current urban employment environment, and the need for more extensive job training and education programs targeting young African Americans. A case study is presented of the implementation of one such program in Ohio, the High Unemployment Population Program. It demonstrates that the most well designed program can fail if staff charged with implementation are not committed to its goals. In the current racially charged environment of the country, this barrier to implementation is likely to affect many new government programs throughout the 1990s. The article concludes with several recommendations for successful program implementation.

INTRODUCTION

A key element of a new urban agenda in the United States is the persistent exclusion of African Americans from economic and employment opportunities. The institutional barriers excluding African Americans from mainstream economic opportunity are onerous: social, cultural, economic and geographic. We turn to government programs as an answer to market failure even though they are weak in their ability to regulate or provide incentives for equal employment opportunity. Government programs designed to redress economic injustice tend to be underfunded, based on faulty assumptions, and designed without careful attention to critical issues of implementation.

This article summarizes research on root causes of higher rates of unemployment among African Americans and presents a case study that illustrates barriers to targeted government employment programs. Common problems that have hindered legislative attempts to redress economic inequity are identified. Reflecting upon these barriers revealed deep divisions among those implementing government programs about the merits of racial equity as a programmatic goal. The article concludes with recommendations for overcoming barriers and points to some new directions in policy.

Race and Unemployment

The higher rates of unemployment and underemployment of African Americans have multiple roots. Both unemployment and underemployment partially can be explained by the changing structure of employment, which has created both a skills and a spatial mismatch.[1] Both have had a profound impact on employment in the black community. Blacks are more likely to be employed in the declining sectors such as manufacturing, and thus have been impacted more severely by restructuring.[2] Those manufacturing jobs that still exist are moving from central cities into the suburbs and even more rural locations.[3] In fact, evidence suggests that many manufacturers leave urban locations that have turned predominantly black.[4]

While manufacturing employment disperses, central city employment is becoming concentrated in high-skill jobs in information-intensive industries that are filled by better educated suburbanites.[5] These economic and spatial trends have led many scholars to contend that high black unemployment rates are partially the result of a mismatch between inner-city residence and the location of jobs.[6] Yet spatial mismatch represents only part of the problem.

The lower educational attainment of blacks relative to whites also contributes to their higher rates of unemployment, especially for black men.[7] Further, the deteriorating quality of education in many urban school systems perpetuates the skills and spatial mismatch.[8]

While it is necessary to improve educational quality and decrease high school dropout rates in predominantly black urban schools, human capital factors alone do not explain racial differences in unemployment and income.[9] The fact that unemployment rates for blacks are more than twice as high as for whites at all education levels[10] suggests that both spatial and skills mismatch are interconnected with racial discrimination.[11]

Patterns of racial discrimination in access to employment range from overt selection of equivalent white applicants[12] to exclusion from social networks through which most employment contacts are made, and to bias in job interviewing and employment testing.[13] Further, discrimination continues once a job is landed, in the form of wage disparity. White college graduates in 1987, for example, were twice as likely to earn $35,000 or more as their black counterparts.[14]

The Failure of Job Training as a Policy Response

The interconnectedness of declining educational attainment, spatial mismatch, skills mismatch and discrimination suggests that policies that address only one aspect of the problem will not be effective. Yet, historically, this has been exactly the approach of most government programs aimed at reducing urban poverty. Whether increasing the supply of education, training, transportation or suburban housing, the Great Society programs ignored the demand side of the employment problem.[15]

The primary federal employment training program, the Job Training Partnership Act (JTPA), for example, has been criticized for not connecting the occupational training it provides with local labor market demand. Further, JTPA perpetuates labor market discrimination through differential assignment to its services, and by ignoring discriminatory hiring practices of firms. Black JTPA participants are less likely than whites to find jobs after completion of training.[16] In fact, race is a better predictor of reemployment success than training.[17] The closest link between training and employment is on-the-job training, through which participants are placed with employers for training. Discrimination in the JTPA system occurs through channeling of white males into on-the-job training, which leads to higher reemployment rates than the classroom instruction in which minorities and women are more likely to be placed.[18] This bias is created by on-the-job-training employers who preferentially select white males for job openings. Selection bias is important because the gain in earnings of those receiving on-the-job-training is higher than for those receiving classroom training. There is little civil rights enforcement to alleviate the bias.[19]

Clearly, the JTPA employment training system is not a sufficient response for lessening racial disparities in access to employment. When interpreted in the context of other findings discussed on the interaction between skills mismatch, spatial mismatch and discrimination, it becomes evident that a more comprehensive solution than that offered by JTPA is needed to address racial inequality in access to training and jobs. Specifically, education and job training should be more closely linked to employment opportunities and affirmative action enforcement.

The State of Ohio's High Unemployment Population Program was developed to counter the above tendencies. Yet the following analysis of its implementation reveals that commitment to equity planning principles does not translate easily into effective outcomes. Thus, this study is an excellent illustration of the difficulty of implementing programs that challenge the predominant model.[20] The lessons derived from this case study are important to policy makers and planners charged with implementation of employment programs.

The case study is based on interviews with key staff involved in the program's formulation and implementation. The second author was deputy director of business development, Ohio Department of Development, at the time the High Unemployment Population Program was initiated. Selection of implementation sites for intensive study were based on questions asked of staff on "best practice" programs. Site visits and extensive interviews also were conducted with representatives from the two programs detailed in this article.

THE OHIO HIGH UNEMPLOYMENT POPULATION PROGRAM

In 1987, a powerful African American Senator in the Ohio Legislature tagged two million dollars onto the budget of the state's industrial training program, and earmarked those funds to serve the hardest-to-employ. Implicit in this earmark was a mandate to serve young black men. The program was called the "High Unemployment Population Program" (HUPP) and was administered by the Ohio Department of Development's Ohio Industrial Training Program (OITP). The program would link employment with education and training by having private sector employers serve as the "home base" for training. Participants would receive on-the-job training in conjunction with classroom instruction leading to a degree or other credential. HUPP would pay all educational fees.

A company that sponsored a HUPP project received complete subsidy for program participants for three years. Firms would be reimbursed for all costs, including loss of salary and training expenses, and would cover the cost of replacement workers needed while the program participant was at school. Child care, transportation, drug and substance abuse counseling, the cost of tools and equipment were all covered by the program. Program funds would even cover the cost of a project manager hired to provide mentoring and case management. In return, the company had to provide a structured, three-year on-the-job and classroom training curriculum that would lead the participant through increasingly responsible positions and certification through school or some other process in a field that promised a career with living-wage earnings. HUPP offered real benefits to firms motivated to participate, and provided the supplementary services lacking in JTPA and other training programs.

Context for Implementation

Challenges to implementing HUPP must be presented within the context of the history and development of the parent program and trends within the broader practice of economic development activities. Throughout the 1960s and 1970s, Ohio's Department of Development (ODOD), in partnership with a group of private utility representatives called the Ohio Economic Development Council, was famous for its notorious "Rhoades Raiders," who "raided" other states for their industrial branch plants. By the late 1970s, however, despite successes in industrial attraction, Ohio's economy was floundering. Like other development departments around the nation, the ODD added several new programs to entice new industry to the state.

One such program was the Ohio Industrial Training Program. It provided plants with subsidy for employee training and was used to attract new plants to the state and to retain existing plants. By the middle 1980s, the state had eighteen OITP field staff throughout the state and allocated around ten million dollars annually to industrial training. As indicated by the program title, the focus was on manufacturing jobs. Regional directors had considerable latitude in allocating funds through an informal process with minimal paperwork.

In the minds of OITP's architects, this type of flexible grant program structure allowed the public sector to respond quickly to opportunities for industrial "attraction" and "retention" with direct subsidy.[21] Economic development professionals, like those at OITP, typically pride themselves on ability to avoid or cut through government red tape, which allows quick response to industrial attraction or retention opportunities. In part, this reflects private sector resistance to paper-intensive federal programs of the 1970s that mandated program benefits to low and moderate income individuals. In part, it reflects the "free market" mentality of the 1980s.

By the late 1980s, new trends in economic development practice were emerging. David Birch's much publicized research on the role of small business in job creation led to new interest in economic development assistance for small businesses. Publicity around the "rise of the service sector" brought demand for development assistance for nonmanufacturing companies. The existence of racial and gender disparities in employment opportunities led to demands for development programs targeting these groups. The strongest constituents for development funds and activities, however, remained committed to industrial attraction and retention strategies and focused on manufacturing firms. As new constituents, programs and procedures developed within economic development departments, opposition to them also developed.

In 1987, a new director was appointed to lead the Ohio Department of Development. Ohio industries had rebounded strongly from the recession of the early 1980s, but like everywhere else, the recovery was uneven. This new director was charged with targeting the Department's resources to those areas and people left out of the state's economic recovery. In addition, he was charged with introducing systems of accountability to the fast and loose world of economic development.

A major priority of the new director was bringing changes to the OITP. Program funds were in great demand and hotly contested. He was approached by legislators, alleging favoritism in the program toward new firms at the expense of existing industries and discrimination against minority-owned firms. There was little empirical evidence to substantiate the accusations since, like most industrial training programs, there had been virtually no evaluations of effectiveness or patterns in allocation. However, a diverse advisory board was appointed and a formal proposal process for fund allocation was implemented. Funds were earmarked for labor unions and for older, existing industries. Existing organizational practices were thrown into change. Field directors' powers were curtailed. Red tape was introduced. Conflict developed.

Implementation Barriers

The HUPP earmark was a particularly explosive ingredient introduced into this programmatic caldron at the ODOD. There were important value conflicts between traditional goals of economic development and an equity-based program such as HUPP. Job training and economic development professionals had tried throughout the 1980s to free their works of the stigma of fiscal and administrative scandals that eventually discredited many of the Great Society programs and their descendants. Individuals within the OITP network had been pioneers of the effort to separate economic development from social welfare programs. The HUPP program undermined what they had been trying to achieve within their field. Their outrage was fueled by concerns of their inherently conservative constituent groups such as local chambers of commerce.

This lack of commitment by staff to the program's goals delayed the implementation of the program. An interagency task force was formed to design program parameters of the HUPP. A year passed and no program guidelines were adopted. Finally, the Department of Development revealed the program's approach. It was estimated that per-participant program costs would be $30,000. While this cost, at $10,000 per participant per year, was only $2,000 higher than some of the targeted JTPA programs, DOD and OITP staff were scandalized at the expense. OITP training subsidies traditionally did not exceed $500 per participant.

OITP staff, who resented responsibility for what they perceived to be a "social" program, came to be solely responsible for developing programs under the bulky guidelines, finding companies willing to participate, and monitoring projects through three years of unfamiliar and unexpected expenses and circumstances. The OITP field staff also went into an uproar about the HUPP program. For example, a key actor in the OITP was a professional who had come from a white Appalachian background. He had overcome many barriers, including poverty and an accent, to achieve his status as a professional. It was his belief that if he could overcome these obstacles without government programs, others could too.

Further, the OITP program manager had no philosophical commitment to the goals of the program and even felt that it represented "reverse discrimination." He hired no additional staff for administration of the program, so existing staff was stretched by the complex new responsibilities. Program guidelines and a request for proposals were not mailed to the field until eighteen months after the funds were set aside (the funds would have expired in another six months, after which point legislative opponents could have successfully argued that the program was obviously a failure and that the set-aside should not be renewed.

The field directors and their staff were uniformly white. They received mixed messages about giving priority to working with this program. They knew the unpopular new director placed priority on it, but the OITP program manager offered no training nor pressure to create proposals. Few field directors took on the hard job of recruiting participants and developing project plans. At least one director went so far as to respond to an inquiry about HUPP by saying that no such program existed. The OITP field network staff were not alone in their failure to work with this program. Program descriptions and proposal application forms were sent to welfare departments, Private Industry Councils, and employment services offices across the state. Of the roughly 150 agencies that received the program Request for Proposal, only two responded.

The program was renewed in the following year, again by legislative fiat in the final hours of budget negotiations. Several steps were taken to improve program performance. In order to implement the program in the face of outrage and resistance, the director hired new staff (from out of the field and out of state) with explicit instructions to ensure that legislative intent, as indicated through the earmarking of OITP funds, would be honored. Layers of new management at the deputy and program level were given explicit instructions from the director to make the HUPP program work. African American staff were appointed to market and then to administer the program. A training session was held for field directors. A minority-owned economic development consulting firm was retained to publicize the program among minority-owned firms and to help them develop proposals for funding.

Approximately twenty-five proposals were submitted, and funds were allocated in a timely fashion. At that point, administrations changed and no further evaluation of the effectiveness of the program was undertaken. In the majority of cases, these proposals were submitted by private minority-owned firms that had heard of HUPP through the grapevine and had not worked with their local OITP field agent in developing the proposal.

Implementation Success Stories

Some companies approached about the program realized immediately that this was a good way to build a loyal work force, particularly in highly desirable fields such as tool-and-die. Others saw it as a source of inexpensive labor for simple projects that could help ultimately lead to genuine company growth. Key staff interviewed for this study identified five programs that exemplified what the program was meant to accomplish. These second-year projects experienced remarkable results. The labor-intensive process of helping hard-to-employ individuals into the work force is illustrated best by the following two projects.

1. R/P International Technologies. Inc.

R/P International (RPI) is a growing minority-owned high-tech firm that provides contract engineering, technical consulting and manufacturing services to the aircraft, aerospace, defense, automotive and electronics industries. The company has fifty employees. RPI is located in Lincoln Heights, Ohio, a predominantly black suburb of Cincinnati. While company policy was to hire local residents as much as possible, this goal was difficult to meet, as few local applicants had the necessary skills for RPI's high-tech operation.

RPI was granted $176,000 to fill twelve training slots in 1989. RPI developed a thirty-six-month program that combined on-the-job training with an associate's degree program. Course work could be completed at Cincinnati Technical College or the University of Cincinnati. During the training period, trainees rotated through the company's sixteen departments on three to four month cycles.

Applicants were recruited through local community groups, employment offices, schools and churches. RPI screened over fifty applicants to fill twelve positions. To insure that applicants possessed both ability and motivation, RPI employed a stringent selection process that included intensive interviewing and drug testing. Once selected, the trainees were subject to the same thirty-day trial period as regular employees.

The commitment of RPI's management team to the project is evident in the amount of time devoted to project administration and coordination. All served as mentors in various capacities, and acted as counselors to the trainees in many areas outside of the realm of job training. Group activities such as company picnics and a softball team were organized to create a sense of belonging for the participants and staff. Many of the trainees had family problems that interfere with good attendance. Many also lacked basic social and work preparation skills, such as how to dress for an interview or work. Management staff reported that addressing these social problems and skills were as essential to the program's success as the technical training.

While RPI managers report that the participants performed well on the job, most participants found that their high school educations left them unprepared to handle the rigorous associate degree programs. Over half of the first-year participants had to take remedial course work before beginning their degree programs. While necessary, the amount of remedial work required will delay completion of the program. RPI had to hire a person to monitor the program. This person keeps track of students' progress through their academic advisors and intervenes as problems occur.

2. Ohio State Building and Construction Trades Council

The building and construction trades have a history of operating highly effective, but racially exclusionary, apprenticeship and training programs. The Ohio Building and Construction Trades Council (OSB&CTC), an umbrella organization representing construction unions in fifteen trades, is working to address past discriminatory practices. OSB&CTC participated in the HUPP program through its Building Trades Minority Development Partnership, a not-for-profit organization. The Partnership was created with the dual mission of recruiting minorities into living-wage residential construction jobs, and meeting the rising demand for affordable urban housing. Once renovated, houses would be rented or sold to low- and moderate-income residents.

Achieving both ends at once required the cooperative planning efforts of the Council with local, state and federal government bodies. The Columbus Department of Human Services assisted the council in identifying properties for renovation. The state's Housing Finance Agency provided loans to cover rehabilitation costs. Long-term financing was provided by Section 203K of the U.S. Housing and Urban Development program. Initial funding for the project came from grants from the local building councils and unions. Continued funding of classroom training was provided by HUPP, the Ohio Building Trades Training Foundation, EDWAA Title III funds, payroll deduction of members, and through a fee paid by contractors who use the union labor pool.

The Partnership recruited minority applicants with histories of prolonged unemployment and it works with minority contractors. The Columbus, Ohio, program worked with a minority contractor in renovating thirty houses in one of the city's poorest neighborhoods, South Lindon. Applicants were recruited through the Ohio Bureau of Employment Services, local churches and community organizations. To further increase community support for the project, minority contractors agreed to retain workers from the project area.

The union-operated training program offered specializations in several construction trades.[22] After completion of the three-year program the trainee achieved residential journeyman status.[23] At this point, trainees had the option of entering a traditional apprenticeship training program or finding employment.

Ten apprentices were employed through the first-year HUPP program. Apprentices worked forty-hour weeks, totaling to 2,000 hours of on-the-job training and 144 hours of classroom instruction per year. Pay was $7.50 per hour, with a full benefits package. Those without a high school diploma earned the GED through the course of the program. There was a 1:1 journeyman-to-apprentice ratio for on-the-job training. Teachers had considerable on-the-job experience in the areas they teach, and updated their skills through semiannual seminars and annual professional development workshops which bring together experts in training and new technologies.

Problems and Possibilities

The HUPP program overcomes several weaknesses inherent in existing federal and state education and training programs in redressing racial disparities. Three interconnected differences are key. First, the program links employment with education. Second, the program offers a longer and more comprehensive plan of study, providing participants with the skills needed for living-wage jobs. Third, the program invests more resources per participant. The implications of these differences are discussed below.

Linking employment with education addresses several problems inherent to the JTPA system. Even if JTPA were to focus on longer-term training, many of those eligible would not be able to participate because no income support is provided during the training period other than Unemployment Insurance. By linking employment with training, participants are guaranteed an income, which enables them to commit to a longer period of training.

Further, the commitment required of participating corporations is similar to that evident in the highly effective German apprenticeship model. There, firms not only have a social obligation to provide apprenticeships, but also assume financial responsibility for such education, regardless of whether they can hire the apprentice upon program completion.[24] Under JTPA on-the-job training, firms are subsidized for providing minimal training to employees they would have had to hire and train anyway.[25] In contrast, HUPP firms devote considerable administrative resources to mentoring and addressing the personal, work and school-related problems of trainees, even though only training costs are reimbursed.

Second, HUPP's longer time frame and broader range of skills training can provide trainees with more employment and education options. In RPI, for example, trainees work in all departments of the production end of the facility, and even learn about business management. Because training is not limited to narrow tasks, trainees finishing the program with an associate degree have the option of entering a bachelors degree program or starting their own business. Likewise, with the Building and Construction Trades program, participants can move into journeyman programs in several areas.

This approach does not come without added cost. Average cost per participant per year is approximately $10,000, considerably higher than the equivalent figure for JTPA. Comparative cost-benefit analysis is premature until the program produces graduates.[26] A preliminary analysis conducted in FY1991, however, showed how difficult it is to reach young black males through the private sector. Of the roughly seventy participants in the first funding round, over fifty percent were white, and over 50 percent were female. Only one-third of the participants were black men. This occurred because participant companies were only encouraged, but not required, to hire black men. The guidelines required only that companies indicate how they planned to reach out to black men and did not provide any mechanism for monitoring hiring practices.

Graduation and placement rates will be the ultimate indicators of success for the HUPP program. Currently, the program receives more applications from firms than can be accepted. Those firms and individuals involved express satisfaction with the program, and are committed to making it work.

SUMMARY AND DISCUSSION

This article began with the claim that current conditions call for a renewed focus on urban policy, specifically for equity-oriented programs to redress racial economic exclusion. The success of these policies and programs ultimately will be determined by how effectively they are implemented. We are a racially divided society, and this division is reflected in the staff of government agencies implementing equity agendas. It is unlikely that the programs developed will be supported by everyone charged with their implementation.

While the HUPP program represents an effort to make racial equity a priority in the state of Ohio, the story of its implementation reveals that getting equity on the agenda is only part of the battle. Indeed, it even may be the easier part.[27] The lesson from this case study is simply stated in Pressman and Wildavsky's classic text on policy implementation[28]: "There is no point in having good ideas if they cannot be carried out." Thus, several observations related to implementation are in order.

1. Without strong and direct leadership from the top, interagency task forces on equity-based programs may not work.

All actors involved in an equity-based program must have clear, self-interested motivation for successful participation. The task force created to develop the HUPP program and make it work in all agencies failed because there were no rewards for making it work, nor penalties for failure, for any agency except ODOD. The governor supported HUPP's goals, and did much to foster its success. However, a governor rarely becomes involved personally in program development, simply because of time constraints. Equity-based programs present such difficulties, however, that top officials must become involved and lend their personal authority to get the program off the ground. Competitive motivation must be created for individuals responsible for implementation. Responsibility must carry with it real rewards and penalties and a system of accountability.

2. Staff with personal belief and/or personal stake in the targeted issue should manage targeted programs.

Empowerment theory has long held that interventions should be wielded by those who experience the effects of those interventions. Not only is this fair, but it overcomes many of the problems recounted above. In the case of the HUPP, all persons involved in fighting for program implementation, including the director of development, were African American or came from families that included African American members. Indeed, the program took off only after an African American program manager was appointed.

3. The field of Economic Development hosts considerable resistance to equity-based programs.

Development departments are frequently singled out as the site for targeted job programs, but the distaste for "social welfare programs" that comes from their constituency renders them ineffective in implementing such programs. Private Industry Councils (PICs) were created to be the nexus between "social welfare programs" (e.g., job training serving the needy) and the business community. This is the natural site for programs like HUPP. PICs need to become far more visible and successful in articulating the competitive advantages of workforce development and equity-based training programs. PIC boards generally include powerful media personnel, who can be very effective in using their status to develop and deliver the message to the local audience.

4. Many private firms have considerable resistance to equity-based programs.

Until firms see training and workforce development as being in their competitive interest, they will not participate in equity-based, workforce development programs.

For one thing, American firms simply do not value their workforces yet, still regarding labor as a cost and not an asset.[29] Many firms are downsizing, and do not see workforce development as a priority, particularly when "strings" are attached to the selection of trainees. Two examples illustrate this problem.

Union and management representatives of a major automotive production plant approached the governor and director of development with a request for $8 million in job training funds to keep their plant competitive. The director explained that the standard training funds were exhausted, but that they could access up to $2 million immediately through the HUPP program. A variety of approaches for using HUPP funds was developed and presented to the company. The human resource director, African American himself, understood the program, but in the end, the plant never used it. Eventually, they were given several hundred thousand dollars in standard OITP training funds.

Neither labor nor management saw long-term workforce development as a competitive issue for the company. Managers probably could see more layoffs, not new hires, with advances in production technology.

There was no competitive reason for the auto plant managers to participate in HUPP. Nor was there a rationale for participation by the union. Their problem was laid-off members, not development of a ready pool of new hires.

A similar situation developed when a large, nonunion insurance firm approached the state for training funds as an incentive not to move out-of-state. A combination of regular training funds and HUPP funds was offered. The company refused to participate in HUPP and eventually was given an inducement package that carried no "strings." In this case, the company could have realized a competitive benefit from workforce development offered by HUPP, and could have enjoyed the financial benefits of participating.

Insurance is an expanding industry, unlike the automotive industry. This is exactly the type of firm that needs to understand why the type of workforce development offered by HUPP presents competitive advantage. Yet these firms and others saw the efforts to get them to participate in the HUPP program as a meddlesome government action. The legislature soon heard about these "social engineering" experiments. Eventually a powerful legislator approached the governor and requested that such large firms seeking incentive funds not be directed to the HUPP program.

5. Equity-based programs, and the leadership to sustain them, take time to work.

While leadership at the top is essential to program success, it also has to filter through the organization and program. Leadership was exhibited by the new staff hired and by businesses such as RPI who became vocal advocates for HUPP. That the program now has more business applicants than slots available is due to the enthusiastic support of middle management and companies satisfied with the program. Such bottom-up support does not happen overnight. Rather, it was generated when skeptical businesses saw that the program could work to their advantage.

The public tends to expect government programs to produce results almost immediately. Yet, although an evaluation of HUPP after its first two years of operation would show a failed program, by year four, the program became a success. This suggests that more time needs to be devoted to examining the process of implementation than in outcome-oriented evaluation.

6. "Implicit" program instructions present structural difficulties to implementation.

The HUPP program was an "implicit" program in that it was a budget set-aside carrying implicit instructions but no legislative mandate, as in a permanent program. Implicit instructions convey a mixed message that hinders implementation. Set-asides generally are temporary. Staff are not hired to administer such programmatic twists because it is expected that funding will expire. A common way to eliminate set-asides is to let the unused, earmarked money roll back into the state coffers at the end of the biennium and explain that the program could not be implemented.

The solution is not to focus on explicitly funding programs targeted to African Americans, since legislators from suburban and rural areas representing primarily white constituents outnumber legislators from city districts where African American communities are concentrated. Resentment for set aside programs is high.

7. Implementing equity-based goals simultaneously with other significant programmatic changes decreases chances of success.

The HUPP was introduced at a time of sweeping administrative changes to the parent program. Field staff had to cope with new procedures and irate clients and constituents at the same time they were expected to implement a very complex, potentially controversial program. Even if all staff had accepted the goals of HUPP, chances are good that it still would have been swept up in the wave of resentment over programmatic changes.

The boom and bust nature of politics makes this factor difficult to avoid. An administration is in office for a limited time. Sometimes the solution is to create an entirely new program to implement the equity-based initiative. The difficulty with this solution is that a new program rarely has time to develop the constituent base that will ensure survival in a change of administrations. Further, an equity-based program, by definition, has a narrow constituency. Therefore, equity-based initiatives should be implemented within existing programs with a minimum of other program changes.

8. The federal government could greatly assist in acceptance of equity-based programs by providing strong leadership in partnership with the private sector and labor unions.

During the Bush administration, several federal initiatives established set-asides similar to that of the HUPP program. States were to develop their own guidelines for use of these funds. In Ohio, the same inter-agency problems that plagued the HUPP implementation process presented insurmountable barriers to working with the federal funds.

Although open-ended federal programs are supposed to encourage innovation at the state level, strong leadership and example is needed to make difficult equity-based programs work. The federal government should establish a tripartite commission, composed of companies, labor unions, and government officials, to promulgate how targeted, equity-based programs could be effectively utilized by companies. Such an initiative should feature a strong marketing and publicity component, clear guidelines about how agencies can work together on such programs, and staff training on the federal, state and local levels.

It only makes sense for the private sector to start undertaking such initiatives. Workforce 2000 warned that the labor force is becoming increasingly female, nonwhite, and non-English-speaking. Supplemental training programs are oriented to ensuring a skilled labor force in the twenty-first century.

Firms that are already experiencing labor market bottlenecks in skilled crafts in urban areas face the choice of moving or training new types of workers. It is far more efficient for the government to lead the private sector in finding ways to use our existing capital and human resources than to allow continued deindustrialization of our cities.

CONCLUSIONS

Equity-based government programs can be created to assist individuals in overcoming barriers to participation in the economic mainstream. Such programs are expensive and implementation is very difficult. Strong leadership is critical to successful implementation. The activity of all participants must be motivated by self interest. Until the majority of us see why equity-based programs are important to our interests, such programs will continue to face insurmountable barriers.

Given the mood of the country revealed in the 1994 elections, this case might be increasingly difficult to make. Yet the strength of equity programs has been their local character—citizens and businesses coming together to solve local problems. This is not a concept alien to conservatives. There clearly is going to be a dynamic tension between those of liberal and conservative ideology. This tension could provide an opportunity for progressive reform.

Ultimately, it might be said that the government's success in intervening through equity-based programs lies in the ability of each one of us as individuals, companies, or agencies to understand why we share in the success of our neighbors, and how that success contributes to our personal, corporate or organizational bottom line. This is not a new message, but it has a new twist. As a nation, our competitiveness is based on preservation and utilization of our resources. As we learned from the practices of total quality control and just-in-time management, elimination of waste is a critical source of increased profits. Equity-based programs contribute to the elimination of waste of human resources, and this helps all of us. We need to market that message, and find a way of holding ourselves accountable for progress in that arena.

NOTES

1. William W. Goldsmith and Edward Blakely, *Poverty and Inequality in U.S. Cities* (Philadelphia: Temple University Press, 1991); J.D. Kasarda, "Entry-level Jobs, Mobility, and Urban Minority Unemployment." *Urban Affairs Quarterly* 19 (1983): 21–40; J.D. Kasarda, "Urban Industrial Transition and the Underclass." *Annals of the American Academy of Political and Social Science* 501 (1989): 26–47.

2. Lori G. Kletzer, "Job Displacement, 1979–1986: How Blacks Fared Relative to Whites." *Monthly Labor Review* 114 (1991): 7–25; Linda B. Stearns and C. W. Coleman, "Industrial and Local Labor Market Structures and Black Male Unemployment in the Manufacturing Sector." *Social Science Quarterly* 71 (1990): 285–98; Loic J. Wacquant and William J. Wilson "The Cost of Racial and Class Exclusion in the Inner City." *Annals, AAPSS* Vol. 501 (1989): 8–25.

3. K. Nelson, "Labor Demand, Labor Supply and the Suburbanization of Low-Wage Office Work." In *Production, Work and Territory,* edited by A. J. Scott and M. Storper (Boston: Allen and Unwin, 1986), 149–71.

4. Gregory D. Squires, "Capital Mobility Versus Upward Mobility: The Racially Discriminatory Consequences of Plant Closings and Corporate Relocations." In *Sunbelt Snowbelt,* edited by L. Sawers and W.K. Tabb (New York: Oxford University Press, 1984), 152–162; W.J. Wilson, *The Truly Disadvantaged* (Chicago: University of Chicago Press, 1987).

5. cf. Kasarda, note 1; Glen G. Cain and Ross E. Finnie, "The Black-White Difference in Youth Employment: Evidence for Demand-Side Factors." *Journal of Labor Economics* 8 (1990): S364–95; Thomas S. Moore and Aaron Laramore, "Industrial Change and Urban Joblessness: An Assessment of the Mismatch Hypothesis." *Urban Affairs Quarterly* 25 (1990): 640–58.

6. J. Vrooman and S. Greenfield, "Are Blacks Making It in the Suburbs? Some

New Evidence on Intrametropolitan Spatial Segmentation." *Journal of Urban Economics,* 7 (1980): 155–67; M. Semyonov, D.R. Hoyt and R.I. Scott, "Place, Race and Differential Occupational Opportunities." *Demography,* 21 (1984): 258–270; Jonathan S. Leonard, "The Interaction of Residential Segregation and Employment Discrimination." *Journal of Urban Economics,* 21 (1987): 323–46; Paul R. Blackney, "Spatial Mismatch in Urban Labor Markets: Evidence From Large U.S. Metropolitan Areas." *Social Science Quarterly,* 71 (1990): 39–52.

7. J. Cotton, "More on the 'Cost' of Being a Black or Mexican American Male Worker." *Social Science Quarterly,* 66 (1985): 867–885; J.E. Farley, "Disproportionate Black and Hispanic Unemployment in U.S. Metropolitan Areas: The Roles of Racial Inequality, Segregation and Discrimination in Male Joblessness." *American Journal of Economic Sociology,* 46 (1987): 129–150. Woody presents evidence that the workplace status of black women has improved relative to black men, but their earning power is still low relative to white women and men. See Bette Woody, *Black Women and the Workplace* (New York; Greenwood Press, 1992).

8. Jonathan Kozol, *Savage Inequalities* (New York: HarperCollins, 1991); Joan Fitzgerald, *The Effect of Education and Training on the Reemployment Success of Displaced Workers in Ohio.* Report submitted to the Ohio Bureau of Employment Services and the Ohio Job Training Partnership (1991).

9. Robert B. Hill, *The Illusion of Black Progress* (Washington D.C.: National Urban League, 1978); David Kiefer and Peter Philips, "Doubts Regarding the Human Capital Theory of Racial Inequality." *Industrial Relations* 27 (1988): 251–262; Daniel T. Lichter "Racial Differences in Underemployment in American Cities. *American Journal of Sociology,* 93 (1988): 771–792.

10. Lester M. Salamon, "Overview: Why Human Capital? Why Now?" in *Human Capital and America's Future,* edited by David W. Hornbeck and Lester M. Salamon (Baltimore: The Johns Hopkins University Press, 1991), pp. 1–42.

11. D.T. Ellwood, "The Spatial Mismatch Hypothesis: Are There Teenage Jobs Missing in the Ghetto?" in *The Black Youth Unemployment Crisis,* edited by R.B. Freeman and H.J. Holzer, (Chicago: University of Chicago Press, 1986), pp. 147–85; M.I. Pomer, "Labor Market Structure, Intragenerational Mobility, and Discrimination: Black Male Advancement out of Low-Paying Jobs." *American Sociological Review,* 51 (1986): 650–659; Daniel T. Lichter, "Race, Employment Hardship, and Inequality in the American Metropolitan South." *American Sociological Review,* 54 (1989): 436–446.

12. M. Turner, M. Fix, and R. Struyk, "Opportunities Denied, Opportunities Diminished in Hiring." (Washington D.C.: The Urban Institute, 1991).

13. Robert E. Mier and Robert Giloth, "Hispanic Employment Opportunities: A Case of Internal Labor Markets and Weak-Tied Social Networks. *Social Science Quarterly,* 66 (1985): 296–309; J.S. Braddock, Jomills Henry, and James McPartland, "How Minorities Continue to be Excluded From Equal Employment Opportunities: Research on Labor Market and Institutional Barriers." *Journal of Social Issues,* 43 (1987): 5–39; H.J. Holzer, "Informal Job Search and Black Youth Unemployment." *American Economic Review,* 77 (1987): 446–452. Harry J. Holzer, *Unemployment, Vacancies, and Local Labor Markets* (Kalamazoo, MI: Upjohn Institute, 1989); Kathryn M. Neckerman and Joleen Kirschenman, "Hiring Strategies, Racial Bias, and Inner-City Workers." *Social Problems,* 38 (1991): 433–447.

14. Bennett Harrison and Lucy Gorham, "Growing Inequality in Black Wages in the 1980s and the Emergence of an African-American Middle Class." *Journal of Policy Analysis and Management,* 11 (1992): 235–253.

15. Bennett Harrison, *Education, Training, and the Urban Ghetto* (Baltimore:

Johns Hopkins University Press, 1972); Michael K. Brown and Steven P. Erie, "Blacks and the Legacy of the Great Society: The Economic and Political Impact of Federal Social Policy." *Public Policy,* 29 (1981): 299–329.

16. cf. Lori J. Kletzer, note 2.

17. J. Fitzgerald, "The Effect of Education and Training on the Reemployment Success of Displaced Workers in Ohio." Report submitted to the Ohio Bureau of Employment Services and the Ohio Job Training Partnership (1991).

18. Gary Orfield and Helene Slessarev, *Job Training under the New Federalism* (Chicago: University of Chicago, Illinois Unemployment and Job Training Research Project, 1986); Duane Leigh, *Assisting Displaced Workers* (Kalamazoo, MI: Upjohn Institute for Employment Research, 1989).

19. Helene Slessarev, *Racial Inequalities in Metropolitan Chicago Job Training Programs* (Chicago: Chicago Urban League, 1988).

20. The second author was deputy director of business development, Ohio Department of Development at the time the High Unemployment Population Program was initiated. Interviews also were conducted with the following people involved with development and implementation of the HUPP program: Sharon LaMarr, assistant deputy director of business development, Ohio Department of Development; Frankie Coleman, state director of JTPA, Ohio Bureau of Employment Services. Site visits and extensive interviews also were conducted with representatives from participating firms, and with program participants.

21. All states provide substantial subsidies to help medium sized or large plants move in or to keep them from moving out. While evidence repeatedly demonstrates these programs do not create jobs or development, industrial attraction and retention programs simply are political necessities. See Harvey Molotch, "The City as a Growth Machine: Toward a Political Economy of Place." *American Journal of Sociology* 82 (1976): 309–332; Bennett Harrison and Sandra Kanter, "The Political Economy of State Job Creation and Business Incentives," in *Revitalizing the Northeast,* edited by George Sternlieb and James W. Hughes (New Brunswick, NJ: Rutgers University Press, 1978).

22. Applicants can choose training as a carpenter, bricklayer, electrician, painter, plumber, roofer, sheetmetal worker or laborer.

23. The residential journeyman status was created for the Building and Construction Trades program. While trainees can find employment upon completion, as a credential it only qualifies trainees for entry into the traditional union-supported apprenticeships leading to high-paying construction jobs.

24. Stephen Hamilton, *Apprenticeship for Adulthood* (New York: Macmillan, 1991).

25. cf. Leigh, note 18.

26. In fact, such a comparison may not ever be possible due to the lack of data on the long-term employment trends and income gains of JTPA participants.

27. Robert Mier and Kari Moe, "Implementing Strategic Planning: Roadblocks to Reform, Economic Development and Equity," in *Harold Washington and the Neighborhoods,* edited by P. Clavel and W. Wiewel (New Brunswick, NJ: Rutgers University Press, 1991).

28. Jeffrey L. Pressman and Aaron Wildavsky, *Implementation* (Berkeley, CA: University of California Press, 1984), p. 143.

29. National Commission on Education and the Economy, *America's Choice: High Skills or Low Wages* (Rochester, NY: NCEE, 1990).

UTILIZATION OF MINORITY EMPLOYEES IN SMALL BUSINESS: A COMPARISON OF NONMINORITY AND BLACK-OWNED URBAN ENTERPRISES

Timothy Bates

Structural changes in the urban economy are causing African-American workers in blue collar occupations to rely increasingly upon the small business sector for employment. This study finds that most of the nonminority-owned small businesses operating in large urban areas do not employ minorities. Even among the businesses physically located within minority communities, the majority of the workers in the nonminority small firms are white. Black-owned businesses, in contrast, rely largely on minority workers even when their firms are located outside of minority neighborhoods.

INTRODUCTION

This study examines the employment composition of small businesses owned by blacks and nonminorities operating in 28 large metropolitan areas. Nonminority owners of small businesses are found to exclude minority employees (including blacks, Asians, and Latinos) quite often while black owners—even when their firms are located outside of minority communities—consistently employ minorities.

Affirmative action employment policies are of little help in combatting the aversion many nonminority small business owners exhibit to employing minorities. Negative white attitudes towards blacks show up regularly in survey data: 65 percent of whites, for example, characterize blacks as lazier than whites.[1] Neckerman and Kirshenman have shown that race serves as a signal of presumed work habits and job suitability for many employers, based upon their general negative stereotypes of blacks.[2] In light of this reality, an alternative strategy for opening up job opportunities in the small business sector is to promote creation and expansion of firms owned by the group—black employers—that has already demonstrated its commitment to minority hiring. The fact that most nonminority-owned small business employers have no minority employees may or may not reflect discriminatory hiring patterns. The geographic distribution of minority and nonminority populations in the United States varies greatly, and minorities live disproportionately in large urban areas. Among Hispanics, 88 percent reside within very large Standard Metropolitan Statistical Areas (SMSAs). Only 27 percent of white labor force participants reside in central cities, versus nearly two thirds of the nation's African-American workers.[3] This study examines the employment patterns of small businesses within 28 large metropolitan areas, and these areas are subdivided, in turn, into minority residential neighborhoods and other urban areas. The purpose of this focus is to examine the employment patterns of white and black-owned small businesses in a manner that reduces uncertainty about geographic proximity of minority employees to jobs. The key finding of this study is that minorities are largely excluded from the payrolls of nonminority-owned small businesses. Even those white-owned small business employers whose firms are physically located in inner-city minority communities employ a work force that is predominantly white. Roughly one third of all such firms in minority neighborhoods employ no minorities whatsoever.

Black-owned firms operating in inner-city neighborhoods, in contrast, employ a labor force that consists almost entirely of minority workers. This study finds that 96.2 percent of the black employer firms operating in urban minority communities rely upon a work force composed largely of minorities. While black firms located outside of minority neighborhoods rely largely upon minority workers, most white-owned businesses in these same areas have no minority employees.

THE GROWING IMPORTANCE OF SMALL BUSINESS EMPLOYERS

Declining blue-collar employment at the nation's largest corporations, and the interrelated phenomenon of shrinking employment of less-skilled workers in manufacturing generally, is weakening employment prospects for such groups as African-Americans traditionally reliant upon industrial jobs. Net creation of low-skilled and blue-collar employment opportunities in recent years has been most pronounced in the small business arena.

Structural changes in the urban economy are causing minority workers in industrial regions particularly to rely increasingly upon the small-business sector for employment. Declining employment in manufacturing, offset by a rise in the service-producing sector, is partially responsible for this trend.[4] Furthermore, a growing body of evidence suggests that the bulk of all new jobs in recent years have originated in the small-business sector. The highly publicized research of economist David Birch proclaims that firms employing fewer than 20 workers "have created about 88 percent of all net new jobs" nationwide in the 1980s.[5] Efforts to replicate Birch's findings have been unsuccessful. More credible studies have pegged the small business share of new jobs at 51 to 56 percent of the employment total.[6] Statistics from the Small Business Administration indicate that firms with fewer than 100 employees were responsible for 53.0 percent of net job creation nationally in the 1980–1986 time period.[7]

Controversy over the role of small business in generating jobs is far from settled, but something of a consensus is emerging regarding employment trends in the manufacturing sector. A recent study of manufacturing employment in the Milwaukee metropolitan area found the employee numbers dropped by 56,800 in the 1979–1983 period and expanded by 5,673 between 1983 and 1987.[8] Looking solely at manufacturers with under 50 employees, Milwaukee-area employment was stable in 1979–1983 (employment grew by a tiny 117 jobs) and it grew by 4,315 employees in the 1983–1987 time period. For Milwaukee manufacturers with 500 plus workers per establishment, employment fell by 46,814 in 1979–1983 and it fell by an additional 3,361 jobs during the 1983–1987 economic recovery period. This pattern of job loss concentrated in the larger establishments and job gains in the small firms typifies manufacturing employment nationwide. Irrespective of the precise overall percentage on job generation by sector, it is clear that urban black workers—particularly males in blue collar occupations—are increasingly limited to employment (and underemployment) with small business.

Until the 1970s, penetration into blue-collar manufacturing had been responsible for widespread income gains for less-skilled employees, especially black male workers. This traditional route to upward mobility has been undermined in many areas of the United States; the massive losses of blue-collar manufacturing jobs in the 1970s and 1980s in nonsouthern regions, furthermore, have effectively reversed many of the employment gains previously captured by black workers.[9]

Black income trends by region highlight the impacts of these job losses. Black family median income in the highly industrialized midwest was $23,671 in 1970, which was 73.4 percent of the median white family income in that region. The midwest has been transformed from the *highest* median income region for blacks (in 1970) to the *lowest* median income region by 1987. In that year, black family income in the midwest region (in constant dollars) stood at $16,755, which was 52.1 percent of the comparable median white family income. High-wage jobs in manufacturing were heavily displaced and the categories for black male workers that registered substantial growth were service employment, unemployment, and labor force nonparticipation. The single line of service employment that grew most rapidly in the midwest was also the least stable, and offered the lowest wages: jobs in eating and drinking establishments.[10]

Largely unprotected by antidiscrimination safeguards, black workers compete for employment in a small-business sector where institutionalized practices tend to undercut their chances of being hired.[11] Small businesses that utilize paid employees are overwhelmingly owned by nonminorities. Among the very small firms in this sector, employees are most commonly either members of the immediate family, relatives, or friends. Employees are likely to be members of social networks that are family based; blacks are not likely to be included in the applicable networks.

Affirmative action, equal employment opportunity law and policies, by their very nature, are not designed to assist the black worker who is seeking employment in this milieu. Consider, for example, the landmark Executive Order 11246, which established rules for nondiscrimination by federal contractors, subcontractors, and construction projects operating with federal assistance. Contractors with 50 or more employees and contracts of $50,000 or more were required to develop and submit affirmative action compliance programs with goals and timetables for the hiring and promotion of minorities. The key phrase here is "with 50 or more employees."

A number of studies have found that young blacks and whites tend to use different job-search techniques. While blacks tend to walk in and apply, whites are more often referred by friends or relatives.[12] A study by Braddock and McPartland found that the quality of employment blacks obtain is directly correlated with the racial composition of their social networks. They found that blacks who attended racially mixed high schools were more likely to live in racially mixed neighborhoods and work in racially mixed job settings. For black workers, Braddock and McPartland conclude that "segregated networks lead to poor paying, more segregated jobs—desegregated networks lead to better paying, less segregated work."[13]

The relevance of social networks to job access helps to explain why the racial composition of the workforce employed by black-owned businesses differs so profoundly from that employed by nonminority enterprises. These small firms largely draw employees from family-based networks, and blacks are commonly not members of these networks. For essentially the same reasons, black-owned firms employ a labor force consisting almost entirely of minority workers.[14]

SMALL BUSINESS EMPLOYMENT PATTERNS IN 28 LARGE METROPOLITAN AREAS

The samples of small businesses analyzed in this section are drawn from the Characteristics of Business Owners (CBO) survey, which was compiled by the U.S. Bureau of the Census in 1987. The CBO survey drew its sample of over 125,000 small business owners from the 1982 Survey of Minority-Owned Business Enterprises (SMOBE). SMOBE, which includes large numbers of nonminority respondents, was used in conjunction with the 1982 Survey of Women-Owned Businesses, to identify firm owners by race, ethnicity, and gender. In the case of multiple-owner firms, all owners were included in the CBO survey. By design, minorities (Asian, Latino, African-American) were heavily oversampled, accounting for over 75,000 of the 125,000 business owners covered by the CBO survey. The response rate was 81 percent.[15] The 28 metropolitan areas examined in this study are SMSAs selected on the basis of black business frequency and certain population characteristics; all of the largest SMSAs are included.[16] The concept of "minority community" is defined at the zip code level in each of these SMSAs: zip codes having 40 percent or more minority inhabitants are defined as belonging to the minority community (or neighborhood). Zip codes with under 40 percent minority residents are defined as nonminority areas for purposes of this study.

For these 28 large metropolitan areas, the incidence of minority employees on the payrolls of small businesses owned by nonminorities and blacks in 1982 is summarized:

	Black firms	White firms
Percent with 50 percent or more minority employees	93.5%	23.3%
Percent with under 50 percent but greater than zero minority employees	4.3%	19.0%
Percent having no minority employees	2.2%	57.8%

TABLE 1
The Incidence of Minority Employees on the Payrolls of Nonminority
versus Black-Owned Firms, by Area, in 1982 (includes small businesses in
28 large SMSAs only).

	Firm located in minority neighborhoods		Firms located in nonminority neighborhoods	
	Black Firms	White Firms	Black Firms	White Firms
Percent with 75 percent or more minority employees	93.1%	29.4%	78.9%	15.5%
Percent with 50 percent or more minority employees	96.2%	37.6%	86.7%	20.4%
Percent with under 50 percent (but greater than zero) minority employees	1.9%	29.4%	10.2%	16.9%
Percent having no minority employees	1.9%	32.9%	3.1%	62.7%
Percent of employers located in each type of geographic area	71.3%	16.4%	28.7%	83.6%

Source: Characteristics of Business Owners Data Base; U.S. Bureau of the Census

These figures certainly reveal very clear-cut differences in the employment patterns of black- and nonminority-owned small businesses operating in major urban areas. While over 93 percent of the black business employers rely upon minorities to fill 50 percent or more of their available jobs, nearly 60 percent of the nonminority employers have no minority employees.

Table 1 breaks down the 28 metropolitan areas into minority neighborhoods and nonminority areas in order to examine small-business employment patterns in greater detail. Looking solely at firms operating in urban-minority communities, Table 1 indicates that 32.9 percent of the white-business employers have no minority workers on their payrolls. Within minority neighborhoods, the preponderance of employees at the nonminority-owned small businesses are white. In complete contrast, nearly all of the black firms utilized minority employees, with 93.1 percent of the employers in minority neighborhoods relying upon minority workers for at least 75 percent of their employees.

Among black employers that are located in nonminority sections of large metropolitan areas analyzed in Table 1, 86.7 percent of them had work forces that were made up of 50 percent or more minorities; most of these relied on minority employees for over 75 percent of their work force. Among the white-owned small businesses in these same areas, most firms had no minority employees whatsoever. Prevalence of minority employees typifies large as well as small black firms, white-collar industries such as finance and insurance as well as blue-collar industries such as manufacturing and construction.[17]

Table 1 documents the fact that black-owned businesses employ minorities predominantly. Among small businesses owned by whites, well over half of those that hire paid workers have no minority workers. Black firms located outside the minority community are clearly much more likely to hire minority employees than nonminority-owned businesses located within minority residential areas.

CONCLUDING REMARKS

Structural changes in the urban economy are causing African-American workers in blue-collar occupations to rely increasingly upon the small-business sector for employment. This study finds that most of the nonminority-owned small businesses operating in large urban areas do not employ minorities. Even among the businesses physically located within minority communities, the majority of the workers in the nonminority small firms are white. Black-owned businesses, in contrast, rely largely on minority workers even when their firms are located outside of minority neighborhoods. This may suggest that unemployment among blacks can be alleviated somewhat by expanding the number of black-owned businesses,[18] but that is not the issue at hand. The evidence presented herein—whites tend to employ whites while blacks tend not to employ whites—is consistent with the hypothesis that the network-hiring propensities of small business owners tend to limit the employment alternatives of black job seekers. Underrepresentation of African-Americans in the ranks of small-business ownership potentially becomes a major obstacle to black job seekers in a world where 1) new job opportunities are increasingly likely to be found in the small-business sector, and 2) white owners of small businesses prefer to draw their employees from networks that contain few blacks. Black-owned firms employed fewer than 250,000 workers nationwide in 1987.[19] If most of the jobs available in the small-business sector are found in white-owned firms, and most of the white-owned firms prefer to hire relatives, family members, friends, and friends of friends—few of whom are black—then it follows that black job seekers will fare poorly in this sector. While this study does not constitute a definitive proof of this proposition, all of the evidence considered herein points toward a small business world of network hiring in which job accessibility is a function of the race of the small business owner. In such a world, expanded black ownership of small business is an option that is worthy of serious consideration.

NOTES

Research reported here was conducted at the U.S. Bureau of the Census, Center for Economic Studies. Findings and conclusions reported in this article do not necessarily reflect the views of the Census Bureau.

1. National Opinion Center, *General Social Surveys* (Chicago: 1991).
2. Kathryn Neckerman and Joleen Kirschenman, "Hiring Strategies, Racial Bias, and Inner City Networks," *Social Problems* (November 1991).
3. These figures, drawn from the 1980 Decennial Census of Population data, are cited in James Lowry, "Set-Aside Programs: Vehicles for Change or Threats to the Free Enterprise System?", in *Selective Affirmative Action Topics in Employment and Business Set-Asides* (Washington, D.C.: U.S. Commission on Civil Rights, 1986).
4. Bennett Harrison and Barry Bluestone, *The Great U-Turn: Corporate Restructuring and the Polarization of America* (New York: Basic Books, 1985). Timothy Bates and Daniel Fusfeld, *Political Economy of the Urban Ghetto* (Carbondale, Illinois: Southern Illinois University Press, 1984).
5. David Birch, *Job Creation in America* (New York: The Free Press, 1987).
6. C. Armington and M. Odle, "Small Business: How Many Jobs?" *Brookings Review* (Winter 1982).
7. These figures are cited in Charles Brown, James Hamilton, and James Medoff, *Employers Large and Small* (Cambridge: Harvard University Press, 1990).
8. Sammis White and Jeffrey Osterman, "Is Employment Growth Really Coming from Small Establishments?" *Economic Development Quarterly* (August 1991).
9. Nationwide data on trends in the occupation and industry of employment illustrate resultant impacts on black men; figures (in percent) represent employment of black men working in:

	1969	1984
a. manufacturing, mining, construction (industry data)	41.3%	33.6%
b. operatives (occupation data)	28.3%	22.6%

While black male operative employment in manufacturing is down across the board, young workers have suffered disproportionately from this trend in job availability. See, Bates and Fusfeld, *Political Economy*.

10. Ibid.
11. Timothy Bates, *Banking on Black Enterprise* (Washington, D.C.: Joint Center for Political and Economic Studies, 1993).
12. Gerald Jaynes and Robin Williams, *A Common Destiny: Blacks and American Society* (Washington, D.C.: National Academy Press, 1989).

13. Henry Braddock and James McPartland, "How Minorities Continue to be Excluded from Equal Employment Opportunities: Research on Labor Market and Institutional Barriers," *Journal of Social Issues* (Spring 1987), p. 12.
14. Bates, *Black Enterprise*.
15. The CBO survey and data base are described in, Timothy Bates, "New Data Bases in Human Resources: The Characteristics of Business Owners Data Base," *The Journal of Human Resources* (Fall 1990).
16. The relevant 28 metropolitan areas include these SMSAs: New York, Chicago, Los Angeles, Detroit, Philadelphia, Houston, Washington, D.C., Dallas-Fort Worth, New Orleans, St. Louis, San Francisco-Oakland, Atlanta, Baltimore, Cleveland, Memphis, Indianapolis, Jacksonville, Milwaukee, Shreveport, Omaha, Columbus, Oh., Birmingham, Newark, Gary, In., Nashville, Kansas City, Richmond, and Pittsburgh. Criteria for SMSA selection are described in Timothy Bates, "Small Business Viability in the Urban Ghetto," *Journal of Regional Science* (November 1989).
17. Differences in the industry distribution of black- and white-owned small businesses are not trivial, with blacks being somewhat overrepresented in service fields and underrepresented in manufacturing. See Bates (1993) for the relevant industry breakdowns.
18. This position is advocated in Bates, *Black Enterprise*.
19. U.S. Bureau of the Census, *Survey of Minority-Owned Business Enterprises: Black* (Washington, D.C.: U.S. Government Printing Office, 1990).

ABOUT THE AUTHORS

Bartholomew Armah, Ph.D., is associate professor of economics at the University of Wisconsin at Milwaukee (Milwaukee, WI 53201).

M. V. Lee Badgett, Ph.D., is assistant professor of public affairs at the University of Maryland (College Park, MD 20742-1821).

Timothy Bates, Ph.D., is a research professor in the College of Urban, Labor, and Metropolitan Affairs at Wayne State University (Detroit, MI 48202).

Marc Bendick, Jr., Ph.D., a labor economist, is a principal in Bendick and Egan Economic Consultants, Inc. (3760 39th Street, NW, Washington, DC 20016-5526).

Elisa Jayne Bienenstock, Ph.D., is assistant professor of sociology at the University of North Carolina-Chapel Hill (Chapel Hill, NC 27599-3210).

Jeremiah Cotton, Ph.D., is associate professor of economics at the University of Massachusetts-Boston (Boston, MA 02125-3393).

Rudy Fichtenbaum, Ph.D., is professor of economics at Wright State University (Dayton, OH 45435).

Joan Fitzgerald, Ph.D., is assistant professor of urban planning at the Center for Urban Economic Development at the University of Illinois-Chicago (Chicago, IL 60607-7035).

Augustin Kwasi Fosu, Ph.D., is associate professor of economics at Oakland University (Rochester, MI 48309-4401).

Paul E. Gabriel, Ph.D., is assistant professor of economics at Loyola University of Chicago (Chicago, IL 60611).

Michael Greene, Ph.D., is assistant professor of economics at the University of North Texas (Denton, TX 76203-4426).

Kwabena Gyimah-Brempong, Ph.D., is professor of economics at Wright State University (Dayton, OH 45435).

Emily Hoffnar, Ph.D., is assistant professor of economics at the University of North Texas (Denton, TX 76203-3408).

Thomas Hyclak, Ph.D., is professor of economics at Lehigh University (Bethlehem, PA 18015-3144).

Charles W. Jackson is a law student at Northeastern University (Boston, MA 02115). He was former Director of Operations at the Fair Employment Council of Greater Washington, Inc. (Washington, DC 20005).

James H. Johnson, Jr., Ph.D., is E. Maynard Adams Professor of Business, Geography and Sociology at the University of North Carolina-Chapel Hill (Chapel Hill, NC 27599-3440).

David A. Macpherson, Ph.D., is associate professor in the Department of Economics at Florida State University (Tallahassee, FL 32306).

Don Mar, Ph.D., is associate professor of economics at San Francisco State University (San Francisco, CA 94132).

Maurice Y. Mongkuo, Ph.D., is assistant professor of public policy and public administration in the Department of Government and International Affairs at the University of South Florida (Tampa, FL 33620-8100).

Paul M. Ong, Ph.D., is associate professor of urban planning at the University of California-Los Angeles (Los Angeles, CA 90024).

William J. Pammer, Jr., Ph.D., is associate professor of public administration in the Department of Government and International Affairs at the University of South Florida (Tampa, FL 33620-8100).

Wendy Patton, Master of City Planning, Department of Political Science, Kent State University (Kent, OH 44242).

Victor A. Reinoso is an MBA student at Massachusetts Institute of Technology (Cambridge, MA 02139). He was former Project Coordinator at the Fair Employment Council of Greater Washington, Inc. (Washington, DC 20005).

Susanne Schmitz, Ph.D., is assistant professor of economics at Elmhurst College (Elmhurst, IL 60126-3296).

James B. Stewart, Ph.D., is Vice Provost for Educational Equity and Professor of Labor Studies and Industrial Relations at The Pennsylvania State University (University Park, PA 16802).

Jennifer A. Stoloff, M.A. is a doctoral student in the Department of Sociology at the University of North Carolina-Chapel Hill (Chapel Hill, NC 27599-3210).

Larry W. Taylor, Ph.D., is associate professor of economics at Lehigh University (Bethlehem, PA 18015-3144).

Andrés Torres, Ph.D., is associate professor at the University of Massachusetts-Boston (Boston, MA 02125-3393).

Roger C. Williams, Ph.D., is assistant professor of economics at Morgan State University (Baltimore, MD 21239).

INDEX

Abraham, Katherine, 249–50, 251, 338, 339
Advertising, job. *See* Media
Affirmative action. *See also* Government programs; Social policy
  assessment of, 107–13, 116–18
  benefits, 101–2, 107, 109
  class/race-based, 56
  and corporation size, 110
  Detroit study (1972), 102–4
  in economic theory, 20, 37–38
  and education, 110
  gender issues in, 101–2, 107–13, 279, 284, 286–87, 293
  and geographical location, 110
  and hiring, 101–2, 107–13
  model for, 104–7, 114nn10,13,14
  and recruitment, 101–2, 107–13
  and stereotypes, 106–7, 109, 112–13
  and unemployment, 278–79, 284–88, 292, 293
  and unionization, 110
Albelda, Randy P., 176–77, 189
Ameniya, Takeshi, 106
Armed forces. *See* Military
Aronowitz, S., 12
Arrow, Kenneth, 17, 21, 26
Ashenfelter, Orley, 107
Asians
  and cultural capital theory, 41–42, 44–45
  in semiconductor industry, 344, 345
  wage differentials for, 62

Becker, Gary, 19, 21, 24, 29–30, 106, 109, 181, 228
Beller, Andrea H., 176

Beller, H., 141
Belman, D., 350
Birch, David, 376, 393
Blanchard, Olivier Jean, 250, 252, 259, 280
Blank, R.M., 350
Blau, Francine D., 141, 176
Blinder, Alan S., 123, 140
Bluestone, Barry, 56
Braddock, Henry, 394
Brauer, John, 325, 326, 329, 330, 331, 332
Breton, Albert, 22, 23, 29, 37–38
Bridefare, 39–40
Bulow, Jeremy I., 166, 167, 278–79
Bureau of Economic Analysis (BEA), 304
Bureau of Labor Statistics (BLS), 191–92, 199, 265, 304
Burman, George, 107
Butler, John S., 328

Census Industry Classifications, 304
Chiswick, Barry, 62
Choudhury, S., 350
Chow, Gregory C., 124, 136n8
Civil Rights Act (1991), 95
Civil rights movement, 20
Clerical occupations, 191–200, 201n6, 203t. *See also* Manufacturing industry; Military; Public sector employment; Semiconductor industry; Service industry; Small business
Community structure, 208–10
Conservatives, 15, 18–19, 20
Contract With America, 53
Corporation size
  and affirmative action, 110
  and employment discrimination, *88t*, 90

and labor demand, 264, 269, 272
Cotton, Jeremiah, 139, 142
Criminal record, 51, 53, 54, 55
Cultural capital theory. *See also* Economic
   theory
   and Asians, 41–42, 44–45
   contextual variables in, 49–53
   criminal record influence in, 51, 53, 54,
      55
   defined, 39
   economic structure in, 45, 53
   education in, 47, 49, 50, 53, 54, 55
   employment discrimination in, 45, 53,
      56
   employment in, 49–56
   familial influences in, 45–49, 54
   geographical influences in, 43, 45–49,
      54
   and Hispanics, 41–42, 43–44, 45
   historical influences in, 43, 45, 54
   human capital in, 39–40, 47, 49–53, 54,
      55
   labor demand/supply in, 41–42
   marital status in, 39–40, 50, 53, 54
   and Multi-City Study of Urban
      Inequality (MCSUI), 40–56
   and social policy, 39–40, 53, 54–56
   social status variables in, 49–53, 54, 56
   values deterioration in, 39, 43, 45, 53
   and welfare, 39–40, 43, 53
Current Population Survey (CPS)
   and geographical location, 239
   and labor demand, 261–62
   and occupational segregation, 191–92,
      199
   and public sector employment, 350,
      352
   and trade-related employment, 300, 304
   and unemployment, 280–81, 288, 290
   and wage differentials, 139, 142, 144,
      167

Danziger, Sheldon, 237
Darity, William, Jr., 61–62, 63, 140
Davis, Stephen, 263, 264
DeBoer, Larry, 291
Defense Conversion Commission (DCC),
   326
Defense industry. *See* Military
Demonstrations, 22
Department of Labor, 111, 176, 268

Desegregation, school, 22–23, 24, 37–38
Diamond, Peter, 250, 252, 259, 280
Dickens, William T., 279
DiFazio, W., 12
Discrimination. *See* Employment discrimi-
   nation; Housing discrimination;
   Occupational segregation; Stereotypes;
   Wage differentials; Women in labor
   force
Displaced Worker Survey (DWS), 261–62
Dixit, A., 301
Donohue, John, 101, 112
Duncan, Beverly, 190, 192, 199
Duncan, J., 302
Duncan, Otis Dudley, 190, 192, 199
Dunne, Timothy, 263, 264

Economic Dislocation and Worker
   Adjustment Assistance Act (EDWAA),
   332
The Economics of Discrimination, 19
Economic theory. *See also* Cultural capital
   theory
   affirmative action in, 20, 37–38
   and black economists invisibility, 15–
      16, 25–26
   collective racial identity model, 17–23,
      25, 26n4, 29–38
   and conservatives, 15, 18–19, 20
   cultural production functions model,
      21–26, 29–38
   employment discrimination in, 17, 19,
      20–22, 25, 33–34
   household production model, 21, 29–38
   human capital in, 23, 33–34, 37, 38
   inadequacy of models, 16–21
   institutionalized envy in, 29, 35
   and legal system, 24–25
   political strategies model, 22, 29, 37–
      38
   reverse tunnel effect in, 29, 35
   school desegregation in, 22–23, 24, 37–
      38
   segregation in, 18–19, 22–24, 38
   and small business, 37–38
   and social policy, 1–2, 15–16, 18, 20,
      37–38
   tunnel effect in, 29, 35
   unionization in, 19–20
Education. *See also* High Unemployment
   Population Program (HUPP); Human